W9-BZW-260

BEYOND BASHERT

BEYOND BASHERT

A GUIDE TO DATING AND MARRIAGE ENRICHMENT

LISA AIKEN

JASON ARONSON INC.
Northvale, New Jersey
London

This book was set in 10 pt. Times Roman by AeroType, Inc.

10 9 8 7 6 5 4 3 2 1

Library of Congress Cataloging-in-Publication Data

Aiken, Lisa.
    Beyond bashert : a guide to enriching your marriage / Lisa Aiken.
      p. cm.
    Includes bibliographical references and index.
    ISBN 1-56821-896-6 (alk. paper)
      1. Marriage—Religious aspects—Judaism. I. Title.
HQ525.J4A57 1996
296.38'563—dc20   95-42432
                                                                      CIP

Manufactured in the United States of America. Jason Aronson Inc. offers books and cassettes. For information and catalog write to Jason Aronson Inc., 230 Livingston Street, Northvale, New Jersey 07647.

This book is dedicated to the memory of Rivka Shapiro,
of blessed memory.
As my first spiritual mentor, she is a partner in everything I do.

May her soul get pleasure
from my efforts to bring *Yiddishkeit* to others,
as she brought it to me.

Contents

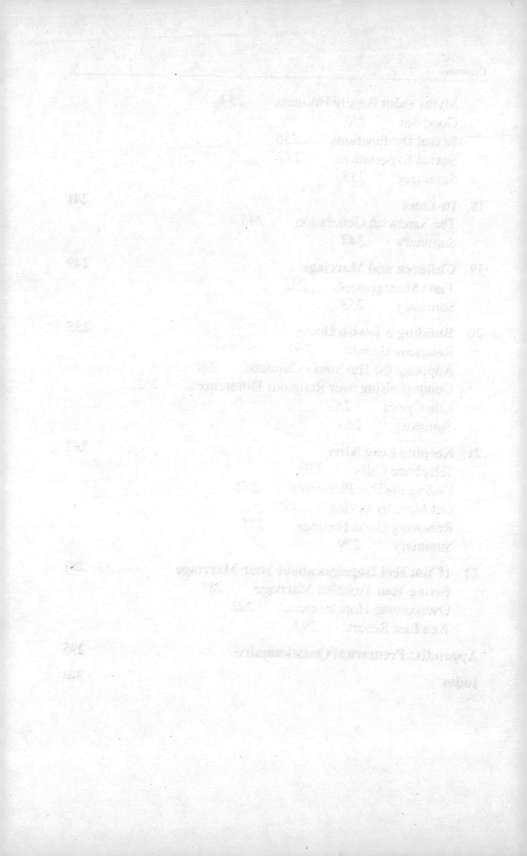

Acknowledgments

My thanks to Rabbi Moises Benzaquen, Shlomit Kossin, and Rabbi Simcha Weinberg for suggesting that I teach Jews concrete information that will help them have better marriages. Rabbi Weinberg also contributed some material to the chapters on marital obligations and Jewish aspects of marriage.

I also thank Tzippora Heller and Abby Lerner for reading the final draft and making helpful recommendations for improving it, and Ira Michaels for his suggestions throughout.

I am indebted to the Almighty for this opportunity to bring people closer to Him, and to each other.

Introduction

We can't choose when and where we are born, who our parents and siblings are, or when we die. But we can choose who we marry and what kind of marriage we have. This will dramatically affect us and our descendants for generations, yet few singles are even minimally prepared to choose an appropriate partner. The majority of married couples do not have the requisite attitudes or skills to work on a marriage, as is borne out by the following alarming statistics:

1. One out of three couples who don't cohabit before marriage get divorced, and three out of four couples who do cohabit first get divorced.[1]
2. Sixty percent of second marriages end in separation or divorce.[2] It has been estimated that 10 percent–20 percent of Orthodox Jews are now getting divorced.
3. The median length of an American marriage in 1988 was seven years, with two out of ten marriages ending before the third anniversary.[3]
4. A 1989 Gallup poll showed that 47 percent of divorces were attributed to "incompatibility"; 16 percent to alcohol or drug abuse; 17 percent to infidelity; 10 percent to arguments over money, family, or children; and 5 percent to physical abuse.[4]
5. A ten-year study of married couples showed that marital happiness has little to do with who people marry and everything to do with how they cope with conflict.[5]

6. Personality traits, compatibility, and similarity do not predict marital happiness or success. How couples handle their differences is what's important.[6]

7. Over 20 percent of American couples hit, shove, slap, or push each other at least once a year.[7]

8. Thirty-eight percent of divorced people were aware of the problems that destroyed their marriage before, or soon after, the wedding.[8]

9. In a large study, half of all American newlyweds had significant marital problems due to unexpected changes in their lives and relationships, even though 85 percent of these couples had had premarital sex, and 54 percent had lived together before marriage. They reported a dramatic increase in the number of arguments they had and the tendency to criticize each other after marriage.[9]

10. Forty percent of American children will have divorced parents by the time they are eight years old, and half will see a second pair of parents divorce by the time the children leave high school![10]

We take for granted that people must spend weeks or months learning how to drive a car, then must pass a test to insure that they have the requisite abilities. Why aren't we as serious about marriage? Couples need only purchase a license (next to the dog license counter) and go through a brief ceremony in order to be married. Society assumes that people somehow know how to communicate, be loving, be responsible, and raise children. Yet this is belied by the astounding statistics above, not to mention the alarming rates of wife and child abuse.

While most religious Jews get some premarital instruction by learning the laws that govern marital relations (*taharat hamishpacha*), they are not generally taught how to judge which characteristics in a potential mate are likely to cause unbridgeable problems, how men and women differ and what this implies, communication and marital problem-solving techniques, and how to relate to in-laws. If couples don't learn all of this, the epidemic of marital discord will continue, since a couple's ability to communicate is the single most important contributor to a stable and satisfying marriage.[11]

Well-written secular books that address these issues abound. Sadly, Jewish books about these topics are superficial or terribly incomplete. This is the first practical, comprehensive guide that integrates research, professional marriage counseling techniques, and Judaism. It gives systematic approaches to choosing an appropriate partner, successfully communicating, problem-solving, and developing love and intimacy. These techniques can help couples create fulfilling marriages, without the expense and inconvenience of seeking professional help and without resorting to divorce.

I take no responsibility for the quality or appropriateness of services or information provided by listed resources, books or agencies.

Throughout this book, names and personal details in the stories have been altered to protect the anonymity of the people concerned. It is purely coincidental if any names or situations correspond exactly to those of real people.

NOTES

1. Michael McManus, *Marriage Savers* (Grand Rapids: Zondervan Publishing House, 1993), p. 23.

2. Michele Weiner-Davis, *Divorce Busting* (New York: Summit Books, 1992), p. 13.

3. McManus, *Marriage Savers*, 105.

4. Ibid., 123.

5. Clifford Notarius and Howard Markman, *We Can Work It Out* (New York: G. P. Putnams's Sons, 1993), p. 20.

6. Notarius and Markman, *We Can Work It Out*, 20.

7. Ibid., 123.

8. McManus, *Marriage Savers*, 123.

9. Ibid., 146.

10. Ibid., 29.

11. Notarius and Markman, *We Can Work It Out*, 21.

I

Who to Be and What to Look For

1

Jewish Views of Marriage

P ersonal ads abound in newspapers and magazines, as singles try to find their ideal mates. Here is a representative sample:[1]

"Beauty Seeking Beast—Bewitching brunette—gorgeous, sexy, smart, honest and loving, Italian ancestry, nonreligious, 30. Desires an intense and sensuous relationship with a cool and reserved, Jewish, late 30s professional who wants his world set on fire. Note/photo."

"Passionate Kisser—Young, 33, intelligent, successful, athletic, warm, thoughtful, good-looking, nonreligious Jewish professional male—searching for one intelligent, attractive, warm, easy to be with, Jewish or nonreligious woman, 28–35, with that extra ingredient—to surprise me for a lifetime. Note/photo please."

"Fabulous, Handsome, Successful—41–year-old Jewish doctor, finally ready for marriage and children. Needs to meet an intelligent, considerate woman, with fun personality and great figure. Prefer ages 26–35. Full-length photo and note a must."

The ads in Jewish newspapers aren't necessarily better, as one man satirized:[2]

"Multimillionaire, drives Jag, *frum* from birth, 6'2", dark, muscular, and extremely handsome, mid-thirties, semi-retired seeks ultra-Orthodox *heimisha* knockout with a Raquel Welch look, Yiddish-speaking, slim, 5'8" +, 18–27–

year-old, for a platonic relationship and dining out in fine restaurants. You should look like a fox, but not necessarily clean my socks. My physical activities include 2 hrs. of daily martial arts, 1 hr. of aerobics, and 5 miles of jogging, with 100 pushups before going to bed. My spiritual side includes Daf Yomi, weekly Chumash, Rashi, and Hebrew numerology. Politically, I'm a right-winger, except for being a vegetarian and a super-easy-going guy. My habits include eccentric poetry, feeding my exotic tropical fish, and autographing my latest book."

One reason why so many Americans get divorced is because they think that a good marriage is about having fun, passion, and romance. Singles are brainwashed by secular books, movies, and songs to believe that they will uncontrollably "fall" in love with someone who "lights their fire" and with whom they will live happily ever after. But strong chemistry only says that our animalistic drive or unconscious side wants someone. It says nothing about whether that person will be a suitable life partner for us.

We "fall" in love (instead of "growing in love") when we think that someone fulfills our fantasy of who we want them to be. These feelings of infatuation are especially strong when we deny someone's shortcomings. As soon as reality intrudes, those wonderful feelings die and we quickly become disenchanted.

Real love is grounded in reality, not in fantasy. It starts by seeing who someone is, then giving to and receiving from them, if there is real potential for marriage. Mature love is an act of responsibility, not an act of desperation or an abandonment to fate, chemistry, or instinct.

People who think that love just "happens" expect the "right person" to enthrall them. They expect to have fun and be happy, then move on to new and more exciting thrills when the good times fade.

Singles who expect a spouse to fulfill their dreams make a shopping list of "needs." They list their ideal mate's height, weight, age, appearance, religious affiliation, title (doctor, lawyer, CEO, career woman, homemaker, etc.), and financial assets. While some criteria are relevant to a good marriage, many important ones are missing. These include being able to handle responsibilities and crises; running a home; dealing with anger and frustration; enjoying and appreciating day-to-day life; sharing meaningful long-term goals, values, and perspectives; communicating well; and (usually) raising children.

THE PURPOSE OF MARRIAGE

God designed our world in such a way that everything has a spiritual purpose. Jewish marriage has financial, physical, and emotional consequences, but its main function is spiritual. While sex to have fun or to foster emotional closeness is a goal for many people, and marriage legitimizes that, Jewish marital relations are supposed to bring God into a couple's intimate life. The *Song of Songs* describes marital intimacy as the "holy of holies"[3] because it allows us to experience God's love. We can't truly love God until we experience marital love because the latter lets human beings feel the deepest intimacy, giving, and merging possible. This is why the Holy of Holies in the Temple was called "the bedroom" (*chedder hametot*). God was present there just as he is in the loving, joyful, intimate union of a husband and wife.

A verse says, "When two Jews who are well-suited to each other marry, the prophet Elijah kisses them and God loves them." This means that when His children live together harmoniously, they hasten the coming of the Messiah, and God becomes part of their union. This idea is illustrated by a story:

Two boys grew up together. As adults, one moved to Rome and the other relocated to Syria. When the Roman Jew visited his Syrian friend, the Roman was arrested as a spy. The king sentenced him to death, but the man asked to go home and settle his affairs, then promised to return.

The king laughed. "Do you think that I am so stupid as to let you go? Once you leave, you will never return."

The Syrian friend then offered to guarantee the Roman's reappearance. "You may imprison me until he comes back and execute me if he's not here by the agreed-upon time."

The king was so amazed that anyone would offer to die for a friend that he consented to the arrangement.

The Roman Jew went home and settled his affairs. He said goodbye to his family, then boarded a boat to Syria. But a terrible sea storm delayed him past the time set for his execution.

The executioner gleefully removed the Syrian Jew from prison and brought him to the gallows. The crowd and the king jeered the man for being so foolish as to believe that his friend would return. They put a noose around his neck and were about to hang him when the Roman Jew ran to the front of the mob. The two friends hugged and kissed and were very happy to see each other. Then the Roman said, "Take my friend off the gallows. It's time for my execution."

The Syrian Jew replied, "No, it's not. We had a deal that if you didn't return in time, I would die in your stead."

"I was caught in a storm," the Roman protested. "I couldn't get back in time. Now get down so that I can receive my sentence."

The executioner was so stunned by their behavior that he didn't know what to do, and finally consulted the king. When the king saw how much the two friends loved each other, he responded, "I'll let you both live on one condition. You must take me in as your partner."

This is how God regards a husband and wife who are devoted to one another. He becomes their Partner if they are dedicated to sacrificing for each other in order to make their marriage work.

Jewish marriage is termed *kiddushin,* meaning "sanctification." A couple brings God's Presence into the world by sanctifying their marriage and making their home a mini-Sanctuary. They create holiness by expressing their inner divinity through their loving, caring, and respectful interactions. They draw down God's Presence by elevating their animalistic drives when they eat, drink, talk, dress, and even have marital relations in ways that God sanctions. They bring holiness into the world by inviting God to be close as they observe His ritual, social, and ethical commandments, in public as well as in private.

Bob is a lawyer who feels God accompany him throughout the day. He won't lie or pad his clients' bills, even when no one will find out. His self-restraint due to his love for God brings holiness into the world.

His wife Miriam is a physician who has studied Jewish medical ethics and lives by them. She brings holiness into the world when she helps patients. She regards herself as God's agent for healing, instead of thinking and acting as if she restores people's health by her own power.

When Bob and Miriam invite guests to their home, people see how harmonious their family is. Their children are considerate of one another and respect their parents. There is a peaceful atmosphere when the parents bless the children on Friday nights. Guests feel serenity and joy sitting at a table set with fine china, silver, and linen, laden with tasty food, and surrounded by happy people singing Sabbath songs. By sanctifying their eating, drinking, speech, and interactions, Bob and Miriam bring God into their home.

When couples share Jewish rituals, Torah study, holidays, and build a Jewish home together, they continually deepen their spiritual and emotional bonds and bring Godliness into the entire world.

When people marry in order to raise a family and insure the future of the Jewish people, their motive is considered "divine."[4] This idea is illustrated by a story about a very wealthy man who died. His will stipulated that his son could inherit his estate only if the son became crazy. The son didn't know what to do, so he went to the Chief Rabbi of Jerusalem. When he arrived, he was appalled by what he saw through the window of the rabbi's house. The rabbi was on his hands and knees, howling and jerking his face like a wild animal. Yet when the rabbi opened the door a moment later, he looked very proper, and invited the man in as if nothing had happened. When the visitor entered, nothing inside seemed out of the ordinary.

The visitor showed the rabbi his father's will. The rabbi then asked if he had peered in the window moments earlier. The man admitted that he had, and that the rabbi had looked quite bizarre.

"And what did you think when you saw me acting that way?" the rabbi inquired. Before the man could reply, the rabbi continued, "You do know what I was doing, don't you? I was playing with my grandchildren. Your father's instructions mean that you can't inherit his money until you get married, have children, get down on your hands and knees, and play with them while acting crazy!"[5]

The father wanted the son to realize that it is pointless to give away money if the recipient doesn't realize that it should go beyond himself. The same applies to marriage. People should get married for reasons that go beyond their personal happiness. Raising children helps couples realize that there is much more to life than personal wants and feeling good. Raising children reminds them of the importance of giving and encourages couples to build a meaningful future.

Many singles think of marriage only in terms of how it will affect them. But if a couple has two children, and each descendant has only two children, they will have over one million descendants twenty generations later! Every marriage can literally create or destroy the world, and can affect the entire Jewish people.[6]

God put us here to fulfill a special, spiritual calling. While some Jews feel emotionally, intellectually, or physically close to non-Jews, we can never be spiritually compatible with them as our marriage partners. Perhaps this is why American Jews who intermarry have higher divorce rates than Jews who marry within the fold.[7]

Gentiles can be every bit as wonderful, bright, and accomplished as Jews, but our life missions are different than theirs. Our mission is to fulfill the Torah and bring spiritual light into the world. We can only do this by marrying Jews and passing on our spiritual legacy to future generations.

In addition, there is an enormous amount of emotional bonding and family cohesiveness that occurs around Jewish rituals, holidays, and the Sabbath. When couples can't share this, an important dimension of marriage is missing. Moreover, mixed marriages give confusing signals to children. They cannot establish a healthy religious identity under these circumstances.

Singles should consider what kind of Jewish life they want, and seek a partner who shares that vision. Jewish children need to be raised with a good religious education, in a vibrant Jewish community. It is easiest to offer home hospitality to guests on the Sabbath and holidays, to host parlor meetings for charities or Jewish study groups, and to be active in communal affairs if a partner supports you.

It is extremely difficult for couples to raise children if they differ strongly in their religious observances and attitudes. If they succeed, it is usually because the less observant spouse allows the more religious one to set the religious tone for the home and to send the children to religious schools.

Singles who are dissimilar in their religious practices and beliefs usually should not date each other because marriages between them tend not to work. It is better not to start such relationships than to go through the torment of separating later. Love does not conquer all, especially where religious differences or children are concerned. (For an elaboration of why we should marry Jews, see the chapters on sexuality, raising children, and building a Jewish home.)

Parents model to their children how God acts and what He expects of us. Parents who only give lip service to Judaism discredit themselves and God. It is critical that both spouses live Judaism, not just preach its beliefs.

SUMMARY

Couples can marry for many different reasons, and hopefully do so for reasons that transcend personal pleasure. They should make homes that radiate sanctity, love, and harmony. By studying Torah, observing the laws of family holiness, keeping a kosher home, and observing the holidays and Sabbath together, couples bring spiritual light into their home and marriage. The more couples reinforce their emotional and spiritual growth, the more they infuse their relationship with depth, intimacy, and holiness.

NOTES

1. *New York Magazine* (Nov. 16, 1992).
2. *The Jewish Week* (Nov. 13, 1992).
3. *Yadayim* 3:5.
4. *Sefer Eliyahu Zuta,* chapter 3.
5. Midrash on Psalm 92.
6. Aryeh Kaplan, *Made in Heaven* (New York: Moznaim Publishing Corporation, 1983), pp. 4–5.
7. N. Goldberg and W. J. Fried, eds., "Jews and Divorce," quoted in *Encyclopaedia Judaica,* 6:136.

2

Marriage as a Partnership

When the author saw a recently married friend, he gushed about his new life. "I'm so happy. My first marriage was terrible because my ex-wife and I both had different agendas. This marriage is great because my wife and I are terrific partners."

What an interesting idea! A good marriage is indeed like a business partnership. Both require partners who are compatible but not identical. Two people must share similar goals but have complementary strengths and shortcomings. Each relationship has basic objectives, mutual responsibilities, and rules for dissolving it if it fails. Both business and marriage partners expect to be loyal and committed and not let outside people or problems intrude. And both partners succeed or fail with the venture, regardless of who put in more time and effort, or who is at fault. No business partner says, "My partner is only putting in 25 percent of the effort needed, so I'll do likewise." The first one will work extra hard to supply what's missing.

Business and marriage partners must take their roles seriously and work very hard, especially when they are getting to know and appreciate each other. They need to respect their differences and iron out problems together. Each must contribute whatever the partnership needs, even if it means giving more than 50 percent of the time, money, or effort required. In both types of partnership, it is a waste of energy to retaliate, rehash past mistakes, or place blame when things go poorly. Instead, focusing on fixing problems and moving forward works best.

Ethel initially thought of marriage as an entitlement program. She expected Sidney to do everything she wanted, and she threw temper tantrums when he didn't. She wanted him to read her mind and guess what she really wanted, then punished him with a cold shoulder when he disappointed her.

Instead of acting as childishly as Ethel did, Sidney showed her how to discuss matters calmly and benefit more in the long-run by being reasonable and accepting compromise. His patience paid off. Ethel gradually stopped reacting to her feelings of the moment and worked for the betterment of their marriage.

Business and marriage partners both need a plan. They create compatible visions of what each will provide and receive from the relationship. Neither assumes that they will be able to change what they don't like in a partner. They assume that what they see will be there to stay.

Neither businesspeople nor singles should say, "I'll look for a partner who is cute and fun to be with. We don't need to share many long-term goals or attitudes as long as we have a good time together." They know that compatibility is important, but fun and happiness can't sustain a partnership indefinitely.

George enjoys Liz's stories about the interesting people she meets at work and her discussions of the books that she avidly reads. He also loves playing tennis and going skiing with her. But Liz intends to stop working once she has children, and is unlikely to have much time for pleasure reading or sports then. She and George won't be able to sustain their relationship a few years from now unless they share deeper ideas, interests, and goals.

Couples and businesspeople should never be too desperate to consider how a new partner will fit into their long-term plans.

People rarely become mature, responsible, emotionally healthy, or adopt drastically different interests and habits after meeting the "right person." If anything, character defects that are annoying before marriage become intolerable afterwards.

Larry was twenty-eight and lived at home when he met Betty. His only responsibility was keeping his car in working condition. His mother did his laundry, shopped, and cooked for him. His father paid the mortgage, utility, and telephone bills. Although Larry worked hard, he never stayed at any one job for long and got into power struggles with his bosses. Betty only noticed that he was handsome, funny, warm, charming, and thoughtful. When he proposed, the furthest thing from her mind was how he would support a family or help her run a household. After marriage, they fought incessantly about his unwillingness to stay at one job, help around the house, pay his bills, or limit his spending. It didn't take long before his charm was irrelevant.

Tammy also lived at home until she got married, but she helped her mother with the cooking and laundry, shopped for the family, and paid her own bills, including what she charged on her credit card. Steve had every reason to assume that she would continue being responsible when they got married, and he was right.

Neither businessmen nor singles should let their emotional needs distort how they see a potential partner. A bad partnership is so terrible that it is worth avoiding at all costs. Someone who has grave misgivings about a potential spouse should make sure to resolve the doubts or else not make a commitment. Dissolving a malfunctioning partnership is so wrenching that it's best not to act hastily in the first place. A bad partnership is not better than no partnership.

A chemist and a teacher met when they were both in their thirties. Despite having Ph.D.s, they approached marriage mindlessly. She was desperate to get married because her biological clock was ticking away. He felt that he should get married because he was tired of his bachelor life, and he finally had met a woman who was interested in him. They knew that they had major differences but got engaged anyway, agreeing to get divorced if things didn't work out. They separated six months later, but it took four years to get divorced. They did not realize how emotionally difficult and legally messy it was to get divorced. This terrible situation ultimately taught them to admit to irreconcilable interests and goals when they resumed dating others, and it also taught them not to force untenable relationships to work.

Rose had poor self-esteem. She wanted to marry a "successful" man so that she could feel special. Baruch showered her with presents, took her out to nice places, and made her very happy. While he normally worked sixty hours a week, he temporarily worked less so that they could spend time together. A week after they got married, he resumed working seventy hours a week to make up for lost time. Rose's initial excitement about being married, furnishing their beautiful home, and getting wedding gifts soon waned. By the end of the year, life without Baruch around bored her. She realized too late that money and possessions were poor substitutes for a loving husband's companionship.

Joseph tended to date women with whom he fell head-over-heels in love, but who weren't especially interested in him. Donna was different. She enjoyed his company, was a good conversationalist, and was not possessive or demanding. They also had great chemistry. It wasn't until Donna had their first child that he realized how dysfunctional she was. She had been a great wife as long as her responsibilities were limited to making dinner every night, shopping twice a week, and doing the laundry twice a month. But raising a child totally overwhelmed her, and Joseph's mother had to do most of it. Only in retrospect did Joseph see that Donna had a life-long pattern of avoiding stress and responsibility. When she made him meals during their courtship, her mother had actually done most of the cooking, or she had bought take-out food. She had complained incessantly of her workload at a job that really did not require much of her. She couldn't wait to get married so that a husband would relieve her of the burden of having to work. She never did cope well when she had to face pressure and managed to avoid meeting most deadlines. When she came home, she spent hours talking to her girlfriends on the telephone. Had Joseph realized that she took almost no initiative and expected to be taken care of by him in childlike ways, he would never have married her.

SUMMARY

Bad marriages can usually be avoided if singles consider marriage as carefully as they would a business partnership. They know when friends have unrealistic expectations or irreconcilable differences with potential marriage partners, and they should be as objective for themselves.

3

Working on Oneself

Singles need a vision of what they want marriage to be like, with ideas about how to make it happen. By considering what they will contribute, they can work on becoming the "right" kind of spouse and can realistically imagine what kind of partner will complement them. Singles who don't think about what they will need to bring to a marriage are likely to be disappointed, because who we are in marriage is every bit as important as who we choose to marry.

Leora was successful in business, beautiful, and very desirable. Unfortunately, she was only attracted to wealthy men who she thought would indulge her real love – spending money. She didn't know how to make herself happy so she spent money to distract herself from her inner emptiness. When she was forty-two, she finally fell head-over-heels in love with a man for the first time in her life. But her ardor quickly cooled and she broke their engagement when he drafted a prenuptial agreement that limited how much of his money she would get in the event of divorce or his death. Leora, like many women with poor self-esteem, will not be happy with any man until she learns to be happy with herself.

People who expect circumstances or other people to make them happy have a chronic undercurrent of misery that surfaces periodically. Marriage can only add to their emotional problems because nothing external can fill their inner emptiness for long. If they can't make themselves happy, no one else will be able to. Marriage cannot provide for all of our emotional needs, unless our needs are few.

Despite what romance novels and movies suggest, marriage doesn't solve emotional problems, and often adds to them. This is why we should strive to *be* the right person, not pin our hopes for the future solely on *marrying* the "right" person.

Sandy was in her mid-thirties, yet could not bring herself to marry her boyfriend of a year. To her, life was a big birthday party, full of delightful presents and attention for her. She could accept that relationships had ups, but not downs; peak moments, but not dull, boring spans that lasted for days or weeks. She had spent years going from one thrilling relationship to another. When each one became dull, she dumped the man and started dating someone new. She lasted a year with Roger only because her therapist had encouraged her to stick it out despite her boredom. As was her pattern, she blamed her recurrent emptiness on Roger instead of addressing her own inner life. When she finally gave up her childlike views of life and accepted Roger as he was, she managed to be happily married. She learned to create her own happiness when he didn't do it for her or with her.

TAKING STOCK OF OURSELVES

While many singles have enormous expectations of a marriage partner, they can be totally oblivious to their own shortcomings. For example, Abe was a religious lawyer who asked a matchmaker to set him up with slim, attractive, bright, interesting, and religious women. The matchmaker gave him the telephone number of a dental hygienist named Laura. He reiterated that Laura had to be slim and was assured that she was.

Laura was shocked when she opened the door and greeted a man who was 5'11" and weighed 270 pounds. On their bus ride to a restaurant, he complained about the many obese women that matchmakers had sent his way. In fact, a recent date was so fat that she took up two seats on the bus! As he ranted about these indignities, his thighs rolled across two seats like a tidal wave. When Abe called Laura for a second date, she told him that she would only consider marrying a normal-weight man. He dismissed her and told her that he didn't need to lose weight.

The Talmud says that a man may not marry a woman who he finds unattractive because he will violate the obligation to "Love your neighbor as yourself." On the other hand, some singles are too focused on others' looks, yet they themselves don't meet their own criteria.

Ellie was gorgeous. She had a gleaming, perfect smile, turquoise eyes, and blond hair. Her twenty-two-inch waist, peaches and cream complexion, beautiful face, and long, slim legs turned heads wherever she went. After six dates, Harry asked if she minded him having a small paunch. (He was twenty-five pounds overweight.) She lied and said that it was just more of him to love. She then asked if he wanted her to change anything about herself. Without hesitating, he replied, "You really need to lose at least five pounds."

Many women are distressed by men's double standards about looks. Men expect women to look stunning, yet the men don't exercise and haul around spare tires that they insist shouldn't bother women. For health and esthetic reasons, men's waists shouldn't be bigger than their hips. (This is especially true after marriage!) Maintaining a normal weight reduces the risk of a heart attack and makes men (and women) more eligible for marriage.

Shlomo had average looks, with a stomach that looked like a mountain made out of a molehill. He was only attracted to women who looked like models and wore a lot of makeup and bright nail polish. Luckily, he worked out his obsession in psychotherapy and is now happily married to a woman who doesn't fit his former criteria.

Singles have many inconsistencies. Jimmy was thirty and sought an intelligent, well-read, interesting, and kind woman. He was usually introduced to professional women, yet refused to spend more than $10 on a date. He considered himself such a scintillating conversationalist that he expected dates to happily share a plate of French fries and a Coke with him—instead of buying them dinner. The fact that he totally monopolized conversations only added insult to injury.

Joni was a thirty-year-old woman who wanted to marry a knowledgeable, religious man who would be a dedicated husband, father, and breadwinner. She had a minimal Jewish background and only observed those religious commandments that she found appealing. She insisted that anyone worthwhile would accept her for who she was. She was quite willing to have higher expectations of men than she had of herself, but then lamented her fate when she stayed single.

When singles make up a "shopping list" of a spouse-to-be's qualities, they should wonder if this person would want them! A woman seeking a sophisticated, refined, well-dressed, and meticulously groomed husband should look this way herself. She should also realize that anyone who is so concerned about looks is likely to be superficial and narcissistic. A man who wants a warm, kind, and nurturing woman should also be that way. Someone who wants a good conversationalist should be an active listener and/or be a good communicator. A person seeking a very observant spouse should be fully committed to an observant lifestyle and Torah study.

Marriage today is a buyer's market, with tremendous competition. Singles who are serious about getting married should make sure to package themselves well. Those who are overweight should lose weight, women should enhance their looks with makeup and attractive clothes, and men should be well-groomed, attractively dressed, speak in a refined manner, and follow proper social etiquette. Women are turned off by men who are self-centered, pick their noses, wipe their hands on their clothes, wear stained or pungent clothes, eat with their fingers or from a knife, and don't open doors or escort her to her door at the end of a date. Men are turned off by women who are self-centered, feel entitled, are overweight, require "high-maintenance," or are emotionally needy.

EGOCENTRIC EXPECTATIONS

In our egocentric society, couples often marry because they hope to get more from a spouse than they have as singles. But unless both partners are givers instead of takers, their love will die of malnutrition.

Children use people as objects. They believe that people and the world exist only to make them happy. As Winnie the Pooh said, "If there is a beehive on top of a tree, it must be there for me [to enjoy the honey]."

After God created the first person, He proclaimed, "Therefore shall a man leave his father and his mother, and cleave unto his wife, and they shall be one flesh."[1] Since Adam and Eve had no parents, this verse implies that the parent-child relationship is unique insofar as parents give unreservedly, while children take. People have to reverse this mentality before marriage by being givers, not remaining takers. This means learning what others need and trying to provide it.

Art thought that he was special and deserved to be admired, although he was really quite ordinary. He spent most of his dates talking about himself, and rarely asked Zelda about herself. When they dated, she expected his narcissism to fade but learned the hard way that character disorders rarely change. When they passed a bookstore, Zelda mentioned that she planned to buy a book in the window on her next payday. On their third date, Art surprised her with a book that he loved. He assumed that if he liked it, she would, too. He ignored her when she told him the previous week that that author's works put her to sleep.

Mary bought her boyfriend an enormous chocolate cake for his birthday, two days after he had told her that he was allergic to chocolate and disliked cake. She got the cake because she found it tasty.

Zalman worked hard, and enjoyed spending time relaxing with Devorah. Meanwhile, she ran herself ragged buying him gifts and cooking elaborate meals that would "earn" his approval and appreciation. But he wanted her to do less for him and to expect less in return, especially since most of what she did "for him" he did not want or appreciate.

We often assume that others have the same needs and feelings that we do. Instead of doing only what pleases us, we should learn what a partner wants and try to provide it. Someone whose gifts and efforts are seldom appreciated may not be giving a partner what he or she really wants. Sensitivity is necessary in order to find out what that person's true desire is.

APPRECIATING DIFFERENCES

Everyone wants to be appreciated and to feel unique and special. We make people feel this way by asking them to share memories, experiences, feelings, and ideas with us, then showing that we treasure them.

A religious Jewish man with a macabre sense of humor dated a conventional religious woman. She loved flowers, classical music, impressionistic art, gourmet food, and trivia. He loved jazz, blues, hard rock, the Addams Family, B-grade movies, and fast food. For her birthday, he bought her a dozen long-stemmed red roses, gave her a book on trivia, and took her to dinner at a fancy, kosher restaurant.

For his birthday, she brought him fried chicken and French fries, gave him a music cassette that he promised never to play in her presence, and surprised him with a dozen long stems from roses, without the flowers. (He had rose fever, and she imitated Morticia Addams by throwing away the roses and keeping the stems.) Each had a wonderful birthday because each acknowledged the other's individuality and unique tastes.

Instead of trying to get someone else to fit our image, we can learn about and appreciate a partner for who she or he is. Many women marry men who they hope to change, while men marry women hoping that the women will *not* change and will accept the men as they are. Everyone yearns to be loved and accepted for who they are. No one wants to feel valued only if they impersonate a fictitious character.

It is hard to accept a partner if we don't have self-esteem and feel secure, because differences symbolize separation and incompatibility to many people. The more insecure people are, the more they feel threatened by differences, and the harder it is to be close to a partner who is dissimilar. A secure woman can love the fact that her husband enjoys reading mathematics, even though she hates it. When he does what makes him happy, she is happy. They can agree to disagree about politics if they have other philosophies and causes to agree about. Their differences can even lead to interesting conversations as they learn from each other and share opposing points of view.

An insecure woman feels threatened by differences because she wants to share "everything" with her husband. She feels inadequate when others appreciate a part of him that she can't. She also worries that he will stop loving her if he meets women who can discuss topics with him that she doesn't understand or appreciate.

Likewise, some men enjoy a wife's career success because it takes an economic burden off of them. They are glad when their wives find work fulfilling, as this makes them happier and more interesting to be with. Insecure men fear women who have fulfilling careers, feeling that, if they married, their wife might stop needing them, or might meet other men who could become rivals. Some men deliberately seek wives who are limited and insular in order to always receive more attention than their wives; thus, their wives will always look up to them.

Most people with poor self-esteem want frequent reassurance that they are lovable and worthwhile, and get upset when it's missing. They expect a partner always to be warm, happy, and uncritical. This is hard for most partners.

Today, people confuse needs with wants. Needy people believe that others must take care of them, and they won't take care of themselves more than is absolutely necessary. Their partners find this dependency draining and exhausting. It is enjoyable to give love and compliments freely, but who wants to have them constantly demanded or expected?

While a good marriage can make happy people more fulfilled, and may take away a certain loneliness, we should not *need* marriage to make life meaningful, give us worth, or be our sole source of meaning. We should want to marry so that we can grow emotionally and spiritually and be able to give of ourselves to a spouse and children. If we are basically unhappy and don't feel that we have much to give, or if we mostly want to take, marriage only compounds our emotional problems and our dissatisfaction with life.

LOVE

People marry for many different reasons, but mostly because they are "in love" and want to spend the rest of their lives with someone special. Healthy love results from ongoing choices that we make to love a partner who has real, lasting, and admirable qualities. Mature people don't "fall in love" as helpless victims of their emotions.

A few hours after Malkie met Milton, she was already fantasizing about marrying him. They talked a lot during the next two days, and she told him all about her life. Milton found her beautiful and vulnerable, and felt wonderful being appreciated and needed. At first, he was so intrigued that he gladly gave her his full attention, but her intensity burned him out by the end of the weekend. He knew that her neediness would be oppressive on a daily basis, so he wisely nipped their relationship in the bud.

Healthy love develops from contributing to a partner's growth, raising a family together, and sharing meaningful ideas, memories, experiences, and goals. It also deepens the more we give and the more we deepen our commitment to a relationship.[2] For instance, a mother loves her baby despite the fact that he never takes care of her. Quite the opposite! He cries, spits up, dirties his diapers, and doesn't talk intelligibly. She loves him because of what she does for him, not because of what he gives her. And the more she does, the more she loves.

We often decide how we feel about something by looking at what we do. If we invest a lot in a cause, we assume that it must be very important to us. The more we do, the more invested we are, and the more we feel committed to it. This is one reason why Judaism requires us to do so many things to serve God. The more we do for Him, the more we love Him, and the more attached to Him we feel.

This same idea applies to marriage. Love results from making the commitment to care for a spouse. When our memories are filled with images of doing for that person, our hearts follow by loving the one to whom we give so much.

We can love others primarily because of what we take from them, or because of what we give. The more partners give to each other, the more it strengthens their relationship. Mature people get pleasure from the "work" and responsibilities of marriage, from sharing and contributing. They don't expect to be repaid measure for measure and don't keep score about who did what.

Unfortunately, many people today expect a partner to heal old emotional wounds and fill lifelong voids. They give in order to get back, and are rarely satisfied with a partner's response because no one can take away such ingrained pain and lifelong emptiness.

Healthy love is built from sharing feelings and communicating wants clearly and sensitively, without expecting a partner to mind-read. In a good marriage, people deal maturely with anger and other feelings. They delay gratification instead of letting their emotions rule them. They get enormous pleasure from making a partner happy, and are willing to put their own wants on hold when necessary for the integrity of the relationship.

Some singles complain that this makes marriage sound like all work and no play. "What about passion and romance?" they challenge. "Why talk about giving? Couples should just relax, enjoy each other, and have a good time!"

Infatuation, chemistry, romance, and having a good time are nice, but they are much more important in dating than in marriage.[3] Married couples need to weather uncomfortable and unpleasant times that sometimes last for weeks or months. They must deal constructively with day-to-day responsibilities, raise children, and resolve tensions and problems. The success or failure of most marriages has little to do with having a good time. In fact, the major reasons for divorce are poor communication and inability to resolve conflicts, especially about money and sex.[4]

Good marriages are made through hard work, they don't just happen. While excitement and infatuation start by "magic," romance and love continue when couples work at it. People who don't know how to deal with the rough spots of marriage will not be able to keep loving feelings alive.

Shari is a well-adjusted woman who had a typical initiation into married life:

"Parts of being married were wonderful, but parts were also miserable. I looked forward to our wedding night for months, but it was a fiasco. My loving feelings towards Al were constantly interspersed with disappointment in him during our first year together. We had to make so many adjustments that it was hard to feel loving a lot of the time. I often felt neglected, and he felt trapped. In fact, he spent time almost every evening reading as his form of escape.

"By the end of our first year of marriage, I had morning sickness and Al was out of work. It took him six months to find another job. We were so stressed by our financial problems that we didn't remember the loving feelings that we once had.

"I learned that married people go through a few good days, weeks, or months, then a few bad ones. We had one terrible spell that lasted an entire year. Then a tragedy became a blessing in disguise. I was hit by a car, and we had unbelievable problems afterwards. While I recuperated, Al was superb and did everything for me. I can't compare the love that I felt for him before marriage with how I felt towards him after we went through that ordeal.

"For years, I questioned whether or not I should have married Al. Since that accident, I've known that I did the right thing. Other men I loved could not have weathered the crises that we've been through as well as he did. I'm lucky that I went for a solid-and-stable type instead of a sophisticated charmer. Those men are great for a short time, but they're too self-absorbed and fickle to be there when the chips are down."

Since giving helps sustain love, it's important to marry someone who can receive what we have to give. That way, even when times are rough, we can still create love.

The biblical story of Jacob and Rachel highlights this. Jacob agreed to work for seven years for Rachel's hand in marriage,[5] and those years seemed like only a few days to him because he loved her so dearly.[6]

We would expect a couple who is deeply in love to want to marry as soon as possible. Every day apart seems like an eternity of delayed gratification. The time flew by for Jacob because everything he did was for Rachel's sake, not for his own. He loved her so much that his own needs were of little concern, and he devoted himself to taking care of her. His pleasure came from making her happy, rather than from gratifying himself, so he wasn't frustrated by waiting years for her to be his wife.

SUMMARY

When God created the first person, He said, "It is not good for a person to be alone."[7] We are incomplete without a partner to give to, provide for, and share with. The Zohar even says, "A man is not called a man until he unites with a woman in marriage."[8]

Singles lack something fundamental, even if all of their physical and material desires are fulfilled. True giving and fulfillment only come by contributing meaningfully to a partner (and children) in marriage.[9] Someone who refuses to marry lives by himself and for himself. When marriage is a labor of love with mutual giving, a couple's union is greater than the sum of their parts.[10]

When we love to gratify ourselves, we stop needing the other person as soon as our wants are satisfied.[11] In addition, we degrade people by seeing them as objects who serve us. The real purpose of marriage is to enable us to exercise our divine image and help a partner do the same.

Singles should ask what they expect to contribute and receive from a spouse, and should assess how realistic that expectation is. Next, they should work on improving themselves and on becoming the kind of person that their desired partner will want. Finally, they need to prepare themselves in order to contribute what such a partner will expect.

NOTES

1. Genesis 2:24.

2. Rabbi Eliyahu Dessler, Michtav M'eliyahu, *Strive For Truth* (New York: Feldheim, 1978), p. 126–127.

3. Clifford Notarius and Howard Markman, *We Can Work It Out* (New York: G. P. Putnam's Sons, 1993), p. 21.

4. Ibid., 56.

5. Genesis 29:18.

6. Genesis 29:20.

7. Genesis 2:18.

8. On Genesis 5:2.

9. Moshe Meiselman, *Jewish Woman in Jewish Law* (Hoboken, NJ: Ktav, 1978), p. 23.

10. *Kohelet Rabbah* 4.

11. *Mishnah Avot* 5:19–20.

4

What We Should Contribute in Marriage

It is easy to tell someone, "I love you and want to spend the rest of my life with you." But intentions mean little if our words aren't backed up by tangible expressions of caring. Who would marry a man who promises to love a woman dearly, but who never does anything for her!?

The secular world emphasizes rights and entitlements, while Judaism emphasizes responsibilities. Marriage entails obligations that go well beyond giving a wife chocolate or flowers periodically or making a husband dinner on a regular basis. Judaism specifies what husbands and wives should do for each other, and assumes that couples will go beyond the legal requirements and do whatever their circumstances require.

All feelings come and go. When love and passion inevitably vanish (even briefly), something else must sustain a marriage. Vague promises of "loving and cherishing" a mate don't keep marriages intact. Love must be expressed in real ways every day to last.

God constantly puts creative energy into the world and sustains the universe moment by moment. Were He to stop doing this for even a second, the world would disintegrate.[1] Marriages also collapse if we stop infusing them with energy. We imitate God by nurturing a spouse every day, and we simultaneously guarantee the vibrancy of a marriage.

A loving marriage requires that we fulfill our obligations. Jewish men have financial, emotional, and sexual obligations to their wives because real love requires taking on responsibilities. We can only love God by assuming religious obligations towards Him, and we do this by following the Torah. Professing faith alone is not enough. The same applies to marriage. Agreeing to make a relationship permanent is not enough. Couples must fulfill responsibilities that sustain and nurture their closeness.

Romance without responsibilities thrives only in fairy tales, novels, and movies. We only need to look at Princess Diana to know that real-life Cinderellas don't necessarily live happily ever after when they marry the prince. Couples who don't work on their marriages and don't do meaningful things for each other become strangers living in the same house.

A HUSBAND'S OBLIGATIONS

Men are obligated to support their wives financially, unless a wife waives this responsibility. Husbands must pay for the family's food, clothing, shelter, and medical care, and buy beautiful clothes, jewelry, and makeup for their wives.[2] If a man lacks the skills or education to earn a living, he must get them.[3]

A husband is also required to make his wife feel cared for[4] and must include her in domestic or financial decisions.[5] Our forefathers did so even 3,500 years ago. For example, before leaving his father-in-law's home and employ, Jacob asked his wives if he should stay. They agreed that it was time to move on.[6]

A man is obliged to buy his wife clothes that will enable her to feel dignified when her parents, siblings, or neighbors visit.[7] He must buy her appropriate outfits for summer and winter that are as beautiful and as varied as those worn by her neighbors.[8]

Jewish law recognizes that women tend to be more sensitive about their appearance than men are. They also tend to be more sensitive to harsh words and readily get hurt feelings. The Talmud says that a man must be careful never to distress his wife because women cry easily.[9]

Men are supposed to love a wife as they love themselves and to honor her more than they honor themselves.[10]

A wife's dignity must be of paramount importance to a husband.[11] He should always help her feel dignified, especially if she spends her days running a home, washing clothes, preparing food, doing errands, and raising children. It pains wives to be asked rhetorically, "What do you do all day?"—as if homemaking and raising children are inconsequential.

Homemaking and mothering are often trivialized, and some women become depressed after leaving prestigious jobs in order to raise children. They lose their self-esteem after experiencing constant disdain by people who regard them as brainless idiots, or they hunger for intellectual stimulation while they raise young children.

Single men may not realize how important it is to help a wife feel respected, intelligent, and valued, especially if she spends most of her time reading children's books, changing diapers, washing dirty clothes, and feeling exhausted. Women need a lot of nurturing, especially when they are mothers, and husbands need to show interest in their wives' conversation and activities, even if they seem mundane.

Both men and women are obligated to light candles in honor of the Sabbath and holidays. However, women customarily light for their household after the husband first puts candles in the candlesticks, lights them to make sure they will burn properly, and then extinguishes them. This custom reminds the couple that the woman has an identity independent of her husband and children.

When a woman prepares her home and her children for the Sabbath, she can easily see herself as only a wife and mother. She must be reminded that she has an inner fire that symbolizes her core identity, and that it needs to be acknowledged, nurtured, and expressed. (Men also have an inner fire that they express independently of being fathers and husbands.) Our inner fires represent our souls' "personalities" striving for actualization. While some women express their uniqueness and individuality as mothers, they should not define themselves only in terms of their relationships with others.

A husband and wife share the candlelighting in order to show that he helps her remember her intrinsic identity (symbolized by the fire), which is independent of her family role. She lights candles to bring her spiritual fire into the world by expressing her Godliness.

A husband is required to develop the couple's friendship by finding out what pleases his wife and trying to provide it. If he knows that she likes flowers every Friday, he should buy them for her if he can. If she loves pizza, and he passes a kosher pizza shop on his way home from work, he should bring her some from time to time. If she feels cherished when he calls her during the day, he should do it whenever possible. He is obligated to nurture his wife emotionally when they may not be physically intimate, by speaking lovingly to her, by writing her love notes or poetry, by being affectionate when they speak on the phone, and by giving her flowers, cards, and little presents.

A husband must fulfill any reasonable promises that he makes to his wife, and must go to a Jewish court to annul any promises that he cannot keep. For example, if he promises to take her somewhere and then changes his mind, he shouldn't think that it is okay to disappoint her.

He must honor her parents and not act or speak about people she cares about in a way that distresses her. He must make it possible for her to see her parents periodically, and must show respect for her by escorting her at least part of the way there.

Husbands who view their homes as refuges from the indignities and abuses of the world should not take out their tensions and frustrations at home. Maimonides said that a husband needs to prepare himself before coming home so that he enters calmly. This means that if he has had a bad day at work, he should get rid of his negative feelings on the way home. If he needs longer to "cool down," he should exercise, learn Torah, listen to music, read, meditate, or relax, then greet his wife nicely.

A man is just as obligated to honor his wife and be sensitive to her feelings as he is to keep kosher and observe the Sabbath. Men are required to listen to their wives, even if they disagree with them or find them boring. A man should never think that he is doing his wife a favor by being nice to her.

A husband is not allowed to criticize his wife for doing her job poorly if she makes an effort to do it well. For example, if it is her job to cook and she makes a tasteless dish that she thinks he'll like, he is supposed to eat it and compliment her for it. (If it is truly inedible, he must reject it sensitively.) In other words, he must be appreciative when she tries to please him, even if the results are disappointing.

He should tell her what he likes in a way that doesn't hurt her feelings. For example, he can tell her a few nights after she serves him overcooked steak that the next time he would like to try it rare. If she washes his white shirts with dark socks and his shirts turn gray, the next time she does the laundry he can ask her to wash the whites and darks separately. Criticizing people when they feel guilty or defensive is counterproductive.

The Bible obligates Jewish men to satisfy their wives physically and sexually.[12] This is included in the *mitzvah* of *onah,* meaning "time." Husbands are required to spend time with their wives, and some of a man's free time actually belongs to his wife. Once married, a man may not reduce the amount of time that he previously implied they would spend together. He may not even learn Torah during "her" time without her consent.

Jewish law views a husband's obligation to spend time with his wife very seriously. During the first year of marriage, he is supposed to spend as much free time with her as possible,[13] and he may not take on obligations that will compromise their time together. This time is to be used to cement their relationship, and build a firm foundation to their marriage. He may never accept a job without her permission if it will decrease their time together.[14] If she is comfortable where they are and he gets a better job elsewhere, he can't relocate without her permission.

The Talmud relates a story about Rabbi Elazar ben Azariah, a remarkable Sage who was nominated for the most prestigious position in Jewish society—head of the Jewish Supreme Court. He consulted his wife about whether to accept the offer, and she advised him to decline since he was only eighteen years old. She did not believe that he would get the respect that he deserved. That night his hair turned white, and he woke up looking like an aged, venerable scholar. His wife then urged him to accept the appointment, which he did.[15]

Some men think that women were put here to take care of them and/or to be mothers. However, both men and women were put here to imitate and serve God. Women should never view being a wife or mother as their entire identity. Nor should a husband foster the idea that a wife is worthwhile only because she takes care of him and their children.

This idea was highlighted in an incident involving the matriarch Rachel and her husband Jacob. Jacob was tricked into marrying Rachel's sister Leah before he wed Rachel.[16] A few years later, Leah had four children while Rachel remained barren. Rachel cried out to Jacob, "Give me children, else I will die."[17] Instead of responding compassionately to his anguished wife, he responded to her with uncharacteristic harshness (for which he was later punished), "Am I in God's place, Who withheld from you fruit of the womb?"[18]

This incident suggests that women have two primary identities: One is as individuals with unique feelings, ideas, drives, and contributions to make. (Men have a comparable primary male identity.) The second is as mothers (derived from Eve's role as the mother of life). Jacob's sharp remark to Rachel was intended to convey that she still had a valuable identity to express even without having children.[19]

Women are good mothers only if they value their womanhood—their creativity, inner divinity, and ability to impact the world, independently of being wives or mothers. Part of a husband's role is to value, nurture, and validate this part of his wife's identity.

A WIFE'S OBLIGATIONS

Jewish wives have obligations that parallel those of their husbands. If a husband supports the family financially, he is entitled to keep whatever his wife earns or finds.[20] If she wants to keep her income, she must first contribute to the household the same amount that he pays for food. That is, if he spends $5,000 a year for food for the family, she must put $5,000 a year into a kitty that is used for household expenses. She may then keep the rest of her earnings. Alternatively, if she buys her own food, she may use the rest of her earnings in any way that she likes.

A husband may not unilaterally decide not to support his wife. Only she may waive his obligation to do so if she wants to support herself or keep her own income.

Couples may keep separate bank accounts, provided they jointly contribute to the family's maintenance. The husband should not use his account to pay for some household expenses while the wife pays for others from hers. Instead, they should have a joint account that is used for household and family expenses. This shows that they are pooling their resources to run a home and raise a family, rather than each having a partial share in their marriage.

If only the husband has an income, he should give his wife discretionary spending money, and they should have jointly owned assets and accounts.[21]

A wife must do, or have someone else do, certain domestic tasks, regardless of whether or not her husband supports her.[22] If she grew up in a home with a housekeeper, or had reason to believe that one would do these chores for her after marriage, her husband must hire help if the wife wants it. If her husband was once poor and promised her that she wouldn't have to do chores if his financial situation improved, she can stop doing them when that happens. If he did not promise, but earns enough to hire help, she may still use his money to do this.

If a couple can afford domestic help and the wife doesn't want it, she must make sure that the house runs properly. Among other things, her husband and children must have clean clothes and prepared meals. The Talmud says that no matter how wealthy a woman is, she must weave cloth for her household's clothing so that she won't be bored.[23]

Women don't have to weave cloth today, but they should not be bored by having nothing constructive to do. Leisure time should be better spent than by playing cards, going out to restaurants, shopping for the latest clothes, furnishings or gadgets, gossiping on the telephone, and watching television.

Wives must also make sure that their husbands are not bored at home because this leads to unhealthy feelings and actions. Couples should have meaningful conversation and emotional sharing every day. Once a husband and wife are emotionally bored with each other, a marriage begins to disintegrate.

Wives are supposed to encourage family members to relate to each other without being couch potatoes or gossipmongers.

If a woman runs the home, she has the final say in all domestic decisions.[24] She determines how the house is furnished, the colors it is painted, what kind of china or dishes they use, and so forth. Husbands are not allowed to invite guests over without their wives' permission. Common sense dictates that a wife consult her husband before making domestic decisions or before inviting guests.

Besides overseeing the running of the home, every wife must personally do "works of love." These show that she is willing to work to make her house a home and to nurture her husband. It demonstrates her interest in him and helps him to feel that he is not living in a hotel run by a maid.

"Works of love" include making his bed, setting the table, and serving him meals. (The original obligations required her also to bake bread, pour beverages for him, and feed and nurse their children. Since we now have bakeries, women can buy bread instead of baking it. If serving beverages makes a wife feel demeaned or taken for granted, she is no longer required to do this, either.)[25]

Whether or not men admit it, most yearn for their wives to nurture them as their mothers did (or should have). Men feel wonderful when wives perform loving acts for them. Although a wife is not a mother-substitute, she can do much to make a husband feel loved and cherished.

Joy's Sabbath guests complimented her on her beautiful china, and she mentioned that she used the same dishes throughout the week. When the guests asked why she didn't reserve her fancy dishes for *Shabbat,* she responded, "I don't believe in treating guests better than I treat my husband. If he enjoys nice china during the week, why should I reserve it for strangers?" This was one of many ways that she made her husband feel special.

A wife must honor and show respect to her husband and his parents. For example, she should never humiliate or criticize him in front of others, including their children. If she disagrees with him, she should do it respectfully in private.

Jews are obligated to "love your neighbor as yourself." The Sage Hillel interpreted this to mean that we shouldn't do to others that which we find hateful, especially if the "neighbor" is our spouse.[26]

SENSITIVITY BEYOND OBLIGATIONS

If a husband buys his wife a gift, or goes to great lengths to please her, she should appreciate his effort and accept his gift graciously, even if she doesn't like it. Many men take a lot of time and make a great effort to please their wives, but they don't do exactly what the wives want. Women devastate their husbands by trivializing or criticizing these presents, not to mention making the husbands feel distant and reluctant to try again.

Ina complained, "Herbie drives me crazy. He buys me gifts that I have to take back to the store because they're never appropriate. Last week he bought me a sweater, but I'm allergic to wool. A few months earlier, he bought me a dress in the wrong size and color. For my birthday, he bought me unattractive earrings. I couldn't even return them because he bought them at a final sale."

Ina had such specific tastes that Herbie could never please her. She lost his goodwill and made him feel inadequate because she never appreciated his efforts. At the very least, she could have given him a list of some very specific things that she would appreciate, such as red roses from the florist down the block, a twenty-inch pearl necklace, a watch with a gold band made by a specific company, a book written by her favorite author, or a specific brand of body lotion or perfume. If Herbie still made mistakes, she should keep the gifts for a while and tell him how wonderful he is and how delighted she is with the presents.

Saul went to several counters in a department store, looking for a birthday present for his wife. He was finally lured to a perfume counter by a huge advertisement suggesting that women feel loved when their husbands give them fragrances. His wife had been too poor to buy perfume before they got married, and he thought that she would appreciate getting some now. He paid twenty dollars for a bottle of a well-known spray, had it gift-wrapped, and attached a loving note. Saul beamed all the way home, having spent three hours looking for the perfect gift to show Tova how much he loved her.

When Tova received her surprise, she was absolutely delighted. She thanked him profusely and sprayed some on her to show him how lovely it smelled, and used it another three or four times during the next month. After her husband no longer remembered giving it to her, she gave it to her sister. Tova never wore perfume because she was allergic to it, not because she couldn't afford it. But she felt that a few hours of discomfort was a small price to pay to avoid hurting her husband's feelings, especially after he went to such lengths to please her.

Marriage requires sensitivity that goes beyond obligations. For example, husbands should help wives who are overwhelmed. Men do this by shopping for food, preparing meals, cleaning the house, doing the dishes, taking care of the children, or doing whatever else is needed without being asked. Men who don't help with domestic tasks should hire someone to ease their wives' burdens.

Many men expect their homes to be spotless when they come home. This is unrealistic for many women, especially those who raise children and/or who work full-time. But men will maximize their chances of having an orderly home if they relieve their wives of some responsibilities, or if they hire help.

Coming home to an attractive wife is also important for most men, and wives are required to look attractive for their husbands, even when they are not allowed to touch.[27] Unfortunately, many women wear dirty housecoats or baggy jogging suits, no makeup, and a *shmatta* (unappealing head scarf) in the presence of their husbands, and then dress up for company or friends. Both husbands and wives should be at least as considerate of each other as they are of strangers. Taking the time and effort to look nice for a spouse does wonders for a marriage, and it keeps both partners from taking each other for granted. With sexual bombardment everywhere, why not make each other feel that neither of you are missing anything by being married? The Talmud even lauded the wife of a Sage who put on her finest clothes before greeting him every evening. She ensured that her husband would never be tempted to look at other women and made him feel special and loved.

Even though wives are entitled to a certain standard of living, they shouldn't insist on it if it will unduly pressure their husbands. Even though Jewish law doesn't obligate women to do certain favors or chores, they should do them if it makes their husband happy without too much extra effort.

Nan grew up in a neighborhood where she and all of her friends wore designer clothes, got manicures every week, and ate out in restaurants on a regular basis. She married Bruce when he was earning a decent living for the first time in four years, but he still owed thousands of dollars in business loans.

A few months later, Bruce's supplier went bankrupt and Bruce was out of work. He tried to make ends meet by taking freelance jobs while Nan looked for a job. Meanwhile, she decided that she needed new clothes to replace last year's wardrobe. Bruce felt humiliated, begging her to make do with what she had, but his pleas fell on deaf ears. In order to make peace, he borrowed money from friends. It strained his friendships and made him resent his wife. Nan should have been more sensitive and should not have forced him into this terrible predicament.

Eli tried to make his wife happy, but Faith didn't attempt the same. She was afraid that the more she did for him, the more he would expect of her, and she didn't want to "mother" him. But it would have enhanced their marriage had she spent the ten minutes a day doing things for him that he wanted, like making him lunches to take to work. She didn't because she assumed that he would expect her to make dinner, too, which she did not have time to do. Instead of doing nice things for him, and letting him know her limits, she kept Eli at arm's length to make sure that he didn't take advantage of her goodwill.

Some husbands work hard to earn money but still struggle financially. Their wives should supplement their income or be sensitive enough not to insist on living beyond their means.[28] Regardless of who earns the money, both should be responsible and sensitive about managing and spending it.

Marital obligations are not a license for spouses to take each other for granted. Although men are obligated to support their wives, wives should still be appreciative when their husbands do this. Husbands whose wives support them (such as *kollel* wives) should not think that they are doing their wives a favor by allowing this. Men should tell their wives how grateful they are for their sacrifices.

A newlywed husband studied in yeshiva all day while his wife supported them by working in an office. When she came home, she cooked and did household chores. Not surprisingly, she was too exhausted to wash the dishes after dinner, but her husband got annoyed that the kitchen was a mess every night. Their friction soon prompted them to see the head of his yeshiva.

The rabbi first heard the woman's story and agreed that it was unreasonable for her to wash the dishes after working so hard all day. The husband then insisted that it was beneath him to wash dishes when he could spend that time learning Torah. The rabbi agreed with him as well. The couple left without resolving the issue.

The next night, the couple was eating dinner when the doorbell rang. They were not expecting anyone and could not imagine who would visit at such a late hour. When they opened the door, the head of the yeshiva stood there.

"What is the Rosh Yeshiva doing here?" the surprised couple asked.

"Somebody has to wash the dishes," he replied as he rolled up his sleeves and made his way to the sink.

SUMMARY

Judaism is very promarriage. The Talmud says, "Any man who has no wife is not a proper man,"[29] and "Any man who has no wife lives without joy, without blessing, and without goodness."[30] Our Sages also taught that "Blessing comes to the home only because of the woman."[31]

Jewish marriages are sustained by both partners fulfilling mutual responsibilities and by doing loving acts for one other. The atmosphere at home should nurture and dignify both partners and keep them from taking each other for granted. The more spouses do for each other, the more each will want to reciprocate, and the more love and goodwill they will create by so doing.

NOTES

1. Morning prayers.
2. Rashi and Tosafot on *Rosh Hashanah* 6b; Maimonides, *Mishneh Torah, Hilchot Ishut* 12:1, 2.
3. See *Ketubot* 61a, and the *Mishneh Torah, Hilchot Ishut* 21:3–6 for husbands' other responsibilities.
4. The Talmud says that this is part of his obligation to feed her.
5. Meiri.
6. Genesis 30:4–16.
7. *Mishneh Torah, Hilchot Ishut*, chapter 13. Maimonides discusses the details of these laws here.
8. *Mishneh Torah, Hilchot Ishut*, chapter 13.
9. *Bava Metziah* 59a.
10. *Yevamot* 62b.
11. *Bava Metziah* 59a.
12. Based on *Exodus* 21:10; see also *Mishneh Torah*, chapter 14 and *Niddah* 71a.
13. Deuteronomy 24:5.
14. *Mishneh Torah, Hilchot Ishut* 14:2.
15. *Berakhot* 27b–28a.
16. Genesis 29:20–26.
17. Genesis 30:1.
18. Genesis 30:2.
19. *Akeidat Yitzchak* on Genesis 30:1.
20. Maimonides, *Mishneh Torah, Hilchot Ishut* 12:2.
21. Shlomo Wolbe, *Binyan Adei Ad*, 111.
22. *Ketubot* 59b.
23. *Ketubot* 59b.
24. Meiri on *Bava Metziah* 59a.
25. For thirty days after giving birth, women are absolved from their wifely obligations. If they miscarry, they have no obligations until they feel able to resume them.
26. *Shabbat* 31a.
27. Rema, *Shulchan Aruch, Even Haezer* 73:1.
28. Eliezer Papo, *Pele Yoetz, Ahavat Ish V'Ishto*.
29. *Yevamot* 63a.
30. *Yevamot* 62b.
31. *Bava Metziah* 59a.

5

The Realities of Married Life

Many singles think that marriage will remove most, if not all, of their unhappiness. They assume that they will never again feel lonely, and will share all of their burdens with a partner who will give them permanent security and bliss.

Many engaged couples are so euphoric that they expect their excitement and ecstasy to last forever. They can't imagine that their love for, and enthrallment with, each other will ever wane. When they are told that the first year of marriage is very hard, they tend to think that is only true for others. Never having been married, they cannot imagine the intense strains they will feel living with a lifelong partner.

Are they in for a rude awakening! Dating under pleasant circumstances makes it easy to have a good time, but life changes after the wedding. Issues that they swept under the rug so as not to offend one another before marriage must finally be confronted. Men tend to spend less time with their wives after they get married, and both men and women tend to criticize each other more. In other words, soon after the wedding most newlyweds go through a period of disenchantment and increased conflict.[1] This is why the first year (or longer) of marriage is a mixed bag of ecstasy and misery for most couples. How they respond to it can make or break them.

Simi's marriage typified how difficult the early years are for most couples:

"When I got engaged, a friend welcomed me to the 'Always Exhausted Club.' I didn't know what she meant until I started planning my wedding. There was never enough time to do everything. In fact, twenty years later I still never have enough time! I worked full-time when I planned my wedding, then went apartment-hunting with my fiancé on weekends. Two weeks before the wedding, we finally found a place, but it needed painting, the floors needed sanding, and it had to be decorated and furnished. My husband and I moved in with only two mismatched beds, one lamp, and a card table. A neighbor donated three broken chairs, and we made a living room 'chair' out of a stack of telephone books.

"The week after our wedding we had *sheva brachot* (celebrations in friends' homes) every night. We never got home before midnight and were totally exhausted. I went back to work the next week and felt like I would never get rested again. For two months, I spent my free time immersing kitchen utensils in the *mikvah* (a ritual bath that is used to sanctify dishes and eating implements), returning wedding presents to a dozen different places, looking for furniture, and writing thank you notes. Meanwhile, we lived in the middle of a stack of boxes and couldn't find anything that we needed.

"When I was single, I almost never cooked. After we got married, I started making dinner most nights, but we didn't finish eating and cleaning up until 10 or 11:00 P.M. We wanted to save our money instead of eating out or spending money on entertainment. It didn't take long before the lovey-dovey conversations that we had shared before marriage turned to discussions of the many tasks that needed doing. Domestic chores and shopping stopped being fun, and we got worn out running around looking for furniture and things for our apartment.

"Meanwhile, Hersh was busy opening new bank accounts, getting us telephone service, having our mail forwarded, unpacking our boxes, and setting up our new home. He also dealt with our plumbing and heating problems and with the moving company. They broke our new china and glassware and damaged the table my parents gave us. Hersh also had to get up half an hour earlier each day than he was used to because our new home was some distance from his work.

"By the time things settled down, I got pregnant. We had a few months of calm until our son was born, then Hersh got a great job out of town. We had just finished furnishing and fixing up our apartment and we were moving again. It was terribly hard relocating with an infant, unpacking again, and trying to make new friends. Hersh's new job kept him at work until 7 or 8:00 most nights, while I stayed home with the baby. I felt lonely and stressed out, and I missed my old job, my friends, and my family.

"I wasn't prepared for any of this. I thought that marriage would continue the wonderful times that we'd had when we were engaged. I didn't believe friends who had warned me that marriage is a lot of hard work and drudgery and that there would be different stresses than when I was single. It's important for engaged couples to know what the first year of marriage is like so that they can anticipate and smooth over the inevitable problems.

"I spent the first two years of marriage wondering if I had made the worst mistake of my life. I realized that my husband and I really didn't communicate well about sensitive issues, and these cropped up often. We could no longer brush them aside. Thankfully, my husband and I now have been happily married for seventeen years, but only because we were committed to working things out. We had a lot of trial and error, and I hope that others are better prepared to deal with the enormous changes that occur with marriage than we were."

Another woman who was finally happy after two years of marriage shared her experience:

"Oren took me to a beautiful ski chalet for our first wedding anniversary. The mountains were covered with pine trees, draped with powdery, white snow. The view from our room was breathtaking, and the burning fireplace and background music in our suite were so romantic. Oren even brought kosher champagne to celebrate our first year together. Yet I was miserable. I kept thinking about how awful our first year of marriage had been and how constantly Oren had disappointed me. He was too quiet for my taste, and I felt bored and cheated of the intimacy that I had expected. That night in the chalet, I sobbed so hard I couldn't stop. I kept feeling that I had ruined my life by marrying him. I couldn't pull myself out of my depression for two days.

"It wasn't until I decided to focus on Oren's good points instead of on how he had failed me that I finally felt good about being with him.

"He still isn't as interesting or as verbal as I'd like, but I value his integrity, his loyalty, his good intentions, and his kindness. He helps me a lot at home, and he's a fabulous father. It took me a long time to value him, and I'm glad that he had the patience to put up with my criticism until I realized what a gem I had."

Marriage takes hard work, perseverance, skill, and patience. It is easy to enjoy picnics in beautiful parks, concerts, movies, strolls through four-star hotels, meals in restaurants, and mood-lifting entertainment. But the glitter eventually stops, and couples must feel good about each other when they face the demands of day-to-day life. Will they feel starry-eyed and excited after a grueling workday, or enjoy each other's company when a baby interrupts their sleep and their routines for years on end? Will they love each other when they shop for groceries, do laundry, pay bills, and clean the house, or only when real responsibilities and problems don't intrude?

Married life challenges couples to make mundane experiences enjoyable and meaningful. Spouses need to enjoy each other whether they're doing household chores or fighting the flu, not only when they dine out or trade presents. Having a sense of humor at a stand-up comedy club or while watching a funny movie is easy. It is more difficult, and critical, to have a sense of humor when your spouse accidentally ruins your favorite outfit in the wash, or your child paints your walls with lipstick and nail polish.

Couples are usually on their best behavior on dates, so that may be a poor barometer of what they will be like in marriage. Few people are as attentive, patient, and loving months or years after the wedding as they were before. Many couples accumulate anger, disappointment, and daily stresses, and they need the tools to deal constructively with them. With the right tools, however, married people can grow more deeply in love by resolving their ongoing differences and problems.

SUMMARY

Jewish couples commit at least five transgressions when they stop working on their marriages:[2] They bear grudges against each other, take revenge, hate their fellow Jew, don't love their neighbor as themselves, and make it impossible for a spouse to live comfortably with them. The resulting tensions may also prevent couples from bringing children into the world.

We create and sustain love by constantly working on a marriage. Couples have different perspectives about life, different ways of expressing themselves, and different needs. Without understanding, good communication, problem-solving skills, and patience, marriages can't survive. Couples need to learn how to make the ups of marriage last while they weather the downs.

Every day is an opportunity to appreciate a partner, learn new things about one another, share new experiences and ideas, relive happy memories, and build intimacy. Marriage is an adventure in which couples can learn to put their disappointments and differences into perspective and come to appreciate the good qualities that they saw in each other during their courtship.

NOTES

1. Michael McManus, *Marriage Savers* (Grand Rapids: Zondervan Publishing House, 1993), p. 146.

2. *Avot D'Rabbi Natan*, chapter 26.

6

Getting to Know a Potential Mate

While singles know that it is important to carefully choose a mate, many select a partner haphazardly. Two good ways to learn about a potential mate are through conversation and observation. When someone's actions contradict their words, actions speak loudest.

We can't objectively evaluate people if we are blinded by our emotions. We tend to see people as we would like them to be or according to preconceived notions, rather than as they really are.

Belinda was a bright, attractive, talented, and interesting woman in her mid-twenties. Unfortunately, she also had poor self-esteem and felt dependent on men. She repeatedly "fell in love" with them after one conversation on the telephone, or after one date, whichever came first. In one year, she fell in love with eight unsuitable men, including one with an alcohol problem, one who turned out to have serious debts, one with psychiatric problems, and five who had no interest in her. She was so desperate for a man to take care of her that she was unwilling to see men as they really were.

Married people who complain about a spouse's bad temper, mood swings, immaturity, emotional unavailability, selfishness, and bad habits usually had plenty of warning signs when they dated. They wanted so much to get married that they ignored these bad traits in the hope that they would magically disappear with time, or that their spouse would love them enough to become a different person.

Unfortunately, drastic changes for the better usually only happen in the movies or in novels.

It is said that we learn everything about a person in the first fifteen minutes after we meet him or her, then spend the rest of our lives forgetting it! In other words, our first impressions of people tend to be quite accurate, yet we ignore our "vibes" because they tell us things that we don't want to hear. Desperate people want others to be the man or woman of their dreams, so they ascribe fantastic qualities to someone they barely know. Naive people uncritically believe what their dates tell them. Many people think that feeling good about the person they're with, and agreeing about major goals, is ample evidence of lifetime compatibility.

People who are easily infatuated should imagine themselves as newspaper reporters the first few times they date someone. They should get objective information and evaluate it dispassionately before deciding if someone has spouse-potential. People should never fall in love with someone until the latter shows serious intentions and realistic potential.

Ian made a terrific impression on Julie because he complimented her a lot and was a great conversationalist. On their fourth date, Julie finally realized that he gave mixed messages. He was charming, kind, and easy-going, but didn't treat her well. He made a good living, bought himself nice clothes, and spent money on himself, but he always took her to cheap restaurants where they went "Dutch treat." When they didn't go out to eat, they went on walks or to free entertainment. Julie realized that talk was cheap and so was Ian!

Michelle was charming, elegant, and refined, and she captivated Morris. He took her to expensive places, then began to wonder if her interest in him was strictly monetary. Instead of continuing their $100 dates, he invited her to go to a botanical garden, a free museum, and a lecture. After going with him on two free dates, she suggested that he spend $60 on tickets to a concert. When he refused, she was reluctant to go on another free date. She confirmed his fears that she was a golddigger and he stopped asking her out.

The Talmud says that we can learn about people by observing how they drink alcohol, handle their anger, and spend money.[1] It's a good idea for singles to arrange opportunities to see a potential spouse in these, and other, situations.

Dating at restaurants, museums, shows, and places where we are spectators usually gives us little information about a potential partner. Yet people can still notice how impatient or angry a date is waiting in lines or sitting in traffic jams. What stresses or frustrates them, and how do they react to unpleasant situations?

Men should notice if a woman expects to be wined and dined. Does she order the most expensive item on a menu or suggest excursions that will break his bank account? Does she spend a lot of money on makeup, clothes, and shoes? Does she shop at expensive stores and hate the idea of buying bargains? Does she complain that she never has enough money?

Women can learn how generous, extravagant, or stingy a man is by where he takes them and how he tips. His car may reflect his financial status and how he takes care of his belongings. But before assuming that someone is well-off because he drives a fancy car, find out if he leases it or borrowed it!

Renee was an unassuming woman who wore simple clothes, no makeup, and lived modestly in a one-bedroom apartment. She owned a six-year-old car, but usually took public transportation to her graduate classes. Greg didn't know until they were engaged that her father was an extremely wealthy businessman and she was a multimillionaire due to his largesse.

Meyer was a strikingly handsome man in his late twenties. He was well-read, expressive, and wrote poetry in his spare time. His romanticism and business acumen attracted Ahuva. She gave him the unconditional acceptance that he wanted, and he loved and appreciated her. He promised to make her rich by marketing her as a jewelry designer and had many ideas about how to do this.

Ahuva's primrose path dead-ended in a mountain of thorns. Meyer was a dreamer who had never succeeded at anything. He had dropped out of college, had a brief marriage when he was nineteen, and went from one freelance job to another. He had great ideas but never carried them off for long. His car was in such bad shape that he had to borrow a friend's car for dates. His prestigious address was a temporary rental that he couldn't afford. He got new business cards every six months because none of his ventures lasted longer than that. Ahuva discovered that Meyer was a troubled man with a warm heart and a vivid imagination, but he couldn't earn a living and had questionable ability to take on the responsibilities of marriage.

Although Ahuva didn't marry Meyer, Ariella did. Ariella was a nurse who made a very good living and didn't care if a husband supported her financially. She wanted a husband with a loving heart, and she found that in Meyer. They were well-suited to each other. He became a lifelong househusband, yeshiva student, and a terrific father, while she supported them and handled their financial responsibilities.

Some people broadcast their financial troubles by asking to borrow money on dates. Con men offer to make women rich, develop their talent, or invest their money in secret bonds, stocks, or business ventures with incredible rates of return. Of course, the deals that seem too good to be true invariably are. People should never give anyone more than $10 unless they are married to them or don't mind never seeing the money again.

Dennis understood how much women want to feel loved and used this to con them. He dated women for several weeks, wined, dined, and lavished attention on them. Then he had a "sudden" crisis, such as being robbed of his rent money, being fired from his job through no fault of his own, or going bankrupt. Women offered to loan him money, then never saw it again. He exemplified the adage, "Men get conned for money, women get conned for love."

Tamara always needed "a few things" from the drugstore. She asked her dates if they minded going with her before they took her home. When she got to the checkout counter, she never had enough money for her purchases, and smiled expectantly, hoping that the date would ante up the $10–$20 for her. Men realized that she expected them to take care of her in unrealistic and inappropriate ways and stayed away from her.

Many singles today are tens of thousands of dollars in debt. They have enormous student loans, outstanding credit card balances, or business loans to repay. A credit check before getting engaged can be a good idea when a date isn't upfront about his or her financial status or if there is reason to doubt the person's credibility.

Alvin was a commodities trader who earned six figures a year. He owned two cars, two homes, and usually spent $100–$200 on a date. Marlene reasonably assumed that he was wealthy, but her best friend did a credit check on him and discovered that he had hundreds of thousands of dollars in outstanding personal loans. Marlene couldn't believe it. She thought it might be an inaccurate credit report, so she verified it herself. She was shocked to discover that Alvin indeed lived beyond his means and had done so for years. He loved living like a wealthy man and had no savings but lots of debts.

Rod and Ellen were married for four months when he discovered that she went on spending sprees whenever she got upset. This happened at least twice a month. He also discovered that she was $40,000 in debt and owed money to everyone from the IRS to MasterCard (at 19 percent interest). He was haunted by her financial problems, and creditors, for years, because he was too polite to look into this before they got engaged.

Aaron and Toby were engaged to be married. Shortly before the wedding, she had a feeling that he had lied to her about his out-of-town business meetings. She wormed out of his secretary that he liked to gamble. She then spoke to one of his co-workers and two of his friends. They confided that Aaron lost about $200 a week playing cards. Toby confronted him and insisted that he see a therapist and go to Gambler's Anonymous. He insisted that he didn't have a problem. She wisely broke up with him.

ALCOHOL AND SUBSTANCE ABUSE

There was a time when being Jewish was synonymous with eschewing alcohol, but this is no longer true. Secular Jews abuse alcohol and drugs as frequently as non-Jews do, and some observant Jews today are alcoholics or substance abusers. One can no longer assume that being Jewish or Sabbath-observant guarantees temperance. And, since 16 percent of divorces are now related to issues of substance abuse,[1] singles can no longer ignore the possibility that their potential spouse has these problems.

Alcoholics and drug abusers don't necessarily look "sloppy" or wallow in gutters. Many have good jobs, dress well, and make a good social impression. A lot of people drink heavily or use drugs only after work, on weekends, or on social occasions.

It is a terrible mistake to rationalize or deny a date's having too much to drink or abusing medication or recreational drugs. People who admit to using drugs or drinking excessively only "once in awhile" can be nightmarish to live with when their ruinous binges occur several times a year, or every month.

Art was an observant Jewish salesman who took clients to expensive nonkosher restaurants. Initially, he ate only fruit or salads, but then he began to drink with his clients once or twice a week. He was soon downing a bottle of wine at Friday night dinners and having a series of "*L'Chaim*'s" (shot glasses of liquor) after synagogue services Saturday mornings. Contrary to many people's ideas about alcoholics, Art made a good living and never missed a day of work.

When Art dated Nancy, he had three drinks over dinner. When she asked him about the kinds of wine he liked, he was quite knowledgeable about the subject and told her where he bought cases of wine. On one occasion when Nancy joined him for a meal, he drank an entire bottle of wine himself. She suggested that he seek help for his drinking problem, but Art insisted that he was a wine connoisseur and denied having a drinking problem. Nancy knew better and stopped seeing him.

Eve was an eighteen-year-old chasidic woman from a good family. She had beautiful character traits, was helpful at home, took care of her younger siblings, taught at a girls' school, and regularly visited hospital patients. She was also addicted to tranquilizers and used them every day to calm herself down. She got prescriptions from four different doctors and had them filled at four different pharmacies. This let her take as many pills as she wanted, while maintaining the charade that she was in perfect control of her emotions.

Charlie came from a good family and was an excellent physician. When he disclosed to Donna on their first date that he had gone to a public high school similar to hers, she joked, "So what drugs did you use?"

Charlie responded, "The usual stuff—pot, hash, Valium, and acid [LSD]."

"So what do you use now?" Donna prodded, expecting him to say "Nothing."

"I prefer Valium, but I drop acid twice a year."

"Aren't you afraid of a bad trip?" Donna wondered, both horrified and curious.

"Nah, I get really pure stuff. I've been using it for ten years and nothing bad has happened yet. It makes the surroundings look really funny, and I get a kick out of it. It's really not as bad as people make it out to be."

Donna had heard that at least one in ten doctors is a drug addict, but she couldn't believe that someone as seemingly normal as Charlie was. She soon discovered that other "normal" Jewish doctors with whom she socialized were addicted to drugs or were alcoholics. Most indulged after work or on weekends, and their habits rarely affected their work. Secretaries and colleagues tended to cover up for the rare ones who came to work drunk or hung over. These doctors were never disciplined or fired for inappropriateness or incompetence.

DRIVING HABITS

Watching someone drive can be enlightening. People show how impulsive, reckless, cautious, or responsible they are by how they drive and how they take care of their cars.

On their first date, Ronna noticed that Ben's car had a dented fender and a broken headlight. She mentioned to him that the headlight wasn't working, and he thanked her for telling him. A month later, the light was still broken. When she mentioned it again, Ben told her that he had not had a chance to take care of it. When she asked where he took his car for maintenance, it was clear that he waited for problems to get out-of-hand before taking the car in for servicing and repairs. On their next date, Ben tried to park in a space that was too small, scratched the car in front of him, then drove off. Ronna decided that she didn't need this irresponsible and reckless man in her life.

Carol remembered that she needed some grocery items as she took Bert home from a charity dinner. She double-parked in front of a convenience store on a main street because she didn't feel like taking a few extra minutes to park in the lot behind the store. Meanwhile, she blocked traffic and forced cars to swerve around her. She saw nothing wrong with this, but Bert decided to find a woman who was less self-centered and more considerate.

When Marla drove Robert to her mother's house for dinner, they got stuck in traffic. She elected not to pass the other cars by cutting in front of the line. She told Robert that being a "mensch" was more important than getting to her destination faster. Robert appreciated her attitude and was glad that she had such fine values.

JOB HISTORY

Even though many singles expect a spouse to earn money, marriage doesn't make people work consistently nor become financially responsible if they weren't that way before. A potential mate's job history is very important. Troubled people tend to change jobs every few months or years and work at jobs that are below their ability or are unrelated to their background and skills. They make lateral moves and leave because of personality or authority problems, inability to handle stress and responsibility, or chronic absenteeism and lateness.

Some people have no goals and drift aimlessly from one job to another. Others are dissatisfied and disillusioned wherever they go. They may get excited initially, then get bored or unhappy as the novelty wears off. People who claim that they left several jobs because someone else created problems for them usually have problems every place they must interact with others.

Jack was creative, brilliant, and won awards for his writing. Yet he never stayed at any job longer than three years. When Rose asked why, he explained, "That boss never appreciated what I had to offer. . . . At that job, someone six years my junior was promoted over me because he played politics well. . . . That agency head was too conservative to let me do what I wanted. . . ." In each case, Jack blamed someone else for his leaving. Rose guessed that Jack had a serious authority problem and was wise enough not to try to fix it.

Debbie was a strikingly beautiful woman who worked as an office manager. Despite her excellent stenographic and typing skills, she never stayed at a job longer than two years. Debbie confided to Dave, "Men harass me everywhere I work so I have to keep leaving." After two dates, Dave realized that she was paranoid, and he stopped seeing her.

Alan had an unusual school history. He skipped a year of high school, completed college in three years, then breezed through law school. He could not find a job so he contemplated starting his own business. Rachel thought that he was an impulsive maverick who needed to be his own boss and work unconventionally. She realized that he might never earn a living but didn't mind his being a househusband while she supported the family. She married him because he fulfilled her intellectually and emotionally. As things turned out, he was great in the kitchen, ran the house well, and gave her the emotional support and love that she needed.

A year after they got married, Alan had a brainstorm and developed a business that made millions. Rachel was very happy about their good fortune but wouldn't have been disappointed even if the story hadn't ended so lucratively.

REVEALING SHORTCOMINGS

Singles needn't advertise their negative characteristics, nor share damaging information on the first few dates. Sensitive topics that must be discussed before a couple gets engaged should be timed and presented in such a way that they can be viewed as minor blemishes in an otherwise desirable partner.

Karen had a kidney problem that resulted in seven hospitalizations when she was a child. Her medical condition improved by the time she was twenty but she could require dialysis or a kidney transplant in the future. When she and Seymour had dated seriously for two months, she summarized her situation to him and mentioned that she could probably have, at best, only one or two children. He was so crazy about her by then that he replied, "You don't even have to tell me this. We'll worry about those things if and when they happen." She was relieved that he cared about her enough to face an uncertain future with her. They are very happily married with their two children and would like to raise Jewish foster children when their own children get a bit older.

Marilyn is a lovely woman with a bipolar (manic-depressive) psychiatric disorder. She takes medication (Lithium) every day, which keeps her from having symptoms. She will probably take it for the rest of her life, except before or during pregnancy, when her symptoms may recur. Her rabbi advised her to tell this to men on their fifth date. If men need more information to decide whether to continue dating, she gives it to them. Most stop seeing her, but she will eventually marry someone who does not mind her having a biochemical disorder.

MEDICAL AND PSYCHIATRIC PROBLEMS

Before getting engaged, singles should disclose their medical and psychiatric problems to each other. They should also get tested for genetic disorders, such as

Tay-Sachs, and, if necessary, for venereal diseases. Tay-Sachs carriers should not marry each other. If singles may pass on other genetic diseases to their children, they should consult a genetic counselor before getting engaged.

Singles need to know how a potential spouse's medical problems may affect them later. For example, many people with ulcerative colitis get part of their colon removed, and must wear a colostomy bag for the rest of their lives. Those who forego surgery may be at high risk for getting colon cancer.

Diabetics must follow restricted diets, and diabetic women may have risky pregnancies. Both diabetic men and women may heal poorly and may be susceptible to gangrene, blindness, strokes, heart disease, nerve damage, and early death.

Shelly's kidneys were weakened beyond repair. She got dialysis three times a week and awaited a transplant. Matt was told about her medical condition and prognosis before he met her, but he didn't care. He found her so special that he married her despite her problems. A year later, she got a kidney transplant and a new lease on life.

Religious Jews in some communities are very misinformed about which medical problems run in families. For example, some religious Jews are reluctant to marry a sibling of a Down's Syndrome child because they believe that such a spouse is likely to have retarded children. That is nonsense. Down's Syndrome is usually related to the mother's age, with women over thirty-five or forty giving birth to a disproportionate number of children with it. Singles should get sound medical advice about a potential spouse's illness or genetic makeup and not rely on old wives' tales.

Psychiatric disorders can be even more debilitating than medical illnesses. Serious mood swings can be devastating and should receive professional attention. Medication, change of diet, and/or psychotherapy can often improve or alleviate many psychiatric symptoms and make life better for all concerned, but they are not without risks and side effects.

Lydia had PMS (premenstrual syndrome) that made her unbearably depressed for two or three days every month. She would call in sick to work, stay in bed until late afternoon, then eat everything in sight. Sometimes she even felt suicidal. When she took medication and ate a diet without sugar, caffeine, or chocolate, her mood improved remarkably. When she ate junk food or ran out of medication, she went back to her former self. As long as Lydia stays disciplined about her diet and medication, her PMS shouldn't interfere with a marriage.

Robin loved Yehuda very much and tried to nurture him through his depressive spells. Being there for him made her feel needed, and she initially liked this feeling. But a year after their wedding, Yehuda was still terribly depressed, despite having a loving wife and being a straight-A student in college. He saw himself as worthless, despite his objective achievements. Much to her horror, Robin came home one night and found that he had overdosed on pills. She regretted that she had minimized the seriousness of his poor self-esteem and depression, which left her widowed at the age of twenty-one.

EMOTIONAL BAGGAGE

Singles should be aware of the emotional baggage that they, and a potential mate, will bring to marriage. Recently divorced people and those from dysfunctional families often have unresolved emotional issues that can ruin a marriage.

Phyllis was overly close to her parents and still lived with them at the age of thirty. Danny was so impressed with her kindness and emotional equilibrium that he never wondered what would happen if she was pried away from her mother. After he married Phyllis, her parents visited every weekend. Phyllis also talked to her mother by phone for an hour every day, sharing the most intimate details of her married life. Mom advised her on how to decorate her home, get what she wanted from Danny, and raise their children. Danny was devastated when he realized that he had married two women, not one. Despite his pleas that Phyllis cut the umbilical cord with her mother, his wife continued breaching their privacy. Danny was sorry that he didn't consider this before they got engaged.

Gary was a twenty-six-year-old computer programmer who was passive-aggressive. Outwardly compliant, helpful, and solicitous of Bernice, he quietly seethed with rage whenever she asked him to do anything. She could suggest that he be on time for a date, wear a suit that she especially liked, or call her at a specific time, but the simplest request reminded him of his overbearing mother. He reacted accordingly, deliberately ignoring her wishes so that she would not control him as his mother had.

Talia seemed to be an independent, twenty-eight-year-old businesswoman, who ran an office of twelve people with an iron fist. Julian didn't realize that her strength and control at work were totally at odds with her personal life. She had a serious eating disorder and alternately starved, binged, and purged. She had no friends and suffered from serious depression. Her desperation to marry Julian prompted her to leave unwanted messages on his answering machine, and to threaten suicide when he didn't respond.

This taught Julian how much better some people function at work than in their personal life. He never again took for granted that success at work implies normalcy in intimate relationships.

MEET THE FAMILY AND FRIENDS

We learn a lot by spending time with people's families. We see how they get along, communicate, and feel about each other. We see what values, traits, and perspectives they share and how they deal with differences. We also see how the family relates to us and can decide if we want to be part of them.

By the time a couple is engaged, potential spouses should be more concerned with responding to each other's needs than to their family's. Yet separating from parents is very hard, especially when parents are critical of the person we love.

Parents may have valid criticisms but should make them without attacking the person or delivering demeaning comments.

Anna was a *baalat teshuva* (returnee to traditional Judaism) whose boyfriend had become increasingly religious during the past two years. Ed observed the Sabbath when they were together, ate only kosher in his house, and prayed most mornings. When he and Anna spent a weekend at his parents' house, she was surprised that his parents hated Judaism so much and was equally shocked by Ed's religious laxity. He explained that he didn't believe that God intended Jewish rituals to break families apart. Since his parents objected to his religious practices, he would never offend them by observing Judaism in their house. This made Anna realize that they shouldn't get married because their religious differences would always cause friction between them.

Naama met Yitz's parents before they got engaged. She was impressed that he helped his mother prepare dinner and was loving and respectful toward her. When Naama asked what his mother thought about her, Yitz said that his mother thought that Naama was cold and aloof. His mother was also concerned that Naama had never supported herself, and was extremely jealous and possessive. Yitz thought that his mother's concerns were valid and was not impressed by Naama's explanations of why these weren't issues.

Soon afterwards, Yitz stopped seeing Naama, then resumed dating her when he thought that he could accept her limitations. They got married a year later, after working through these issues.

Before getting engaged, couples should see if they feel comfortable with each other's friends. If not, they should wonder if it is because the couple has more differences than they thought. If close friends have strong reservations about someone's "intended," their concerns should be considered.

Laura dated Roger for a few months and was excited about introducing him to her friends. Her best friend was especially impressed and wished that she could find such a husband. Laura never met Roger's close friends because they all lived far away. Shortly after their marriage, Laura discovered that Roger was a fraud who had no friends, and he verbally and physically abused her.

When she went to her friends for emotional support, most of them told her that they had sensed that Roger was evil. They had never told Laura because she wasn't receptive to hearing any criticism about him. Had she been more open to their opinions, she would had been spared a lot of anguish.

Ken and Cecille dated for a month before they visited each other's parents. The couple was observant but had different orientations to life. His parents were wealthy, modern Orthodox Jews and hers were blue-collar and non-religious. Ken couldn't talk to Cecille's father, and there was always tension between them. Things were no better between Cecille and Ken's parents. His mother was opinionated, snobby, and pushy, not to mention critical of Cecille. The two women had nothing in common, and both were relieved when their encounters ended.

Instead of wondering why they felt so uncomfortable with each other's parents, Ken and Cecille ignored it and got married. They soon had serious problems because Ken wanted his parents' materialistic lifestyle while Cecille wanted the simplicity of her family's background. Neither was comfortable with the other's family and friends. It was not until they had children that Ken and Cecille realized that what they hated in each other's parents was an integral part of their spouse. If only they had seen that before they got married!

SUMMARY

A rabbi (the Chofetz Chaim) had dreams of changing the people of Warsaw. When that failed, he decided to scale down his vision and try to change his congregants in Radin. When he saw how fruitless that was, he endeavored to change his family. Finally, he realized that he could not change anyone else, so he decided to change himself. We can learn from him how risky it is to try to change others.

A good psychotherapist or a wise rabbi can help people gain realistic expectations of marriage, know which incompatibilities are significant, and which issues are not negotiable. Instead of planning to change a spouse after marriage, learn as much as you can about the person before you get engaged. If you can't accept someone as he or she is, don't get married to that person.

NOTES

1. Michael McManus, *Marriage Savers* (Grand Rapids: Zondervan Publishing House, 1993, p. 123.

2. *Eruvin* 65b.

7

Determining Compatibility

There are endless incompatibilities that seem to make couples miserable. These include differences in goals, styles of relating, religious orientation, child rearing methods, spending and personal habits, intellectual and emotional needs, socio-economic backgrounds, and lifestyles. This is why couples must seriously consider who they are, what their goals are, and what kind of partner will mesh with them before they get married. Differences *per se* do not cause irreconcilable marital conflicts, but if differences make someone so uncomfortable that she or he will not tolerate them, they are likely to result in ongoing, and unnecessary, friction.

We can't choose a partner realistically without knowing whether our goals and lifestyles will be complementary for the next fifty years. Reacting to how we feel about someone today may not predict what a relationship will be like many years from now.

The Torah tells us to love our fellow Jew as we love ourselves.[1] This means overlooking someone's shortcomings so that we can value their good qualities, but it does not imply ignoring a potential spouse's character defects or their incompatibility with us. We must be realistic about how we will feel about someone's traits, attitudes, lifestyle, and habits after many years of living with them.

People sometimes insist that their spouse changed after marriage in ways that could not have been foreseen. While this is sometimes true, people usually give enough information for us to evaluate our compatibility with them if we:

1. Have them talk about themselves: their personal and social background, relationships with family members, how they did in school and/or occupation. What are their leisure activities, hobbies, interests, goals, and anticipated lifestyle?[2]

2. Observe how the person reacts in a variety of settings, remembering that someone's nature is expressed more by how they act than by what they think.[3]

3. Don't get blinded by emotions.

4. Investigate someone's background and check out stories about him or her.

5. Consult friends, relatives, and/or references who know the person *well*.

Some behaviors or traits should never be whitewashed, such as being prone to temper outbursts or to violent rages. These will ruin a marriage, not to mention being potentially dangerous for a spouse and terrible for children.[4] Women, especially, have to be careful to stay away from men who have a tendency towards violence and who can't control their anger. Men will sometimes reveal violent tendencies when asked how fathers should discipline their children or how a husband should react if his wife disrespects him.

There is now an excellent premarital questionnaire called "PREPARE" that predicts with 86 percent accuracy those couples who are likely to get divorced. The 125–item questionnaire asks each partner to rate their compatibility in areas such as religious beliefs, sex, expectations, personality, interests, and so forth. It is filled out separately by the man and woman, is computer-scored, and the results are then discussed with a trained counselor. "PREPARE-MC" is for couples who were previously married and have children. For a list of qualified counselors in your area, write to: PREPARE, P.O. Box 190, Minneapolis, MN 55440–0190. Ask them to give you the names of professional family therapists who are not priests or ministers, and who are trained to administer and interpret the test.

CAREER CONSIDERATIONS

Our career choices affect who we marry and what kind of marriages we have. Many single women seek men who earn a lot of money without realizing how lonely they will be living with a man who is rarely home or whose mind is always at work.

Rena and Bill were both successful professionals. When Rena was on a career track, she did not mind Bill's working fourteen hours a day because she did the same. But when they had their first baby, she decided to stay home and raise her. Bill's ongoing absence became a serious problem, and Rena felt unloved and lonely as she raised their children by herself. One day their four-year-old daughter put her doll to sleep saying, "And if you're very good this week, Daddy will spend some time with you."

The little girl once answered the phone when Bill's best friend asked, "Can I please speak to your Daddy?"

Bill was at work, even though it was Sunday morning.

The girl replied, "I don't have a Daddy."

Wealth comes with tremendous sacrifice for most people. A beautiful home, a few glamorous evenings a year, and a semi-annual vacation are scant consolation for a husband's chronic absence for ten or twenty years. The prestige of being a doctor's wife hardly makes up for one's husband getting called to the hospital on a rare evening out. Having a lot of money does not seem to matter when a husband brings work with him on every vacation and has a heart attack in his fifties.

Some men erroneously assume that professional or business women will make poor mothers and homemakers. Sometimes these women's problem-solving abilities, organizational skills, and broad knowledge serve them well as homemakers and mothers, make them more interesting mates, and their income eases a man's financial burden. Some careers, such as teaching, even let women take leaves of absence for two or three years to raise each child. Many professional and business women work part-time or from their homes when they have children.

Pat, Marlene, and Gitty were all successful career women. Pat became a partner in her law firm after working hard for seven years, during which time she had two children. By the time she had her third child, she took a year-long leave to enjoy raising her daughter. She found that she enjoyed it so much that she started her own law practice in her home.

Marlene had terrible morning sickness when she was pregnant with her first child. She decided to leave her job as a systems analyst and become a full-time mother and housewife. When her youngest child reached school age, Marlene started a consulting business at home. Her husband was grateful that she had saved money before they got married because it took pressure off him as their family grew. They had the financial advantages of her career combined with the flexibility to raise a family.

Gitty was in her last month of medical school when she had her first child. Over the next six years, she brought her three children with her to the hospital several times a week so that they could spend time together. She then found a job working three days a week that gave her career satisfaction, money, and a generous amount of free time with her family.

Some single men eschew "career women" because they assume that secretaries, office managers, computer programmers, or teachers will be more inclined to stay home and raise children, but that is not always true. Some single women view marriage as a chance to hire a housekeeper to run the home and raise their children. Not having a career does not imply dedication to raising children or to being a devoted housewife.

Until they have children, many women don't really know if they will want to stay home raising them. Nevertheless, singles should discuss their ideas about childrearing and working outside the home, rather than make assumptions about what will happen when they have kids.

Women tend to have sequential lives, unlike men. They may have a career, drop out of the work force for ten or more years so that they can raise children, go back to school, and/or start a second career. While most men would not think of leaving a lucrative or meaningful career in order to raise children, many women expect to do exactly that.

GEOGRAPHICAL ISSUES

"Geographically undesirable" singles live far away from each other. "GU" couples who end up getting married usually have flexible schedules, money for travel and long-distance phone calls, and the emotional stamina to weather a few intense days together, followed by weeks or months apart.

It is important for "GU" singles to get to know each other on their "home turf," as well as at work, with friends, and with family, if possible. Relationships that rely mostly on letters and telephone calls can lead to misguided conclusions.

Roy met Jill on a visit to Chicago, and they spent five days together before he went back to graduate school in New York. They kept in contact until Roy returned six weeks later. But Jill wasn't as excited to see him as he was to see her. Their relationship began too intensely for her. She wanted to date him one or two nights a week, not several days on end. They agreed to part ways.

Cheryl lived in Los Angeles, where she met Michael at a friend's party. The friend knew Michael well and had only positive things to say about him. The new couple spent four days getting to know each other, during which time Michael met her parents. He quickly felt like part of the family and reluctantly went back to school in Miami. Meanwhile, he and Cheryl spoke every day for the next two months, and she spoke to his parents by phone. When he visited Cheryl during his spring break, they got engaged.

Mike and Cheryl didn't need to spend a lot of time together because they came from similar backgrounds and had similar styles, goals, and personalities. They were honest with each other and quickly knew that they were right for each other. They have been happily married for twelve years.

Some people feel very strongly about living in the suburbs or in the city, in New York, in Israel, near their family, or in a place where they can make a lot of money. Singles who are wedded to living in a specific place should not date people who are equally wedded to living elsewhere.

Mimi planned to live in Houston so that she could stay near her parents. Fred lived there while he worked on a temporary job assignment but planned to move back to Detroit to be near his widowed mother when his position ended. After a few dates, they realized that neither would change their feelings about where to live, so they stopped seeing each other.

Barbara got a wonderful job in Washington, D. C., where she enjoyed the city's cultural and social activities. When she and Neil got engaged, he lived in Baltimore but hated it. His dream was to live in a small Jewish community near mountains and pristine forests. As her love for him grew, his idea of moving to a rural setting started to appeal to her. When they got married, they moved to Denver, with its access to the Rockies and national parks. Unlike Neil, Barbara was never wedded to the idea of living in any particular place, so it was very easy for her to pick up and move where he wanted.

PERSONAL COMPATIBILITY

Opposites attract, yet we tend to be most comfortable with people like ourselves. Couples from dissimilar cultural, intellectual, and socio-economic backgrounds have higher divorce rates and less marital happiness than similar couples. For example, Sephardic (Mediterranean) and Ashkenazic (European) Jews have many cultural differences, especially in their attitudes towards women and raising children. This is why marriages between Sephardic men and Ashkenazic women usually fail. Marriages between Sephardic women and Ashkenazic men tend to be much more successful.

Whatever differences couples have before marriage usually intensify afterwards, even though the couple tends to become more similar in other ways. For example, people with lots of energy tend to stay that way and want a partner who will do things with them. Someone who has to push to keep up with an energetic partner before marriage shouldn't think that the partner will become a homebody after marriage.

Extroverts enjoy socializing and group activities. Introverts prefer spending a quiet evening at home reading, watching television, or eating dinner with a spouse. If these differences are problematic before marriage, they tend to worsen later.

"Couch potatoes" rarely become social butterflies, initiators, and leaders, nor do they look for responsibilities and lively activities. People whose energy is gone by 9:00 P.M. don't suddenly develop inner Duracells that work all night. Our daily energy cycles ("biorhythms") tend to be stable, with some people having their peak energy in the mornings ("larks") and others peaking in the late evening ("owls"). "Owls" feel energetic just as "larks" are getting ready for bed. When these types marry, they enjoy joint activities most that occur in the middle of the day.

"Mismatched" couples are not necessarily doomed, but they do need to work hard to adapt to their differences. Husbands can watch late-night movies alone or read, having spent time earlier with their now-asleep wives. Wives who jog at 6 A.M. should not expect "owlish" husbands to join them, nor to be great conversationalists at breakfast.

A punctual husband can get upset every time his perpetually-late wife makes them tardy. Or, he can suggest that they go separately to social functions, or ask her to get ready an hour earlier than necessary. Alternatively, he could relax, read, balance the checkbook, and make phone calls while she gets ready, taking the perspective that it doesn't matter if they get there on time or not.

Singles have to decide which differences they can live with and adapt to, and which are completely unacceptable.

Some people hate living with a mate who is messy, disorganized, or unfocused. Comedies have been written about neat-freaks who live with slobs, but it's not so funny if you are one of the players.

More important than having differences is how well couples accept and adapt to them. For example, a messy wife can have a place at home where she can be a slob, while her neat husband sets up an orderly space for himself. They can keep common areas moderately neat. (This often means that he tries to keep it clean, while she leaves her papers, dishes, and clothes strewn about.)

People's personality traits and energy levels tend not to change much, as Judy's situation illustrated:

Judy was a twenty-six-year-old secretary who hated her job. She had a few friends but dated little. She was so depressed that she stayed in bed several days each month, and psychotherapy and medication had little effect. Finally, she moved to Israel and underwent a personality change. She got married and was happy for the first time in years.

Ten years later, Judy was miserable again. She was in dire financial straits, her sister had a brain tumor, and Judy's depression was as bad as ever. Her "miraculous" personality overhaul had lasted less than a year, and her depression returned quickly because she never developed good coping skills. Changing where she lived made her happy temporarily but did not teach her how to deal with life.

SHARING ACTIVITIES, OR GOING IT SOLO

While couples should share many goals and values, they don't have to share everything. One spouse can take aerobics classes, jog, play tennis, ski, watch sports, listen to opera, or enjoy shopping without the other. In yeshiva communities, wives often go to movies, exercise classes, and concerts with each other while their husbands learn Torah, stay home with the children, or work. In such circles, it is assumed that wives will often socialize with other women instead of with their husbands. There are no hard and fast rules about which activities couples should share, so singles need to decide which are essential to them and which are not.

Some vegetarians are happily married to dead-animal eaters, while others couldn't countenance such an arrangement. Some "couch potatoes" feel agonized about socializing with an extroverted spouse's friends, while others enjoy staying home when the spouse goes out without them. More important than the actual differences is the way each partner feels about them, and whether they can communicate and compromise around them.

RAISING A FAMILY

Singles who hope to raise a family must consider what kind of parent a potential mate will be. Would you like your children to be like this person?

Couples must agree about basic childrearing methods, values, and attitudes. They must also respect each other or their children will divide and conquer them.

Marie spoke French to her daughter Isabelle, while Misha spoke his native Russian to her. When Isabelle wanted something from Marie, she asked in French. If her mother refused her, Isabelle went to Misha and pleaded with him in Russian. How well she understood manipulation at the tender age of two and a half! Luckily, Misha and Marie agreed to always back each other, making sure that their children could not pit one parent against the other.

Couples who expect to have children should have basic agreement about:

1. Values and goals they want to model and teach their children.

2. Discipline. Children get confused when they are allowed to play a laissez-faire parent against a strict one. They need parents to set reasonable limits, stick to them, and not be excessively harsh.

3. The kinds of peers and intellectual, social, emotional, and spiritual influences they want for their children.

4. Religious education for children. Children can go to public, private, and secular schools; to Hebrew, Sunday, or Jewish day school; or to a variety of yeshivas. The time to discover that the wife wants her daughters to go to Bais Yaakov and the husband insists that they attend a day school is before marriage, not when the children are entering first grade.

Some singles who seem like poor parent material can be good parents if they are loving and have common sense. They may simply need to learn some concrete skills. People who are impatient, short-fused, rigid, undisciplined, or "too intellectual" tend to be poor parents, unless they overcome these limitations. Watch a potential spouse relate to his or her nephews and nieces or to children whom she or he likes. That is a good gauge of how she or he is likely to be with your children.

Couples who are planning to get engaged should discuss what they will do if they have fertility problems, as almost one in five couples now does. They should also discuss how they will respond if they have a handicapped child. It is unpleasant thinking about these matters, but it can avoid disasters later.

Bernie and Shoshana dated for several months and were contemplating getting engaged. Shoshana asked Bernie what they should do if they could not have children. He told her that he would still love her and would want to stay married. He adored children, so she assumed that they would adopt if need be, but they never discussed it. Ironically, two years after their wedding she still had not conceived, and Bernie turned out to be hopelessly infertile. (Men have almost half of the infertility problems.) He wouldn't hear of adopting. After five years of waiting for Bernie to change his mind, Shoshana finally divorced him.

Ted and Dina were a secular Jewish couple. A few months after she became pregnant, she had an amniocentesis. Much to her horror, her fetus had Down's Syndrome. She and Ted had never discussed what they would do if this happened, and she had an abortion against Ted's wishes. He felt violated and angry. Their resulting unresolved tensions destroyed their marriage, and they got divorced.

Baruch and Shulamis were twenty years old when they met. They had dated for two months when she was hospitalized with terrible abdominal pain. She was found to have a huge uterine tumor and her uterus was removed. Baruch asked her to marry him soon afterwards and suggested that they adopt or raise foster children. He loved her so much that he thought it only fair to share their love with others. Shulamis loved him beyond words for his sensitivity and unselfishness.

SUMMARY

The Talmud describes two kinds of marriages: "A man who finds a woman finds goodness,"[5] and "I find that a woman is worse than death."[6] In ancient times, bridegrooms were asked which type of marriage they had.[7] In the first kind of marriage, the man found goodness by deciding that he married the right woman and was committed to working things out with her. In the second, he always harbored doubts that he had married the wrong woman and consequently felt worse than death.

Our Sages advised us about which characteristics to look for in a spouse. They recommended that a man have more achievements than his wife,[8] but not so many that she feels inadequate.[9] They suggested that a man who marries a wise and understanding woman has acquired everything,[10] and that a wealthy man is one "whose wife's deeds are beautiful."[11] On the other hand, they warned that a woman who is too intellectually superior to her husband might become contemptuous of him. And if he marries a woman primarily for her beauty, he will pay a heavy price for it later.[12]

Singles should decide which characteristics are important in a mate and marry accordingly. Look for someone who is a mensch (or menchette), communicates well, and is adaptable to change. Whoever you choose, you'll be miserable if you focus on what you didn't get once you are married and obsess about how much better someone else would have been.

NOTES

1. Leviticus 19:18.
2. Shlomo Wolbe, *Binyan Adei Ad*, 32.
3. *Sanhedrin* 107a.
4. *Orchot Tzaddikim*, "On Anger."
5. Proverbs 18:22.
6. *Ecclesiastes* 7:26.
7. *Berakhot* 8a.
8. *Yevamot* 63a.
9. *Kiddushin* 49a.

10. *Zohar, Vayikra* 52.
11. *Shabbat* 25b.
12. *Sefer Chasidim* 378.

SUGGESTED READING

Gottman, John. *Why Marriages Succeed or Fail.* New York: Simon and Schuster, 1994.

II

Transition to Marriage

8

Engagement

Congratulations! You are now engaged! You'll be in a whirlwind during the next few months as you plan your wedding, look for a place to live, enjoy this special time with your fiancé/e, and share your excitement with all of your friends and family.

You will probably attend one or more engagement parties and bridal showers given by friends and coworkers. On the Sabbath before the wedding, the bride will be feted at a *Shabbos Kallah,* an afternoon gathering with female friends and family. The groom will have an *aufruf,* where he gets an *aliyah* (is called up) to the Torah in the synagogue. The fiancée or family fills small bags with candies and distributes them to the congregants, who throw them at the groom when he finishes his *aliyah.* This symbolizes the wish that the new couple have a sweet and fruitful marriage. The groom or his family usually sponsor a *kiddush* (a buffet of sweets or heartier fare) after the services.

Soon after getting engaged, couples should make up guest lists so that they, their friends, and family can plan the many celebrations ahead. Couples must know approximately how many guests will be attending each party and the wedding before other plans can be made. Friends who sponsor celebrations like bridal showers or the nightly celebrations after the wedding will need guest lists a few weeks in advance in order to extend invitations and prepare food.

In between celebrations, there are many things to do. Most people find it helpful to keep lists of what needs to be done. Couples have to find a place to live and buy furniture and furnishings. They may want to register for china, silver, crystal, linens, appliances, and housewares they hope to receive as wedding or shower gifts. Brides who don't want to register should give their "wish list" to their mother, a close friend, and/or to the hostess at the bridal shower. She can share this information with friends who want suggestions about what presents to give. The list-keeper can also keep track of which items on the list were already bought.

Brides shouldn't assume that friends and relatives will give her what she requests. People are notorious for giving gifts that please themselves and often spend as little money as possible to fulfill their obligation to give something. The following scenarios are familiar to many newlyweds:

A couple registered for china, silver, and crystal service for eight, plus forty-five household items. They got three china plates, two silver forks, four knives, and two crystal glasses as wedding gifts, and none of the household items they needed. They did, however, get twelve huge wine glasses (they don't drink), six cheap flower vases, service for eight in defective china that was not returnable, nine candy dishes (they don't eat candy), four picture frames they didn't want, and checks ranging $18 to $25 from a few couples who gave cash.

A religious bride's coworkers gave her a nonkosher party. She could eat nothing there and drank only seltzer. They also presented her with a wedding gift that they collectively bought—a hideous, framed, velvet picture. When she tried to return it, the store refunded only half of the purchase price because the secretary who bought it was so sure that the bride would love it that she didn't get a receipt. The saleswoman had to assume that it was bought on sale, which it wasn't.

One bride received four teakettles, despite the fact that neither she nor her husband drank hot beverages. When she diplomatically asked a friend where she had purchased the kettle she gave, the friend admitted that she had saved over fifty useless wedding gifts from her own wedding several years before. She palmed them off one by one on her newly married friends.

One bride received a scratched silver-plated tray from a millionaire aunt. The aunt was so cheap that she had taken it off her living room table and polished it herself. The pink paste was still stuck to the bottom!

Other unforgettable wedding gifts:

- Items that come gift-wrapped in Bloomingdale's or Saks Fifth Avenue boxes—to make the couple think that the gifts were expensive. When the bride tries to return them, she discovers they were bought elsewhere!
- Gifts that can't be returned, like a "custom-made" stoneware platter in a color and shape resembling an oversize pickle. Equally appreciated are useless gifts from stores that went out of business during the early seventies.
- Gifts that brides spend an entire day returning, only to discover that the model was discontinued, only cost $20, or was bought too long ago to get a refund.

- Gifts from close friends or family, which violate your taste, but which you are expected to appreciate and use. When Aunt Selma comes to visit, you make a mad dash to find the purple, pink, and green striped hand towels that she bought at a final sale. You normally hide them but put them on display when she visits.
- Gifts that the bride hates, but the groom loves and wants to keep. Or vice versa.
- Useless gifts from people, who asked what you wanted and were told that you wanted cash.
- Embarrassingly intimate apparel given at a bridal shower.
- Intimate apparel or nightwear that three people could wear — simultaneously.
- Useless gifts that people give after an older, or previously married couple, says they don't want or need anything.

Brides often get shower gifts that they can't use and, in some cases, can't even recognize! It is helpful for a good friend to sit next to the bride and tell her what that Tupperware gadget, the hand-crocheted "thing," and other nondescript objects are. Above all, the bride should keep smiling and make the givers think that she is tickled pink by their thoughtfulness, no matter how she really feels!

The nicest wedding gifts are those that are wanted or needed, or are pleasant surprises. If people ask what you want, consider the following:

- Ask people to make contributions to a charity like Yad Eliezer. They make weddings for needy Israeli couples. There may also be a local charity in your community that dowers poor brides.
- Ask people to contact you two weeks after the wedding and see what you still need.
- Cash in lieu of gifts.
- Small household items that are overlooked until they are needed. For example, *havdalah* (a ceremony marking the end of the Sabbath) and Sabbath candles, bottles of wine for the first few Sabbaths, a basket of hand soaps, toothpaste, toothbrushes, deodorant, shampoo, and other toiletries for use while yours are still packed in boxes; wall clocks, mezuzah scrolls, and a calendar.

Keep a box of alphabetized index cards on which you write the name of each guest to be invited to the bridal shower and/or wedding. Include their address and telephone number. As you receive gifts, note each one on the respective giver's card and the date when you sent a thank-you note. This helps keep track of what you received. It also helps you to send thank-you's that mention the specific gift in a timely way.

Don't return unwanted gifts immediately after you get them unless the store will only take them back within a short time after purchase. Call stores and ask how long you can wait before bringing gifts back for exchanges or refunds. Time permitting, return unwanted merchandise a few weeks after the wedding. By that time, most of your gifts will be in, and you'll save time batching gifts and returning them once, instead of every time you get one.

Don't feel insulted when you get presents that are disappointing or grossly inappropriate. You can have hours of entertainment during the first months of marriage sharing stories with other couples about the wedding presents you received!

THE BRIDE'S AND GROOM'S GIFTS

Speaking of gifts, this is when the groom buys his bride an engagement ring and wedding band. (More about that in the chapter on "Money.") Find a friend or relative in the jewelry business who can get it for you wholesale! Learn about the Four Cs (color, carat, cut, and clarity) and consider your budget before you shop. There is a custom among some religious Jews to buy the bride a beautiful watch instead of a diamond ring. Some women prefer a colored stone, such as a sapphire, instead of a diamond, especially when they are on a very limited budget. It is customary for religious grooms to also buy their bride silver candlesticks and a platter to set them on. They typically give them to the bride in the seclusion room after the wedding ceremony.

The bride buys the groom a *tallit* (prayer shawl). While it is nice to surprise him, many religious men are particular about the type of fringes, the length of the garment, the color of the stripes, or the fabric. Ask if your groom would prefer to shop for this with you. One bride spent $200 on a silver collar for her groom's *tallit,* only to discover that he hated having a heavy strip of silver around his neck.

A kosher *tallit* should cover at least half of the man's body, have kosher fringes, and preferably be wool. Although they are widely sold, polyester *tallitot* are not preferred and are invalid if they are less than about three feet wide.

It is also customary for couples to buy each other a prayer book (*siddur*) before the wedding.

MAKING ARRANGEMENTS

The date for the wedding should be at least one week after the bride expects her period to end that month. This will allow her to immerse in a *mikvah* shortly before the wedding, so that the couple can be physically intimate on their wedding night. (See the chapter on "Sexuality" for more about this.) Unfortunately, many brides get their period on or shortly before their wedding day, despite the most careful planning. While it was once common for brides to take the birth control pill for three months prior to their wedding in order to regulate the timing of their periods, this is not recommended.

There are certain times of the year when Jewish weddings may not be held. These include the Jewish holidays, the Sabbath, the three weeks between the seventeenth of the Hebrew month *Tammuz* until the ninth of *Av* (usually mid-July until early August), and for most of the seven weeks between Passover and the

Feast of Weeks (Shavuot). If you don't know when these dates are, consult an Orthodox rabbi before setting a date.

Ask both sets of parents if your tentative date for the wedding is okay before finalizing plans. You don't want to make nonrefundable deposits on a wedding hall, band, or invitations, only to find out that the bride's parents have already bought plane tickets to Israel that week, or that the groom's father must be away on business. (The author planned her wedding around her mother's doctoral exams!)

Once you have one or two tentative dates, find a wedding hall, caterer, band, videographer, photographer, and rabbi to officiate. Ask your married friends or your friends' parents to share their experiences and advice with you. It can save lots of time and will be invaluable. A friend may know that the hall you wanted has a dance floor that is too small for the 150 guests that you expect, despite what the manager says. You may find that the caterer you wanted has the best prices, but the food is not tasty. Look through friends' wedding pictures to get ideas about how a florist can decorate the wedding canopy or to see what halls look like. Asking friends about their experiences with bands may reveal that the one you thought you wanted has mediocre musicians, or that you must pay extra for the specific musicians you want.

Once you narrow down the choices of where to hold the wedding, see if it is available when you want it. Some places are booked two years in advance. Many large synagogues require you to use their caterer or charge a fee for their rabbi and cantor, even if you don't want them.

If possible, see the hall when it is set up for a wedding. Some plain halls look magnificent when they are decorated, while others seem cramped when guests actually mill around or dance there. Some places look gorgeous but have terrible acoustics, especially when outdoor courtyards or large halls are used. Sometimes the guests cannot see the ceremony because pillars or the wedding canopy obscure their view. Some wedding halls now use huge video screens that simultaneously show the ceremony so that all of the guests can have front-seat views, but you may not want to resort to that.

Get sample menus and prices when you are choosing a caterer. Find out if they charge extra for wine and liquor, bartenders, and corkage. Caterers who allow you to purchase your own alcoholic beverages and charge only for bartenders can save you hundreds of dollars. Religious Jews tend to drink little wine and liquor, so don't pay a caterer for what you don't need.

Tell the caterer that you'd like to see them cater a wedding and/or sample the food. (This is the best part of choosing a caterer!) Some menus sound great on paper and the foods look great at a buffet, but they don't taste nearly as good as they appear.

Once you've chosen a caterer, pick a menu and the kind of service that you want (French, carving stations, hors d'oeuvres, etc.). Decide if you want them to provide the liquor. When you agree about the details, you will have to sign a contract that itemizes the services to be provided, the costs, a guranteed minimum and maximum number of guests, and so on. Most places require a small nonrefundable deposit to confirm the agreement, usually $100 or so. Reserving a hall or synagogue might require a more substantial deposit.

Audition bands by hearing them play at a wedding, or ask for an audiocassette of their wedding music. When you have narrowed down your choices, see if the musicians you want are available on your wedding date. You will need to sign a contract stipulating how many musicians they will provide, how many hours they will play, and how much they will charge for overtime. Most Jewish weddings have a minimum of four or five musicians, for a minimum of four hours. The bandleader will ask for a nonrefundable deposit when you sign the contract.

A few weeks before the wedding, know who will be in the processional, and in what order they will walk down the aisle. Discuss with the bandleader specific pieces of music that you want at the smorgasbord, ceremony, and reception, and/or ask him for suggestions.

Once you've chosen a caterer and hall, you are ready to select a florist. Ask your caterer and friends for recommendations. Some couples prefer to rent silk flowers from charitable Jewish organizations. The caterer, wedding hall manager, or local Orthodox synagogues can advise you about making such arrangements.

Decide what kind of bridal (and bridesmaid) bouquets and table settings you want. If you want the *chupah* (wedding canopy) decorated with flowers, make sure that the florist knows how to do this. Ask to see pictures of *chupahs* that he has already done.

Once you've selected the date and the place, you can design the wedding invitations. The bride and groom should construct separate guest lists, then pare them down if necessary. You'll need one invitation for each couple, plus one for each single guest. When you have a rough idea of how many invitations you'll need, order twenty or twenty-five extra. You will probably discard some because the envelopes were addressed incorrectly, and a few "forgotten" guests will invariably need invitations that you didn't originally plan to send.

Mail out invitations four to six weeks before the wedding, but try to order them at least three months in advance. This will give you time to see proofs and correct any mistakes. You don't want to discover, after it's too late to do anything about it, that the invitation has an incorrect time or date, or that the groom's and bride's parents' names were reversed or misspelled.

If you address the envelopes yourself, check an etiquette book in order to do it properly. It will tell you how to address singles who want to bring a significant other or fiancé; two doctors who are married to each other; a Mr. or rabbi who is married to a doctor; a wife of a married couple who might use her maiden name, and so forth. If a friend or calligrapher is addressing envelopes, make sure that she or he knows the rules.

Ask the wedding hall manager for a stack of direction cards with maps that tell the guests how to get there. Put one in each invitation. Make your own if you are getting married in an unconventional place that doesn't have its own cards. This will keep you from getting a barrage of phone calls from people who don't know how to get to your wedding.

Put a number next to each guest on your list and put the same number on your respective response cards. This will tell you who sent back the RSVP replies with no names.

You will want to order *bentschers* for the wedding. These are small booklets containing the special grace that is said after the wedding meal and at the *sheva brachot* (nightly celebrations) the week after. Order them directly from a printer, unless your caterer can get them cheaper. The covers are usually custom-printed with the couple's name, the date, and place of the wedding. If there is a logo on the invitations, this goes on the *bentschers* as well.

Guests like to take *bentschers* as souvenirs, and half of them may disappear as the guests do before grace is even said. Ask the caterer how many *bentschers* to order (you don't need one for each guest), then add ten or twenty to this number. When you get the *bentschers* from the printer, save the extra ones for you and your family. Collect any *bentschers* left over after the wedding and use them at the *sheva brachot*. Ask your *sheva brachot* hostesses to collect them each night, then take them with you for use the next evening.

BUYING A GOWN

The bride needs to select and get fitted for a wedding gown and veil, hopefully at least three months before the wedding. This will allow time to make necessary alterations. A minimum of three weeks (and often longer) is usually needed after each fitting, and at least three fittings are usually necessary. If bridesmaids will wear special gowns, the bride will have to know their sizes and arrange fittings well in advance.

Beautiful bridal gowns can cost thousands of dollars, but there are five excellent ways of saving money when buying them:

1. Buy a sample gown and/or veil. They usually look as nice as nonsamples, but cost 50 percent less. They may need to be cleaned or may require minor mending, but this is easily done when the alterations are made. If you don't see samples that you like on the rack, ask the saleslady to show you some. (When the author got married, she found a stunning $600 gown for $300, and the saleslady marked down a $150 headpiece to $75 because it was the end of the season. These were more beautiful than the $2,000 gowns and $500 headpieces.)

2. Buy a less expensive gown and have a dressmaker alter it. A good dressmaker can tell you where to buy matching lace or satin for $30–$40, and for another $50–$100 can make sleeves, fill in a low-cut bodice or back, or change the style of the gown.

3. Rent a gown. A gown that sells for $2000 may rent for $500. If you must get married in an expensive gown of your dreams, this is one way to do it.

4. Borrow a gown from a friend, relative, or charitable organization that loans wedding gowns to brides.

5. Find a used gown from a newspaper ad at a thrift or antique clothes shop, or at a flea market. Many are in excellent shape and can be had for as little as $100. If it needs alterations, see number 2.

The groom will need to buy a wedding suit if he doesn't already have one. Either he, or the rabbi, will need to supply a *kittel* (a white tunic) for him to wear under the wedding canopy.

RELIGIOUS CONSIDERATIONS

The bride and groom will need to take group or individual instruction in the Jewish laws that govern marital relations. These are given separately to men and women, usually as five or six lessons in as many weeks, and should be completed at least two weeks prior to the wedding.

Meet with your rabbi at least once before the wedding, preferably at least a month in advance. He should have enough time to get to know you as a couple, and you should feel comfortable discussing any concerns that you have about your marriage or wedding.

Some rabbis give premarital counseling, including suggestions for dealing with parents and in-laws. Some may recommend professional counseling or, in rare cases, postponing or canceling the wedding if the couple can't resolve important issues.

The rabbi must also ascertain if Jewish law allows the couple to marry. For example, a *cohen* (a man of priestly descent) may not marry a convert or divorcée, and Jews may not marry Gentiles. A convert is considered Jewish only if she or he was converted according to Jewish law. This requires committing oneself to the observance of all of the Torah and rabbinic commandments.

Couples need to show the rabbi proper documentation if either party converted or is divorced. They should also know how to spell their Hebrew names so that the rabbi can ensure that the marriage documents are written properly.

A previously married bride or groom must have a Jewish divorce certificate, known as a *get*. A civil divorce alone does not permit a Jew to remarry. When a *get* cannot be obtained, an observant rabbi who is expert in Jewish marital laws may know legitimate legal loopholes that permit remarriage.

THE KETUVAH

Obtain a civil marriage license and a Jewish marriage document a few weeks before the wedding, both of which will be completed by the rabbi at the wedding. Ask your rabbi if he has a preference about which type of *ketuvah* (Jewish marriage contract) you should get before ordering it. He may want it worded in a particular way, or tell you that the $300 *ketuvah* you planned to commission is invalid. No matter how beautiful a *ketuvah* is, it must be written according to Jewish law. A Jewish couple is not allowed to live together without a properly written and witnessed *ketuvah*.

A *ketuvah* is primarily a legal–financial document that spells out the husband's obligations to his wife. It has become common, though, for couples to buy an elaborate, custom-made one that they frame and display in their home. These can cost hundreds of dollars. Elaborate, printed ones can be bought for $36 or more in Jewish bookstores, while a plain *ketuvah* can be bought for as little as two dollars.

Two observant Jewish men who are unrelated to each other and to the couple must sign the *ketuvah* just before the wedding ceremony. The groom gives the *ketuvah* to the bride under the wedding canopy, after giving her the wedding ring and saying the ancient pronouncement of marriage to her: "Behold, you are consecrated to me according to the laws of Moses and Israel."

SHEVA BRACHOT

The week after the wedding, couples have *sheva brachot* every night and may have them twice *Shabbat* afternoon. Make a list of the men you want to honor by having them say the marriage blessings under the wedding canopy and after the wedding meal. Give the list to the rabbi or to the person coordinating the wedding details. Let the honorees know your plans in advance so that they will be at the ceremony on time! Have back-up honorees if your designated ones are detained.

Friends and relatives will want to sponsor the *sheva brachot* at their homes or at a kosher restaurant. Two or three weeks before the wedding, give each hostess a list (with phone numbers and addresses) of guests you'd like invited. At least seven men must eat a meal with bread, and up to three men can eat dessert only for each *sheva brachot* meal, at which a minimum of ten men must eat with the bride and groom.

Some couples go on a honeymoon after the week of *sheva brachot*. Plan this several months in advance if you are going during a popular vacation time or to a popular place. You don't have to stay only at kosher hotels if you rent a condo or an efficiency with a kitchen and pack kosher bread, cheese, yogurt, meat, frozen meals, and the like. You can go to exotic locations, supplement what you have with local fruits, vegetables, and fresh fish, and eat in your vacation kitchen. Bring paper plates, plastic cups, knives, forks, spoons, and bowls, aluminum foil for double-wrapping foods that you'll cook in the oven, and Saran-wrap for food you'll heat in the microwave. Take a vegetable peeler and a sharp knife, and you'll eat like a king and queen!

ENGAGEMENT FIGHTS AND FEARS

While engagement is a very exciting time, it is also exhausting and stressful for most couples. When couples must make decisions together, plus accept input from both sets of parents, it can easily strain a relationship.

The author has told many engaged couples, only partly tongue-in-cheek, "Don't think that the wedding is for you. You're just supposed to show up. Your parents (and sometimes your spouse-to-be) will control much of what happens." If the bride's parents pay for the wedding, they usually expect to have a strong say about everything, which can be very distressing to the couple. Even when the couple pays for all or part of the wedding, parents can exert enormous emotional pressure to do what the parents want. Matters are even more complicated when one or both sets of parents are divorced or remarried.

Few engaged couples are prepared for the many fights that occur during this time, especially if the couple has never quarreled before. Many couples break their engagement because they now see irreconcilable differences or traits they don't like in their partner. Some break their engagement privately while they try to work things out. But even couples who initially felt ecstatic about getting married usually have periods of tremendous confusion, misery, anger, and anxiety during this stressful time.

Some couples who had felt happier than at any other time of life question whether they are making the right choice of partner. They vacillate between love and hate, anger and conciliation, security and mistrust. Their expectations of future wedded bliss may be marred by second thoughts about their fiancé/e or in-laws. Couples then wonder if these issues will disappear after the wedding, or if they are about to ruin their lives.

How can someone know if their engagement jitters are normal or if they are legitimate warnings to call off the wedding?

Having second thoughts is a normal part of being engaged. Almost every engaged person asks, "Do I *really* want to spend the rest of my life with this person?" People have reservations for many reasons, some unimportant, some very serious. Many of these can be dismissed after talking to a reassuring, sensible married friend or to a premarital counselor. If your parents give good advice, you can talk to them. Unfortunately, many parents are themselves a source of strain on an engaged couple. Their vested interest in a child's marriage or breakup disqualifies many of them from being objective or helpful.

It is highly recommended that couples take the "PREPARE" questionnaire that was mentioned earlier and discuss the results with a qualified counselor. Apart from the unresolved conflicts that each couple might discover they have as a result of this test, other common reasons for engagement panic are:

1. *"Sometimes I have no feelings for my fiancé/e."*
Singles often think that couples should be madly in love with each other most of the time, but that doesn't happen in real life. One married woman told a friend, "My husband and I have a good marriage, and I think that my feelings are pretty typical. I feel that he's terrific three or four days a week, I feel neutral another two or three days, and he really gets on my nerves about one day a week."

People often panic when they feel "nothing" for their spouse-to-be, even if they know that they are right for each other. Feelings are like waves. They go up and down, come and go, even if we generally love someone. We can stay in a relationship because we *know* that is the right thing to do, not because we always feel that way at every moment. It is normal to feel intensely close and in love for a few hours or days, then to have a period of relative detachment. If you continue to act loving even when you feel distant or angry, don't do hurtful things to each other, and stop worrying about whether your feelings will come back, you are likely to rebuild your closeness in a few days.

Many people panic when they stop "feeling in love" after getting engaged or soon after marriage. Loving feelings often go away temporarily if we are afraid or are questioning whether or not to go ahead with the wedding. Panic is such a strong feeling that it makes it hard to feel anything else.

If specific issues bother you, talk them over with an insightful friend and/or with your fiancé/e. If you are sure that you want to marry this person, do relaxing and enjoyable activities together for a few weeks without evaluating whether you are right for each other. If your loving feelings still don't return, discuss your concerns with a therapist.

Yosef was petrified about marrying Linda, and he tested her by asking her to do some errands for him. Linda was already overwhelmed working full-time and planning the wedding, so his errands were not a priority for her. When she did not buy him the tie that he wanted that week, he took it to mean that she would never put him first. He felt angry and cold, then wondered if he might not really love her. Two meetings with a therapist, the second of which included Linda, were enough to convince Yosef that they were well-suited to each other. The therapy taught him to verbally communicate his need for reassurance and nurturing instead of testing her and expecting her to read his mind.

Six weeks before the wedding, Iris and Don had a terrible fight on the telephone. His parents insisted on inviting ten more guests than her parents were willing to pay for. Iris' parents couldn't afford ten more guests, and the small hall couldn't comfortably accommodate yet another table. Don told her that they should pay for the extra guests out of their wedding gifts and be a little crowded at the reception. Iris was furious about Don's selfishness and concern with his parents' wishes. Her love for him vanished, and she considered calling off the wedding. She asked Don to see a rabbi with her. The rabbi's objectivity and experience helped them see each other's point of view instead of only defending their own positions, and this led to each validating the other's feelings, with a resulting compromise. When Iris saw that Don really did care about her, but that they both needed to communicate better, her love for him resurfaced.

Losing feelings for a fiancé/e is more serious if you often lose interest in people once they become interested in you; if you are angry with, or hurt by, your fiancé/e over matters that aren't getting resolved; if you now see serious problems with your fiancé/e that you whitewashed before; if you are fighting a lot about wedding or marriage plans; if you or your fiancé/e are having problems with commitment, intimacy, or cutting apron strings to the family.

Two months after Marlene and Ezra got engaged, he still had not bought her an engagement ring. He "never had time" to make up a guest list for the wedding. He hadn't gotten around to looking at apartments with her, so they still didn't have a place to live. His lack of real commitment soon overcame her love for him, and she suggested that they see a rabbi or therapist together. Ezra refused, so Marlene went by herself. The rabbi told her that if he wouldn't even come for premarital help, she shouldn't marry him. She took his words of advice and broke their engagement.

Sandy was gorgeous, smart, and successful. She had dated all kinds of men but typically pined for those who wouldn't commit to her and disdained men who were good marriage material. When she was thirty-two, she felt her biological clock ticking away and got engaged to Seth. He was attractive, was emotionally stable, made a good living, came from a good family, and adored her. Yet she felt uneasy. The strong chemistry that had first attracted her to him had dissipated. He was no less wonderful now than he was when they first met, yet she didn't feel excited about him anymore. He met all of the right criteria for a good husband, yet something didn't feel right to her. She decided that if she didn't feel more passion after marriage, she could always get a divorce.

Sandy needed professional help for her emotional problems. She had spent her life trying to rescue men who had terrible emotional problems and found men who were emotionally healthy boring. She did see a therapist and worked through her emotional conflicts in a few months. She was then able to appreciate Seth, and they got happily married later that year.

Hanna and Reuven were ecstatic when they got engaged after ten dates that consisted of eating out and telephone conversations. As she met his friends and family, she began to respect him less and less. His family told disparaging stories about Reuven's irresponsibility, unreliability, and embarrassing behavior at work. His friends saw him as a buffoon and didn't take him seriously. None of his friends' sisters had been willing to go out with him. Hanna realized that her idealistic view of him was based more on fantasy than on reality. She listened to her misgivings because they were well-grounded and broke off their engagement.

2. *"My fiancé/e and I fight a lot."*

Arguments and fights are a normal part of most marriages, but if they happen so often or in such destructive ways that they undermine the love, the relationship will sour. Most people are on their "best" behavior when they date, and they avoid issues that might create conflict. Once couples get engaged, they can no longer do this. It is normal and healthy to have differences of opinion and style, but a fight needs to follow some basic ground rules:

It should address the specific issue at hand and not digress to extraneous issues, the past, personal attacks, nor involve violence, threats, insults, screaming, or humiliation.

It should be done in a respectful and validating way, where matters eventually get resolved, or else you can live with the differences. If either person harbors anger that resurfaces later, the issue wasn't really resolved.

It is done with each party really listening to the other, not being two mutual monologues where each person only tries to get his or her point-of-view across.

The goal is to compromise and apologize when necessary, not to try to win and make your partner lose.

Fighting should not be a primary way of getting attention or connecting. Couples who fight more than they express warmth and love need counseling. Happily married couples have at least four times as many warm and loving interactions as negative ones.

Couples should choose their battles, not fight about every difference they have. We need to live with some differences and not expect our spouse to always think, feel, and act the way we think is best.

Fighting should ultimately bring a couple closer and be done with a sense that they are both playing on the same team. It should not result in couples seeing each other as enemies or idiots.

Learning how to communicate properly is critical to fighting in a way that resolves issues and brings couples closer. Most couples need to develop these skills. See the "Suggested Readings" at the end of the chapter for help in this area.

3. *"I'm worried that my fiancé/e will turn out to be different than she or he seems."*

This is a normal fear and should motivate couples to do some serious thinking about whether they have good reason to worry that their fiancé/e will change in unacceptable ways.

People who have learned a lot about a spouse-to-be in a variety of settings should be able to make a reasonable assessment about who she or he is. We rarely have total knowledge before making any decision, but we can usually do reasonably well with the information that we have or can easily get.

People who have followed this book's suggestions know a lot about the person they plan to marry. They have met the person's family and friends and have talked to people who could warn them about serious problems. They have discussed their feelings and observations with a trusted friend who can give objective advice. If you still have concerns that a fiancé/e will change in important ways, discuss this with a therapist or counselor.

Avi was very wealthy and worried that Laura acted so perfectly because she wanted his money. He spent six months getting to know her, her family and friends, and heard stories about her that gave him reason to believe that she would be a wonderful wife. After they got engaged, he had many fears that she might change for the worse once she had a ring on her finger. He could not guarantee that Laura would stay warm, loving, and patient, as she had been for years, and he drafted a prenuptial agreement to protect himself. He felt better once they signed it, and they went ahead with the wedding. They have now been happily married for thirteen years, and he has never had to use the document.

Stan became a *baal teshuva* (an observant Jew) a year ago and got engaged after dating Jan five times. He wondered if he had been a bit hasty and questioned how well he really knew her. He decided to speak to a rabbi who counseled *baalei teshuva*. The rabbi encouraged him to stay engaged without setting a wedding date. He agreed that Stan really did not know Jan, her family, or friends, and that he should take more time to do this. During the next two months, Stan discovered that Jan had serious family problems, was extremely insecure and possessive, and had unrealistic expectations of marriage. Despite the social pressure to go ahead with the wedding, he wisely broke off their engagement.

Roberta dreamed of having a beautiful house in the suburbs where she could live an upper-middle-class life. Moshe was a businessman who sometimes did well financially, but, at other times, he verged on bankruptcy. Roberta said that she really didn't care how much money he made, yet her behavior belied this. She loved to eat out in restaurants, go on pricey vacations, wear beautiful clothes, and so on. Truth be told, she wouldn't dream of lowering her standard of living. Moshe recognized the discrepancy between what she said and how she lived. She would be miserable if they had to tighten their belts for several years in a row when he didn't have money to indulge her tastes. He broke their engagement.

4. *"Maybe if I wait a little longer, someone better will come along, and I'll regret marrying now."*

People who worry about this are usually in one of three camps: One group does not like making decisions and rarely trust their judgment. They are afraid that any decisions they make will turn out badly. They often stay single well into their thirties or forties because no one seems quite right. People who are characteristically indecisive should see a psychotherapist.

A second group is afraid of marriage. They fear that they will relive their parents' disastrous marriages or be dominated by a spouse who is as overbearing as their mother or father was. They think that intimacy will strip them of their freedom and independence and force them into giving up their identity. They equate tying the knot with tying a noose around their necks. Professional help can enable them to work out these conflicts.

Bonnie was a thirty-year-old woman from a dysfunctional family. She met Mark at a party, and they dated for two years before he proposed to her. After she accepted, she had second thoughts. "He's a wonderful guy, we're very compatible, he's sensitive, warm, and a good communicator," she admitted, "but he has some annoying habits. He's usually late for dates, he bites his nails, and he doesn't dress fashionably. I love to ski and he hates cold weather. I love the beach, but he can't stay in the sun. Maybe I should wait another year and see who else comes along."

Bonnie's misgivings about Mark obviously had more to do with her fears of marriage than with something that was wrong with Mark. Bonnie needs to admit that she is terrified of marriage and to work out her feelings about this.

A third group wonders if they have "settled." While some rare individuals marry a partner who has everything on their "wish list," most people don't. They have to decide whether the pros of marrying an individual outweigh the cons, and then deal with ongoing differences.

What one person can realistically hope to find in a spouse may be completely unrealistic for someone else. For example, a twenty-six-year-old *cohen* (man of priestly descent) may easily meet many suitable, potential partners, while a forty-year-old *cohen* will find his choices limited because a *cohen* may not marry a woman who is divorced or who has slept with a non-Jewish man. A man who earns a meager living will have fewer prospects than a man with a better income. An attractive woman is likely to have more prospects than someone who is heavy and unattractive. Someone with a debilitating handicap may also have limited choices.

Singles with poor self-esteem or with bleak marriage prospects (such as older religious women and *cohanim,* young single mothers, or women with many children) sometimes make big compromises in order to get married. People who have second thoughts about "settling" should ask if they are reconciled to what they are giving up. Will they resent the spouse later, or compare him or her unfavorably to others, or be chronically disappointed?

People who marry just to be married or to have children often regret it later. They should find enough qualities to love and respect in a spouse or not get married.

Not being physically attracted to a spouse-to-be, or feeling no chemistry, *are* valid reasons not to get married. *Why* you're not attracted may be something to discuss with a rabbi, wise friend, or therapist. Some religious people think that they should be "above" considering looks when they choose a marriage partner. Looks should not be the primary reason to marry a spouse, but the rabbis deemed physical attraction important enough that they forbade men to marry women whom they had never seen. If you're not physically attracted to someone, have a platonic friendship, not a marriage.

Ilana, a thirty-four-year-old woman, confided to a friend, "I'm getting cold feet about marrying Ben. I don't know what's wrong with me. He's kind, he brings me flowers and little gifts, he's considerate, he'll do anything for me, and he worships the ground that I walk on."

Her friend asked, "Can you imagine being physically intimate with him?"

Ilana blushed, then shook her head. "No, I don't have those kind of feelings for him." Her friend advised, "Either resolve your feelings about him or don't marry him." This conversation helped Ilana identify what made her so uneasy about marrying Ben. It also validated her feeling that she wasn't being petty for wanting to marry a man whom she found attractive.

Her friend suggested that Ilana ask Ben to speak to her husband. He advised Ben to get contact lenses, fashionable clothes (for the first time in twelve years), lose twenty pounds, and work out. He also suggested reading Ilana romantic poetry once a week and sharing his loving feelings with her. For the first time,

Ilana saw Ben as a man instead of as a platonic friend, and they got married a few months later.

Carol was very religious, accomplished, and thirty-five years old. She had dated many religious men, none of whom were appropriate for her. Meanwhile, she and Ken, one of her nonreligious, Jewish coworkers, became good friends, and he showed interest in her way of life. Six months later, he told Carol that he was willing to keep kosher, observe the Sabbath, and follow the laws of family purity if he ever fell in love with a religious woman. It wasn't long before he and Carol discussed marrying each other. He was willing to send their children to a religious school, although he had no strong commitment to learning more about Judaism himself. When he proposed, she accepted. She felt that, at her age, it was better to have a wonderful husband and father who had some religious limitations than to stay single indefinitely.

When her religious friends criticized her for "settling," Carol had second thoughts. She wondered if someone better would come along in the next five years. Perhaps she should have faith that God would send her a more religious husband. She finally decided that the possibility of finding someone "better" was too remote to give up what she had. Carol and Ken have worked very hard to make their marriage happy, and they have raised wonderful children together. Neither of them has any regrets about their decision.

Raizy was twenty-two, and most of her friends were already married. Her friends and relatives kept telling her what a "catch" she found when she got engaged to a "terrific" *yeshiva bachur* (rabbinical student) who was touted as one of the most brilliant "learners" in the yeshiva. They had identical religious beliefs and practices, he came from a prestigious family, and his family liked her. Yet she wasn't thrilled about marrying Yudi.

She confided to a friend, "People keep telling me how wonderful Yudi is and how lucky I'll be to have the merit of supporting him in his Torah learning. But I'm just not as enthusiastic about him as others are."

Her friend asked, "Besides being a good learner, and coming from a nice family, what else do you like about Yudi? Is he nice to you? Do you sense that he understands and appreciates you? Does he show interest in your thoughts and feelings and want to know how to make you happy? Does he make you feel special?

Raizy began to cry. "Most of the time, he talks about himself, what he wants, and what he thinks. I'm not convinced that he loves me. Maybe he just wants me to support him, make a nice home for him, and raise children. I don't get the sense that he knows how to provide emotionally to a woman, or that he understands me. He's not very warm, and he seems aloof when I talk about my feelings."

Her friend validated her, "The fact that someone knows how to study Talmud is no reason to consider him a good marriage partner. A husband needs to have good character traits like patience, warmth, an even temper, and be caring. If he's very self-centered and overly intellectual, he's not ready for marriage."

Raizy's community and family had pressured her to marry a Torah scholar at all costs. It never occurred to her to look for a warm mensch (a decent human being). Despite opposition by her parents, his family, and the head of the yeshiva, she broke the engagement. It took her another four years to meet her husband, a religious businessman who learns Torah every day after spending time with his family and helping her put the children to bed.

5. *"My parents or friends disapprove of my fiancé/e. Maybe they're right."*

Some people are happily engaged until their parents or friends object. Some objections are well-founded; many are not. Try to find out specifically why people oppose your choice of partner. Then decide if their reasons are well-founded and relevant to you.

Kevin was a convert to Judaism, and Arlene's parents vehemently disapproved of him. They insisted, "You don't want your children visiting his parents and learning their values. You won't be able to go to your in-laws during Jewish or Gentile holidays, and you'll never be comfortable in their home. When they offer to babysit, you'll be sorry if you say 'yes' or 'no.' Kevin's a wonderful man, just don't marry him."

Arlene was very upset that her parents would not accept Kevin, but she didn't want to create a rift with them. She considered calling off their engagement, then realized that her parents' objections weren't relevant to her. She didn't care much that Kevin's parents weren't Jewish. They were very nice people with good values who would never interfere with the way she raised her children. She couldn't always say the same about her own parents. Kevin and his parents also had a warm relationship with mutual respect, and they loved Arlene like one of their own children.

Arlene didn't want to have to choose between her parents and the man she loved, but they forced her to do exactly that. She married Kevin against their wishes. It hurt her terribly that her father didn't come to the wedding and refused to speak to her for a long time, but she never regretted her decision.

Henya was not an intellectual, but she was warm, caring, and had a lot of common sense. She went to work at eighteen to help support her family and never had a chance to go to college. Bill's friends warned him not to marry her because she was obviously no intellectual match for him. It troubled him that most of his friends thought of Henya as "dumb." It was true that she was not sophisticated and often sat on the sidelines when he was with his intellectual and educated friends. When he did some soul-searching, though, he realized that he didn't need an intellectual wife. He could get intellectual stimulation at work. He wanted a homemaker who would give him and his children lots of love and attention. He married her and he has not been disappointed.

Mat was a naive twenty-one-year-old who was madly in love with Evelyn. One night, they were at his parents' house for a family dinner, and it came up in conversation that she was a carrier for Tay-Sachs disease. Mat was also a carrier, meaning they had a 25 percent chance of having a Tay-Sachs baby with each pregnancy. The parents told Mat privately that they would advise him not to marry Evelyn because having a Tay-Sachs child would be so devastating. Mat had a lot of second thoughts and finally decided to be pragmatic and realistic instead of naive and noble. He sadly broke off their engagement.

Jon coped poorly with stress. When he and Peggy got engaged, she told him that she had endometriosis and might not be able to have children. That was fine with Jon. He really didn't want to have children and figured they could adopt if he ever changed his mind. A month later, Jon and Peggy were with friends of his who were having infertility problems. In the course of conversation, Peggy shared her problem with Mel and Sally. After dinner, Mel took Jon aside and warned, "Peggy's a nice girl, but neither of you are emotionally prepared for what you will go through when she wants a child." Jon was very upset by the prospects of breaking up with Peggy, so he dismissed Mel's advice. Unfortunately, Mel knew what he was talking about. Jon and Peggy were happy for their first two years of marriage, but became miserable soon after she decided that it was time to get pregnant. They have been on an emotional roller coaster for the past six years, and Jon has become a workaholic to avoid facing her constant depression.

6. *"I'm not sure that I'm ready for the responsibilities of marriage and children."*

Few people are before they get married. Many couples discover that, no matter what they expect marriage and children to be like, nothing fully prepared them for the reality. Some couples do need time to mature, others need to learn self-control and communication skills, still others never become ready because they are unwilling to do the emotional work necessary to take care of a spouse and children.

If you are not ready yet, what do you think needs to happen before you'll feel ready? Do you think that if you only finish an educational degree, travel more, date more people, live on your own, or establish yourself in a career that you will be ready? What will make you feel differently about marriage then? If you marry now, can you do things that are important to you afterwards? You might want to discuss these issues with a rabbi, a wise friend, a sensible parent, or a counselor.

If you think that you don't have the skills to be a good spouse, read some good books about the topic (see "Suggested Readings" throughout this book), and observe how happily married couples interact. Identify skills, attitudes, and feelings that you need to work on, as well as your current strengths. Ask yourself and a few close friends how to develop what you are missing.

Many first-time parents don't know a lot about raising children. They learn by trial-and-error, from their pediatrician, from other parents, and from books as the children grow. You don't have to know all there is to know about raising children before you get married, or even before you have them. You have to be open to learning, though, and be flexible, because you will learn mostly from on-the-job training.

Share concerns about being a financial provider with your intended spouse and/or with a financial counselor or accountant. If you need help finding a good job or getting out of debt, ask a mentor, vocational counselor, or accountant for advice. You may need job training, a realistic budget, or people with whom to network for a better job.

If you are concerned that you don't manage time or household responsibilities well, ask a trusted friend or relative how to improve. Married people might be able to teach you some useful "tricks" that make running a home much easier.

Some people have emotional barriers to marriage. They don't want to grow up. They don't want to take care of someone else. They don't want to listen to a spouse's problems. They don't want to be tied down. People who have these emotional barriers do not suddenly get better by throwing themselves into marriage. If anything, they resent a spouse and children for taking away their freedom. If you have these issues, work them out with a professional before you get married and then hope for the best.

7. *"I can't put my finger on it, but something doesn't feel right."*

This vague, uneasy feeling typically arises for one of several reasons: The first is that someone has confused emotions and can't sort out which are situational, and which are more lasting and significant. For example, you and your fiancé/e may be compatible, yet be physically and emotionally exhausted, overwhelmed, and stressed. You may feel pressured to please others, or wonder if your fiancé/e is really there for you. You may fight about lots of trivial issues related to the wedding and setting up a new home. You may wonder if it is normal to have to work so hard on a relationship or to compromise so much. With all of this emotional turmoil, you might feel detached and wonder if you really love each other.

Engagements are tumultuous for most couples, especially once they start planning the wedding. Almost every couple has arguments and disagreements during this time. See if you can work through these tensions by putting matters in perspective but not by ignoring them or shoving them under the rug. Your wedding day is just one day of the rest of your lives, but the issues that it precipitates can be portents of future conflicts and communication problems.

Ina and Bert initially dreamed about their wedding day, but now it seemed like a nightmare six weeks away. She found the perfect wedding gown, but he disapproved when he heard how much it cost. He wanted the women and men to sit at separate tables at the reception, while she wanted mixed seating. She didn't want bridesmaids, but her mother insisted that her sisters and her nieces walk down the aisle. Ina wanted to invite only fifty close relatives and friends; her father invited an additional thirty cousins and thirty business associates. She dreamed of walking down the aisle while a friend played the guitar; her fiancé vetoed it. Finally, Ina was so hurt, angry, and upset that she cried for two hours and threatened to call off the wedding.

If a couple can communicate well as they plan and compromise about their wedding, they can continue to use these same skills once they are married. But some couples will find that they lose sight of the importance of their relationship,

or they whitewash their feelings in order to make peace, while harboring resentments. A wedding can be wonderful, but the next forty years are much more
important. Planning a wedding can allow couples to see how they handle conflict
and whether they sacrifice their relationship or dismiss each other's feelings when
issues arise that are important to them. It is critical for couples to empathize with
each other and see a partner's point of view, as well as be able to express one's own
feelings in such a way that they are heard and validated. Couples who deal with
these differences by wallowing in hurt and anger, sulking, attacking each other, or
withdrawing, are likely to continue these negative interactions after the wedding.
The longer these counterproductive patterns continue, the harder they will be to
change later, and they may even cause irreparable damage in the long-run.

In other words, disagreements over the wedding can reflect a couple's basic
inability to communicate and resolve differences. If they feel that something is
wrong with their relationship but can't put their "gut feelings" into words, they
should not dismiss their sense of being mismatched. They should try to identify
what is wrong and talk these issues out with the fiancé/e and a married mentor.

Gail and Bob were a month away from their wedding when she suddenly got
panic attacks. Something told her that he wasn't trustworthy. She talked to a
perceptive friend about her misgivings, and her friend recommended that she
investigate Bob. She was shocked to discover that Bob had lied repeatedly about
where he had been many nights that he had said he was working. He tried to
convince her that she was mistaken, but she had incontrovertible proof and broke
off the engagement.

Dov and Dora got engaged. Over the next two months, she sensed that he had
misrepresented himself to her. When she confronted him with her feelings, he
admitted that his commitment to Judaism was very different than hers. Although
he observed the requisite rituals, he did them out of habit, not because he believed
that it mattered. He hadn't told Dora this because he wanted to marry her and
thought this might dissuade her. It did.

Steve and Denise seemed to be the perfect couple, but she always felt uneasy
about their engagement, without knowing why. Steve told her several times a day
that he loved her. He tried to make her feel better when she felt blue. He bought her
personal gifts and had a great sense of how to make her happy. They seemed to
have similar values and long-term goals, and he was very supportive of her.

She confided her misgivings to her brother, who joined them for dinner later
that week. Her brother told her later, "Steve is very smart, and he does a lot of nice
things for you, but he also tends to put you down. When he disagrees with you, he
says that he is right and you are wrong. He didn't seem to respect any of the
opinions you voiced, except for those that agreed with his. Maybe what you're
sensing is that he trivializes a lot of your feelings and ideas, even though he
obviously loves you.

Denise realized that her brother was absolutely right. When she told Steve that
he often dismissed her feelings and gave him a few examples, he even dismissed
her comments by saying that his comments shouldn't bother her! After a number

of failed attempts to convince him that this was a serious problem, she broke off the engagement.

A third reason people feel that something isn't right is because of their inner conflicts. As their fears of commitment and compromise surface, their loving feelings recede. If they can't resolve this on their own, they should talk to someone who can help them.

James believed that he should find a wife who was so compatible with him that she would agree to everything he wanted. After he and Debbie got engaged, he felt panicked. He liked her, and they had dated for a year and a half, but she was now trying to change him. He had put on thirty pounds during the past two years, and he agreed that he should diet but didn't feel like it. He was months behind in paying his bills and got frequent calls from collection agencies, yet he continued to procrastinate. He was prompt for business meetings, but was invariably fifteen to thirty minutes late for dates with her. She told him that his behavior in these areas wasn't acceptable.

When he discussed this with a therapist, the therapist suggested that he take control of his life. James was already thirty-five years old, and it was time to act like a responsible adult. James was really afraid that Debbie would force him to grow up, and he didn't want that. He went through another year of therapy before he was ready to marry Debbie and accept adult responsibilities.

8. *"She or he doesn't have the right image for me."*

Many people have an image of the person they want to marry. Men may want a beautiful, warm, supportive woman who is always calm, who says and does the right things. Instead, the woman they grow to love is ten pounds overweight, moody, and has frequent bad hair days. She is a good person, but he really wanted a woman who he could proudly show off in public.

Many women want a tall, handsome husband who is sophisticated, strong, sensitive, and caring. Instead, he is short, with thinning hair, and looks more like the Pillsbury doughboy than Superman. Her mind says that looks really shouldn't be so important, but her feelings say that she is disappointed.

No spouse is perfect. If you can't accept a spouse's shortcomings and focus mostly on his or her assets when you are engaged, it's unlikely to happen when you're married.

On the other hand, someone's image can express warning signs that make you uneasy. When that happens, dealing with misgivings now is much better than when it's too late.

Liz loved Eric, but his image made her uneasy. She once showed his picture to a perceptive friend, who said that he was surrounded by a cloud of anger, tension, and depression. It showed in his face and stance and made the friend wonder how often he lost his temper and hurt people. Liz discovered that Eric had been fired from a number of jobs, apparently for arguing with his bosses.

Rena and Sylvan got engaged. He was very nurturing, stable, helpful, and interesting, and she felt lucky to have him. On the other hand, she felt embarrassed when he was with her friends. Instead of being suave and diplomatic, he always seemed to put his foot in his mouth. His social *faux pas* didn't bother him, but they bothered her enough to consider calling off the wedding. She saw a therapist who helped her appreciate Sylvan's good points while accepting his limitations. Rena stopped expecting Sylvan to be the envy of all of her friends, and she decided to marry him because of his nurturing qualities.

ADJUSTING TO IN-LAWS

It takes time for most couples to get used to their in-laws, while many in-laws find the transition equally difficult. Adult children want their parents to see them as adults, while their parents may find separation painful. They may fear that their child will no longer need or want them, their advice, or their love, and may blame the new spouse to the extent that this happens. Parents also want to know that their son- or daughter-in-law treats their child well. If the parents feel their child is being short-changed, parents can be rejecting or critical of the spouse.

If parents and children separate well, they can accept and appreciate each other's autonomy and choices. If not, they can feel as if they are in a tug-of-war between a child's loyalty to the spouse and to the parents. As a rule, the more each feels he or she doesn't have to choose sides and the more accepting the parents are of the new spouse, the easier this adjustment is.

One challenge of engagement is deciding what to call in-laws. Many use the same names they use for their parents, such as Mom and Dad, Imma and Abba (Hebrew), or Mommy and Tattie (Yiddish.) But others feel awkward sharing this intimate title with anyone else but their parents.

Calling in-laws "Mom" and "Dad" becomes natural for those who truly admire, love, and appreciate their in-laws, and for whom these feelings are reciprocated. But those who don't feel this way may prefer to use a more formal or less intimate title. Consider the following:

1. Soon after announcing your engagement, ask your fiancé/e what your future in-laws would like you to call them. Ask for a few choices and let your fiancé/e know in advance which ones you won't be comfortable with. This is less confrontational than having your in-laws tell you how to address them.

2. If you don't want to call them what you call your parents, try similar names. For example, if your parents are Mother and Father, call your in-laws Mom and Dad. If you call your parents Mom and Dad, try Imma and Abba for your in-laws.

3. Some in-laws suggest, or are comfortable with, their children's spouses calling them by their first names.

4. You can't avoid addressing your in-laws by some title forever. Try mentally rehearsing a different one each week until you find one that's comfortable. It's embarrassing and insulting to call in-laws "Um," "you," or "Mr. and Mrs. – – –" indefinitely. Once you decide what to call them, it becomes more natural over time.

SUMMARY

The introduction to *A Tale of Two Cities* could be applied to an engagement: "It was the best of times, it was the worst of times." The excitement of finding a life partner, of being the center of attention, and of planning a wedding make engagement one of the happiest times you'll ever have. But the stress of trying to please both sets of parents, a fiancé/e, and oneself can also create enormous misery.

How you resolve second thoughts about a fiancé/e could have repercussions for the rest of your life. Talking about your concerns with an objective and insightful rabbi, therapist, friend, or relative can be enormously helpful and can save you years of grief and regrets later.

If you manage to weather your engagement successfully, you'll be ready for your long-awaited wedding day, and be better prepared for years of married life! *Mazel Tov!*

SUGGESTED READING

Notarius, Clifford, and Markman, Howard. *We Can Work It Out*. New York: G. P. Putnam's Sons, 1993.

9

The Wedding

Many Jewish wedding customs are modeled after the Jewish people's "marriage" to God when He gave us the Torah. The Almighty betrothed us to Him forever, with "fairness, justice, love, and compassion." Jewish brides and grooms pledge the same to each other.

Although a Jewish marriage is a celebration, it is also a solemn time for introspection and for beginning life anew. To this end, couples observe a private Day of Atonement from sunrise on their wedding day until the wedding ceremony. They say special penitential prayers from the Day of Atonement services, ask God to purify them from their past sins, and pray that He grant them a happy life together. Some people also read the entire book of Psalms. Unless a wedding takes place on the New Moon, or on a day when fasting is prohibited, couples also fast until they drink wine or grape juice during the wedding ceremony. Someone who repents on his or her wedding day is forgiven for all their past sins.

It is customary for the bride and groom not to see each other on the day of the wedding or even the entire week before. A "guardian," usually a series of friends, roommates, and/or close relatives, keeps the bride and groom company during this time so that neither is alone.

Since they are not supposed to see each other until the *badeken* (veiling of the bride), the bride and groom sit in separate rooms at the wedding hall. About an hour before the ceremony, guests start greeting them. The bride usually sits on a "throne" in the smorgasbord, or hors d'oeuvre, room, while the groom sits at a table in a room where light refreshments are served. His male friends keep him company while the rabbi presides over the signing of the betrothal and wedding documents.

The betrothal document is called the *tenaim,* meaning "conditions." In ancient times, this was signed a year before the wedding. Today, it is usually signed by witnesses and acquired by the bride just prior to the wedding. It contains the verses, "May this match flourish and grow like a verdant garden. He who finds a wife finds good, and obtains favor from God who is good, and who says the match is good." After two observant Jewish men sign the *tenaim,* the mothers of the bride and groom break a china plate together. Among other things, this symbolizes how terrible it would be if the couple's relationship dissolved. It also reminds those present of the destruction of Jerusalem at this joyous time.

The pieces of china are usually distributed to single women as a good luck omen for marriage. This is the Jewish equivalent to catching a bride's bouquet, except that anyone who wants one can have a piece of the plate. No one feels left out.

Once the bride accepts the betrothal contract, the couple needs a *get* (Jewish divorce) to end their relationship. Only men can initiate a Jewish marriage, and women either accept or reject this unilateral contract. Once a woman formally accepts it, the husband must give her a Jewish bill of divorce if either party wants a divorce. Since he initially made the contract, only he can abrogate it, although he can do so only with her consent.

PRENUPTIAL AGREEMENTS

If a married Jewish woman wants a divorce, and her husband refuses to grant it, she may ask a Jewish court (known as a *bet din*) to require her husband to give it to her. Jewish law empowers Jewish judges to do whatever is necessary to convince a recalcitrant husband to give his wife a *get* if she wants one. If all other forms of persuasion fail, judges may even beat him until he agrees to divorce her. If he still refuses, they are allowed to hit him until he dies, thereby releasing her from her marriage vows as a widow.

Unfortunately, civil laws prevent Jewish courts from using effective means to ensure that recalcitrant Jewish husbands will divorce their wives. This has resulted in the sorry state of many Jewish women now being married against their will. These women are known as *agunot,* meaning "chained women."

Jewish men today have many ways to avoid divorcing their wives when they should. Men go to a different community or country, ignore the summons of the local *bet din,* or even blackmail the wife and her family for exorbitant amounts of money in exchange for giving a *get.* Although progress has been made in states like New York, civil courts rarely enforce a Jewish court's ruling that a man must give his wife a religious divorce.

If an *agunah* has sexual relations outside of marriage, she is an adulteress, even if she is civilly divorced. All Jewish children born of an adulterous union are bastards (*mamzerim*), according to Jewish law, and may not marry Jews of legitimate birth.

Some men also face extortion by wives who refuse to accept a *get* unless the husband pays them a lot of money. Some women refuse to accept a *get* out of spite. But since Jewish law allows polygamy but not polyandry, a man whose wife refuses to accept a divorce can remarry. He does this by overriding the rabbinic prohibition on polygamy by getting permission to do so from one hundred rabbis in three countries. If he does this, he must leave a *get* for his wife with a *bet din* before he may remarry; his wife may accept the *get* at any time thereafter. He may have legitimate sexual relations with a second wife after obtaining this kind of permission to remarry.

All Jewish couples should now sign a prenuptial agreement protecting them from such disasters. Ideally, they should sign it and have it witnessed before the wedding. At worst, they can still do it when the Jewish marriage documents are prepared before the ceremony. A portfolio, including the prenuptial agreement, *ketuvah,* and *tenaim,* are now available, along with guidelines for implementation, from the Rabbinical Council of America, 305 Seventh Ave., New York, NY 10001, (212) 807–7888.

Following is an example of a prenuptial agreement:

PRENUPTIAL AGREEMENT[1]

a. Husband's Assumption of Obligation

I. I, the undersigned, _____, husband-to-be, hereby obligate myself to support my wife-to-be, _____, in the manner of Jewish husbands who feed and support their wives loyally. If, God forbid, we do not continue domestic residence together for whatever reason, then I now (*me'achshav*) obligate myself to pay her $ _____ per day, indexed annually to the Consumer Price Index for all Urban Consumers (CPI-U) as published by the US Department of Labor, Bureau of Labor Statistics, beginning as of December 31st following the date of our marriage, for food and support (*parnasah*) from the day we no longer continue domestic residence together, and for the duration of our Jewish marriage, which is payable each week during the time due, under any circumstances, even if she has another source of income or earnings. Furthermore, I waive my *halakhic* rights to my wife's earnings for the period that she is entitled to the above-stipulated sum. However, this obligation (to provide food and support, *parnasah*) shall terminate if my wife refuses to appear upon due notice before the *Bet Din* of _____ or any other *bet din* specified in writing by that *bet din* before proceedings commence, for purpose of a hearing concerning any outstanding disputes between us, or in the event that she fails to abide by the decision or recommendation of such *bet din.*

II. I execute this document as an inducement to the marriage between myself and my wife-to-be. The obligations and conditions contained herein are executed according to all legal and *halakhic* requirements. I acknowledge that I have effected the above obligation by means of a *kinyan* (formal Jewish transaction) in an esteemed *(hashuv) bet din.*

III. I have been given the opportunity, prior to executing this document, of consulting with a rabbinic advisor and a legal advisor.

IV. I, the undersigned wife-to-be, acknowledge the acceptance of this obligation by my husband-to-be, and in partial reliance on it agree to enter into our forthcoming marriage.

Groom	Bride
Signature: _____	Signature: _____
Name: _____	Name: _____
Address: _____	Address: _____
_____	_____
_____	_____

Signed at _____ Date _____
Witness _____ Witness _____

To obviate some legal battles over custody, division of property, alimony, and child support, couples are also urged to sign a prenuptial arbitration agreement. It stipulates that both parties will submit their disputes to a *bet din* in the event of their separation or divorce.

The following is an example:

b. Arbitration Agreement between Husband and Wife[2]

Memorandum of Agreement made this day of _____57_____, which is the _____ day of _____, 199_____, in the City of _____, State/Province of _____, between _____ the husband-to-be, who presently lives at _____ and _____ the wife-to-be, who presently lives at _____. The parties are shortly going to be married.

I. Should a dispute arise between the parties after they are married, Heaven forbid, so that they do not live together as husband and wife, they agree to refer their marital dispute to an arbitration panel, namely, the *bet din* of _____ for a binding decision. Each of the parties agrees to appear in person before the *bet din* at the demand of the other party.

II.   The decision of the panel, or a majority of them, shall be fully enforceable in any court of competent jurisdiction.

III.   (a) The parties agree that the *bet din* is authorized to decide all issues relating to a *get* (Jewish divorce) as well as any issues arising from premarital agreements (e.g., *ketubah, tenaim*) entered into by the husband and the wife.

> [The following three clauses (b,c,d) are optional, each to be separately included or excluded, by mutual consent, when signing this agreement.]

(b) The parties agree that the *bet din* is authorized to decide any other monetary disputes that may arise between them.

(c) The parties agree that the *bet din* is authorized to decide issues of child support, visitation, and custody (if both parties consent to the inclusion of this provision in the arbitration at the time that the arbitration itself begins).

(d) In deciding disputes pursuant to paragraph III b, the parties agree that the *bet din* shall apply the equitable distribution law of the State/Province of _____, as interpreted as of the date of this agreement, to any property disputes which may arise between them, the division of their property, and questions of support. Notwithstanding any other provision of the equitable distribution law, the *bet din* may take into account the respective responsibilities of the parties for the end of the marriage, as an additional, but not exclusive, factor in determining the distribution of marital property and support obligations.

IV.   Failure of either party to perform his or her obligations under this agreement shall make that party liable for all costs awarded by either a *bet din* or a court of competent jurisdiction, including reasonable attorneys' fees, incurred by one side in order to obtain the other party's performance of the terms of this agreement.

V.   (a) In the event any of the *bet din* members are unwilling or unable to serve, then their successors shall serve in their place. If there are no successors, the parties will at the time of the arbitration choose a mutually acceptable *bet din*. If no such *bet din* can be agreed upon, the parties shall each choose one member of the *bet din* and the two members selected in this way shall choose the third member. The decision of the *bet din* shall be made in accordance with Jewish Law (*halakhah*) and/or the general principles of arbitration and equity (*pesharah*) customarily employed by rabbinical tribunals.

(b) At any time, should there be a division of opinion among the members of the *bet din,* the decision of a majority of the members of the *bet din* shall be the decision of the *bet din.* Should any of the members of the *bet din* remain in doubt as to the proper decision, resign, withdraw, or refuse or become unable to perform duties, the remaining members shall render a decision. Their decision shall be that of the *bet din* for the purposes of this agreement.

(c) In the event of the failure of either party to appear before it upon reasonable notice, the *bet din* may issue its decision despite the defaulting party's failure to appear.

VI.   This agreement may be signed in one or more copies each one of which shall be considered an original.

VII.   This agreement constitutes a fully enforceable arbitration agreement.

VIII.   The parties acknowledge that each of them have been given the opportunity prior to signing this agreement to consult with their own rabbinic advisor and legal advisor.

In witness of all of the above, the Bride and Groom have entered into this agreement in the City of _____, State/Province of _____.

Groom	Bride
Signature: _____	Signature: _____
Name: _____	Name: _____
Address: _____	Address: _____
_____	_____
_____	_____

Acknowledgments

State/Province of
    County of   } ss.:

On the _____ day of _____ 199_____, before me personally came _____, the groom, to me known and known to me to be the individual described in, and who executed the foregoing instrument, and duly acknowledged to me that he executed the same.

_____

Notary Public

State/Province of
    County of   } ss.:

On the _____ day of _____ 199_____, before me personally came _____, the bride, to me known and known to me to be the individual described in, and who executed the foregoing instrument, and duly acknowledged to me that she executed the same.

_____

Notary Public

Once both parties are protected by having a copy of these agreements, they should put them in a safe place and, hopefully, they will never have to use them.

THE KETUVAH

After the *tenaim* ceremony, two witnesses sign the *ketuvah,* or marriage contract. It spells out the husband's obligations toward his wife, including his need to honor and cherish her, and give her food, clothing, shelter, time, and sexual gratification. It also stipulates how much money he must pay her if he dies or divorces her.

The rabbis instituted the *ketuvah* some two thousand years ago to protect women, although the Torah requires the husband to provide for his wife even without the document. A couple may not live together if the wife, or her agent, does not have a valid *ketuvah.*

A standard *ketuvah* for a first marriage is written in Aramaic and says:

On the _____ day of the week, the _____ day of the month of _____, the year from the creation of the world, according to the way we count here in _____, the groom, Mr. _____, son of _____, said to this virgin, Miss _____, daughter of _____, "Be my wife according to the law of Moses and Israel. I will work, honor, feed, and support you in the manner of Jewish men, who work, honor, feed, and support their wives faithfully. I will give you the marriage settlement of virgins, 200 silver *zuzim,* which is your due according to Torah law, as well as your food, clothing, necessities of life, and conjugal needs, according to the custom of the world."

Miss _____, this virgin, agreed, and became his wife. The dowry which she brought from her father's house, whether in silver, gold, jewelry, clothes, furnishings of the dwelling, or bedding, Mr. _____ accepts upon himself as being worth 100 silver *zekukim* altogether.

And thus said Mr. _____, our groom, "The obligation of this *ketuvah,* this dowry, and this additional amount, I accept upon myself and upon my heirs. It can be paid from the best part of the property and possessions that I own under the heavens, that I now own or will own in the future. It includes possessions that can be mortgaged and that cannot be mortgaged. All of it will be mortgaged and secured to pay this *ketuvah* document, this dowry, and this additional amount from me, even taking the shirt off my back, during my life and after my life, from this day and forever."

And the obligation of this *ketuvah* document, this dowry and this additional amount was accepted by Mr. _____, our groom, upon himself, in the strictest manner of all marriage documents and additional amounts that daughters in Israel are accustomed to, that are made according to the enactments of the Sages, of blessed memory. This is neither a speculation nor a sample document.

We have made an acquisition from Mr. _____, son of _____, our groom, to Miss _____, daughter of _____, this virgin, about everything that is written and spelled out above, with something that is appropriate to make this acquisition.

And everything is proper and established.

(Signed) _____ son of _____ witness
(Signed) _____ son of _____ witness

Some rabbis give couples English summations of the *ketuvah,* signed by the groom, after he gives the *ketuvah* to the bride. The following is one such antenuptial agreement:

ANTENUPTIAL AGREEMENT[3]

This contract is a summary of the husband's obligations to his wife. It is given to assure that the husband fully understands his obligations, and underscores the value nature of the *ketuvah* as a contract. This also facilitates adjudication in the secular courts of the United States.

This agreement is binding on _____, hereinafter referred to as the husband, and his estate, until all clauses are fulfilled.

I. If the husband dies, or this marriage is terminated by a legally valid divorce according to Jewish (Torah) and civil law, a lump sum equal to the monetary value of 100 pounds of silver, or the amount specified in the *ketuvah,* whichever is greater, shall be paid to _____, hereinafter known as the wife. In addition, any monies, articles of value, and real estate contributed by the wife to the joint property of the couple are to be returned in full value to her. This includes all marriage gifts from her family and friends, all property she owned at the time of marriage, or acquired later by independent means, plus any wedding expenses that she, or her family, paid.

Any dispute as to the true value of the wife's estate is to be submitted to binding arbitration in a rabbinic court.

II. Until complete dissolution of the marriage, the husband will pay for the wife's:

1. Food and clothing, in keeping with the social and economic status of the husband and the previous economic standard of the wife;

2. Living accommodations commensurate with the social and economic status of the family;

3. Full medical expenses;

4. Burial expenses;

5. He will also ransom her if she is kidnapped.

If the husband dies, the wife may remain in the marital home and receive from the estate all benefits in Article II until she remarries or accepts the settlement sum in Article I.

If the couple separates, all of the above obligations remain in full force until the completion of all divorce proceedings, and all impediments to the wife's remarriage are removed. Any residual restrictions to such remarriage, be they secular or religious, maintain the support provisions of this agreement in full force.

Signed _____ Date _____

Name _____

Witness _____

Witness _____

THE BADEKEN AND WEDDING CEREMONY

Ater witnesses sign the *ketuvah,* the groom and male guests usually pray the afternoon or evening service, depending upon the time of day. When they finish, the male guests escort the groom to the bride amid great fanfare. The veiling ceremony that follows is usually an emotional highlight of the wedding.

When the groom reaches the bride, he lowers her veil over her face. This is called the *badeken,* and symbolizes the groom setting aside the bride as his wife. It also makes sure that he marries the intended bride instead of an imposter. When our forefather Jacob thought that he was marrying his beloved Rachel, her sister Leah was actually behind the heavy veil. He didn't discover that he had married the wrong woman until the next day![4]

The bride's father and guests traditionally bless the bride. The father says, "May the Lord make you like Sarah, Rebecca, Rachel, and Leah," and then says the priestly blessing: "May the Lord bless you and guard you. May the Lord shine His face towards you and be gracious to you. May the Lord lift His face towards you and grant you peace."[5] The guests say, "Our sister, may you be the mother of thousands of myriads."[6] The men then usher the groom to the place where the wedding processional will begin, while the guests find their seats for the wedding ceremony.

Male and female guests traditionally sit in separate pews before the processional begins. When the groom walks down the aisle, either his father and father-in-law, or his parents escort him. He dons a white tunic (a *kittel*) under the wedding canopy, which he also wears on the Day of Atonement. It symbolizes his spiritual purity. The bride is escorted down the aisle by both of her parents, or by her mother and mother-in-law. She comes to the wedding canopy last because "the last one is the most precious."

The bride and groom are likened to a king and queen on their wedding day, so the guests rise in their honor as each walks down the aisle. Some parents carry lit candles as they escort the bride and groom. Fire symbolizes light and joy. If the couple's relationship is a tranquil and sacred one, they will give light like candles. If not, they will destroy each other like unbridled flames.

The Hebrew words for man, *ish,* and woman, *ishah,* have the word *aish* at their root. *Aish* means fire. The remaining two letters, the *yud* from *ish,* and the *heh* from *ishah,* spell God's Name. If the couple has a harmonious relationship, they direct their inner fire to draw God's Presence into the world. If God is absent from their relationship, and/or they don't get along, all that remains is destructive fire.

When the bride reaches the wedding canopy (*chupah*), she walks around the groom seven times, followed by her mother and mother-in-law. This circling symbolizes the bride's building a wall of protection around her husband. Since a bride's and groom's prayers go "straight to Heaven" on their wedding day, they often pray for themselves and their friends at this time. When the bride finishes circling the groom, she stands to his right, which is the side that symbolizes love. This shows that she will always be there to help him.

The rabbi says two blessings of betrothal at this point. He first sanctifies a cup of wine (or grape juice), then sanctifies the couple's relationship through the marriage rituals. The couple then drinks from the cup.

Next, the groom takes the wedding ring and places it on the index finger of the bride's right hand. He recites the ancient formula in front of two designated witnesses: "Behold, you are consecrated to me with this ring according to the laws of Moses and Israel." Once he does this, she becomes his wife.

The bride and groom show their commitment to each other by his giving her an object of value, and her accepting it. The ring symbolizes eternal love and the protective wall that a husband builds around his wife.

The *ketuvah* is read after the ring ceremony, and the groom then gives the *ketuvah* to his wife. The officiating rabbi may address the couple at this point, although this is not required. When he finishes, he and/or several appointed guests recite a series of seven wedding blessings under the *chupah.* These blessings thank God for creating humanity, for the joy of the bride and groom, and for the future rebuilding of Jerusalem and the Messianic Era. After the last blessing is said, the newlyweds drink from the cup of wine. Then the groom steps on, and shatters, a glass wrapped in cloth. This shows that even when Jews experience their greatest joy, they remember that the holy Temple is in ruins and that their happiness is not complete.

The bride and groom then proceed to a special room where they are secluded (*yichud*) to symbolize the consummation of their marriage. They end their personal Day of Atonement by breaking their fast there. Meanwhile, the guests go to the banquet hall to begin the wedding meal.

When the couple leaves the *yichud* room (after at least six or seven minutes), the photographer usually takes pictures of the couple and their families. When the photosession is finished, the couple rejoins the wedding guests. Between courses, the men dance with the groom and the women dance with the bride, with the bride occasionally going to the men's side and sitting with her husband amid the male entertainment.

Guests usually go to great lengths to entertain the newlyweds. They perform acrobatics, dance with sparklers, wear outrageous and funny costumes, and so on.

The men do Cossack dances, walk on their hands, wear special hats that are aflame, carry the bride and groom on chairs in the air, and dance with men on their shoulders. Women often bring long jump ropes, or make them by tying cloth napkins together. The bride and female guests dance, jump rope alone, or in tandem. They do traditional dances, replete with Maypoles and streamers, pompoms, costumes, and lots of antics. The more merrymaking the better, and it typically continues for hours.

When the wedding feast ends, the guests thank God for the delicious food by saying the grace after meals together. This is followed by repeating the same Seven Wedding Blessings that were said under the *chupah* in the company of at least ten men.

When it's over, the couple says good-bye to their guests, changes out of their wedding clothes, and leaves to start their new life together.

WEDDING DISASTERS

Everybody loves a wedding—unless they're worried that something will go wrong. When your wedding day approaches, remember:

1. Have a good time and enjoy yourself.

2. No matter how carefully you plan, something is guaranteed to go wrong. An infinite number of problems can arise, so don't expect everything to go perfectly.

3. You'll laugh in retrospect when things do go awry, so don't let it ruin your wedding day.

Here are a few illustrations of what can go wrong, no matter how carefully you plan your wedding:

As one couple stood under the wedding canopy, the bride whispered to her new husband, "Are those men reciting the wedding blessings your relatives?"

"No," he responded, "Aren't they yours?"

"No," she replied, "I've never seen them before in my life."

"Neither have I," he confided.

They later found out that some important rabbis happened to be nearby, so the officiating rabbi invited them to participate in the wedding ceremony. No one asked the couple if they wanted to substitute these rabbis for the friends and relatives they had planned to honor with saying the blessings.

One bride was determined to keep her gown spotless. She made sure that the florist took off every pollen-laden pistil from the lilies in her bridal bouquet. She reminded the rabbi and the caterer three times to use white grape juice instead of red wine for the wedding ceremony so that it could be easily cleaned if it spilled on her dress. She stayed away from children with dirty hands and guests bearing sauce-laden plates at the smorgasbord.

When she and her new husband finally broke their fast in the *yichud* room, he opened a bottle of Coke, and it sprayed all over the front of her gown. So much for her careful planning.

Many a bride has ripped open seams on her gown while dancing. Others have had their train ripped when guests stepped on it or placed a chair on it, not realizing that the train was underneath.

One bride lost her shoes just before walking down the aisle. She ended up getting married in a hastily-discovered pair of white ballet slippers.

One couple paid $400 for a *ketuvah*, only to discover before the ceremony that it was invalid. An officiating rabbi confiscated another couple's *ketuvah* while they were in the *yichud* room, because the rabbi just found out that the groom had been previously married and did not have a copy of his *get* to prove that he had been properly divorced.

More than one woman has had her engagement ring stolen by waiters or guests when she took it off to wash her hands before the meal. There have also been incidents of guests or relatives stealing cash gifts out of the groom's jacket when he took it off during wild dancing and of wedding gifts being stolen from the bride's room.

At one wedding, an elderly guest had a massive heart attack on the dance floor. The guests whisked the groom out of the room because he was a *cohen* (of priestly lineage) and could not be in proximity to a corpse. Meanwhile, the bride sat by herself in the midst of total chaos.

If your wedding disaster is minor compared to these, count your blessings. Rarely does anyone have an uneventful wedding, so be prepared to roll with the punches.

WEDDING JITTERS

Getting married is truly wonderful for some couples, but it is scary and overwhelming for others, especially for those who have last-minute jitters. It is common to hide such panic behind mechanical smiles and a social mien, as couples wonder if they are making the worst mistake of their lives. Many couples are grateful that they got a video of the wedding because they were too anxious to notice what was going on while it was happening!

Don't be surprised if you're scared witless. That is par for the course. If need be, find a close friend to reassure you, take a tranquilizer, and think about what you love and enjoy about your spouse-to-be. Remember how terrible you felt all those years that you were single. And if all else fails, remind yourself that your panic will be over in a few hours, and things will probably be better soon.

Before you get married, talk to some happily married friends about how they felt on their wedding day. You might be shocked to hear how scared some of them were before they married the spouse who seems perfect for them now.

Having terrible misgivings on your wedding day is not necessarily an indication that you should call things off. Feelings are not facts, and we have to know when fears come from our imaginations instead of from reality.

Gail was mistrustful of people. She spent most of her time alone in her apartment, doing freelance writing. Despite her reclusiveness, she dated Morris for a year and happily accepted when he proposed to her. He was very good to her, but the idea of marriage petrified her. She knew intellectually that Morris was a good partner for her but couldn't stop obsessing about all of the things that could go wrong after tying the knot. On her wedding day, she took medication to keep her anxiety attacks under control and repeated to herself, "I just have to make it until 2:00 . . . I know that I'm making the right decision . . . I'm not going to die . . . Morris loves me and I love him. . . . " It was one of the worst days of her life but, once the ceremony was over, she relaxed and enjoyed the rest of the celebration.

HELPFUL HINTS

Talk to some married friends about how to make your wedding day less stressful. For example, ask a trustworthy friend, relative, or wedding hall director to help ensure that everything runs smoothly. If the room where you want to keep the gifts is locked when the guests arrive, that person will find someone to unlock it. If the caterer can't find the liquor that you bought, that person will track it down. If you left your contact lenses on your bathroom counter at home, that person will somehow get them for you.

When the author got married, a recent bride from her synagogue had compiled seven pages of helpful hints for brides-to-be. She happily gave copies to anyone who asked. New brides then annotated their copies and passed them on to engaged friends. See if anyone in your community has such a list.

A few suggestions: Copy the seven wedding blessings in large Hebrew letters, or in English transliteration, onto seven index cards. Give respective copies to whomever will recite that blessing at the marriage ceremony and at your *sheva brachot*. Collect each card after the ceremony and meals and use them the next day. These cards are extremely helpful for people who cannot read Hebrew, or who left their reading glasses at home.

If you expect nonobservant guests to attend your wedding, type a one- or two-page explanation of the day's events, and make enough copies for each guest to have one. If you like a fancier look, you can decorate the blurbs with beautiful designs or have them printed and bound. Put them near the seating cards or on the seats in the wedding hall. Letting your guests know what to expect and what the rituals mean will make the day more meaningful to them if they aren't familiar with Jewish traditions.

Ask a relative or friend to collect the wedding gifts and bring them to your home a few days later. Make sure that the gifts are kept in a locked or supervised room at the wedding hall. Don't tempt unscrupulous people to walk off with your crystal, silver, and cash.

Now that VCRs are so popular, having still photographs of the wedding is not that important if you have a limited budget. Still photos are nice for relatives or friends, but it is a lot cheaper to give them copies of the video at $10–35 a piece. Hiring a still photographer can cost $1000 or more.

The bride and groom rarely have a chance to eat after they leave the *yichud* room. They are so busy getting photographed, dancing, being entertained, and greeting guests that they have little time to enjoy the meal. Those who have the time may be too nervous to eat! In any case, consider asking the caterer to wrap and refrigerate your meal. By the time the wedding is over, you will be ravenous and can finally eat alone together.

No wedding is complete without considering the less fortunate. Donate left-over food that you can't use to a *Tomchei Shabbos* organization. These charities give food to needy Jews in a community. If your town doesn't have one, contact a local Meals on Wheels, homeless shelter, *Bikur Cholim* (organization of Jewish volunteers who visit the sick and homebound), or your local synagogue and make advance arrangements to have the food picked up and distributed.

Another beautiful practice is to make a charitable contribution to enable other Jewish couples to get married. *Yad Eliezer* will sponsor an entire wedding for a poor Israeli couple, including hundreds of guests, for only $1,000. Since the average American wedding costs $16,000,[7] and half cost more, it is not a lot of money to pay to really share your joy with the less fortunate.

After your wedding, consider donating the wedding gown and veil to an organization that outfits poor brides. *Yad Eliezer* does this in Jerusalem; most large Jewish communities throughout the world have local groups that do the same. If you are too sentimental to give your gown away, consider loaning it to single friends who get married. In any case, have your gown and veil cleaned soon after the wedding to keep the fabric from being permanently stained. Heirlooming them will keep the fabric from deteriorating or turning off-color over time.

NOTES

1. Courtesy of the Orthodox Caucus. My thanks to Rabbi Basil Herring for providing the text.
2. Ibid.
3. Courtesy of Rabbi Moshe Tendler. Reprinted from Lisa Aiken, *To Be a Jewish Woman* (Northvale, NJ: Jason Aronson, 1992), pp. 149–150.
4. Genesis 29:23, 25.
5. Numbers 6:24–26.
6. Genesis 24:60.
7. Michael McManus, *Marriage Savers* (Grand Rapids: Zondervan Publishing House, 1993), p. 121.

SUGGESTED READING

Aiken, Lisa. *To Be a Jewish Woman.* Northvale, NJ: Jason Aronson, 1992. Contains a wealth of information about Jewish marital obligations and rights, sexual intimacy, and Jewish views of birth control and abortion.

Auman, Rabbi Kenneth, and Herring, Rabbi Basil, eds. *The Prenuptial Agreement: Halakhic and Pastoral Considerations.* Northvale, NJ: Jason Aronson, 1996. A project of the Orthodox Caucus.

Herring, Basil. "Putting an End to the Agunah Problem." In *Amit Woman,* September 1994, pp. 17–21. Explains the importance and structure of the Orthodox Caucus's prenuptial agreement. Required reading for any engaged couple.

Kaplan, Aryeh. *Made in Heaven.* Brooklyn, NY: Moznaim Press, 1983. An excellent book for those interested in knowing about the marriage ceremony and the spirituality of marriage.

Wallman, Lester, and McDonnell, Sharon. *Cupid, Couples and Contracts.* New York: MasterMedia, 1994. For couples who are interested in prenuptial financial agreements.

10

Adapting to Marriage

Adapting to marriage has never been easy. Even the first couple, Adam and Eve, had problems. God made Adam a life partner after Adam realized that he was lonely. Within hours, she gave him forbidden fruit to eat, and Adam blamed her for getting them expelled from the Garden of Eden![1]

Marriage often changes how we see, and relate to, the person we married. A roommate's or friend's personal habits or shortcomings might annoy us, but our blood pressure skyrockets when we realize that a spouse's bad habits, friends, and family might torment us for a lifetime! This is partly why half of all newlyweds have significant marital problems, even when they were blissfully happy until, and throughout, the wedding.[2]

While certain people get married in order to have security, it makes people lose some independence. It is easy to build resentments about that, while losing sight of what we once appreciated in the person we now have to accommodate to, and share our turf with, permanently.

This is why good communication and a willingness to change are the foundations of marriage. Without them, marriages quickly deteriorate under a sea of unresolved anger, conflicts, and disappointments. One reason why divorce in America is so rampant these days is because people are used to "doing their own thing," not compromising and doing for others.

We live in a throw-away society that is based on instant gratification and entitlement. If we can't find exactly what we want at one store, we get it at another. Markets cater to our every whim and want. The media constantly tells us that we deserve pleasure, an easy life, comfort, and that we should "have it all."

Our society does not stress patience and delayed gratification. We live with fax machines, overnight mail, messenger service, and instantaneous telecommunication. If we want money from a bank any hour of the day or night, we can get it from a 24–hour machine. We are surrounded by supermarkets, pharmacies, and drug stores that never close; we can order whatever we need from 800–telephone lines. If we want something we can't afford, we buy it with a credit card so we don't have to wait. If we don't like the bother of depositing paychecks or paying our bills, the bank will do it for us. And, if we aren't inclined to cook or shop, we can always order take-out food and have it delivered. Today, most Americans have become impatient and intolerant of even small discomforts.

As if all this weren't enough, commitment and permanence are now anathema to us. Many of us change schools, jobs, and/or residences every few years. We may get new cars and personal computers every two or three years. We eat ready-made food, buy products in throw-away containers, and use disposable plates, utensils, and napkins. We discard razors, paper tablecloths, hospital gowns, and even cameras after only a few uses!

We no longer repair broken answering machines, Walkmen, toys, household furniture, appliances, and old cars because it is much cheaper and easier to get new ones.

Living this way makes it very difficult to think that we shouldn't discard a "broken" marriage partner, or one who does not make us happy. Living with a marriage partner is often anything but comfortable and enjoyable. We have to be patient and invest a lot of time and energy into resolving our conflicts. Marriage requires not leaving as soon as we stop being happy or when we need to repair the relationship. We have to believe that building a marriage is worth more in the long-run than being comfortable now.

American "egalitarianism" says that couples should split responsibilities fifty-fifty, but this rarely happens. It is well-known that wives usually spend at least twenty more hours a week doing domestic chores than husbands do, even when both work full-time. One partner (usually the wife) also tends to put in much more emotional and physical effort than the other. People who expect marriage to be a fifty-fifty proposition usually end up having half a marriage or no marriage at all.

Each partner should feel that his efforts are totally responsible for the marriage's success or failure. When couples fight, even if one person is 95 percent responsible, the other should take responsibility for his or her 5 percent contribution. When a partner's efforts fall short, we can keep the marriage viable by helping the other person get back on track. Seeing a marital problem as only one spouse's fault and being unhappy until she or he changes is a good prescription for divorce.

The Torah requires us to do what is "good and right,"[3] not just live by the "letter of the law." Marriages crumble when people stand on principles and refuse to do more than their "fair share." Both spouses should try to do as much as possible, not as little as they can, to make their marriages vibrant. They should also consider what role they played in any marital dispute or conflict.

Marriage is an investment. The more we put into it, the more we are likely to get out of it, although it may take years to fully reap the benefits. We should not keep score as to how many times we made our spouse happy, then stop being nice if we don't quickly get rewarded.

It surprises some people that Americans who live together before marriage get divorced 50 percent more often than do couples who never cohabited before the wedding. We expect the opposite to occur, since cohabiting couples know what living together is like. But unless they are committed to staying together and changing when new situations warrant it, and they learn and practice the skills to make marriage work, conflicts over their differences will inevitably arise. The same feelings that brought them to live together, instead of getting married first, may make divorce a comfortable way out. Their early physical intimacy often masks the lack of emotional and spiritual intimacy that inevitably surfaces in time.

This illustrates the fact that a couple's attitudes about marriage and their communication skills are much more important than how innately "compatible" they are.[4] Couples must know how to talk and listen to one another, not vent their anger or disappointment in destructive ways. They must resolve problems and know what a spouse needs and can't tolerate. If couples have the right attitudes and skills and then give 100 percent of themselves to make sure that their marriage succeeds, they are likely to fulfill their expectations.

Many animals, like lobsters, have shells that protect them from predators. At the same time, their shells also keep them from growing. As they mature, they must shed their comfortable protection and grow new shells to become stronger and better adapted to their environment. But this temporarily makes them completely vulnerable.

The same process happens in marriage. The challenges of marriage make us uncomfortable, but we need them to grow. At the same time, we instinctively hold onto our comfortable, secure habits and ideas when we feel vulnerable or challenged. However, this interferes with our becoming "one" with a spouse, and we must let go of our old, individual shells in order to grow new ones that suit us as a couple.

We resist doing this because we like familiarity and stability. While change can be an exciting challenge to some people, it makes others feel vulnerable, insecure, and frightened, especially if it means giving up parts of our identity or our comfort. The more we believe that a spouse wants to change our identity, not just get us to modify a few behaviors, the more tenaciously we hold onto our "self."

We see how uncomfortable change is when we make even tiny alterations in our daily habits. For example, if you usually wear a watch on your left wrist, wear it on your right arm for a day or use your left hand to do things that you usually do with your right hand. If such small changes feel strange, it's no wonder we resist big changes so much!

Vicky was a designer and Warren was an engineer. Their esthetic tastes were so different that a friend asked Warren if it wasn't horrible living with someone who was so different.

He replied, "It's awful if your attitude is, 'I must have things my way.' It's an exciting challenge for us because we try to see how much we can compromise for each other."

Ultimately, we can fight change, resign ourselves to it, or grow by learning new ways of communicating, negotiating, and compromising. Like Warren, we can think of adapting to married life as an exciting challenge, or as a threatening, anxiety-provoking nightmare. It's all in our perspective.

There is a story about a man who goes to the next world. He is given a choice of going to Heaven or Hell, and asks to see both before choosing. An angel first takes him on a tour of Heaven, where the residents are quietly sitting and enjoying themselves. "What a bore," he says to himself.

He then goes on a tour of Hell. Its residents are laughing, partying, and having a great time. What an exciting place to be! Without hesitating, he tells the angel that he wants to go to Hell and is whisked there in a flash. Much to his shock, it bears no resemblance to what he just saw. The heat was unbearable, and suffering people screamed constantly. He was ordered to do backbreaking work. The pain was intolerable.

"Wait a minute," he shouted to the angel. "This is not the place that you just showed me. What happened?"

The angel smirked, "The Hell that I showed you before was what the tourists see. Now you're a permanent resident."

Some people liken this to marriage. There is a saying that marriage is not as wonderful as singles imagine it will be, nor as awful as married people say it is.

Being single, and even living together, gives people an unrealistic view of what marriage will be like. From the time of engagement until a week after the wedding, the couple is the center of attention. They are showered with gifts, they go out a lot, they celebrate, and they talk on the telephone until the wee hours of the morning. They walk on clouds and believe that their partner is wonderful and can do no wrong.

This continues until the honeymoon is over, and the "real world" intrudes. Instead of going out and being entertained, they clean the house, cook, wash dishes, do laundry, and pay bills. The glamour of doing chores together fades. Instead of giving each other gifts, they spend hours returning unwanted wedding presents, furnishing their home, and unpacking boxes of belongings. Sensibility replaces romance.

Then spouses develop flaws that "weren't there" before. He snores, she looks terrible without makeup. He's got a terrible temper, she gets wicked mood swings.

He's a slob, she's never ready on time. They both stop being polite and appreciative. As tensions crop up and disappointments mount, couples may lose sight of what attracted them to each other in the first place. When they feel angry and tense, couples start to criticize and retaliate, rather than work at loving. Without making a continual effort to build their love and affection for each other, they will grow distant, bored, or hostile.

Staying in love is an art that takes ongoing work. It begins by carefully listening to a spouse, understanding what motivates him or her, learning to speak in a way that he or she is receptive to hearing, and finding out what the other one needs. We each come to marriage with a story and with personal dictionaries, which express how we uniquely see the world and relate to others. We want our spouse to read us from cover to cover, and we should be willing to do the same with them.

Even though couples who are destined to marry share two halves of the same soul, husbands and wives are never identical. It is a challenge for each spouse to develop emotionally and spiritually, while meshing with the other in complementary ways that overcome differences.

The *Ethics of the Fathers* says, "It is not up to you to complete the job, but neither are you free to desist from trying."[5] The job in marriage is not to concentrate our efforts on "perfecting" our spouse; it is to work on ourselves and our marriages in such a way that we can grow. A challenge, yes, but one that is well worthwhile.

It is much easier to see a spouse's shortcomings than to notice our own. We like to see ourselves as wonderful and basically wholesome, while our spouse needs to change annoying habits, attitudes, and so on. Since we can't change others, we need to recognize how our behavior influences our spouse's responses to us. We should change ourselves if we want to encourage a mate to change.

Janet needed Sonny to complete some forms so that she could get a student loan. She nagged him repeatedly, but he refused to do it. Finally, she forged his signature and sent the forms out herself.

While living with someone like Sonny is maddening for a responsible person like Janet, nagging won't change him. If anything, he'll respond by taking even longer to do the task. Janet learned to ask him once or twice to do things by a certain deadline. If he still has not done them, she does them herself. He now does 25 percent of what she wants, which is better than the zero percent that she got by nagging.

Francine's husband was neither warm nor demonstrative. She was tempted to give him a cold shoulder until he gave her the cuddling and affection that she wanted. Had she done this, he would have been even more withdrawn in response to her rejection. Instead, she showed him extra warmth and affection. By modeling in an accepting way what she liked, he learned to be warmer.

Marriage is like riding a tandem bicycle. If we lead one way, our partner may have no choice but to follow. If we angrily try to force a partner to do what we want, we can topple both riders.

NOTES

1. Genesis 3:12.
2. Michael McManus, *Marriage Savers* (Grand Rapids: Zondervan Publishing House, 1993), p. 146.
3. Deuteronomy 6:18.
4. Clifford Notarius and Howard Markman, *We Can Work It Out* (New York: G. P. Putnam's Sons, 1993), p. 20.
5. *Mishnah Avot* 2:21.

SUGGESTED READING

Arond, Miriam, and Pauker, Samuel. *The First Year of Marriage.* New York: Warner Books, 1987.

11

Marital Expectations

The *Ethics of the Fathers* asks, "Who is rich? One who is satisfied with his portion."[1] People feel content when their marital expectations are fulfilled and feel disappointed, depressed, and angry if their reality falls short of what they hoped for. Their misery is multiplied by their sense of entitlement to what they lack.

A man was very happy with his wife, even though she wasn't spectacular in any way. He explained, "I'm a simple man. I expect my wife to make me dinner at night, keep a clean house, take care of the children, and speak nicely to me. Most of the time she does this, so I am happy. When she does more than this, like being especially affectionate, buying me a little gift, or making me special food, I am ecstatic."

Meanwhile, his next-door neighbor was miserable. He expected his wife to keep the house spotless, to always look stunning, to drop everything she was doing whenever he came home from work, to make him specific foods at least three times a week, to manage the family finances, to take care of the children and help them with homework every night, never to get upset, to go wherever he wanted for weekends and vacations, and so forth. His expectations were so high that he was almost always disappointed.

Our expectations and attitudes largely define our contentment with marriage. What our lives are objectively like is much less important than how we feel and what we tell ourselves about our circumstances. One person lives in poverty and is quite happy with her life. Another person in the same situation feels miserable. If we set expectations that are out of reach, even if they are realistic for someone else, we feel deprived and impoverished. When we get more than we expect, we feel rich.

People have many expectations about how a spouse should act, feel, and think. For example, most Americans expect a husband to be the family's main breadwinner and expect wives to raise the children and run the home. We expect spouses to be considerate and thoughtful; to share many of our values, interests, and opinions; to build our egos; and to make us feel desired, special, and important. Some people assume that everyone shares these expectations, but they don't.

For instance, some Jewish wives support their families financially while their husbands study Torah full-time. Some husbands are more involved with child rearing and domestic chores than their wives are. Some wives expect to have little in common with their husbands and get their primary companionship from women. Some husbands expect their colleagues, not their wives, to build their egos and make them feel important.

Some people don't even expect a spouse to be nice to them! A "Dear Abby" letter said that a woman's husband was an ex-prisoner, did not support her financially, and cheated on her. She loved him because "he is wonderful to my children from my first marriage." Not most people's cup of tea, but she was content to stay married to him.

Our expectations of a husband or wife reflect cultural norms, as well as our emotional wants and needs. For example, some women are content with a husband who earns $25,000 a year, while others think $200,000 is not enough. Some men expect their wives to be overwhelmed, exhausted, and disorganized while they raise children, yet others expect to come home to *House Beautiful* every night.

Izzy was a good provider, a loving husband, and an excellent father. He treated Rachel well, went anywhere she wanted, and adored her. But he wasn't sophisticated and had poor social skills. When they hosted guests or went to social functions, she felt humiliated by his social ineptitude and inability to discuss politics, literature, art, and music.

Instead of focusing on his wonderful qualities, Rachel kept telling herself that she had been cheated and deserved much better. She spent hours thinking about her friends who had the sophisticated husbands that she "should" have gotten, while she got stuck with a "booby prize." By constantly generating negative thoughts about her husband, she created a constant dissatisfaction that ultimately led to a wrenching divorce.

Motty had even more "liabilities" than Izzy. He stuttered, always looked unkempt, and was shy and awkward around strangers. Yet Nechama thought that he was wonderful. She adored him because he was a loving husband and father. He was helpful at home, had impeccable integrity, set aside time every day trying to become a better person, and learned Torah. Her cup overflowed because she valued what he was and attached little importance to what he wasn't.

Every spouse has pluses and minuses. Happily married people put their disappointments on a back burner and don't expect a partner to be what she or he isn't. They modify their expectations and appreciate what a partner is and provides, rather than being constantly disappointed with how she or he falls short. They cope with disappointment by reminding themselves about what they love and appreciate in a mate, and they don't harp on the shortcomings. In other words, what we tell ourselves about a mate determines our feelings about him or her much more than the objective reality does.

This idea was illustrated by Avishai, four, and Shimi, eleven. As soon as Shimi announced that he was going outside to play with his friends, his tag-along brother chimed in that he was going, too.

Shimi protested, and his mother intervened. "Avishai, you can't play with Shimi and his friends, but you can play with your friends Yoni, Shmuli, Benni, and Yehuda."

Avishai wanted what he couldn't have, but contented himself with what was available. Like Avishai, we need to accept not having exactly what we want and appreciate what our spouse can provide.

Lolly complained that her husband, Michael, sometimes scrapped their romantic plans when his friends came into town. She asked her therapist, "Why does he put his friends ahead of me?"

The therapist explained that Michael was a very loyal person, and being good to his friends was very important to him. Even when he would have preferred to spend the evening alone with his wife, he felt a responsibility to be a good host to friends whom he hadn't seen in a year. In fact, Michael's loyalty was one of the things that Lolly loved about him. The same way that he was loyal to her, he was also loyal to others he loved.

Lolly mulled this over and agreed. "I guess I'm lucky that he's so loyal." She quipped, "It seems that I married a golden retriever!" Now able to put aside her anger, she went home and told Michael how disappointed she was when he dropped their plans and spent the day with friends who came to town. He agreed that it wasn't right to do that. He now sees his friends only if they call him ahead of time so that he doesn't have to cancel dates that he's already made with his wife.

We can evaluate the reasonability of our marital expectations by putting ourselves in our partner's shoes, not by comparing our spouse with others.

Sylvia wanted Henry to spend more time with her. After all, her friends ate dinner with their husbands most nights, while she and Henry only ate together on Friday nights. Instead of dwelling on how much better her friends had it, she thought about how grateful she was that her husband provided so well for her and their children. Instead of being angry about the sixty hours a week that he worked, she focused on the fact that he spent most of his free time with her. Neither of them wanted him to take a pay cut or find a new job, so it was pointless to rue the fact that he didn't work less. Instead of complaining or nagging when he took an occasional hour to read and relax, she hired a babysitter one night a week so that they could go out together after he had a little time to unwind. She couldn't get what she ideally wanted, so she contented herself with the next best thing.

In most marriages, spouses can choose to see their cup as half-empty or half-full. Their perspective can make the difference between filling a cup more or draining it because they feel that there's not much there, anyway.

Annette worked full-time and also ran the home. Alex wanted her to launder and iron his shirts because it wasn't convenient for him to drop them off at the Chinese laundry. Instead of getting angry when she told him she didn't have time, he put himself in her shoes. He realized how burdened she was already and tried to iron the shirts himself. After scorching one and wasting fifteen minutes doing a poor job on another, he learned that it was best to keep taking them out.

Shana wanted her husband to share her tastes. She played classical music at home, hoping that Ike would come to like it, but he still preferred jazz. She asked him to watch "oldie but goody" movies with her, even though they bored him. He wanted to watch science fiction. He liked steak and French fries, but she made him salads, brown rice, and tofu so that he would be healthier. He couldn't even sit in his favorite chair without her telling him that he was slouching. He finally felt so tortured that he asked her to stop trying to "improve" him.

He asked Shana how she would feel if he forced her to live with his tastes. Instead of assuming that married couples must share the same likes and dislikes or assuming that her likes were better, his comment helped her realize how terrible it was to force a partner to live her way. Once she stopped telling herself that Ike must change, she stopped shoving her tastes down his throat. She discovered that he was willing to share her tastes once in a while, but only if she didn't make him do it.

Martin loved to watch Sunday football on television. Shulamit found this very annoying. Instead of pitying herself for being a football widow and asking him to give it up, she realized that this was his only time to relax all week. She put earplugs in her ears, curled up next to him, and read books, with a fire burning in the fireplace, as he watched the season's games.

Before expecting a spouse to be like you and enjoy what you enjoy, remember that he or she is an individual who wants his or her tastes and choices respected. No one likes to feel that he or she is "broken" and must be fixed. Couples aren't supposed to be the same, and not all differences must be bridged.

MAKE YOURSELF HAPPY

Most people want to be happy. Contrary to popular belief, our happiness depends on how we react to life, not on how well we control the people around us. We choose how we react when a partner is difficult, frustrating, or hurtful, and our reactions can lead to greater intimacy or cycles of negativity. How much we focus on a partner's shortcomings largely determines how much they disturb us and how we feel as a result. For example, we can react to their quirks as comical or endearing and take them in stride or be furious, indignant, and hurt.

How we perceive things affects us much more than the actual events do. We don't have to be thrilled about upsets and disappointments, but we don't have to make them worse than they already are. We make ourselves miserable thinking that our marital happiness depends upon a spouse changing to be what we want or harping on the fact that we didn't get the spouse we thought we deserved. As long as we choose to stay married, we have to live in the real world, not in a fantasy where our expectations are completely fulfilled. If a spouse has serious character flaws, terrible problems, or is abusive, we may need to get divorced. But if we decide to stay and live with typical marital conflicts, dwelling on how awful things are keeps us from appreciating what is good. Rather than focusing on what our partner needs to improve, we should consider how we can improve ourselves and be happy, regardless of whether or not our spouse changes.

Many women expect their husbands to spend more time with them than their husbands are willing to spend. The husbands want time to "do their own thing" and feel smothered spending "too much" time with their wives. Some wives unrealistically think that if their husbands only loved them enough, they would spend more time together. While this is sometimes true, the amount of intimacy a woman wants is often more than a husband is willing to provide, and the amount of time that she wants to talk may be much more than a husband feels is necessary or desirable.

Some husbands will agree to reserve specific times to take a walk, go for a drive, go out to eat, or go on a "date" with their wives. Some couples arrange satisfying, uninterrupted time together early in the morning or after the children go to bed. Couples who don't spend at least fifteen to thirty minutes of loving time together every day may need counseling and/or help managing their time better.

Often women have a stronger need for intimacy than men have, while men have a stronger need for independence, power, and individualism. When men's need for intimacy is satiated, they tend to pull away, slay a few dragons, and/or assert their independence. Men can go through cycles of closeness and aloofness for a lifetime, yet be totally devoted to a wife. "Neglected" wives shouldn't panic, feel rejected, or be devastated when husbands want to spend time alone, as long as the couple also spends some quality time together. Giving husbands space when they need it will encourage them to want closeness a few hours or days later.

When wives feel threatened by a husband who pulls away, they tend to pursue their husbands, or become needy and critical. This encourages men to stay away longer and connect less and less. No one wants to be around someone who is needy or aggravating. The less needy and critical wives are, the more men are likely to want to nurture them and be nurtured in return.

This is but one reason why it is important for most wives to socialize and enjoy some activities without their husbands. They can do volunteer or paid work, take classes, pursue hobbies, and have female companionship and conversation. They can go to sisterhood and charity meetings, book reviews, movies, concerts, shows, gardens, craft fairs, and museums without their husbands. When wives can't be happy without their husbands, it is unlikely that they can be truly happy with them.

Many women are initially horrified at the prospect of taking classes, exercising, watching movies, visiting museums, or going to eat alone. Once they try it and get used to it, they usually find that it's not so bad and can even be quite liberating! Getting out of the house usually makes them feel better and makes them more interesting to be with. What man wants a boring wife, who keeps bemoaning her solitude? When a woman's emotional needs are limited enough that her husband can fulfill them, he feels good. Men try to avoid wives who are so needy and unsatisfied that they make the man feel inadequate.

Men who don't receive enough intellectual stimulation from their wives should suggest that their wives read, socialize, take classes, attend lectures, or study with them or on their own. When this is not possible, husbands should get their intellectual stimulation on their own or from others.

Husbands who feel neglected by wives who have too many responsibilities at home should recognize that their wives are probably overwhelmed. Be more attentive, helpful, and/or hire help or babysitters. Husbands who feel neglected by wives who are social butterflies should ask if there is anything they can do to make their wives enjoy being with them more.

Leah went to a parlor meeting every week, to class on Monday nights, and a *simcha* (celebration) or school function a third evening most weeks. Albert finally asked her, "Don't you enjoy eating dinner with me?"

Leah carefully answered, "Most of the time I don't. You spend most of our time together telling me about your day, but you don't seem very interested in mine. I'd like to hear your feelings and ideas, but I also want you to be interested when I share mine with you. It's boring just listening to the details of your accounting sheets, then have you tune me out when you're done."

Although it hurt him to hear this, Albert took her sobering comment to heart and started asking her to relate what she learned and felt after each evening out. When they spent evenings together, he made a point of not giving her a business report about his day, and instead, asked her to talk about herself. For the first time, he asked her what she would find interesting about his day. She replied that she would like to hear how he felt about his work instead of hearing dry details. Within two months, their relationship was much better, and Leah only went out once a week.

ASK FOR WHAT YOU WANT?

When are our expectations of a spouse inappropriate?

Aidel had a very painful childhood. Her mother died when she was an infant, and her father put her in foster care when she was six. While Yochanan was sympathetic to her emotional fragility, he felt drained by her constant requests for reassurance and love. She needed to address her feelings in therapy, not expect her husband to make up for, and listen to, a lifetime of emotional deprivation.

Frances was a biochemist and Rich was a mathematician. He wanted her to read his calculus books every night so that they could "share" his interest. Instead, she preferred to read romance novels. Rather than expecting Frances to be a computer, Rich needed to be more romantic with his wife. Once he was, she was willing to discuss calculus with him from time to time.

Even though some people think that we should always ask for what we want, Judaism teaches us not to make unrealistic requests of a spouse if it will make them feel bad as a result.

Tehilla always liked to please Emanuel. When he asked her to make him apple strudel just like his mother's, she didn't want to say "no." But she already had too much to do and didn't have time to bake. When she offered to buy strudel at the bakery, he declined the offer. Finally, she made it for him in the wee hours of the morning because she wanted so much to please him. While she should learn to say "no," he should have the sensitivity not to put her in situations where she feels she can't turn him down.

NOTES

1. *Mishnah Avot* 4:1.

12

Daily Life

Couples only know what day-to-day married life is like once they experience it. Adjusting to marriage can be especially difficult for people who have previously lived with others without having to compromise or communicate well.

Moving into one spouse's apartment or house usually causes more problems than moving into a home that is new to both of them. In the former situation, one person already controls the living space, and the newcomer automatically upsets the *status quo* every time he or she tries to change things.

Arleta moved into Andrew's apartment when they got married. She had never told him what she really thought of his "early attic and late relative" decorating, but assumed that she would fix up the place after moving in.

She embarked on her mission a week after the wedding. She started by asking him to throw out his old newspapers and magazines. He resented her telling him how to live in his own place, and the papers stayed where they were. She reminded him several times, but the piles around the living room and bedroom just grew higher and higher.

Arleta decided that she'd had enough of his bachelor ways and took matters into her own hands when he was at work one day. She filled a huge garbage bag with his periodicals and left it for the garbage collectors to recycle. Elated with her progress, she threw out the stained pillows on the sofa, his worn slippers, and lots of his "junk." She replaced two of his paintings with her posters. She turned his ugly towels and bedsheets into dust rags. She made up the beds with designer sheets and put lace-bordered towels in the bathroom. She went through his closet and threw out most of his socks and underwear because they had holes in them, then discarded his stained and outdated ties. She left his polyester shirts and suits in a pickup spot for Goodwill.

When Andrew came home to a place he no longer recognized, he felt violated and outraged beyond belief. Arleta didn't understand why he didn't appreciate how much better their home looked. But all Andrew could think of was how much better it would look without her in it!

Most couples have to accommodate a partner's tastes in clothes and home furnishings. It doesn't matter if your spouse has objectively terrible taste. You still have to address his or her feelings about losing meaningful personal possessions. If you don't take a spouse's feelings into account, unresolved tensions can simmer for years.

Spouses should consult each other before decorating and furnishing a home, unless one gives *carte blanche* to the other to do as she or he pleases. When couples can't agree, Jewish law gives the woman authority to decorate as she pleases. Practically, though, some husbands and wives feel better if each has a room to do with as they please, and they compromise about the rest of the house. This may foster more domestic peace than the wife doing everything her way.

Husbands and wives should discuss the matter before discarding each other's belongings. What seems like an eyesore or junk to one person often has sentimental meaning to the other. Each may feel violated if his or her feelings are dismissed without due consideration.

Some people find it easier to part with comfortable and familiar possessions once their marriage feels secure and comfortable. It may help to wait a few months before asking a spouse to part with treasured mementos, even if you can't imagine why anyone would like such "stuff" in the first place.

WHAT HAPPENED TO THE PERSON I MARRIED?

Newlyweds are often shocked by how differently a spouse treats them than they expected.

Jodi assumed that Jerry would join her for breakfast every morning, buy food when it ran out, and make dinner when he got home before her. In other words, she expected him to treat her as considerately as she treated him. She soon discovered that his ideas were very different from hers.

The first week of marriage, Jerry joined Jodi for breakfast every morning. But instead of chatting with her, he buried himself in the newspaper. He had no need to talk in order to feel close to her and was quite content to sit silently in the same room. She could not understand why he found stock market quotes and baseball scores more interesting than her. Her perspective made her feel rejected and isolated. She mistakenly assumed that every loving husband would want to talk to his wife as much as possible. She didn't realize that men don't have the same need to talk that women do. Nor did Jerry know that women expect their husbands to talk to them. After all, none of his male roommates ever cared if he talked to them or not. They were good buddies without much conversation.

Jodi learned that men and women have different ways of getting their needs met, and she stopped seeing Jerry's behavior as personally insulting. She told him that she didn't mind him reading during breakfast but asked if he would spend a few minutes talking to her, too. He agreed. This arrangement gave her the intimacy that she needed, without depriving him of a chance to enjoy his morning paper.

Normally, Jerry went to work before Jodi did, and she cleaned up the breakfast table and washed the dishes. One morning, she left earlier than he did. When she came home, Jerry had washed his dishes but had left hers on the table. She was devastated because this was a sign to her that he didn't care about her. Instead of barraging him with her upset feelings, she thought about what to do. She realized that he might not know that husbands are supposed to be more considerate of wives than they are of roommates. She calmly told him that wives have different needs than roommates do, then gave him some practical suggestions: He should offer her food when he took some for himself; he should set the table for her when he sat down to eat; he should cook enough food for both of them when he made meals; and he should ask if she needed anything before he went out to the store. He was grateful that she had enlightened him instead of getting angry at him for doing things that he didn't know were inappropriate.

THERMOSTATS

A comical part of newlywed life is adjusting to incompatible thermostats. Most wives feel cold when their husbands are comfortable, and their husbands perspire when wives are in their element. Battles over air-conditioning, heat, and open windows commonly occur until couples find compromises that both can live with, or until the wife enters menopause. If they personalize these issues or make them into power struggles, they'll never resolve their differences.

Aaron can't tolerate more than a jacket in winter, while Roberta gets chilled when the temperature drops below seventy degrees. When she sets the heat at seventy-two, he melts, and when he sets it at sixty-five, she freezes. If they compromise at sixty-eight, neither is comfortable.

When they first got married, she thought that he exaggerated his discomfort so that he could set the thermostat his way. Setting the thermostat quickly turned into a power struggle between them, until she spoke to other couples who told her that most of them had the same dilemma. She and Aaron compromised: she dresses like an Eskimo when they are home during the winter, and he drinks a lot of iced tea when they are home during the summer. Not everyone's solution, but it works for them.

They were also quite surprised to discover that even though women are usually colder than men, women have much greater tolerance for hot objects. Roberta would put hot dishes on the table with her bare hands, while Aaron would scorch his hands touching them. After making him a hot mug of tea, Roberta would hold it first and get the pleasure from warming her hands. Once she gave it to Aaron, he was pleased that the temperature was just right. Instead of being only a nuisance, their temperature differences encouraged her to snuggle up to him to get warm, and he loved holding her cold hands when he felt too warm. Learning how to use this difference to enhance their relationship taught them the value of not being exactly the same.

SLEEPING HABITS

Couples have many adjustments to make in the bedroom. Jewish law prohibits couples from sleeping in the same bed when the wife is *niddah* (when she gets her period until she immerses in a *mikvah* twelve to fourteen days later), but they may share a bed at other times.

Sharing a bed seems romantic, but it is uncomfortable for many couples. People normally change positions forty to sixty times a night,[1] and one partner's restlessness often disturbs the other. Couples who do share a bed should buy one big enough for both of them to be comfortable. Religious couples often buy narrow twin beds, then later regret not buying wider ones. Some couples prefer one bed that they share when they can be together and a second, narrower bed that one uses when they must sleep apart. Two large beds take up too much space for most bedrooms, although some couples prefer this option.

This is an excellent illustration of the fact that there is no "right" way to bridge most marital differences. Each couple can find out what other couples do, but, ultimately, each couple must choose which of many possible solutions works best for them.

Snoring is a serious problem for many couples. It has been estimated that 60 percent of men between the ages of forty and sixty-four snore heavily, and the noise can be as loud as jackhammers (eighty to ninety decibels)![2] (Men tend to snore more than women do.) Since people snore loudly only when they sleep on their backs, it helps to sew a tennis ball into the back of a snorer's pajama top. It will keep him from rolling onto his back when he sleeps, making snoring unlikely.

Some people need to read in bed or listen to music in order to fall asleep. If this disturbs a partner, they can read in another room or use a small, focused lamp or flashlight to read in bed. Earphones are useful, if tapes, music, or radio talk-shows disturb your mate.

EXPRESSING PREFERENCES AND DELEGATING
RESPONSIBILITIES

Because marriage melds two different people, respecting each other's individuality is important. People have preferred ways to shop, cook, clean, pay bills, file papers, and the like. It is useful to discuss these preferences before the husband ruins his wife's white lingerie by washing it with his black socks, and she messes up his bookkeeping by writing checks without noting them precisely as he likes in the ledger. If one spouse doesn't like the way the other does things, the one who is more particular should communicate how she or he wants things done. If one partner makes several attempts and can't get it done to the other's satisfaction, then the more painstaking one should do it himself or not criticize the other's efforts.

Sarita hated to shop for food, but Alan didn't mind. The first time he did it for them as a couple, he bought many items that weren't on the list that she gave him. He also went to the most expensive supermarket in the neighborhood because the checkout lines there were shortest. From then on, Sarita shopped when she wanted to save money and refrained from criticizing Alan when he saved her time.

If one spouse has a specific way she or he wants something done, she or he should let the other know what it is. For example, a wife can tell her husband before he goes shopping, "Don't buy the blueberries if they cost more than $1.69 a box, and don't get whole milk if they don't have skim." When the husband comes home, she should compliment him for his help, not criticize him or get angry with him for the things he didn't do the way she wanted.

Every spouse has strengths and weaknesses. Engaged couples and newlyweds should discuss which tasks each does well, and which ones each likes and dislikes. Then they can delegate responsibilities.

Newlyweds have a lot to do after the wedding. They must unpack their belongings and wedding gifts, write thank-you notes, return unwanted gifts to stores, furnish their home, set up bank accounts, get telephone and utility services connected, resolve problems with the superintendent or landlord, and so on.

In addition, they have the usual responsibilities of marriage, including buying food and household items, cooking, washing dishes and laundry, cleaning the house, paying bills, gardening or mowing the lawn, and preparing the house for guests. The list expands exponentially when they have children.

Some couples post a list of items to buy, things to do, and a schedule calendar in a convenient place, such as on the refrigerator. This lets each spouse know what needs to be bought or done and reminds them of their individual and joint plans.

Art is a vegetarian but Sherri is not. He is a good cook and enjoys working in the kitchen, but he hates to clean up. Sherri is a mediocre cook but is willing to clean up, although her allergies prevent her from dusting around the house. They decided that he will cook, vacuum, and dust, while she will buy groceries, wash the dishes, and do the laundry. He leaves her a very specific list of foods that he wants her to buy every week and where she should buy them. Meanwhile, she showed him how to vacuum and dust in places that he would normally ignore.

Artie and Risa both enjoy cooking and entertaining, but neither likes to clean, shop, or pay bills. They have different tastes in foods and different standards about how to do housework. They decided that the spouse with the more demanding standards will do that task. Since Risa is constantly dieting and is health conscious, she buys and cooks most meals. Artie is particular about cleaning, so he does that. He also pays the bills and keeps their financial records in order.

Once couples agree about who will do which tasks and how they should do them, the other spouse should not criticize the partner's efforts. For instance, it was Artie's job to do the laundry, but Risa forgot to tell him not to wash her silk blouse with the rest of the wash. Unfortunately, the blue dye bled all over the other clothes. The next time she was careful to be specific.

If, after a few honorable attempts, the spouse whose chore it is can't or won't do it as requested, the other person (to whom it is most important that it be done a specific way) should do the chore himself or herself.

Conflicts arise when couples disagree about who should do which chores. This is a major source of arguments for couples. For instance, Simona and Ethan both worked forty hours a week, and she assumed that they would share the housework equally. Meanwhile, he expected her to do most of it. She made a chart listing each chore and how much time it took. It showed that she spent fifteen hours a week running their home, shopping, cooking, and cleaning, while he spent an average of one or two hours a week paying bills and doing household repairs. Even though he initially thought that his wife would do all of the domestic chores, the chart made him realize that she needed help. Instead of arguing about *who* should do various chores, they defined the problem as having chores and needing to figure out how to get them done. He agreed to shop, vacuum, and wash the dishes whenever she cooked. He still believed that his wife *should* do all of the housework and cooking, but the important point was that the problem got solved.

SUMMARY

Our Sages debated how *mezuzot* (parchment inscribed with biblical verses) should be placed on the doorposts of Jewish homes. They ruled that we should place them in the upper third of the doorpost, inclining inward. This was a compromise that took various opinions into account.

The placement of *mezuzot* reflects the importance of compromise as a foundation of a Jewish home. The rabbis wanted to stress to couples the importance of respecting one's partner and taking a partner's feelings into account. Knowing that each person has strengths and worthwhile ideas helps make the transition to marriage a lot easier.

As couples adjust to daily life, they often have a misconception that they must share the same perspective about what needs to be done and how. Not only do they waste an enormous amount of time and energy trying to do this, it often results in a lot of anger, with the chores still not being done.

For example, Adrian wanted Ira to volunteer to clean the bathroom and take out the garbage every week and to do so without complaining. Ira was willing to do these chores, but he hated doing them. She battled with him every week about his grumbling, so he stopped doing them altogether.

She also argued with him about how he should *want* to spend time with her family and be eager to help her host Sabbath guests. He insisted that he was *willing* to do both, and he put on a nice social mien so that neither her family nor their guests knew that he wasn't excited about socializing. Why couldn't she accept that she got what she wanted without him having to feel about people the way she did?

Almost every couple has times when they have to choose to either get what they want or convince their partner to agree with them. Getting what we want is much easier than changing a partner's feelings, attitudes, and beliefs. If a partner is willing to do what we want, even if he or she does not share our feelings about it, we should be grateful and accept that. Insisting that a spouse feel the way we do or agree with our perspectives is largely a waste of time. While it is certainly okay to express our feelings and our hopes, we should not try to impose them on a spouse. If we insist on doing that, we are likely to lose his or her goodwill, not gain agreement anyway—and the tasks will probably not get done.

NOTES

1. *Jewish World* (September 11, 1992), pp. 23–25.
2. Ibid.

III

Enriching a Marriage

13

Communication Skills in Marriage

We are distinguished from animals by our ability to speak.[1] If we use words constructively, we can exercise our inner divine image and build bridges to others. By doing the opposite, we destroy the world and act worse than animals.

The Torah repeatedly stresses the incredible power of words. For example, God created the world with ten phrases: "Let there be light . . . Let there be a firmament in the midst of the waters . . . Let the waters under the heaven gather together in one place, and let dry land be seen . . . ," and so on.[2] He also revealed the Torah using ten phrases, called the Ten Commandments. Thus, He used words to create physical and spiritual worlds.

The Third Commandment, which prohibits us from taking God's Name in vain, teaches us not to trivialize our power of speech. God gave us this faculty so that we would use it productively, not gossip, lie, and hurt other people's feelings or reputations.

One way that we can use speech constructively is by talking to our spouses (and children) in ways that foster domestic harmony. The Mishnah says that bringing peace between a husband and wife is so important that we "enjoy its interest in this world, but its principal [reward] remains to enjoy in the World-to-Come."[3]

While "freedom of speech" is extremely important to liberal Americans, fostering harmony should be more important to Jews than being brutally honest and exercising our "right" to say whatever we want. Judaism does not allow us to say whatever we feel like saying, even if it is true. We can potentially violate fourteen positive and seventeen negative commandments by saying derogatory things to people and about them, even if what we say is true![4] We are supposed to censor our speech if we would otherwise hurt people's feelings, damage their reputation, or focus ourselves primarily on their shortcomings instead of allowing ourselves to recognize their positive qualities.

Secular society advocates saying and doing whatever feels natural. Many people still believe "If it feels good, do it" and "Don't keep your feelings in, especially anger. Share them." This is an excellent way to ruin any relationship, especially a marriage. No one wants to be assaulted by someone's anger or be subjected to brutal criticism. Spouses often become so comfortable "sharing" their uncensored feelings that they do irreparable harm to their partner. Studies have shown that one devastating comment can undo the goodwill and love created by at least twenty loving acts, and that invalidating a spouse's feelings is a major factor in the collapse of marriages.[5]

A potential convert once asked Hillel to teach him the gist of Judaism while standing on one foot. Hillel responded, "What is hateful to you, don't do to others."[6] This expresses the essence of how we fulfill the commandment to love our spouse as ourselves.[7] The medieval Jewish philosopher Ibn Gavirol eloquently expressed this idea by saying, "When the roots of love are deeply set in the heart, its branches manifest themselves on the tongue."

We like others to treat us with tact and diplomacy, and we usually do this with strangers. But many couples think that it is okay to be so relaxed and comfortable with each other that they treat their spouse worse than any stranger. Instead of anticipating how their words will affect a spouse, they speak freely. They justify this by saying that the spouse doesn't mind or that it is okay to say whatever's on their mind because they are married.

Children talk naturally. They say exactly what they think and feel. They can be charming or mortifying when they do this. No one appreciates honest, but tactless, statements like, "I hate you and wish you were dead," "I'm sorry I ever met you," or "You look really ugly." Children and adults must learn to stop being "natural" and tactfully censor themselves.

God modeled the need to carefully measure what we say by choosing every word in the Torah to convey a moral lesson. For example, before bringing the Great Flood, He told Noah to take "seven animals of every species that is ritually clean and two of every species that is not clean."[8] It would have been more succinct to term the latter species "unclean." God used extra Hebrew words to express this idea so that we would learn to go out of our way to use refined language, even when coarser or undiplomatic language feels more natural.

People don't realize that good communication is supposed to feel *unnatural!* This is because we have to engage our brains before speaking and consider how our words will be heard. Then we must decide if, how, and when to say something. We are not accustomed to constantly pausing and thinking before speaking, rather than impulsively saying what we feel.

Richard told Aliza, "You think you understand me so well. The truth is, you don't understand me half as well as my sister does."

Richard's words were absolutely accurate, but they devastated his new wife. Since this kind of statement could not possibly have a positive effect, he should have kept it to himself.

The goal of marital communication is to enhance the relationship, not to be brutally honest and truthful. We are supposed to ask ourselves, "How is my spouse likely to receive what I want to say?" If there is no way that we can word the message so that it will have a positive effect, we shouldn't say it.

The talmudic Sages even addressed whether or not we should lie when someone else's feelings are at stake. They contemplated the following scenario:

Guests at a Jewish wedding customarily sing, "This is how we dance in front of a beautiful and gracious bride!" But what if the bride is ugly? Should the guests lie and sing the standard words anyway?[9]

Hillel's disciples ruled that some "truths" are relative or subjective, and that diplomacy should be the rule. Since every groom thinks that his bride is beautiful and gracious, we can describe reality as he sees it, even if we don't share his perceptions.

Some people think that it is hypocritical to say or do what we don't feel or believe. Judaism tells us we must sometimes act contrary to our natural feelings and beliefs when they misguide us or are inappropriate. When we go against our feelings and do the right thing anyway, our feelings will eventually become more appropriate. We shouldn't worry about seeming hypocritical. We should do the right thing even if it feels awkward.

While Torah teaches us objective truths about how to live, there is rarely only one right way to see, or deal with, relationship conflicts. This is why, when you have two Jews, you get three opinions! We should expect husbands and wives often to have different views of the "truth," as happened in the following anecdote:

A couple with a marital problem went to their rabbi. When the wife reported her side, the rabbi responded, "You're right." The husband then defended himself and presented a completely different perspective.

The rabbi thought for a moment, then replied, "You're also right." The rabbi's assistant quietly pulled him aside and asked, "Rabbi, how can they both be right?" The rabbi pensively stroked his beard and exclaimed, "You're right, too!"

Some issues are black or white, true or false, right or wrong, but most relationship conflicts are not. They are shades of gray, and matters of opinion, style, or preference. It is rarely productive to tell a spouse that we are right and he or she is wrong, that our view is true and theirs is false. Even if we *are* right about some factual matter, who wants to be told that they are wrong?

We naturally get defensive, hurt, or angry when we are told that we are wrong, stupid, or mistaken. We feel humiliated having our shortcomings pointed out to us and may even defend our egos by becoming more wedded to our point of view. After we feel attacked or humiliated, we rarely agree that we made a mistake or see someone else's point of view.

Although some situations involve facts that are true or false, right or wrong, two people can both be right about many issues because there are at least two sides to every story. Husbands and wives can perceive the same event differently, with each believing that his view is the "real" truth.

Couples need to learn that it doesn't matter who is more "right," and that it is fruitless to debate such matters. What matters is that couples find a way to live peacefully with their differences, or they will erode their loving feelings for each other.

Zelig was a difficult man. He never admitted making a mistake and even denied obvious facts to avoid conceding that he was wrong. For example, Ruchama complimented him on how nice he looked, then added, "Did you know that your tie has a stain on it?"

"No, it doesn't," he insisted, as he stared at the glaring, quarter-sized blotch.

It would be pointless for Ruchama to keep insisting that his tie is dirty if Zelig is determined to deny it. If she wants him to change ties, she should just tell him that she would prefer him to wear a different one and ask if he would change for her.

Zelig was extreme in his denial, but most of us feel defensive when someone tries to prove us wrong. Rather than acknowledge a criticizer's point of view, we usually feel more determined to stand our ground.

When we try to prove that we are right and our spouse is wrong, we may win a few battles, but we will lose the relationship war. Being "right" and lonely is not much of a victory.

This is why being right is not that important in marriage. We often have to choose between two conflicting goals: speaking the "truth" or getting our spouse to see the "truth," and resolving the problem. Ironically, doing the former often precludes doing the latter.

Harry worked diligently for two years in Eddie's store. Eddie rewarded him by making him a limited partner. A year later, Harry decided that he should run the business. Eddie refused to consider this but did give Harry a modest bonus.

Harry was very angry that Eddie did not treat him the way he wanted and complained bitterly to Marie about it every night. She loved him but thought that he was totally unrealistic. When she tried to tell Harry why his perspective wasn't justified, Harry felt even more humiliated and he resented her siding with Eddie.

Objectively, Harry's view of himself was grandiose but, emotionally, he wanted Marie to acknowledge his hurt feelings and lack of recognition. As long as Marie tried to get him to see her "truth," without giving him the support that he wanted, he became even more wedded to his position. Her response was truthful but useless.

People who are upset can only hear another point of view and resolve their problems if we first empathize with them. Pointing out how wrong they are only convinces them that we don't understand them. We have to take away their pain before they'll listen to reason or advice.

Marie should have empathized with Harry's upset feelings about Eddie's lack of appreciation. After bandaging his ego's wounds, she could add, "He's lucky to have you as a partner, and you're lucky that he let you join him." At some future point she could add, "I understand what you want from Eddie, and it must be so painful to you that he doesn't seem willing to give it. Do you think that it makes sense to drop the issue for now, and broach it with him again next year? Then you'll feel confident enough to open your own business if Eddie won't give you what you want. You'll have leverage then that you don't have now."

Marie shouldn't tell Harry that his perspective is "wrong" because he won't hear it. Taking an opposing point of view when a spouse wants empathy makes him or her feel that we are an enemy. They only feel that we are on their side if we validate their feeling now and gently suggest a different approach later.

Two husbands who have been happily married for over fifty years told the author the secret of their success: Each feels secure enough not to argue with his wife about trivial matters. One said, "If my wife says that it's cold outside and I'm sweltering, what difference does it make? If she says it's late, and it's only nine o'clock, I just say, 'Yes, dear.' Why should I waste time arguing with her about issues that aren't really important? Life is too short for that."

Most issues that get played out on marital battlegrounds are not very important in the long-run. They become important because they symbolize emotional issues like being understood, respected, and controlled, and having power. It's not worth creating distance with a spouse for an entire day over the socks on the floor, forgetting to buy milk, or who said what in the last argument. It's best to put the matter into perspective and move on.

Aaron and Harriet went for a walk around the neighborhood. As they came home, she asked, "How far do you think we just walked?"

Aaron was an accountant, and precisely answered, "About nine-tenths of a mile."

"No," Harriet replied, "that's not possible. It couldn't have been more than seven-tenths of a mile. I know how long it takes me to walk on the treadmill, and we just walked about the same distance that I go in fifteen minutes."

Aaron got annoyed. "Look, our *shul* is exactly one mile from the house, and it takes me twenty minutes to walk there on *Shabbat*. This just took us eighteen minutes, so it had to be nine-tenths of a mile."

This exchange continued for forty-five minutes and left them both feeling tense for the rest of the day. It would have been wiser to agree to disagree.

ANGER

Secular psychologists and self-help books urge us to get in touch with our anger and "share" it with the person who "made" us angry. Anything seems to be a valid reason to get angry today: your mother criticized you thirty years ago; you can't afford what your neighbors have; you had to stand in line for twenty minutes; your spouse didn't do what you wanted . . .

It is not really other people who make us angry. It is our reactions to them. What we tell ourselves about how awful others are fans the flames of our anger. In other words, we usually feel angry when life doesn't go as we expect it should. Instead of assuming that people and life should always live up to our expectations, we can grow by having more realistic expectations and changing our reactions when things don't go our way.

One mother constantly got angry at her four-year-old son. He was never ready for school on time, and it took at least half an hour every night to get him into bed. Instead of changing her expectations and accommodating him, she kept getting angry that her son acted like a normal four-year-old.

Many people have the same reaction to a spouse. They get themselves angry thinking, "If only my partner would change, everything would be fine." And if we had wheels instead of legs, we wouldn't have to ride the bus! We can start becoming less angry by seeing what we do to perpetuate our spouse's behavior and by having more realistic expectations of him or her.

Some people think that only their way of seeing the world and acting is "right." They believe that a spouse who does differently must be wrong and should do what's "right"—in other words, what they want. When the spouse continues in his or her ways, the other one may assume that their partner is deliberately ignoring their wishes or is irreparably "messed up." They react to this with anger or hopelessness.

Barraging a spouse with anger may feel good at the moment, but it destroys marriages. Before responding with our feelings, we should first analyze why we are angry. Do we have unrealistic expectations of our spouse, given who she or he is? Do we feel hurt, unloved, controlled, or disrespected? Could we have misinterpreted our spouse's words or actions? Should we hear his or her side of the story? Is what happened really so bad, or are we reacting to an accumulation of hurts and disappointments, some that have built up since childhood?

Asking these questions helps us put matters into perspective and gives us a better idea about how to deal constructively with the situation.

Since how we feel depends upon how we interpret events, and what we tell ourselves about them, people have very different reactions to the same circumstances. For example, depressed people don't have objectively worse lives than those who aren't depressed. They just view their problems as more distressing.

Many people get annoyed or angry having to stand in line for an hour to buy something they need, while others don't mind. They listen to a Walkman, write letters, chat with a friend, relax, or work out a problem in their head while waiting.

Some husbands get upset with wives who start cleaning the house for Passover a month ahead, while others get upset with wives who don't. Some husbands feel comfortable living in a pigsty, while others get angry if one toy is on the living room floor. Some women get angry if their husbands don't help them in the kitchen, while others get angry if their husbands invade their territory.

People who are often upset may not be able to change their life circumstances, but they can change their reactions, attitudes, and expectations in order to be happier.

NEGATIVE THINKING

Healthy people can feel conflicting emotions such as anger and love at the same time. Emotionally-limited people can't. When they feel angry with someone, they cannot feel love at the same time. As soon as they feel angry at a spouse who disappoints or hurts them, they lose sight of the spouse's positive qualities. The more they harp on the spouse's shortcomings, the more they fuel their anger and hatred.

Stuart and Lucy went out with friends. When Lucy made an insensitive comment about Stuart, he quickly fueled his pyre of hatred through the following cycle of negative thinking:

"I can't believe that Lucy attacked me again. She does this every time we're with other people. She just doesn't care about my feelings. I can't trust her and never should have married her. I don't love her anyway. How could I? She's so stupid, and she embarrasses me when I'm with my friends. Maybe I should just leave her. We're just incompatible."

By overgeneralizing ("she does this *every* time we go out), globally trashing her ("she's stupid"), mind-reading ("She doesn't care about my feelings"), and making statements of hopelessness ("we're incompatible"), Stuart completely negates the positive aspects of their relationship and quickly convinces himself that she is his enemy.

A better way to react in these situations is to think constructively about them, in a way that can lead to a positive outcome. For example, Stuart could think:

"Lucy really hurt my feelings just now. I wonder if she realizes that. When I've told her in the past that I'm hurting, she tends to react with compassion. I guess I should ask her later what she meant by her comment. If I understood it the way she meant it, I'll let her know that it embarrassed me and ask her not to do it again. She may not realize that she was insensitive."

People who generate a lot of negative thoughts about their marriage, or their partner, need to practice generating positive thoughts about incidents that otherwise lead to hostility. If they do this when the incident is not overwhelming, they will learn how to think constructively in situations before they get overly upset.

By the time people get emotionally flooded, it is very hard to change how they feel. "Flooded" people need to tell a spouse, "I am so upset right now that it won't be productive to talk to me. Let me calm down for an hour and I will set a time with you tonight or tomorrow to discuss the matter further."

When we notice that a spouse is emotionally flooded, or verging on rage, we should call a time-out. That is not the time to pursue an uncommunicative spouse and encourage them to open up! Talking about an explosive topic to someone who is already emotionally flooded is counterproductive. If they already perceive you as an enemy, your very presence will keep them upset. If they want to withdraw or leave in order to cool their heels, give them the space to do it.

Much of the emotional upset that couples experience is due to their interpretation of what happened with a spouse and to their continuing thoughts that reinforce the injury. If they conclude that a spouse deliberately hurt them, they react by feeling angry and upset. Yet many of these negative feelings come from mind-reading or from judging a spouse's behavior and intentions without hearing their side of the story. We can avoid a lot of anger and upset by checking things out with a spouse before concluding that they were deliberately insensitive or hurtful. Otherwise, we will misinterpret their words and actions by distorting them through our emotional filters. This will only add fuel to our emotional fire.

Jeannette and Rudy agreed to go to a museum at 10:00 A.M. He drove off at 9:30, and was still gone half an hour later. She was furious, and began fuming about his inconsideration. She fueled her anger until she was a cauldron of rage, by remembering a dozen incidents in which he had wronged her during their four years of marriage.

At 10:30, Rudy walked in the door. Jeannette started assaulting him verbally: "Why are you so inconsiderate? Why can't you ever be here on time for something that's important to me?"

When she walked into the hallway to confront him, he silently gave her a bouquet of flowers. "I'm sorry I'm late. I drove all over town trying to find a florist that was open on Sunday. I wanted to call you when I saw that I would be late, but there were no telephones anywhere. I finally got these flowers at the supermarket a mile away and figured it didn't pay to call you from there to tell you I'd be home in five minutes."

Jeannette had the humility to apologize and thank him for his thoughtfulness. The next time he did something that made her angry, she reserved judgment until she had a chance to discuss it with him.

Many marital fights are rooted in misinterpretations. If couples would only take the time to clarify what happened, they could avoid many arguments and bad feelings.

Shari was chatting with her best friend on the telephone. Barnett overheard her say, "He makes me so upset . . . I don't expect much from him any more . . . He has no manners, smells bad, and desperately needs a bath. Days like today he makes me so sick I want to throw him out of the house."

Barnett felt devastated, then angry. How could she talk like that about him? What had he done to make her so angry? His usual response when he got angry at her was to give her a cold shoulder and withdraw into his den.

When they ate dinner, she acted as if nothing was wrong. For a change, Barnett decided not to withdraw and asked, "Shari, are you angry with me?"

"No," she said, looking surprised. "Why do you ask?"

"Well, I couldn't help but overhear your conversation a little while ago. I heard you say some pretty nasty things about me, like you want to throw me out of the house."

Shari burst out laughing. "You thought that I was talking about you? Jeri and I were talking about our dogs! Hers just threw up all over her new carpet, and ours chewed up my favorite nightgown this morning."

Barnett felt sheepish, seeing how badly he had misjudged his wife. It taught him to reserve judgment about her in the future.

Jews are required to judge each other favorably.[10] We are not allowed to assume the worst about a spouse when it is possible to give him or her the benefit of the doubt. The best way to dispel doubts is to discuss incidents and hear our partner's side of the story.

As Nita and Andrei strolled down the street, they ran into some of her friends. She introduced her new husband and they all chatted pleasantly. Before parting, Andrei told a story with some off-color words that embarrassed Nita. Later, Nita asked why he was so inappropriate.

"What are you talking about?" Andrei asked innocently.

Instead of assuming that he deliberately embarrassed her, she retreated and asked, "Do you know what ----- means?"

"Sure," he replied, and proceeded to incorrectly define the off-color words. Poor Andrei! He had tried so hard to master English, but sometimes he said disastrous things in an attempt to be sophisticated. After Nita explained that he had confused two words, he never made that mistake again!

BEING UNDERSTOOD VERSUS TAKING REVENGE

When someone hurts us, we often feel torn between two desires: we want the other person to understand us, but if he or she doesn't, we want to get even. Apart from the fact that Judaism prohibits us from taking revenge against other Jews,[11] getting even hurts our character and damages our marriages. It also ensures that we won't get the understanding that we wanted in the first place. No one feels bad for someone who tears them apart and hurts them.

Burt often worked until 9 P.M. When Hanna asked him to come home earlier, he didn't. She tried getting back at him by ignoring him when he came home, so he came home even later. Finally, she started taking exercise classes, lost ten pounds, and tried greeting him in a sexy outfit. She stopped complaining about problems as soon as he came in the door and didn't nag him. As she became more pleasant, interesting, and happier, Burt preferred coming home to staying late at the office.

There are many ways to get what we want, but we usually get more with honey than with vinegar.

Dealing with disappointments and upsets in a way that fosters closeness is one of the greatest challenges of marriage. Taking revenge, proving how wrong a partner is, trying to hurt a spouse as much as we have been hurt, and bearing grudges may feel good in the short run but always hurts us in the long run.

Adelle spent a lot of time cooking for Noah. He ate whatever she made, but never thanked her. Not surprisingly, she felt taken for granted. She stopped cooking and cleaning the house, starting the day that Noah's parents were supposed to come for dinner.

Noah's lack of appreciation was inexcusable, although perhaps remediable. What Adelle did was self-defeating and violated the biblical prohibition against taking revenge. Had she discussed her feelings with Noah and extended herself a little longer, he might have showed more appreciation. He didn't realize that she had felt taken for granted, and he felt bad that he hadn't communicated how grateful he truly felt.

If a discussion, and a few reminders, still didn't help, Adelle could stop extending herself then. Her vengeful actions did not get her more appreciation in the long-run.

EXPRESSING HURTS

When a spouse apologizes after we say we were hurt, we lose our desire for revenge and feel understood. On the other hand, if he or she keeps defending his or her position instead of validating our feelings, we may get angrier. Such interactions usually escalate to a point where one or both spouses withdraw, keep battling, or explode. As long as this happens, neither person gets the love and understanding he or she wanted all along.

When a spouse upsets us, we should train ourselves to put our anger aside and calmly explain that we feel hurt. Saying that we are hurt is likely to get us more sympathy than saying that we are angry. Focusing on our anger usually makes a partner defensive and less likely to acknowledge our feelings.

People also tend to be more sympathetic when they feel guilty rather than attacked. When we tell a receptive spouse that we feel hurt, he or she is likely to feel guilty or sorry and try to make us feel better. Telling a spouse how angry we are is likely to make them feel attacked. Then, they are less likely to value our feelings and may tune us out.

By thinking before we speak and tuning in to a spouse's feelings, we can communicate hurt in a way that is most likely to get us validation.

Esti was very disappointed that Howie forgot her birthday. She fueled her anger by reliving her outrage until she exploded: "After everything I do for you, I expected you at least to remember my birthday. Don't you care about anyone besides yourself?"

Her attack resulted in Howie defending himself instead of soothing her feelings. "I was so busy at work, I didn't have a chance to buy you a card or a gift. Besides, I do lots of things for you. I don't see why you have to get so bent out of shape about this."

"You'll never understand anything, you're just a rotten husband," Esti screamed, as she ran up the stairs into the bedroom and slammed the door.

Howie's defensiveness instead of empathy added to Esti's anger and hurt. She felt invalidated and dismissed.

Despite her outburst, Esti was torn between two feelings. She wanted her husband to make her feel loved but also wanted to hurt him so that he would know how she felt. Her reaction succeeded in hurting him, but she never got the satisfaction of feeling understood and loved.

It would have been much better had she said, "It hurt me terribly that you forgot my birthday today."

If Howie is a caring but forgetful husband, he will probably respond, "I'm so sorry. I guess I got so caught up in work that I forgot to look at the calendar this week. I feel terrible. What can I do to make it up to you?"

By emphasizing her hurt instead of her anger, Esti won't get even, but she is likely to feel understood and get the nurturing that she really wanted.

Linda felt frustrated and neglected when Emil watched hours of football on television. She wanted him to spend that time with her. One Saturday night, he took her to a show and dinner at a nice restaurant. She thought that he enjoyed their closeness so much that they would spend the next day together. But, as usual, on Sunday afternoon, Emil spent three hours parked in front of the TV watching a Redskins game. When it was over, he asked, "What's for dinner, honey?"

While he was relaxing in front of the television, she was busy fueling her anger. What kind of a husband would rather spend time watching a bunch of men smashing into each other than spend romantic time with a wife? He was just like his father, who also neglected his wife. Even if he didn't feel like being romantic, at least Emil could have helped her with chores so that she had less work to do. Instead, he ignored her until he wanted something from her! Let him take care of himself. After all, he didn't mind her taking care of herself. . . .

Without an awareness of the inner monologue that Linda had been having for the last three hours, Emil was completely baffled by her explosion when he asked about dinner.

"That's up to you. I'm not cooking," she declared. She plopped herself down on the sofa and read a magazine. Emil responded by shutting down emotionally and watching another sports program. He chalked up her response to PMS.

Linda had enjoyed their night out but was hurt that Emil gave football more attention than her the next day. It would have been better to tell him how much she enjoyed their evening together and how difficult it was to lose that closeness the next day. She could have suggested that he tape some, or all, of the game on the VCR so that they could spend Sunday afternoon together. He could then watch it at night.

Alternatively, she could tell him that she wanted them to spend more time together and he could respond, "I enjoy being close to you, too, but I also want some time to be by myself. I love you, and I want to have a nice dinner with you tonight. How about if I spend the next three hours alone, and then we'll have a romantic evening together?"

Linda's inner monologue destroyed the closeness they had enjoyed and distanced them from each other for the rest of the week. She should have spent her time and energy generating positive and constructive statements about their relationship and thinking about how to approach him productively. For example, she could tell herself, "Men have such different needs than women. I guess Emil gets satisfaction from football the way I get satisfaction from watching a ballet or having a great conversation with my friends. If Emil doesn't want to spend the whole day with me, I'll call one of my girlfriends and we'll see that new romantic comedy. When Emil and I see each other tonight, we'll both be happy about how we spent our day."

Instead of yelling at a spouse or throwing tantrums, we are most likely to get comfort and sympathy by emphasizing our disappointment, hurt, and yearning for closeness. If we can't get everything we want from our spouse, we should think about how we can get it with others, or by ourselves.

THE A,B,C'S OF COMMUNICATION

Effective communication requires one spouse to send a clear message which a second spouse correctly receives and understands. A telephone with two speakers and no receivers gives no communication. Neither do conversations with two spouses trying to be heard at the same time while neither is listening. When two people both expect the other to hear them, they are having mutual monologues, not *co*mmunication. Real communication takes place only when someone is listening with the goal of understanding the partner, not thinking about how to refute their position, solve a problem, defend oneself, or gain understanding at the same time.

Unfortunately, most people like to talk more than listen. We focus on what we want to say rather than on what our partner is saying, and we don't make them feel understood.

This is why the first step toward good communication is being a good listener. Our bodies were designed to teach us this. We have two ears and only one mouth so that we'll listen more than we speak.

When we listen to a spouse, we need to hear what our partner is really saying. We should not read their minds nor interpret their words according to what we want them to mean.

Noreen told Daryl that she was unhappy. As many men do when a wife complains, he thought that she was blaming him for her unhappiness. This made him feel threatened. Instead of empathizing with her, he gave her advice about how to make herself happier. She was hurt by his lack of support and felt brushed off.

Listeners often have to choose between making a speaker feel understood or offering advice and solutions to a problem. Unless a spouse says that he or she wants advice, we should assume that he or she wants first to feel understood.

If we are not sure why a spouse is talking to us, we should ask. For example, we can say to a spouse, "I'm not sure why you're telling me this. How would you like me to appreciate or respond to what you just told me?"

If your spouse looks perplexed, you can clarify, "I'm not sure if you want me to understand how you feel, suggest ways to change the situation, or if you just wanted to share this information with me."

Since Daryl didn't ask Noreen to clarify why she was unhappy, he incorrectly assumed that she was blaming him. Had he first asked her what she meant, he would have discovered that she was feeling blue because she didn't feel challenged at work, and she felt better when she shared her feelings with Daryl. She didn't expect him to do anything about it, she just wanted him to listen compassionately and show that he understood.

Daryl could say, "It must be so frustrating for you to feel that you have so much to offer at work, but not to have an opportunity to show it."

Poor responses would be:

1. "I guess it's time for you to find another job. Why don't you check the 'Help Wanted' section of today's paper?"

This is not helpful because it offers advice before Noreen feels understood. This will make her feel that Daryl doesn't care about her and is dismissing the seriousness of her problem.

2. "Whenever you get blue, it doesn't last too long. I'm sure you'll feel better soon."

This is counterproductive because it makes Noreen feel brushed off. If Daryl really took her feelings seriously, he would not try to "fix" her problem so dispassionately.

3. "Yeah, I know what it's like to be unhappy at work. I've been feeling that way for the last fifteen years. Let me tell you about the latest fiasco that happened to me . . ."

This is not helpful because it focuses attention on Daryl instead of supporting Noreen while she feels upset.

4. "It's not good to dwell on these things. By the way, did we get any interesting mail today?"

This makes Noreen feel that Daryl isn't interested in her feelings. He tries to distract her instead of facing her discomfort.

5. "Unh-huh . . . (while reading the newspaper)"

This shows that he simply isn't interested in her feelings.

6. "Can't you see that I've had a bad day, too? Why do you have to tell me about your problems when I come in the door?"

This response will make a wife feel discounted and unimportant. He can communicate nicely by saying, "I care about your feelings, sweetheart, but my head is still buzzing from work right now. Would you please tell me more in half an hour, when I'll be able to give you the full attention that you deserve?"

Daily stresses and distractions make good communication difficult. We tune people out when we're overloaded, preoccupied with other matters, or trying to be understood ourselves.

Steven settled down in the den after a tiring day. Meanwhile, Elena made dinner. He perfunctorily asked her how her day was as he read the newspaper. She didn't think he was listening, so she responded, "The neighbor's house burned down, the dog died, there was an armed robbery at the butcher's this afternoon, and I'm grilling cockroaches for dinner."

"That's nice," he said as he turned the page, looking for the continuation of the article. "When are we eating?"

There is no point telling a spouse anything when he or she isn't paying attention. The best you can do is to plan a time to have a real conversation.

A man owned a donkey who knew how to do arithmetic. A skeptic asked the donkey how much two plus two was, but the animal didn't respond. The owner told the man to bring him a two-by-four, and the puzzled man complied. The owner promptly swatted the animal on the rump with the board, then told the man to repeat his question. As soon as he did, the donkey pawed the ground four times.

"How come your donkey can add now?" the puzzled man asked.

The owner explained, "The animal knows how to add, but first you have to get its attention!"

Most of us have the potential to be good listeners, but we have to pay attention. It is pointless to discuss important matters with a spouse who is preoccupied, self-absorbed, or half-asleep. When you want to have a meaningful conversation, you may need to ask a partner to set a time in the next day or two when he or she will be receptive instead of assuming that he or she will listen when you are ready to talk.

Good times to avoid talking about important topics are when someone walks in the door from work, when he or she is hungry, angry, or exhausted, or is totally preoccupied with other matters.

PERSONAL DICTIONARIES

People use the same words to mean very different things. Each of us has a personal dictionary that results from our culture, our upbringing, our experiences, and our personality. We should never assume that a spouse understands general terms in precisely the same way that we do.

Corey was working on lesson plans one Sunday morning and asked Sid not to bother her. He left wordlessly to play racquetball. When he returned, he took a shower, used his electric shaver, went into the kitchen, and made a milkshake. He smashed the ice tray on the counter and poured a handful of cubes into the blender, then whirred it for a few minutes.

Corey appeared and said, "You have been making so much noise that you could wake the dead! I asked you not to bother me. Why are you doing this?"

Sid responded, "Why are you upset? I didn't bother you. I didn't talk to you, and I stayed away from the bedroom while you were there."

To Corey, "Don't bother me" meant "Don't make any noise," while to Sid it meant, "Don't talk to Corey." When he disturbed her, she should have clarified what she wanted before getting angry.

At the end of their Judaism class, Rami introduced his wife Muriel to Arlene, a fellow student. He thought that Arlene and Muriel would enjoy meeting each other, and the women exchanged phone numbers.

On their way home, Muriel chatted, "Arlene seems so lovely. By the way, is she religious?"

"Yes," Rami replied.

When Muriel called, Arlene invited her to lunch at a nonkosher restaurant. This surprised Muriel, and she invited Arlene to her home for *Shabbat* dinner instead.

That night, she asked Rami why he had said that Arlene was religious.

"But she is religious," Rami protested. "She's just not observant."

To Rami, a "religious" person was someone who felt close to God. To Muriel, it meant being Sabbath-observant.

Ralph was mild-mannered and conservative everywhere except in his car, when he drove like a Grand Prix contestant. Lena asked him to drive more carefully, and he agreed. The next time they went for a drive, he sped along at seventy-five miles an hour.

"I thought that you were going to drive more carefully," she commented.

"I am," Ralph said defensively. "I usually go eighty-five here. I slowed down for you."

"Driving carefully" obviously meant very different things to each of them. Ralph could only know what Lena wanted if she translated it into behavioral terms. She needed to say, "Ralph, please don't drive faster than the posted speed limit when I am in the car with you."

Lois asked Buddy to be more sensitive to her feelings. He assumed that she wanted him not to criticize her, but that's not what she meant. She wanted them to do more activities together that she enjoyed and him to consult her before he made plans. She should have specified that, instead of using a vague term like "being sensitive" to describe what she wanted.

Sometimes we say things that are so ambiguous they lend themselves to many possible interpretations.

Norbert asked Estelle if she wanted to go out Saturday night. She replied, "Last time we went out to a Chinese restaurant I got food poisoning."

This could have many possible interpretations. To name a few:

1. He could think that she was accusing him of choosing restaurants poorly, since he had suggested the Chinese place.

2. He could think that she was angry at him for taking her to a restaurant where she got sick.

3. He could think that she wanted to go out but not to a restaurant.

4. He could conclude that she was willing to go out to eat but didn't want Chinese food.

Without checking it out with Estelle, he couldn't know what she meant.

He wisely asked, "I'm not sure how to understand your comment. Are you saying that you don't want to go out with me, that you don't want Chinese food, that you're mad at me for what happened last time, or what?"

She responded, "I'm not angry at you. My getting sick wasn't your fault. I would like to stay away from restaurants for awhile, though. How about going to some place where we don't have to eat?"

IMPROVING LISTENING

Couples can improve their listening abilities by practicing the following exercise. The more they practice it, the less awkward and artificial it feels and the better their communication will be.

Set aside five to fifteen minutes to talk when you won't be interrupted by visitors, children, or phone calls. Have one index card that says "speaker" on it, and a second card that says "listener" on it. Decide who will speak first. (If you can't agree, flip a coin. Heads gets the "speaker" card, while tails gets the "listener" card.) The speaker discusses a topic of his or her choice for two or three minutes. It can be about the day's events, a problem, a memory, feelings, and so on. It can be happy, neutral, sad, upsetting, or enjoyable.

The "listener" should listen attentively without interrupting. When the speaker finishes, the listener summarizes what was said without interpreting, elaborating, becoming defensive, or criticizing.

The speaker then says that he or she feels understood, and compliments the listener. They then switch cards and roles.

If the speaker does not feel understood, he or she reiterates what he or she would like the listener to understand, as many times as are necessary for the listener to paraphrase it to the speaker's satisfaction.

Susan told Joe about her day. She was upset that her boss gave her more work than she could possibly finish before a deadline. That stressed her, then she came home and found that the children had decorated her bedroom walls and curtains with chocolate pudding. To make matters worse, the kids also took huge chunks out of the chocolate cake that she had made for the sisterhood meeting that night.

When she finished, Joe recapped, "You feel stressed by your overwhelming day. Your boss expected too much from you, and the kids destroyed the house and the cake that you worked so hard to make."

Susan responded, "That's very good. That's exactly what I meant."

Alternatively, Joe could have distorted what she said and replied, "You're explaining why you're in a bad mood tonight, and warning me that we'll need to find a new babysitter who is more conscientious than the one we have now."

Susan would then reply, "No, that's not what I said. Let me tell you again." She then reiterates her story as many times as necessary for Joe to summarize it to her satisfaction.

Let's say that Joe was supposed to have taken care of the kids when they destroyed the house and the cake. He might respond defensively, "It wasn't my fault that the kids messed things up. You should keep sweets on the top shelf of the refrigerator where they can't reach them. I can't keep my eyes on them every second."

Susan would then say, "I'm not accusing you. I'm telling you how I feel. You are supposed to summarize my feelings, not defend yourself. Can we try this again?"

Susan would then repeat herself, and Joe would respond, "You had a pretty terrible day. Your boss made impossible demands, and the house was a shambles when you came home."

Susan would then acknowledge Joe's good summary.

They then repeat the exercise with Joe telling Susan what's on his mind and Susan summarizing it to his satisfaction.

Properly summarizing what each person says sensitizes a couple to listen carefully. It also trains them to clarify what a spouse really meant instead of jumping to conclusions about it.

In this exercise, couples must not respond to the implications of the speaker's message, defend themselves, nor try to solve problems. The goal is to listen to each other and not get derailed by personal interpretations or agendas. Until a couple can listen well, they won't communicate or solve problems. Careful listening with the goal of simply trying to understand each other makes two people feel like allies. That is a prerequisite for productively solving problems together.

SENDING MESSAGES

Besides listening well, we must also send messages effectively. We do this by thinking about who is listening and how we need to say something for them to hear it properly. By first considering what our goal is in communicating, we can plan what to say and how to say it.

Our Sages often did this. One striking example occurred when King Ptolemy wanted a personal library containing a Greek translation of every book that existed. Until then, the Jewish Scriptures had never been translated from the original Hebrew. But Ptolemy was so intent on reading the Bible that he imprisoned seventy Jewish Sages in seventy separate rooms and ordered them to translate the Torah into Greek, on pain of death.

The Sages reluctantly did as they were told, but didn't translate the Torah literally. They were afraid that the Greeks would misinterpret the Torah's true meaning in line with their idolatrous beliefs. So each Sage deliberately mistranslated certain passages in such a way that the Greeks would understand the Torah's intent, not its literal meaning. (Miraculously, when each Sage finished, each translation was identical, including the mistakes.) This is how the Septuagint came into being.

Communicating with a spouse in a way that leads to peace is so important that God even distorted the truth to preserve a couple's domestic harmony.[12] This happened when a divine messenger told the patriarch Abraham that he and his wife Sarah would have a child together at the respective ages of one hundred and ninety.[13] When Sarah heard this, she exclaimed, "After I have become old, shall I have [the] pleasure [of children], [considering] how old my husband is?"[14]

God later asked Abraham, "Why did Sarah laugh, saying, 'Will I really give birth, [given] that I am old?' "[15] The Lord deliberately omitted telling Abraham that his wife had said that he was old so that He wouldn't disturb their peaceful relationship.[16]

These illustrations remind us how important it is to keep in mind how a listener will hear us.

Jonathan's wife thought that her hips were too big. She had tried many diets and exercises, all to no avail. In an effort to make her feel better, he put his arms around her and said, "I'm so happy I married you. You're beautiful, sexy, and smart." Not surprisingly, she was very pleased. Had he said, "It's okay that your hips are too big. I love you, anyway," she wouldn't have been very happy.

Elisha knew that Lorraine had poor self-esteem. She was a good wife but, unfortunately, was a terrible cook. She made flavorless food night after night, but he complimented her anyway because he knew how hard she tried to please him.

Finally, instead of asking her to take cooking lessons, which would have hurt her feelings, he told her that he wanted to try a special diet to give him more energy. He invited her to learn how to make "unusual" foods with him. By cooking together, she learned how to make delicious food without feeling put down or criticized.

Most of Donna's friends were going to resorts for Passover. Brian felt very bad that he didn't make enough money to even hire help, let alone go anywhere for the holiday. Donna was about to tell him where everyone else was going when she realized that it would only make him feel bad. She told him, "You know what, Brian? It's a lot of work preparing for Passover, but I'm glad that we're going to be in our own place for the holiday. It's so much more special that way, and we can do things just the way we want at the *seders*."

When one spouse wants to communicate about a problem with the other, the speaker should first decide on a goal. For example, Clara wants Carl to talk to his mother less frequently. She brainstorms some possible ways to do this:

1. She could ask him to talk less to his mother.

Since Carl loves his mother, this is likely to hurt his feelings, and make him feel threatened. He will not like feeling that he has to choose between his mother and his wife, so this is not a good option.

2. She could criticize him for the many hours that he spends talking to his mother.

He will feel attacked and not be receptive.

3. She can tell him that she admires him for being such a devoted son, then express concern that his mother often criticizes Clara to him, leading to his being

upset with Clara. Clara would appreciate it if he would refuse to continue conversations when his mother criticizes her, or tell his mother to work out her upsets directly with Clara and not use Carl as a middleman.

This is a good option. It compliments Carl, doesn't ask him to sever a relationship with his mother, and also conveys Clara's concerns about the way the mother drives a wedge between Clara and Carl.

4. If number 3 doesn't work, Clara can tell Carl that she is concerned because he gets upset with her after he talks to his mother. Can they resolve the problem together?

MIND READING

Some people erroneously assume that a caring spouse should magically know what they think, feel, want, and need. When a partner doesn't mind-read, they misinterpret it to mean that she or he isn't understanding or loving. But unless people are psychics or have crystal balls, no one can read minds. We should be mature enough to tell a spouse what we need and feel.

Mimi is a very moody woman, and Lloyd long ago gave up trying to anticipate her moods and reactions. She could be loving and compassionate one moment, enraged and hypersensitive the next. She would expect Lloyd to intuit her feelings and respond exactly as she wanted, but when he'd ask how she was, he never knew if she would appreciate his concern, be unpredictably angry at him, or be depressed. She even expected him to know from day to day what he did that provoked her wrath or disappointment.

Instead of being so childish, she should take responsibility for her mood swings and outbursts, tell him how he can make her happy, and be appreciative when he tries.

Jenny loved flowers and chocolate and assumed that Herb knew that. After all, he gave them to her before they got married. She wished that he would still buy them for her, and felt hurt that he didn't. He gave her little gifts every few months, but Jenny preferred flowers and chocolate. Unless she tells him, he won't know they mean so much to her, and he won't have the pleasure of making her ecstatic.

Peter believes that a loving wife will clean the house, get the kids ready for bed, and have dinner ready before he comes home. It upsets him terribly that Shoshana rarely does this. When he walks in, she is usually chatting on the telephone, the kids are running around, and dinner is still an idea.

Instead of discussing this, he assumes that Shoshana knows that every man wants what he does, and that she can't be bothered to make him happy. He decides that he won't make her happy if she won't make him happy! He responds by being cold and aloof, which only reinforces their distance. She has no idea why Peter acts this way but assumes that he is reacting to stress at work.

Peter's mother was a full-time housewife who lived for her husband and children. He assumed that all loving women were like that. It never occurred to him that most families, including Shoshana's, weren't like his. She grew up in a home with two working parents and seven children. Their house was never orderly for long, schedules were not a priority, and weeknight dinners were catch-as-catch-can. Shoshana has no clue that Peter expects their home to be other than as it is.

We should ask a spouse to clarify their expectations and wishes, and we should clarify ours, rather than making assumptions and misinterpretations. Since this seems so obvious, why don't spouses tell each other how they feel and what they want?

First, many people expect a spouse to know what they want and need, just as their parents knew what they needed when they were infants. Some adults expect a spouse to mind-read this way.

Second, some people think that their needs are obvious, or that everyone feels the way they do. People who do that feel deliberately ignored and hurt if a spouse violates their expectations. We rarely look for other explanations if we think that something is self-evident.

Third, saying what we want makes us vulnerable. It hurts more to be deliberately ignored or rejected than to secretly yearn for something and never get it. Some people are so afraid of rejection that they live with disappointment rather than ask for what they want. They create a self-fulfilling prophecy.

Fourth, some people think it is less meaningful if a spouse does what we want after we've asked for it. To the contrary, a partner who is willing to do what they would not otherwise do for us is making a strong statement of caring.

COMMUNICATING FEELINGS, WANTS, AND NEEDS

One way of telling a spouse what you want or feel is by using "I feel . . . ," "I want . . . ," "I need . . ." statements.

Raizy wanted Ephraim to spend at least an hour of uninterrupted time with her every night, but never told him this. He usually busied himself with his computer instead of talking to her, and she felt short-changed.

She needed to set an appropriate time to tell him, "I enjoy your company so much that I want to spend more relaxing and loving time together. Could we work on that?"

Instead of assuming that he knew that she was miserable but didn't care enough to make her happy, she gave him the benefit of the doubt and told him what she needed.

Gila has little need to go out at night or on weekends, but Alan does. He says, "I really enjoy being home with you, but I also need to go out sometimes. How about our going out to eat on Sunday nights and getting away for a weekend sometime during the next month?"

Notice that these expressions are very specific and detailed. It is not useful to make vague requests like, "I want you to be more attentive and loving," or "I'd like to go out more." The more we specify what we want from a partner, the more likely we are to get our needs met (providing that the requests are reasonable and doable).

Examples of "I feel, I need, I want" statements are:

- "I need to feel that you respect me. I feel that way when you do _____ or say _____ to me."
- "I need to feel more secure about your love for me. When you criticize me in front of others or yell at me, I don't feel loved. I need you to stop doing that."
- "I need you to appreciate what I do. I would like you to tell me at least once a week that I did something to make you happy. I would also like you to thank me when I cook for you."
- "I need your help in the house doing chores and taking care of the children. I feel overwhelmed doing so much myself. Would you do the laundry every week and help me get the kids ready for bed every night?"
- "I feel unloved when you don't buy me flowers at least once a month."
- "I want you to acknowledge how hard I work to make a living. I'm exhausted working ten hours every day at my job. I need you to thank me when I give you my paycheck and ask me once a week how my day was."
- "I want to feel that my home is a haven where I am protected from the abuses of the world. I want you not to barrage me with problems or criticize me as soon as I walk in the door. If you need to discuss problems with me, please wait at least forty-five minutes after I've come home and have had a chance to eat dinner."
- "I want you to respect my need to be alone at times. I'm not rejecting you, but I feel stifled when I have almost no time for myself. I'm with people all day long, and I need a half-hour to breathe when I come home."

Sharing our wants and needs with a spouse helps us get more of what we want, although we won't always get exactly what we requested.

CRITICISM

When we are upset, we tend to think more about how we feel than about how our spouse feels. But this is when we need to be especially careful not to tear a partner down and to measure our words carefully. Following a few rules can keep criticism constructive:

1. *Don't criticize when very angry.*
Angry people often make the "medium the message." That is, they attack or explode in such a way that the spouse only hears the anger, not the words.

Attacking people erodes their self-esteem and makes you their enemy. They will respond by retaliating, defending themselves, tuning you out, or walking away. The angrier you seem, the worse others will react.

Judith asked Armand to get some medication for her while she took their son to a play-date. When she came home, Armand was still in the living room. She exploded, "You never do anything around here! You're so lazy!" Venting her anger in such a global, destructive way won't get him to be more helpful.

We get sympathy by showing our hurt and vulnerability, not by sending missiles of anger. A reasonable spouse will feel bad and want to help if we say that we are hurting and need them, but will get defensive if we stress our anger.

Judith could have said, "You work so hard all week and I know that you like to relax on Sundays. But I have a terrible toothache, and the pain is unbearable. Please help me by getting my medication now so I can take it when I come back."

Had Armand realized how urgent the situation was, he would have readily helped out.

2. *Preface and follow criticism with a compliment.*

People hear criticism best when they feel secure and loved, appreciated, and admired. We make them feel that way if we preface criticisms with compliments. For example, "I love you very much, and I appreciate how good you are to me. But I feel very upset about _____. If you would do _____ in the future, I would appreciate it. Thanks for hearing me out. You're so wonderful."

Complimenting a spouse also reminds us of our spouse's good qualities, instead of allowing us to focus only on their shortcomings. That helps us criticize more gently and makes them more receptive to hearing us.

If we can't give our spouse at least one compliment, we are too angry to criticize in a constructive way.

3. *Be constructive and brief. Criticize a specific behavior and say how you want it changed.*

Don't criticize someone's traits or personality. Don't be global or vague. Don't tell a spouse that he or she is bossy, obnoxious, controlling, sloppy, inconsiderate, and so on. Specify a behavior that you don't like and say what you'd prefer. For example, "Would you please wash the dishes and clean up the kitchen after you cook or eat?" is a nice way to criticize. Saying "You're such a slob" is not.

Rather than calling a wife a nag, it's better to say, "I appreciate your conscientiousness because you run our home so well. On the other hand, I get upset when you tell me what to do and when, several times a day. Ask me once to do something. Thanks, cutie."

Criticism should never attack a person, dredge up past history, or digress to extraneous matters. This means not talking about how your husband is just like his father, how your wife has been doing the same thing ever since you've known her, diagnosing your spouse with the latest psychobabble, or talking about every upset that you've been through during the past four years.

Address the present, identify a specific behavior, and say how you want it modified. For example, "I'm enjoying your company at this restaurant, and I'd rather be here with you than with anyone else in the world. Could you do me a little favor, though, and please not eat with your fingers? Thanks."

Try to limit criticism to, at most, three or four sentences so that it doesn't sound like a lecture or chiding. Also, avoid using phrases like "You always" and "You never." No one can change an eternity of undesirable behavior.

Mark came home at the end of a tiring day and yelled at Joan: "You never clean up the kids' toys! I nearly break my neck every night when I come home! This house always looks like a condemned project. None of the women in your family know how to keep a clean house!"

Mark's reaction was destructive, global, and vague. He attacked his wife and destroyed her dignity, leaving her feeling defensive, hurt, and angry. Had he only showed that he appreciated how hard she worked taking care of the house and children, she wouldn't have felt taken for granted and would have been more likely to do what he wanted in the future.

Joan picked up the toys that night, but she resented Mark for days, and the problem continued.

A better criticism would have been, "Joan, I appreciate how hard you work keeping after the kids all day long. I couldn't do what you do. But it upsets me when I look forward to seeing you at the end of the day and I walk into a minefield of toys. Would it help if I called you before I leave work so that you and the kids can put away the toys?"

4. *Don't criticize what a partner can't change, and don't blame.*

Rosalyn and Ted unpacked at their hotel when she realized that her wallet was missing. She asked if he had it, and he said that he saw it lying on the dresser at home. He thought that she had deliberately left it there.

"I can't believe that you saw it there and didn't say anything," she said in a nasty tone of voice.

"Well," Ted said defensively, "I asked you to check and see if we had everything before we left."

"You should have known that I would never have left my wallet home."

"How was I supposed to know that? I can't read your mind." And so on.

It is a waste of time to cry over what can't be changed or to blame a partner. When Rosalyn realized that the wallet was at home, she could have complimented Ted on how well they got everything else together, then asked him to let her know if she ever left her wallet home again before they went out anywhere. Then they can brainstorm together about how to deal with the fact that their theater tickets were in her wallet.

5. *Build a spouse's self-esteem; don't humiliate, insult, or curse.*

Humiliating people may silence them but it won't convince them of your point of view.

Bobbie was twenty pounds overweight, and Ruby had asked her many times to get back to an appropriate weight. When they attended a *bar mitzvah,* she devoured two plates of hors d'oeuvres, then headed to the carving station. Ruby said, "Don't you think that you've eaten enough for a few days? If you keep this up, you'll be getting your own zip code soon."

Bobbie was so humiliated and angry that she continued to stuff herself and took home a doggy bag of cake and petits fours as well.

A better strategy would have been for Ruby to say something positive to motivate Bobbie to stop eating: "I think that you're the most beautiful woman here, but you'll be an absolute knockout soon if you don't overdo it tonight. Let me know if I can help you become as svelte as you were on our wedding day."

Bobbie may still be tempted to eat like there's no tomorrow, but her pangs of conscience may curb her appetite and reinforce some self-control.

6. *State what you want in positive, not negative, terms.*

It is better to emphasize what we like and want, rather than what we dislike. For example, "Your other dresses are so much more flattering than the one you wore yesterday. Would you wear them instead?" A poor critique would be, "What an ugly dress you're wearing! Where in the world did you get it? Please don't ever wear that again."

Marty would like Charlene to stop spending so much time talking on the telephone to her friends. Instead of telling her that she spends too much time on the phone, he can say, "I would like to spend more time together at night without being interrupted by phone calls. Can we make eight to nine o'clock our time, and let the answering machine take calls then?"

7. *Be realistic about what a spouse is willing to change. Choose your battles, and don't criticize too much at once.*

The more reasonable a critique is, the more likely someone is to heed it. Some people (typically women) try to "overhaul" a spouse's personality as soon as they are married. Rather than constructively criticize a habit or a behavior every few weeks, their reconstruction plan attempts to "fix" a spouse as soon and as thoroughly as possible.

Helene told Morris how unfashionable his clothes were and asked him to discard them and buy new ones. A few hours later, he sat down to read a magazine and munched on a candy bar. She promptly told him that he shouldn't eat sweets. When they had dinner, she wanted to make plans for the weekend, but he was too tired to discuss it. She told him that he should go to sleep earlier and not read in bed.

She should have constructively criticized only one or two things at a time, preferably things that he could change rather easily: "Morris, I bet that you would look fantastic in a navy suit. Would you mind if I bought you one?" When Morris was used to the new outfit, she could ask if he would mind if she bought him a few other suits. If he's agreeable, he might gradually give away his unattractive outfits as he gets used to the new ones.

Instead of expecting him to give up sweets "cold turkey," she can make him healthy desserts and offer them as occasional substitutes for junk food. Instead of lecturing him about how bad sugar is, she should make healthy alternatives more appealing.

If he is often tired, she can ask if there is anything that she can do to make it easier for him to get a good night's rest. Would a backrub help him unwind? Would he like more time to decompress after work? Would it help if she didn't talk to him so much before they went to sleep?

She should not make a bunch of suggestions/criticisms at the same time. A spouse may be willing to change three or four behaviors over a few weeks but not in two days. Asking for too much, or criticizing too often, undermines a spouse's feeling of adequacy. It makes him or her feel broken, infantilized, and controlled.

The more we identify something as "us," the more we feel threatened if someone tries to take it away. Most people are willing to modify a few behaviors but not give up their personality or identity.

Frank doesn't mind Brenda criticizing his clothes because they don't express his identity. If she tells him what she'd like him to wear, he's happy to dress as she likes.

Gerald feels differently. When Ada asks him to dress conventionally, he feels that she is trying to change his identity. She thinks that his mustard and olive suits, loud ties, and white socks look dreadful, but he thinks otherwise. The best that she can do is to tell him how attractive he is, and ask if he might be willing to wear a specific outfit that she likes once a week.

Requests that accentuate what's positive are much more likely to be heeded than those that sound negative.

DIPLOMACY

Good communication is easy when we are happy and calm, but not when we are in a bad mood, angry, or caught off guard. The more we train ourselves to communicate lovingly instead of saying what we feel, the easier it will be to respond constructively when circumstances are not ideal.

Suzanne was still twenty-five pounds overweight three months after having a baby. Nursing gave her a voracious appetite and she never found time to exercise. So, she felt depressed about her looks. Lenny also found her unattractive but kept that to himself because there was nothing constructive that she could do with that information.

One night she asked, "Do you find me attractive now that I look like a cow?"

Lenny chose his words carefully. "You must feel so pained losing the body that you once had, but you're still beautiful and I love you." Later that evening he suggested, "If you'd like, I'll take care of the baby any night and Sunday mornings so that you can work out. Your well-being is important to me, and I want you to be happy."

Tom told Carol that he needed a new suit, and it pleased her that he was going to replace the outdated ones that he had worn since high school. He saved up $175 of their hard-earned money and bought a suit that he loved at a final sale. When he modeled it for her, she hated everything about it, including the waste of a week's take-home pay.

"So what do you think?" Tom asked, with an ear-to-ear grin.

Carol knew that the clothes could not be returned, and they obviously made him happy, so why spoil his pleasure?

"I think that it suits you well," she smiled. "Wear it in good health.

Feige was very proud of her first batch of *challah* (bread baked for the Sabbath and holidays). She had spent four hours making it and was so proud to serve it to her husband. It was as hard as a rock, burned on the bottom, and raw and doughy on top. As her husband tried to chew it, he discovered that she had used four tablespoons of salt instead of the four teaspoons that the recipe called for.

"How do you like it?" Feige asked expectantly.

He smiled and affectionately told her, "There's nothing like homemade *challah*. Thank you for being such a wonderful wife."

Our words should enhance a spouse's self-esteem, even if we must bend the truth. Protecting a spouse's feelings and acknowledging his or her efforts are more important than being "honest."

MARITAL STYLES

Some couples have stable and fulfilling marriages, despite having volatile, raging arguments.[17] Couples who argue passionately over many issues can still have strong marriages, provided they resolve their differences, laugh a lot, and share a lot of love, romance, and passion. If they attack each other, or reduce their marriage to endless bickering or violence, the marriage is likely to dissolve.

Some couples "conspire" to avoid conflicts. They agree to disagree and try never to discuss matters that will end up unresolved. They make light of their differences instead of working them out, focus on what they love and value in each other, and stress what is positive.[18] The downside of marriages that avoid any kind of conflict is that they lack real intimacy and can't resolve serious conflicts that can't be dismissed.[19] In other words, all couples have differences. As long as you and your spouse have congruent ways of dealing with them, you can have a fulfilling marriage.

When this doesn't happen, couples need to examine their respective styles of handling conflict. Women complain most about husbands not communicating, while husbands complain most that they want less fighting. What this means is that many couples have one spouse who withdraws when there is a conflict, while the other tends to keep pursuing the one who withdraws in order to communicate about the problem. Not surprisingly, about 80 percent of withdrawers are men and 80 percent of the pursuers are women.

Many men avoid arguing because it gives them high blood pressure and a "fight-or-flight" reflex that floods them with stress hormones. If they don't know how to argue productively and don't want to be violent, the only way they know to feel better is to shut down and be quiet. Ironically, their dropping out of arguments usually infuriates their wives, who see this as a sign that the husband doesn't take their complaints seriously. The women assume that they must express themselves louder and more elaborately, and thus they hound their withdrawn husbands.[20]

Ultimately, this does not work. What does work is for the pursuer to stop pursuing and to bring up issues in a way that the withdrawer feels he will not be attacked, insulted, or made to feel inadequate. If the withdrawer needs time to compose himself, he should tell the pursuer, "I'm too upset to discuss this now. Let's try it again in an hour [or at some time in the next day]." Withdrawers need to understand that withdrawing from conflict does not solve these kinds of problems. Pursuers need to know that escalating conflicts when a withdrawer feels flooded will be counterproductive.

There are good and bad ways to fight and argue. Couples who keep fights manageable use kind or flippant comments to soothe their spouse and keep the conflict from becoming total chaos. For instance, a wife who notices her husband becoming emotionally "flooded" can cool him down by saying, "Wait a minute. I'm not blaming you," or "It looks like you're feeling attacked. I'm discussing this with you so that we can feel close again."

A husband might cool things down by quipping, "I wish that I could have your PMS this month so that life would be easier for both of us," or, "Did I just become an army general? It looks like I started World War III. How about if we try this again?"

Couples who don't de-escalate hostilities usually get emotionally and physically "flooded." They quickly reach a physical boiling point and feel like exploding. Men usually do this much more often, more rapidly, and for longer periods of time than women do. When women let go of stressful states and think that the issues are forgotten, men are usually still boiling and obsessed with revenge. They also tend to stay this way for a long time.[21] This is why a husband's stress level (physiological arousal) is the best predictor of how unhappy both partners are.

People who are flooded can't process information, and it is futile and/or destructive to keep trying to communicate when they are in this state. Successfully married couples become adept at soothing each other and keep each other from becoming unduly worked-up when they address problems and communicate. Couples that repeatedly "flood" tend to lose their fond memories of each other and almost invariably get divorced.[22]

One exercise to help couples communicate more safely is to set a time when both are willing to discuss an issue without interruption, for not more than thirty minutes. They begin by flipping a coin to decide who will be the first speaker, unless only one person wants to address an issue. Meanwhile, each person has an index card with a happy face on it, a second card with a neutral face on it, and a third card with a frowning face on it.

As the speaker says what she or he wants to communicate, the listener holds up one of the three cards, depending upon how the listener feels about what she or he is hearing. The listener's feelings change as the discussion does and she or he changes cards accordingly. When the listener holds up a frowning face, the speaker asks what it was about his or her comment that made the listener unhappy.

For example, Zack listened as Lydia spoke:

"I had a wonderful time watching you with the kids today. You have such a nice way with them." (Zack holds up his smiling-face card.)

"On the other hand, I was upset that you gave them lollipops, especially after we discussed how bad it was for them to have junk food." (Zack switches to a frown card.)

Lydia asks, "Tell me how you're feeling."

Zack replied, "I don't like hearing criticism about the way I treat the kids."

Lydia questions, "How can I discuss with you my upset about the kids eating candy?"

Zack substitutes the neutral card for the frown. "How about if you just say that you don't want them eating candy, instead of criticizing me for giving it to them?"

Lydia clarifies, "Would it be okay just to ask you not to give the kids lollipops in the future without discussing what you did in the past?"

Zack switches to a smiling card. "Yeah, that would work a lot better with me. I have such a strong association to my mother making me feel like a bad boy when I did things that she didn't like. This way will bypass my bad feelings."

Using these cards as one person speaks gives him or her instantaneous feedback about what kind of message the receiver is getting. If couples key in to each other's reactions as they happen, they can often resolve communication issues as they arise, instead of knowing the effect of their words only after they are already derailed from a productive discussion or are flooded.

Bronna gave Kalman what she thought was helpful advice. When he held up the frown card, she knew immediately that he didn't see her comment as positively as she did. When he shared some fears with her, he expected her to hold up the frown card. When she held up a smile, he discovered that she appreciated him opening up to her. He had assumed that she would think that he was a wimp if he showed any weakness. This kind of feedback enabled them to clarify issues that had been difficult for them to resolve before.

The goal of these exchanges is to find out how each spouse impacts and reacts to the other. By learning what feels good and what doesn't, they can do more of what's positive and less of what's negative.

BALANCING CONFLICTS WITH LOVE

Studies have shown that no matter where couples are from, or what their socio-economic levels are, all satisfied couples make sure that there are approximately five times as many positive events and interactions as negative ones.[23] This means that if couples fight during breakfast, they will shower each other with affection for the rest of the day, or at night. If they give one criticism, they will make sure to give five validating and loving comments before giving another critique.

This does not mean that it is okay for couples to insult, humiliate, curse, or denigrate each other, as long as they have five positive interactions afterwards. The damage from *destructive* fighting is not readily erased.

Couples who ultimately divorce average one put-down or insult out of every ten comments they share. They zing each other with five times as many cruel and invalidating comments as happy couples do. This negativity usually takes on a life of its own until they can't get through a week without major blowups.[24]

A word to the wise – if you think that your way of speaking to your spouse isn't hurtful or overly critical, ask your mate. If you want a good marriage, remember that criticism is ultimately in the eyes of the beholder.

PRIVACY

Secular society encourages people to share everything, even one's most private feelings and experiences. Television talk shows like Oprah Winfrey, Geraldo Rivera, and Phil Donahue are extremely popular because they make strangers privy to the most intimate details of other people's lives. People no longer appreciate the importance of boundaries.

We should know better than to be overly revealing. Before sharing personal information with a spouse, ask, "What will he or she do with this? Will he or she be empathic and keep it confidential? Will he or she find it overwhelming or inappropriate? Will this be constructive?"

Wanting to disclose personal information does not justify doing it. If a spouse won't appreciate our secret thoughts and feelings, we should keep them to ourselves.

Naomi had an abortion before she became religious. Her husband didn't know this because he had never asked about her premarital sex life. He assumed that she had had relations with other men but was not interested in the details. She was told that her abortion should not impair her fertility and wisely decided not to disclose it to her husband unless he asked.

The Bible teaches us not to trivialize how information might affect us. God commanded Adam and Eve not to eat from the tree of "knowledge of good and evil."[25] When they partook of knowledge that they were not equipped to handle, it ruined them.

Most people think that getting knowledge is always good, but that is not true. Knowledge is only good if we can use it productively. Sharing some kinds of information with a spouse may hurt their feelings or make them think ill of us. We should not gratuitously share information if it will destroy someone's love for us.

A story is told about the Chofetz Chaim, a revered European scholar and rabbi who lived a generation ago. He was famous for writing books that censured gossiping, and he was scrupulous never to speak or listen to negative comments about others.

While traveling on a train, the rabbi sat next to a Jew who was going to visit the saintly Chofetz Chaim, and who didn't recognize the rabbi sitting across from him. The simple man gushed about how wonderful the famous rabbi was.

"I know him well," the Chofetz Chaim said humbly, "and he's not the saint that you think he is, nor the greatest Jew of this generation."

The man was outraged. "How dare you put him down! Everyone knows what a pious scholar he is."

The Chofetz Chaim continued his self-effacement. "Don't be fooled by appearances. You don't know what he's like deep down."

This dialogue continued for several minutes with the man getting more and more incensed. Finally, he was so outraged by this stranger's insults to the Chofetz Chaim that he hit him.

When they arrived at the train station in Radin, a crowd of Jews eagerly awaited a dignitary. "Who are all these people waiting for?" the traveler asked.

"The Chofetz Chaim is on that train, and we're here to greet him," a stranger answered. "Oh, there he is!" With that, the stranger pointed to the man whom the traveler had just assaulted.

The traveler was horrified about what he did and ran to the Chofetz Chaim to apologize. "I'm so sorry, I had no idea who you were. Please forgive me."

"That's okay," the Chofetz Chaim replied. "I just learned a lesson. It's not only forbidden to speak badly about others, it's even forbidden to speak badly about oneself!"

If we want a spouse to respect us, we should not say or do things that destroy that respect. A rabbi once warned, "If a man confides to his wife that his friends mocked him, she will also scorn him in her heart." We lower a spouse's esteem for us by divulging stupid or degrading things that we said or did. No one wants to be married to a failure or to an idiot. If we want support when we feel low, there are healthy ways to get it.

Edie did not like her looks, but Steve found her very attractive. She constantly made derogatory comments about the size of her nose, her overbite, and her being *zoftig*. It didn't take long before Steve stopped seeing her as beautiful and began seeing her as she saw herself.

Loren worked hard and made a good living, but he was socially inept. One day, he told Vera that he was turned down for a promotion at work because of a series of stupid mistakes he had made bookkeeping. This made her angry, and she lost respect for him. Before he shared this with her, Vera at least respected him as a provider. Afterwards she saw him as a failure there, too. Since she did not know that he was being considered for a promotion, there was no reason for her to know he was turned down.

Cathy was a good mother, but doubted her maternal abilities. Instead of asking Walter for reassurance, she deprecated herself. Walter began to wonder if she really was an unfit mother. Soon, all he saw were signs of her inadequacy, even though she really was a terrific mother.

Everyone makes mistakes and has imperfections, but a loving spouse will either overlook them or see them as a minor part of an otherwise wonderful person. When we keep focusing on our shortcomings, it is hard for a spouse not to do the same.

We shouldn't share information that will lower a spouse's esteem for us unless we must. We should never make a spouse question our stability, fidelity, or trustworthiness because we want reassurance or are trying to make conversation. Nor should we share family secrets, information about previous intimate relationships, past abuse, or emotional problems without considering how it will impact our spouse.

Terry had a very bad relationship with her family until she married Ozzie. That was a turning point in their relationship, and her parents finally started treating her respectfully. She sometimes wanted to tell Ozzie about how abusive her parents had been to her but realized that it would make him hate them and ruin the warmth that the family finally shared.

People like Terry should work out their feelings in therapy, if they need to. Sharing them with a spouse can permanently destroy a good relationship with in-laws. Even if Terry feels good telling Ozzie about her past, he will not be able to be civil to people who hurt the woman he loves.

Jordan was hospitalized for two weeks with depression when he was thirteen. He saw a psychotherapist for the next three years and came to terms with his feelings about himself and his parents. By the time he went to college, he was better adjusted than most people and never had another bout of depression. Ten years later, he married a very sweet but unsophisticated woman. There was no reason to tell her about his teenage suicide attempt because it would prompt her to question his present stability. Unless his depression resurfaces, he is better off not sharing this part of his life with her.

We should never share fantasies about the opposite sex, fond memories of past lovers, or intimate details of our premarital (or other marital) relationships with a spouse.

People who have recurrent thoughts of violence, but who would never harm anyone, should not alarm and frighten a spouse by sharing their fantasies. Many women with postpartum depression think about abandoning, or even killing, their infants but would never do it. Their feelings change when their depression lifts. Some people who have no intention of ever committing suicide express their sadness or pain by telling a spouse, "I wish I were dead."

Sharing these feelings can seriously damage a marriage, even if the listener should know not to take these comments at face value. People who have these feelings should seek professional help and preferably not divulge these feelings to a spouse.

Adelle had recurring thoughts about strangling her newborn for two weeks after giving birth. She would never do such a thing, but she made the mistake of telling Eli. Although her depression soon resolved, Eli found fault with her mothering from then on. Eventually, the seed that Adelle planted in his mind became a tree. He divorced her a year later because he convinced himself that she was an unfit mother, despite her being quite normal and well-adjusted once her depression passed.

Akiva was a religious man who confided to Reva that he yearned to smoke marijuana as he did before he became religious. Although he would never use drugs again, his comment made her lose respect for him and she questioned his emotional stability.

Manny shared with Zahava a lascivious dream that he'd had about his secretary and laughed about how funny it was. But Zahava didn't think that it was funny at all, and she started to question his fidelity. She never fully trusted him again.

If need be, this kind of sensitive information should be shared with an objective professional, such as a rabbi or a therapist. Doing it with a spouse can destroy your marriage.

Nor should couples discuss their spouse's shortcomings with their friends or family, unless the latter are extremely talented at resolving marital problems. Most spouses will feel betrayed if they find out that you shared their personal life with outsiders without their permission.

It is also difficult for your friends or family to be objective when you say negative things to them about your spouse. Parents, especially, find it hard to ever forgive someone who hurts their child and are likely to think badly about your spouse from then on. Even if you remember to tell a parent or friend that your spouse is better now, it is unlikely to change their unfavorable point of view. Long after you have gotten over the upset, your confidant is stuck with a negative view of your spouse.

Nora told her mother that Sol took antidepressant medication that alleviated his mood swings. Her mother thought that only crazy people took psychiatric drugs, and she was not excited about her son-in-law, anyway. But after hearing this, she saw Sol as defective and disturbed, even though he acted perfectly normal.

George told his friends many "newlywed" stories about Paula that poked fun at her bad points but mentioned none of her good ones. He painted a terrible picture of her before his friends had a chance to like her. Some months later, things were much better, but his friends continued to see her as a brainless "ditz." They thought that he was crazy for marrying her, and refused to socialize with them as a couple because they disliked her so much.

SUMMARY

Speech can be our best ally or our worst enemy.[26] The idea that "Death and life are in the power of the tongue"[27] is especially true in marriage.

Good communication usually takes a lot of work, but it can bring couples closer, resolve tensions and problems, and foster mutual understanding. This sometimes requires putting anger on hold, giving a spouse the benefit of the doubt, and humbling ourselves to see things from a spouse's perspective rather than taking revenge.

We must sometimes lie diplomatically in order to preserve harmony with a spouse[28] and must remember that our spouse has vulnerable feelings when we are angry or upset with him or her.

Communication is the bedrock of marriage. It should convey 80 percent affection and positive sharing and not more than 20 percent criticism and arguing.

By noticing when a spouse gets upset during disagreements, we can be sure to soothe him or her before things get out of control.

It may take a long time to lay the groundwork of a marriage, but it is worth doing well from the start. If that didn't happen, it is never too late to start again.

NOTES

1. *Targum Onkelos* on Genesis 2:7.
2. Genesis 1:3,6,9; *Mishnah Avot* 5:1.
3. Based on *Shabbat* 127a.
4. Chofetz Chaim, *Guard Your Tongue*, part 2, chapter 1:2.
5. Clifford Notarius and Howard Markman, *We Can Work It Out* (New York: G. P. Putnam's Sons, 1993), p. 28.
6. *Shabbat* 31a.
7. Leviticus 19:18.
8. Genesis 7:2.
9. *Ketubot* 17a.
10. Leviticus 19:15.
11. Leviticus 19:18.
12. *Yevamot* 65b.
13. Genesis 18:10.
14. Genesis 18:12.
15. Genesis 18:13.
16. Rashi on Genesis 18:13.
17. "A Lens on Matrimony," *U.S. News and World Report* (February 21, 1994), pp. 66–9.
18. "Success in Marriage May Be a Matter of Style," *USA Today* (April 4, 1994), p. 4D.
19. Ibid.
20. "A Lens on Matrimony," 68.
21. Ibid, p. 67.
22. Ibid, p. 68.
23. Ibid, p. 67.
24. Ibid.
25. Genesis 2:17.
26. *Arakhin* 15b.
27. Proverbs 18:21.
28. "On Flattery," *Orchot Tzadikim*.

SUGGESTED READING

Hendrix, Harville. *Getting the Love You Want*. New York: H. Holt, 1988.
Notarius, Clifford, and Markman, Howard. *We Can Work It Out*. New York: G. P. Putnam's Sons, 1993. This is one of the best books available on improving a couple's communication and resolving conflicts. A must for couples who are having trouble communicating!

14

Differences between Men and Women

God deliberately created two different sexes so that each can contribute to the other what the other lacks. Judaism values the differences between men and women and urges us to use them constructively.

What men want to contribute to marriage may be very different from what women need, and vice versa. Since we may not feel comfortable providing what a spouse needs, we can grow by stretching ourselves to develop new skills and ways of giving.

The differences between men and women are much more than physical. Men and women have different ways of speaking, thinking, relating, experiencing, and responding to life. This chapter will generalize about how men and women do this, and many people will not fit these stereotypes. Some men may act and react with "women's" emotional depth and sensitivity, while some women may react more like men. Some people will have a mixture of characteristics. That is fine. What matters is that couples recognize the legitimacy of their differences and deal with them constructively.

Men and women tend to have different primary needs. Men primarily need respect and admiration.[1] They get this by "slaying dragons," making their mark on the world, and having a wife's approval and acceptance. Men value their independence and ability to accomplish tasks without anyone's advice or help. They tend to compete and like to show off their competence. Their greater need to be respected than loved allows many men to put work (or achievements) first and family second.

Women have a primary need to be loved.[2] While men feel worst when they aren't respected and admired, women feel worst when they aren't loved, especially by their husbands. Women collaborate and bond with family and friends because they need to be loved and give love. Unlike men, few women can find the emotional fulfillment in a career that they seek from intimacy with a spouse. While women want respect, getting love is more important when they have to choose.

The most blessed state for a woman is to be emotionally, physically, and spiritually close to a mate. She cherishes this "oneness" so much that she cannot imagine anyone wanting to give it up. Yet intense and prolonged intimacy makes many men feel that they are losing their autonomy. They escape this tension by pulling away periodically.

Most men have their fill of intimacy after a few hours or days of closeness with a wife. They feel restless and withdraw in order to regain their independence. This is part of a man's nature and happens regardless of how "good" a wife is. Yet it makes some wives panic because they think their husbands no longer love them. If the women would only allow their husbands some space, the men would lose their emotional satiety and want nurturing again. If a wife nags, criticizes, interrogates, or gets angry, the husband won't feel lonely, and will stay away longer because closeness feels bad.

When men want to be alone or to pursue healthy interests by themselves, wives should let them, then offer closeness and connection when they want it again. Men think that their cycles of intimacy and independence are normal, and they expect to come back to a loving and accepting wife, not to confrontations and criticism.

Men often distance themselves when women are getting their fill of intimacy. If women are patient and non-pressuring, husbands usually come back and are loving again in a few days. If men are welcomed back, reconnections can be intimate and satisfying. If wives are hostile or confrontative, the men are sure to withdraw again soon.

It is important for couples to discuss their respective needs for space and intimacy and to compromise about them. A husband may be unwilling to hold his wife all night but may be willing to do it for an hour. He may be unwilling to give her a weekly backrub for thirty minutes, but may be happy to cuddle with her for the same amount of time. He may feel trapped spending an entire week in a hotel with "nothing" to do but may find the same vacation delightful if they can go out for some entertainment and recreation.

Husbands want to feel that they can uniquely provide what their wives need, but wives should be independent enough not to expect men to fill all of their emotional needs. Men are turned off by clinginess and neediness. Needs should be limited enough that a spouse can fulfill them in the course of daily life. For example, a woman can expect her husband to spend at least half an hour of "quality" time with her every day, but when he must work overtime, she may have to accept talking by phone instead of in person. She may be unwilling for him to go on vacation without her for a week, but should not mind him going for a day here and there. She may resent his going out three nights a week to study Torah with a partner, but may be happy for him to do it if he first helps put the children to bed and spends time with her. Couples need to creatively find ways to fulfill each other's needs.

Needy people have unlimited desires that they expect a partner to fulfill. Compromises frustrate them because they don't get everything they want, and they can't enjoy what they do get. When a spouse pours energy into a partner who is like a bottomless pit, the appreciation received never equals the effort made. Sooner or later, some giving spouses become angry and resentful giving this way and stop making the effort.

CONVERSATIONAL STYLES

We can talk to a spouse for many reasons, such as to share information, experiences, memories, feelings, needs, and wants; to solve pragmatic problems or ease emotional tensions; to feel close and be understood.

. Men and women often have different agendas when they talk. "Women-talk" makes connections, establishes rapport, shares feelings, and solicits support, while "men-talk" usually gives information about the world or relates details of daily life. Women seek goodness, connection, and intimacy when they talk, while men are more concerned with truth, objective reality, and showing their individuality and independence. Some men feel comfortable arguing and disagreeing with those closest to them, while this irritates and threatens women, who feel that they are talking to an adversary, not to a loving ally.

Men talk to show their competence, knowledge, and power; to get attention, respect, and admiration; and to show their mastery of the world. When men share their opinions or offer advice, they want to be appreciated for their knowledge and expertise, not be told that they are wrong or don't understand the person to whom they are giving advice.

Women talk to create emotional bonds, while many men only talk if they have something concrete to talk about. Men don't like feeling pressured to talk when they have nothing to say and usually want to talk less than women do.

Wives most need to talk when they are at home, while men find silence at home refreshing. Women feel punished or abandoned when their husbands are silent, while men enjoy silence because it means not having to confront or impress anyone.

We often assume that others want and need what we do. Men who are comfortable being silent and "doing their own thing" assume that a wife also finds that satisfying. Men don't know that silence kills a marriage because women need frequent emotional connections via words and loving gestures.

Comfort with silence is anathema to women, who create rapport by sharing feelings and agreeing with each other. The first woman was called "Chava,"[3] which means "conversation" in Aramaic. This alludes to the fact that conversation played a pivotal role for Eve and her female descendants.

"Adam" comes from the Hebrew word for "earth," and suggests that he and his male descendants have a passive, quiet side to them. Men often seek serenity by withdrawing and secluding themselves when they are troubled or trying to solve a problem. Meanwhile, their wives try to connect to them by talking, but the men may not want reassurance and support through conversation. Men would often rather be left alone to ponder and collect themselves than have to talk through their problems.

Women who don't know this try to get a withdrawn or silent mate to "open up," or they punish him for his silence. Women who talk to troubled husbands as a way of showing support make many men feel badgered, smothered, or intruded upon. The men then retreat even further into silence or leave the room.

Most men don't want to talk about their problems until they have solved them. Wives should ask their husbands if they want privacy before assuming that a withdrawn man really wants to converse. Otherwise, a man who wants to be alone is bound to feel irritated when his wife keeps hovering nearby attempting to get him to talk. He should tell her that she can help him by accepting his need to work things out by himself. If he wants to withdraw, he should tell her that he needs some time to be alone and let her know when he expects to be more available. If she asks if something is wrong and he says that everything's fine, she should not interrogate or criticize him, nor hover nearby until he "comes out of it." She can ask how much time he needs to be alone, respect his need for privacy, and "do her own thing" in the meantime. When a man wants to withdraw, he should reassure his wife that she has done nothing wrong, that he loves her, and that he will come out of his "think room" when he is ready.

As a practical matter, he should not completely withdraw for more than a day at a time. Even if he wants to be alone to ponder some problems, he should still make time by the end of the day to converse with his wife about other matters.

While men withdraw to deal with their problems, women often complain to a husband or friends to get support. Men assume that if someone complains, there must be a problem that needs to be solved. Since men are trained to be problem-solvers and "doers," they often offer solutions when their wives complain, rather than give support and understanding.

Most wives who complain do so as their way of sharing feelings. They trust their husbands enough to be vulnerable with them. They want to be heard and get empathy and validation for their feelings, but don't want their husbands to do anything about the problem. They especially don't want advice. They want love and support and will find their own solutions later. Wives who get advice without empathy and validation complain that their husbands don't listen to them. The men obviously do hear them, they just don't give wives what they need.

Wives also feel ignored when a husband listens to them while simultaneously doing other things, like watching television or reading. Wives want, and deserve, undivided attention. They need a husband to make loving gestures and smile, say "Um-hm," and make eye contact when they talk. Women want reassurance that they are wonderful, loved, and worthy of a listening ear. They can't feel that way when a husband is distracted or seems indifferent.

When women talk and complain in order to get reassurance, understanding, and love, big doses of TLC usually give them the security they need, and they feel better within a few hours or days. Men show that they understand a woman's feelings by not suggesting solutions unless a wife specifically asks for them. Giving wives solutions when they feel hurt or sad makes them feel angry and misunderstood. Men are most helpful giving empathy and love without suggesting ways to fix a problem.

When men minimize or ignore a wife's unhappiness or distress, try to convince her to feel differently, or offer advice, she feels misunderstood, lonely, patronized, and frustrated. Women want a husband to listen to, and agree with, their distress, not try to talk them out of it.

While men find "women-talk" baffling, many wives find "men-talk" frustrating, boring, and superficial. Instead of discussing feelings, men tend to relate impersonal details. A major complaint by wives is that their husbands don't talk to them. This means that men don't talk to them about feelings.

Some men think that talking about feelings is a sign of weakness or childlike dependence. They keep a "stiff upper lip" because they think that talking about feelings makes an upset person even more upset. Some men even think that wives discuss problems and feelings as a way of manipulating husbands to give them more attention. Instead of offering support, which would gratify a wife and take away her need to complain, some men do the opposite. They try to "toughen her up" by ignoring or minimizing her upset. Almost nothing could be worse because women who don't get emotional support feel alone, unloved, misunderstood, and desperate. They then complain louder and more frequently to get their husbands' concern and caring. If this fails, they may withdraw in pain and anger.

Men often support each other by minimizing a friend's problems. For example, they say, "I'm sure you'll get over it soon," "Things can only get better," or "I have confidence in you. You'll deal with it." Sometimes, men even show support by changing the subject when a friend feels "down."

Women find these comments and reactions insensitive and hurtful. They feel put down and not taken seriously when they are treated this way. Women show support by validating each other's feelings, encouraging troubled friends to talk about their problems, and staying close until the person feels better. In other words, most men show concern and support in a way that makes women feel uncared for, while women normally show concern and give support in a way that makes men feel disrespected and infantilized.

Since men are solution- and outcome-oriented, not feeling-oriented, they try to make others feel better by giving advice. Women, however, are more attuned to the *process* of getting support and will not resolve problems until they feel understood. No one who is upset listens to advice until his emotional pain is soothed. Men need to know that they do something very important whenever they empathize with a wife's feelings. Husbands who don't understand this are baffled, hurt, or angry when a wife ignores or rejects their advice, or is angry at them for giving it!

Both women and men want their feelings validated and understood, but they express this differently. Men want a wife to believe that they can solve problems on their own, and that they are independent and self-sufficient. Wives want husbands to take them seriously, agree and empathize with their distress, and support them while they solve their problems.

Shuli ran a business that was struggling to get off the ground. She told Daniel that a customer convinced her to sell a product below cost, and she was very upset for letting herself get hoodwinked. Daniel got angry with her for being so unassertive and told her that she must learn to be firmer with people. She contemplated showing her assertiveness by telling him how angry his lack of support and empathy felt!

Daniel thought that if Shuli would only take his advice, she would become stronger. He felt devalued and angry when she rejected his good recommendations. She felt that he didn't understand how painful her failures were to her.

Daniel should have said, "Oh, Shuli, I'm so sorry about what happened to you. It's so infuriating to be taken advantage of, then feel helpless to do anything about it."

She would have replied, "Yeah, it really was pretty awful." After a few minutes of elaborating her feelings, she would conclude, "Now I feel so much better. Thanks for listening and being so understanding."

Instead, Daniel's response got him a cold shoulder for the rest of the evening.

Lily took a train to work, and it broke down for forty-five minutes. She sweltered in the oppressive summer heat with no air conditioning. When she finally arrived at work, the work assignment that she had wanted was given to someone else. When she came home and made dinner, she forgot to take the steaks out of the broiler until they were burnt and the kitchen was filled with smoke.

When she told Leon about her day's disasters, he gave her practical recommendations that he thought showed sensitivity and thoughtfulness: "This is the fourth time that you've had problems with the train. Why don't you carpool with Marissa and Ella? . . . And by the way, please be more careful in the kitchen. You could have set the house on fire."

Leon's well-intentioned remarks made Lily's blood boil, and she thought about what else she might set on fire. She felt completely misunderstood and even more distressed than she had been before talking to him.

A better response would have been, "I'm sorry you had such a terrible day, Lily. I feel so bad for you. I've never been trapped on a train, but I imagine that it must have been awful. And I can't believe that they gave your work assignment to someone else. Boy, when it rains, it really pours, doesn't it? Come here, let me give you a hug." This kind of emotional support helps wives get over their pain and distress quickly. They will figure out what to do about their concrete problems once they feel emotionally soothed.

When we don't feel validated, we keep reiterating the same idea in the hope that a partner will understand if we just explain ourselves better. Once we feel validated, we move on. When a partner keeps explaining himself, we need to make him or her feel understood. Until and unless we do that, she or he won't solve the problem.

Toni and George reversed the typical ways that men and women respond to each other. They were discussing his job, which he was considering leaving because it was so stressful and he got so little appreciation there. She was very concerned that another job would not pay as well.

George: "I had another horrible day at work today. I don't know how much more of this I can take. I spent the last two weeks doing a special project for my boss, and not only didn't he acknowledge what a good job I did, he criticized me for something I didn't even do!"

Toni: "So what are you going to do?"

George: "I've got to find another job. In fact, the only thing that allows me to get through every day is knowing that I can leave."

Toni: "Oh, you don't want to do that. [This is called invalidation.] We have a mortgage to pay, we need to get another car, the kids have school tuition. . . . Why don't you just take a different attitude about your job?" [She's giving advice.]

George: "You just don't understand how difficult things are for me. I can't stay where I am."

Toni: "Sure you can. Lots of other people stay at jobs they don't like for years. They have golden handcuffs."

George: "Well, lots of other people stay in a rat race and end up as dead rats. I don't want that to happen to me. Do you realize what I've been through for the last six years?"

Toni: "I think that you're overreacting to your boss. Don't take him so seriously, he's a jerk."

George: "He's a jerk who's ruining my life. Just yesterday, he gave me another ridiculous assignment."

Toni: "Come on, George, don't be so sensitive . . . "

George keeps trying to get Toni to empathize with how he feels about work, but she doesn't want him to leave. The more she invalidates him by saying it's not so bad, he shouldn't take things so seriously, he's overreacting, and so on, the more he reiterates how terrible things really are. Conversations like this can go on for a very long time, with each side reiterating their feelings without acknowledgement. George will end up feeling frustrated and misunderstood, while Toni will feel that he is acting like a baby and overreacting.

WOMAN-TALK AND WOMANLY WAYS

Another way that women and men speak differently is that men express themselves forthrightly, while women make indirect requests.

Louis drove Sherry home after a pleasant day canoeing. They had not eaten for hours, and Sherry was ravenous. When she saw a road sign announcing a Howard Johnson's, she asked, "Would you like to stop for some ice cream?"

Without hesitating, he replied, "No, thanks, I'm not hungry," and kept driving.

Sherry was floored. Her question was a polite way of asking Louis to stop so that she could eat. It didn't occur to her that he took her literally and did not read between the lines. She concluded that he was oblivious to her feelings and she got angry.

He didn't understand why she suddenly became so cold and aloof for the rest of the drive home. It never occurred to him that her question was a way of saying that she wanted ice cream. Had he known that, he would have gladly pulled over.

Rina planned to visit her parents for a few days and had a 7 A.M. flight on a wintry Sunday morning. Avigdor offered to drive her to the airport forty minutes away, but she told him that it was silly for him to do that when she could get a taxi. Besides, the roads were icy, and it would not be pleasant driving. When he agreed to let her take a taxi, she was furious. She couldn't believe that he wouldn't take her to the airport and didn't override her protest. She expected him to read her mind, not listen to what she said.

Another source of marital tension is women's use of the word "could." They ask their husbands, "Could you take out the garbage?," "Could you do me a favor?," "Could you take care of this?" Some husbands take this literally and answer, "Yes." They *could* do what their wives ask, but they have no intentions of *actually* doing it. This infuriates women.

Women should ask men if they *will* do something, not if they could do it. They should also make their requests direct and brief, such as, "Will you please take out the garbage before dinner?" not "Could you take out the trash?," "Do you mind taking out the garbage?," or giving a five-minute explanation of why the garbage needs to be taken out.

Women also confuse men by nodding their heads, or saying, "Mm-hmm," to show that they are listening. This does not necessarily mean that they agree with what is being said. When a wife does this, the husband thinks that she agrees with him, and then he is surprised or angry to find out that she doesn't.

For example, Sarah nodded her head when Noam said, "You really need to sharpen these knives." The next night, they were as dull as ever.

"Did you forget to sharpen the bread knife?" Noam asked.

"Oh, no," Sarah replied. "I don't want the knives sharper. I'm afraid that the kids will cut themselves if they are honed."

Her nodding showed that she was aware that the knives were dull. It didn't mean that she planned to remedy the situation.

Until husbands and wives learn each other's languages, they need to be explicit about what each wants and means.

Since men and women don't speak the same language, they should expect it to take a long time to learn a partner's language. Here is a dictionary of "woman-talk," followed by the responses wives expect from husbands:

Wife: "Would you like to take out the garbage?"

Please note that this is a rhetorical question.

Correct answer: "Of course, dear, more than anything in the world."

Wife: "Would you like to try the new restaurant that just opened?"

Correct answer: "If that would make you happy, I'd love to."

Wife: "Can you give me a hand cleaning up the kitchen?"

Correct answer: "Of course, honey. I'll be right there."

Wife: "Did you like the new shirts I bought you?"

The husband hates them.

Correct answer: "They're great. Thank you for taking such good care of me."

The husband can either not wear the shirts, wear them at home, or return them a few weeks later. If she asks about the shirts after he returns them, he can say that they were too small and the store didn't have his size, so he found some other shirts that fit better.

Most wives assume that a husband will do what they want if he only knows what it is. When he doesn't do it, they assume that they didn't express themselves clearly. They then ask again, with a more detailed explanation of what they want, and why. If he still doesn't do it, they "remind" him, or try to explain again, and louder. Men call this nagging.

There is a coffee mug that says, "It's not that I didn't hear you. I'm ignoring you." Most men dislike being told what to do, and many assert their autonomy and independence by ignoring a wife's nagging. They view a wife's requests as attempts to control them, even when a wife has neutral or loving intentions. Some men avoid confrontations by agreeing to do what a wife asks, then proving they are "real men" by not doing it.

Women often don't know that their attempts to show caring make men feel controlled or infantilized.

Laurel was a sweet woman who respected Glen, who was proud to be the family breadwinner. When he had a debilitating accident, she tried to help him by paying the bills, keeping the children away from him, and making family decisions. Instead of being grateful for her concern and love, he felt angry and emasculated. She unwittingly had stripped him of the very role that made him feel like a man, and he wanted his responsibilities back.

He needs to tell Laurel how he feels and get back his sense of control by reappropriating tasks that make him feel important and capable.

Isaac had a very demanding job and Yael worried that stress was ruining his health. He went to work at six every morning and came home exhausted twelve or more hours later. In short order, he developed neck pains, put on fifteen pounds, and had no time to exercise.

Being a loving wife, Yael went on a "nurturing" spree. She made him a chiropractic appointment and bought him a special contoured pillow for his neck. She enrolled him in a health club so that he would exercise and bought him books about heart disease and stress. Finally, she planned a "relaxing" weekend, a mere three hours' drive away.

When she surprised him with all of this, she was shocked that he blew up at her. She thought that he would appreciate the many hours that she had spent trying to help him, yet he fumed that she was trying to run his life. It never occurred to her that he would feel controlled. Since then, she has learned to ask if he would appreciate these kinds of "favors" before assuming that he would.

WAYS TO SHOW A MAN LOVE

Although both men and women want to be loved, the things that make each feel that way can differ. The following are some ways to show a man that you love him:

1. Look attractive. Ask your husband how he would like you to dress, and wear what pleases him. If he wants you to wear clothes that aren't suitable in public, wear them at home.

2. If you cover your hair, do it in an attractive way. A modest woman is supposed to look dignified and attractive, but not *attracting*. If a modestly dressed woman wants to wear comfortable clothes, she should do so without looking like a washerwoman. Don't dress better for strangers or friends than for your spouse.

3. Ask your husband if he wants you to wear makeup and perfume, and wear what he likes.

4. If it is important to your husband to live in a tidy house, try to keep things that way. If you need outside help or his cooperation, work on it together.

5. Try to plan Fridays so that the house will be clean and the children will be ready for *Shabbat* by the time you light the candles and he goes to synagogue.

6. Ask your husband when he likes to eat dinner and try to have it ready on time.

7. Make him food that he especially likes.

8. Put a love note in his lunch.

9. Buy him a treat that he wouldn't buy himself.

10. Manage your time so that you're not too tired or too busy to give him some undivided attention at night.

11. Give him time to be alone when he wants it.

12. Join Weight Watchers and start exercising if you need to lose weight or are out of shape.

13. Don't humiliate, nag, or criticize him when he makes a mistake or forgets to do something.

14. Make him feel like the center of your life at least once a day.

15. Greet him at the door when he comes home and show that you are excited to see him.

16. Compliment him.

17. Call him at work to say that you love him.

18. Tell him that you appreciate how hard he works to support you and the family.

19. Give him a backrub.

20. If he enjoys it, draw him a bath and wash his back.

21. Ask him to help you make a list of joint activities that he likes and do one every week.

22. Plan a vacation that includes activities he likes.

23. Ask him to discuss parts of his life that he finds meaningful, such as his work or his Torah studies.

24. Refuse to let the telephone, children, or friends interrupt when your husband is talking to you or when you are eating dinner together.

25. Buy him a birthday present that he will like, not what you think he should have.

26. Make his bed and leave a chocolate on his pillow.

27. Bring him a snack or cup of tea, coffee, or hot chocolate if he likes them.

28. Make him breakfast.

29. Arrange the children's schedule so that he can have time alone, take a nap, or relax for an hour.

30. Ask him if it is a good time to talk before assuming that it is.

31. Tell him some specific ways in which he makes you happy.

32. Thank him when he helps you around the house or with the children. (Don't tell him what he needs to do, or should have done, at the same time.)

33. Tell him at least five times as many things that he does that you appreciate than you criticize.

34. Be affectionate. Smile at him and give him a hug when you walk past him.

35. Let him know why he is special to you and how lucky you are to be married to him.

36. Wear something sexy to bed.

37. Tell him that you find him sexy and desirable.

38. Initiate lovemaking with him sometimes and be enthusiastic when he initiates it. If his hygiene needs improvement, suggest taking a shower together.

39. Empathize with his work stress without telling him how bad your day was at the same time.

40. Tell him how proud you are of his accomplishments.

41. Display a picture of him on your nightstand, or carry his picture in your wallet.

42. Compliment him in front of guests, friends, and family.

43. Remind yourself of what initially attracted you to him and what you now love about him. Share these memories and feelings with him.

44. Ask if you have a habit that he would like you to change and offer to work on it.

Every few weeks:

1. Buy a magazine, book, or newspaper that he likes.
2. Make a lunch or evening date with him.
3. Give up your Saturday nap and watch the kids so that he can recoup from an especially hard week.

Every few months or once a year:

1. Buy or make him a special present that you know he will like, such as a bathrobe, a new recliner chair, balloons that say, "You're the greatest," accessories for his computer or stereo, or books that he wouldn't buy himself.
2. Pamper him one day for no special reason. Make him breakfast, screen phone calls for him, wear his favorite outfit for you, and let him choose a place to go together for the day. If you can afford it, spend the night at a hotel or country inn.
3. Share an activity that he enjoys. If he skis and you don't, have lunch and aprés-ski together at the lodge. If he wants to go to a baseball, basketball, or hockey game and you aren't interested, take a good book or things to do and share his enthusiasm, or encourage him to go without you and have a good time.
4. Farm the kids out to your parents or friends so that you can spend a weekend alone together.
5. Tell him that you are all his for a day, and ask him how he would like to be taken care of.
6. Send his parents birthday, Mother's Day, holiday, anniversary, and get-well cards.

WAYS TO SHOW A WOMAN LOVE

While some men assume their wives know that they love them, most wives need this love reaffirmed several times a week or, preferably, every day. Men sometimes think that if they work forty hours a week to support the family, their wives should experience forty hours' worth of love, but this is not how women's emotions work. Work is something that has to be done, but time spent there doesn't create affection.

When we give charity, it is better to give smaller donations every day than one lump sum every year. This is because daily giving makes us more conscious of its importance and makes us more giving.[4]

This idea also applies to marriage. Giving tends to be part of a woman's nature, and most wives and mothers give freely and often. Men may need reminders or encouragement to do the same, but the more they give, the more loving they become.

Most wives would rather have husbands say, "I love you," give them hugs and kisses, and say words of appreciation for a total of five minutes every day than give them one big gift every month. Women expect a husband to do loving acts for them every day. Men are surprised that a wife may appreciate getting flowers every week more than getting a new dress every few months, even if the dress costs much more. Men are also shocked that the thrill and appreciation they get for giving an extravagant gift like a fur coat, expensive piece of jewelry, car, vacation, or home appliance only lasts for a few days. Women then expect a husband to give more expressions of love. Women's emotions are nurtured by the frequency of loving interactions and gifts, not by how much money or how many hours were spent buying them.

Couples need to regularly put deposits into their relationship account. Just as batteries slowly lose their charge with time and need recharging, our emotional batteries drain if they aren't recharged. Women recharge a husband's batteries by supporting and listening to him, cooking for him, making a comfortable home for him, and the like. Women need a husband to do much more than earn money, provide basic material needs and comfort to feel loved. Women need many personal "extras" to feel cared about. Below are some ways that a man can show his wife that he loves her. (It is great if men can do at least three or four of these every day):

1. Tell her that you love her.
2. Hold her for a few minutes before you get out of bed or before going to sleep if she likes this.
3. Have breakfast with her while giving her your undivided attention. Ask her about her plans for the day. Tell her that you'll miss her when you are at work.
4. Clear off the table after breakfast or dinner instead of expecting her to do it. Don't wait for her to ask for help.
5. Keep her company and talk to her as she cooks or cleans up the kitchen.
6. Have dinner together and let the answering machine or children take messages.
7. Tell her that you thought about her during the day.
8. Call her from work and tell her that you miss and love her.
9. Give her a hug and a kiss when you come home before doing anything else. Give her a hug and a kiss before leaving in the morning.
10. Tell her how pretty she is.
11. Compliment her. Notice when she wears something different, like a new perfume or a new dress, or when she goes out of her way to look attractive.
12. Notice when she puts up new decorations, buys new linens, pictures, and so forth.
13. Ask if she needs anything done around the house and do it without grumbling.
14. Help her do chores that you know are hard, distasteful, or tiring for her.
15. Make breakfast for her, even if it's just a cup of coffee.
16. Ask her about her day, and show interest in what she says.

17. When she complains, tell her, "I'm sorry things are so difficult for you." Empathize without getting defensive or offering solutions.

18. Make her a candlelit dinner. (If you can't cook, bring in take-out food and light candles.)

19. Make a picnic, preferably near a secluded stream, lake, or in a wooded glen where you can have privacy. Take a bottle of champagne (with unbreakable, plastic champagne glasses) for a romantic touch.

20. Read her poetry or a romantic chapter from a book.

21. Take her to a botanic garden, park, lake, or other romantic setting. Row her to the middle of a lake and propose to her.

22. Leave her love notes.

23. Write her poetry (Even three or four lines is fine).

24. Put your arms around her while she washes the dishes.

25. Give her a backrub or body massage. (If you don't know how, ask her to show you, and/or borrow a how-to book from the library.)

26. Caress her hand or cheek when you sit together.

27. Take her hand and give it a squeeze or a kiss when you are driving.

28. Wear clothes that she likes.

29. Put on her favorite music and dance with her at home.

30. Buy her presents that she would like. They don't have to be expensive. If you don't know her tastes or clothes size, check her wardrobe or ask her before making purchases.

31. Ask her what she'd like to do together and do it.

32. Tell her what a good cook she is.

33. Show appreciation when she does your laundry.

34. Make time to be alone with her without interruptions.

35. Offer to watch the kids or take them out so that she can have some time for herself.

36. Bring home her favorite dessert or other food.

37. Give her a hug when you pass by her in the house.

38. Make eye contact and smile at her. Blow her kisses when you are on the far side of the same room.

39. Tell her how happy she makes you.

40. Tell her how much you love her when she does something nice for you.

41. Tell her that she is very sexy.

42. Ask if there is anything you can do to make her happy.

43. Read her articles that will interest her while she is cooking, or nursing the baby.

44. Read to her at the end of the day. Choose something light, funny, romantic, or emotional, depending upon what she likes.

45. When she is tired or overwhelmed, clean up the kitchen and put the kids to bed so that she can take a relaxing bath. Surprise her with some bubble bath or fragrant oil.

46. Go for an evening stroll together. Hold her hand or put your arm around her.

47. Watch a sunset together.

48. Shovel the driveway, steps, and walkway after a snowstorm so that she doesn't have to do it.

49. Ask if there's anything that she would like to talk about.

50. Ask if you have one habit that she would like you to change and offer to work on it.

51. Help her on with her coat.

52. Speak warmly to her, then caress and kiss her for at least ten minutes (and preferably longer) before initiating foreplay.

53. Ask her to show you how she would like you to kiss and caress her.

54. Hold her after you make love.

55. Take her out to dinner and/or give her flowers after she goes to the *mikvah*.

It is a good idea for men to do one or more of these every few weeks:

1. Bring her flowers, candy, or a special treat. Greeting cards (homemade or commercial) are also nice. If you're on a limited budget, a rose on a pillow is nice. Make a paper rose if you can't afford the real thing.

2. Plan a date for the two of you to go somewhere that she would enjoy. If you don't know when your wife will be free, or what she would like to do, ask her before making plans. Make necessary reservations or buy tickets yourself instead of expecting her to do it.

3. Take care of the baby in the middle of the night so that she can sleep.

Things to do every few months or once a year:

1. Make all the arrangements for a vacation or a weekend getaway. If you can, pack her bags for her.

2. Ask her to choose a day when you will do whatever she wants.

3. Arrange a treasure hunt for her. Post a stick-it note on her bathroom mirror that gives a clue about where her first present is. When she finds the first present, note number two is attached. It will give a hint where the second "treasure" is, and so on. Hide between five and ten gifts, ending with the most extravagant one. For example, post note number one on her bathroom mirror. It says that it's time to toast your happy marriage. She goes to the toaster oven, where waffles are waiting for her. Note number two is on top of the toaster and tells her that listening is a lost art. She finds gift number two, a cassette tape, inside the stereo tape deck. The attached note cues her that you never know what goes on behind closed doors. She goes to her closet and finds gift number three, a new hat. She reads the clue for gift number four: "Some like Italian, some Russian, some French. But this has more to do with wood than with salad." When she looks inside her dresser ("dressing"), she finds three of her favorite magazines, and a clue about gift number five: "Roses are red, violets are blue, flowers are nice, and they're waiting for you." She goes to the florist, where she finds a bouquet of flowers waiting for her (already paid for,

of course). The note there gives her a clue to go to her favorite restaurant ("Let's meet for lunch"), where she and her husband eat a meal. The next clue leads her to a book of coupons, each of which is redeemable for one hour of time with her husband. The final clue directs her to the bedroom, where a gift-wrapped, beautiful nightgown awaits her. What a wonderful day of surprises!

4. Give her a gift certificate to get pampered in a beauty parlor with a beauty makeover, manicure, pedicure, massage, facial, and/or body wrap.

5. Offer to go shopping with her and buy her something that she likes.

6. Buy her a nice piece of jewelry.

7. Surprise her with a beautiful dress, coat, or scarf (if she wears them). (Take a full-length picture of her to show a saleswoman if you need help.)

8. Remember her birthday and your anniversary with a singing telegram and special gift. If you can afford them, champagne or a nice bottle of wine, a dozen red roses, a meal in her favorite restaurant, a special show or concert, or an evening cruise are all nice. If you go out, carry her over the threshold when you get home.

9. Send her balloons or flowers for no reason.

10. Tell people how wonderful she is in her presence.

Both men and women can give their spouse a short list of loving things that they'd like to do together or receive from each other. If you want to receive love notes and your spouse isn't comfortable writing them, model how to do it by writing them first. Buy, or borrow, a poetry book from a library and read to your spouse first if you'd like him to read to you.

If you want your spouse to buy you something that he or she has never bought before, detail precisely what you want. For example, instead of saying, "Can you buy me some chocolate?" try, "I would love for you to bring me a bag of chocolate kisses for Mother's Day. They sell them at the grocery store on the corner." Or, "Would you buy me a flower bouquet for *Shabbat?* There's a great florist next to the bakery, and he will put a beautiful bunch together for less than fifteen dollars."

Be sure to let your spouse know that you appreciate what he or she does for you, even if the result isn't exactly what you wanted. Don't assume that a good husband or wife will intuitively know what you want without any guidance. As a spouse learns what pleases you, and you reinforce their efforts, they are likely to give more spontaneously.

RESPECT

As was mentioned earlier, husbands usually need more respect than wives do. Husbands feel devastated when their wives compare them unfavorably to other men, belittle their achievements, or don't respect how hard they work. Unfortunately, some women don't realize how much their casual and critical comments hurt their husbands. For example, many men are offended when their wives disagree with them, especially in front of others. If you do this, ask your husband if it bothers him.

When couples disagree, it is better to mention your points of agreement, or at least acknowledge your partner's position, before voicing your differences.

A friend asked Marcia and Hal how they liked a new foreign film. Hal said, "What a stupid, boring movie. Don't waste your time or money seeing it."

Marcia liked the film and wanted to say, "It was a great film, but Hal doesn't know anything about French culture so he couldn't appreciate it." Instead she said, "Hal and I agree about most things, but we have different tastes in movies. He likes fun films, I like heavy mood-setters. This was a heavy film."

If either partner knows that making comments in front of a spouse will only provoke an unpleasant scene, they should keep their opinions to themselves. They can share them with friends when the spouse isn't around. (Derogating the spouse to friends or family is never okay. Sharing opinions about issues that one partner finds inflammatory can be reserved for more neutral settings.)

Allie was outspoken and frequently contradicted or disagreed with Israel. This made him feel insulted and humiliated, but he never let her know that. He just seethed inside while she thought that he appreciated her forthrightness.

Most husbands feel disrespected or insulted when a wife contradicts or disagrees with him, or shows greater knowledge or expertise than he has, especially if she does it in front of others. Women may not feel as injured if their husbands do this to them, so they may not know how painful most men find this, whether the men admit it or not.

Women should apologize when they disrespect their husbands, or their husbands will stay hurt and be distant. (Husbands, of course, should do the same if they hurt their wives' feelings.) Most men cannot love if they feel disrespected, and they are likely to withdraw or retaliate when they are hurt.

Justin tried to carve a hot turkey, which fell apart as he cut it. Liz knew that if she suggested waiting until the turkey cooled down, he would feel insulted and challenged and insist on doing it his way. So she said, "I forgot to season the turkey. Let me do it now, before you finish carving it." She dawdled in the kitchen until the poultry was cool, then brought it back to the table. Her sensitivity kept him from losing face, not to mention that it salvaged the meal.

Blair and Jordana planned a car trip to Washington. He insisted on driving, but refused to get directions. "I know how to read a map," he maintained. An hour later, they were hopelessly lost. He still refused to ask directions because that was tantamount to admitting his ignorance.

Jordana asked him to stop so that she could use a ladies' room. At the rest stop, she got directions and casually shared them with Blair when she got back in the car. He wasn't willing to ask a stranger for directions, nor let Jordana ask while he was with her, but he was willing to use the directions once she had them. Her womanly wiles preserved his dignity and got them to their destination.

Bob bought an "easy-to-assemble" bicycle, feeling proud that he saved $35 over the pre-fab model. After spending half a day trying to assemble it, he had made a Rube Goldberg contraption. He wouldn't get advice about how to fix it since his ego was on the line.

Jocelyn surreptitiously hid some small pieces, then showed him that something from the diagram was "missing." She offered to get the parts from the store later that week. Bob no longer felt that it was his fault that he couldn't assemble the bike, and he abandoned the project without losing face. Jocelyn took the bike back and paid to get it assembled.

Men's need for respect at home is so important that Jewish law institutionalizes it. Men are the heads of the household in many respects, and they perform many rituals for the entire family. For instance, they normally make *kiddush* (sanctification of the Sabbath and holidays over a cup of wine) for the family, say the blessing over bread on the Sabbath and holidays, lead the grace after meals, and head the Passover *seders*. A wife and children also follow her husband's religious customs if his family traditions differ from hers.

It is very important to some men that their wives ask about, and respect, their opinions and do what the men want. Consideration dictates that spouses consult each other about issues that affect each other or that involve their children.

Many husbands feel disrespected when a wife doesn't do what they ask, while women are more likely to interpret a husband's not doing what they want as a lack of love or concern. Both may assume that a spouse will do what they want if the spouse only considers them important enough.

Men often think that a wife expresses her feelings for him by how she takes care of him and their home, and they are apt to feel slighted if dinner is not ready when they come home, or if the house is messy. Religious men often expect the table to be set, the wife to be beautifully dressed, and the children ready to go to the synagogue when the Sabbath starts on Fridays. This doesn't happen in most homes, yet some men take it personally when it doesn't.

Wives, like husbands, would like appreciation and respect for what they do. Yet some men can't understand what they should appreciate about a woman who stays home "doing nothing" all day. If they would switch roles, they would see why cooking, doing housework, running errands, and taking care of children is so difficult, especially if they have paid jobs at the same time.

Wives feel respected when husbands value their wives' time and help them. When a husband shops, cooks, cleans, and/or takes care of the children, his actions express his appreciation and say that her time is important. Husbands should never give their wives the message that housework and childrearing are beneath men, or that women are not capable of anything better. Husbands must make wives feel loved and dignified, and wives must make husbands feel respected and loved.

DIFFERENT STYLES

Since men are trained to be independent and competitive, they solve their problems by withdrawing and focusing on issues as they block out everything else. Their inability to focus on multiple tasks leads to their getting irritated by interruptions at home and makes their wives angry that they don't see the totality of what needs to be done in running a house and raising children.

Women are adept at juggling many projects simultaneously, like taking care of children, running errands, making phone calls, cooking, cleaning, and tending to a husband. They don't understand why men feel overwhelmed just filling a woman's shoes for a few hours or days. But the answer is simple—men aren't women!

Someone in a competition must block out distractions and be single-minded about achieving a goal. Someone who is trained to collaborate, as women are, must be aware of the totality of a situation and the many factors that need attention at once. Thus, most women can focus on and complete many tasks simultaneously, while most men find the many distractions and disruptions of running a home and raising children very difficult to handle. This is illustrated by the fact that we take for granted mothers who work full-time, manage a home, and raise children, but are impressed when a father does the same.

Part of men's independence is that they feel humiliated asking for help or information. They think that means they are incompetent, stupid, and ignorant, so some tend not to ask for their wives' opinions and advice. Meanwhile, wives want to be asked because it makes them feel included and valued. They feel discounted if a husband doesn't think enough of them to consider their thoughts and ideas.

God made Eve an *ezer kenegdo,* a "helping opponent," to Adam.[5] This means that part of a woman's nature is to want to nurture a husband and help him. When she does this in a way that he doesn't appreciate, such as by offering helpful suggestions that he doesn't want, he feels offended, infantilized, disrespected, or controlled. At such times she is like an opponent, not a helper. Men like to think that they can accomplish goals on their own. It hurts their egos when a wife thinks they need improvement, advice, or help. Men (and women) want lots of acceptance, encouragement, and admiration, and little criticism and recommendations.

Max didn't like to answer to anyone and saw no reason to let Yaffa know when he went to play tennis, jogged, ran errands, or visited his friends. This made her feel excluded and ignored. When Yaffa brought this to his attention, they worked out a compromise that suited them both. Max told her his plans in advance, and she encouraged him to do what he wanted without criticizing his choices.

Many women complain that husbands don't spend enough time with them. Some wives think that if their husbands only loved them enough, they would put their work and hobbies on a back burner and spend more time together. But men who are emotionally invested in their work or other activities won't slow down until they retire or get debilitated. Men's strong need for achievement cannot be fulfilled through personal relationships alone. A wife's love and support is important, but it is fulfilling in a different way than work is. Some men even feel smothered or distressed by spending more than minimal time with their wives.

Sometimes consulting a rabbi or therapist will encourage a man to spend more time with his wife. At other times, a wife will have unrealistic expectations and need to give her husband more space. In either case, women who can't get enough time with their husbands must create alternatives to intimacy or companionship with him. They can do this by socializing with girlfriends, taking classes, working on community projects, and enjoying activities alone.

SHARING KNOWLEDGE

Most spouses like to feel they have something unique to offer a partner, and they enjoy sharing what they know. Asking a spouse to teach us makes him or her feel good and also benefits us.

Danielle is not very assertive and feels uncomfortable asking for help. She was at wits' end using her computer but was afraid to ask Julius for help because she didn't want him to think that she was stupid. When she had no choice but to ask him how to use her program, he felt pleased that he could teach her, and she felt grateful for his support.

Herman was a wealthy businessman who was ashamed of his learning disability. Only his wife knew why he avoided reading letters, books, and newspapers. He was fiercely independent, but by allowing his wife to read to him, they grew closer. She felt needed, trusted, and valued, and he felt indebted to her for opening up a world that had been closed to him for most of his life.

HELPFUL EXERCISES

The following exercises are helpful for couples who want to bridge their differences. Do one exercise at a time, and implement it for a week before going to the next one:

1. Discuss which phrases you each use that your partner misunderstands or finds irritating or upsetting. Are there better ways to say what you mean?

2. Tell your spouse between one and three things that he or she says or does that make you feel disrespected. The spouse should listen without defending him- or herself, apologize for hurting your feelings, and ask what to say or do differently.

3. Together, review the ways that men and women show love (earlier in this chapter) and check off those items that you would like to do for your spouse, and what you would like him or her to do for you. Add items that aren't on the list. Do at least three items on your partner's list every day.

4. Tell your spouse one thing that you would especially like during the next week. (It should be specific and reasonably doable.)

5. Discuss your needs for intimacy and independence/space. Try to work out ways to fulfill each other's needs while respecting your differences.

SUMMARY

By recognizing how men and women differ, couples can accept and work around their differences. Mutual respect, good communication, compromise, hard work, and a good sense of humor are useful ingredients in this process.

NOTES

1. Rambam, *Mishneh Torah, Hilchot Ishut* 15:19–20.
2. Ibid.
3. Genesis 3:20.
4. See *Avot* 3:15; Rambam, Mishnah Commentary, ad loc.
5. Genesis 2:20.

SUGGESTED READING

Freeman, Arthur, and DeWolf, Rose. *Ten Dumbest Mistakes People Make and How to Avoid Them.* New York: Harper Collins, 1992.
Gray, John. *Men Are from Mars, Women Are from Venus.* New York: Harper Collins, 1992.

15

Solving Problems

Couples' problems have many aspects to them. Some are logistical or pragmatic, such as when a wife wants her husband to tell her where to buy items that he needs. Some are social, such as deciding how early to leave a party without insulting the host, or determining what is a reasonable amount to spend on a gift. Many problems have emotional overtones, such as when a wife wants her husband to tell his parents that they can't visit as planned. And some issues are spiritual, such as deciding if a butcher or a restaurant is reliably kosher, or finding a rabbi who is acceptable to both husband and wife.

Few marital problems fit neatly into one category. Even when problems seem to be logistical, spiritual, or social, emotional issues usually play a role, too.

Couples can't solve problems unless they recognize what the real issues are and communicate on the same wavelength about them. For instance, a husband may be satisfied with a logical solution that is emotionally unacceptable to his wife, or she may opt for a spiritually satisfying solution that makes no sense to him. They will not resolve these conflicts until they address the issues on their spouse's terms.

Don thought that he was making a straightforward request when he asked Helen to reschedule her parents' visit. He didn't want them around when he came back from an exhausting business trip. He needed a few days to unwind first.

But Don's practical solution raised emotional issues for Helen since it involved her parents. She was looking forward to seeing them for the first time in four months. If they came a few days later, they would have little time together. She also believed that Don was using the business trip as a pretext to avoid seeing her mother, with whom he didn't get along.

Helen and Don will reach an impasse as long as she sees this as an emotional issue and he approaches it logically. He has to acknowledge her annoyance and disappointment and admit that he would feel the same way if he were in her shoes. She needs to acknowledge his need to decompress.

Once they offer this kind of understanding, they can solve the problem by compromising. If he is adamant about not wanting Helen's parents to come as planned, he can offer to treat everyone to dinner if his in-laws come a week later, and let them stay as long as they wish. Or, he can offer to pay for them to stay in a hotel if they come at the already agreed-upon date.

We don't solve some problems if we miss what our spouse is really trying to convey and only speak our language, not theirs. Is she or he trying to share information? Is she or he asking for a practical suggestion, or looking for emotional support? Since women often converse in order to make emotional connections, husbands may not realize that their apparent requests for information or help are really efforts to feel close. Women may not realize that a husband's description of his day is a search for affirmation, not advice. Before trying to resolve an issue, couples should ask what kind of response their partner is looking for (support, suggestions, agreement, and so on). Then they can address the real issues.

A wife who complains usually wants support or a listening ear and will feel better when she gets it.

Alice had a very difficult pregnancy. She had morning sickness, felt tired, and slept poorly at night. Whenever Marty asked her how she felt, she usually said, "I'm tired," "I'm not feeling great," or "I'm nauseous." His impulse was to tell her to eat differently, to take vitamins, or to try taking a warm shower before going to bed. But he knew that everyone else gave her advice and she didn't need that from him. Instead, he made her feel loved and taken care of. He said, "I'm so sorry that having our child is so hard on you. I wish that I could make it easier." His support was exactly what she needed, so she didn't feel the need to elaborate on her aches and pains. She changed the subject and talked about more pleasant matters.

Many men get annoyed when wives complain instead of fixing their problems. When women complain repeatedly, some husbands stop listening or dismiss their wives' complaints. Instead, men should offer "chicken soup" — words and gestures that show concern and caring. Women who want nurturing will stop complaining once they get it and will talk about something else.

Men should never tell women that their feelings are exaggerated or unwarranted, even if objectively that is true. It makes women feel belittled and ignored. People who overreact to "minor" issues often have a strong need to be in control, and/or tend to lump many upsets together. (Sometimes people also overreact because they have a biochemical disorder or are exhausted.) Ideally, people who frequently overreact should learn to put matters into perspective, see upsets as individually manageable, and modulate their responses. Spouses, though, are rarely the ones to help someone do this.

Empathizing with spouses usually disarms them and takes away their upset and anger. If a spouse is upset with us, he or she won't hear our side of things until we first show that we appreciate and understand his or her feelings. Remember, when two people simultaneously try to get their feelings across so that each feels understood, they are having mutual monologues, not communicating. Communication requires one speaker and one listener, not two speakers. When we listen and validate our partner so that he or she feels understood, we can ask our partner to appreciate our feelings about an issue. Only after both sides feel understood are we likely to find a workable solution to the problem.

Couples commonly miscommunicate when one person wants emotional validation (usually the woman) while the other wants to solve a logical problem (usually the man). We can only resolve practical problems by first dismantling a spouse's emotional barriers and making that person feel that we are their friend and ally. As long as one or both spouses see only their differences, or don't feel understood, they will feel like enemies. Even if we disagree with a spouse's perspective, we can only resolve conflicts by first showing our spouse that we understand how he or she feels.

Robert bought Ida a cassette tape, some makeup and makeup brushes, and costume jewelry for her birthday. She was pleased to get the tape but not the other gifts.

"It was sweet of you to remember my birthday," she began, "but I'm not sure what these other gifts are for. You know that I already have all the makeup and jewelry that I need."

"Well," Robert smiled, "This was my way of suggesting that you try a new look."

Ida got angry. "I resent your using my birthday to make me over. I've told you many times that your taste in makeup and clothes doesn't suit me. I already wear what you want around the house, even though I don't like the way it looks. A birthday present is supposed to be what the recipient appreciates, not what the giver wants for himself."

"So take it all back and get what you want," Robert barked angrily.

"No. Why should I have to return stuff that I never asked for . . . ?"

This interaction will be unproductive as long as Robert feels unappreciated and attacked and Ida feels manipulated. Let's see how they can get back on track:

Robert can start by sincerely apologizing. "I'm sorry, Ida, but I did want to make you happy. I guess that I was selfish, and I shouldn't have used your birthday to get what I wanted. I *would* like to get you a present that you'd appreciate. What can I buy you?"

Ida's anger melted when he apologized and validated her. "Actually, I love the tape, and that's enough of a present. I don't need you to get me more things. How about if we go out for a romantic walk on the seashore? I'd rather have your company than gifts."

Note that Robert did not defend what he did this time because that would have escalated the conflict. He suppressed his desire to say, "What's the big deal about dressing the way that I like?" Had he done that, it would only have made her feel misunderstood and egged her on to counterattack, "I think that your tastes are ridiculous. You have a problem if you don't think that understated makeup and classic clothes are attractive." And so on, *ad nauseum*.

Robert successfully disarmed Ida by apologizing for hurting her feelings, even though he didn't believe that he did anything wrong. He actually thought that she was pretty insensitive for reacting the way she did, but he didn't get caught up in justifying himself because that would have perpetuated the conflict. He had to choose whether to be right or to resolve the conflict. He chose the latter. He did this by having the humility to admit that she had reason to be upset. Tuning into her hurt feelings allowed her to tune into his hurt and try to make him feel better.

Had he insisted that she was "too" upset, or given examples of his friends' wives who wore the kind of makeup that he liked, or explained why his tastes were fine, it would have escalated their conflict. Pointing out how right we are when our partner doesn't feel understood only leads to greater distance and anger.

After letting this issue rest for a few days, Robert said, "I know that you find my tastes in makeup, jewelry, and clothes repulsive." (Even though it's hard to say this, we foster compromise by acknowledging our partner's point of view.) "I don't want to impose my tastes on you, but it would make me really happy if you would dress the way I'd like when we go out. If you would do that for me, I'll go anywhere you want for the evening."

By (1) acknowledging a spouse's feelings, and (2) offering something a spouse wants in return for doing what we want, we maximize our chances of getting satisfaction.

Some problems cannot be solved by giving a spouse what he or she wants. When that happens, we should still validate their feelings and soothe them emotionally.

Bezalel's wife was embarrassed by driving their ten-year-old car, and hated the nuisance and expense of getting it repaired every month or two. She told him that she wanted another car, but they could not afford one.

He could have said defensively, "What's the matter with you? We don't have money to throw away on a new car! It's not the end of the world for you to drive an old one. In my family, we always keep the same car for at least twelve years." Doing that would only have hurt her feelings and led to a fight.

Instead, he acknowledged her by saying, "Jeanie, I wish that I could buy you another car, and it upsets me that you have to drive our jalopy. You really deserve better. As soon as we can save enough money, let's get you a better car."

Even though he can't give her the object that she wants, he gave her the support and understanding that she wanted, which was the next best thing.

It can't be stressed enough that the major reason that couples don't resolve problems is that they don't address each other's feelings about issues. We often have to choose between being "right" now and being happy in the long run. Proving ourselves right or our partner wrong is not productive. What's important is understanding and validating a spouse's feelings and perspective so that we can both be happy and have a generally satisfying marriage.

SPEAKING A SPOUSE'S LANGUAGE

Before we try to resolve conflicts with a spouse, we must know what the real issues are. Otherwise, we will spin our wheels addressing matters that are irrelevant. A good way to do this is to ask a spouse what feelings or perspectives are motivating their responses to us.

Ingrid asked Marc to make the kids tuna salad, corn, and vegetables for dinner, but he wanted to relax. Without discussing his feelings with her, he ordered pizza from a take-out store. Ingrid got very angry and proceeded to give a long explanation about why the children needed nutritious food, thinking that this would convince Marc to make dinner. Since the real issue was that he didn't want to be bothered preparing food, her logical arguments got them nowhere. He didn't care if eating pizza was less nutritious than eating tuna and vegetables. She would have discovered what the real issue was by asking Marc, "What did you think of my request that you make the kids dinner?"

Once she finds out that he wants to be comfortable, she should acknowledge his feelings, then ask if he will do her a favor and help her out. That is likely to be much more productive than giving him a nutrition lecture.

Jeff explained to Cindy that she was too lax about keeping kosher, but she insisted that her standards were fine. He tried logically to convince her otherwise, but it didn't work. Until he recognizes that she has an emotional barrier to changing, he will waste his time giving her logical arguments.

We can be motivated by "truth," logic, or feelings. When couples have different values and motivations, we are most likely to get what we want by asking our spouse to do us a favor or by speaking to his or her values and motivations. We are least likely to achieve our goal by convincing our partner to see things from our point of view if it is very different from theirs.

Dick and Nurit agreed that they needed a dining room table, but he wanted a sturdy, durable, and reasonably priced one. She was most concerned with how pretty it was and how well it would fit the decor of the house. The table that she wanted cost $800, while his cost $300.

They thought about this from their partner's point of view: She could not convince him that her table was worth the extra $500 because it was not better made. However, he convinced her that the table would be covered most of the time, anyway, so they might as well buy the cheaper table, and cover it with beautiful lace tablecloths. Since Dick valued cost and value and she valued esthetics, they found a compromise that took both into account.

Asher is forty pounds overweight, eats unhealthy food, and leads a sedentary life. His wife can't understand why he won't take better care of himself and see the long-term consequences of what he's doing. All he thinks about is his present comfort. Even though she believes that he is setting himself up for health problems, lecturing him about heart attacks, cancer, and strokes will be a waste of time. Since he is motivated by comfort, urging him to do uncomfortable things and trying to reason with him will be fruitless. However, since he tends to eat whatever is in the house, the best way to get him to change is by stocking the house with healthy foods that he finds tasty and asking him to walk with her a few times a week. He is unlikely to be philosophically swayed to her way of life, so she might as well put her effort into changing his environment so that he will act differently.

Jo enjoys smoking cigarettes. Her husband has shown her articles about the dangers of smoking, but she thinks these disasters will never happen to her. Facts won't convince her to give up her cancer sticks, but her daughter's upset feelings about it might. Only emotions that are stronger than the pleasure she gets from smoking will dissuade Jo from continuing. Facts and information will not.

Some people procrastinate, act self-destructively, or passive-aggressively to avoid discomfort. We won't convince them to act differently by pointing out that their behavior creates terrible problems in the long run. People who want to avoid discomfort now don't care about the future. They are only concerned with the present.

Phillip had a mild pain in his tooth that got progressively worse until he had no choice but to see the dentist. By the time he went, he needed a root canal. The dentist told him to come back in three months and maintain scrupulous dental hygiene. Since the dentist had relieved his immediate pain, Phillip ignored the advice and didn't go back for another two years. By that time, he needed six fillings and periodontal surgery. Phillip is the kind of person who will never take preventive action as long as the disasters he creates can be fixed. His wife will waste her time trying to convince him that his behavior is self-defeating. The best she can do is to make it more comfortable for him to be responsible now.

Margaret managed money poorly. Balancing the checkbook made her anxious because she had to confront how little money she had. So she didn't pay bills for a few months at a time in order to accumulate savings, while she charged as many expenses as possible to her credit card. She liked this because it gave her the illusion of having more money. Being responsible was much less important to her than feeling comfortable. Lecturing her about ruining their credit and describing how awful it is to get nasty letters and phone calls from collection agencies will be useless. Sammy should limit how much she can spend by cancelling their credit card and closing their joint account, then paying the bills himself.

Greg needed to change jobs, but he couldn't bear the thought of being rejected, so he avoided sending out a resumé or going on interviews. Bella felt angry about this, but knew that it wouldn't be productive to make Greg feel even more inadequate. She conquered her impulse to put him down or lecture him about how irresponsible he was; she realized that his poor self-esteem was the real problem. The only way that he would apply for a new job was if he felt better about himself and his abilities.

Bella asked if they could work on his job search together, and he was willing. She told him that he underestimated his strengths, and suggested ways that he could highlight them on his resumé. Her support and understanding, instead of criticism, made him feel better. Next, they brainstormed about how he could minimize his one weakness (having only a bachelor's degree in a field where most people had a master's degree) and locate potential employers who would count experience and ability. Later that week she suggested rehearsing in mock interviews, and they spent an evening doing role plays. She played Greg, and he played interviewers. She showed him how to respond positively to difficult questions, then they switched roles. Two weeks later, Greg sent out some resumés and got an interview the following month.

They rehearsed interviewing the night before, and Bella encouraged him to see the meeting as a learning experience, not an evaluation of his worth. Although he didn't get that job because they wanted someone with skills he didn't have, he realized that he had catastrophized how bad interviewing would be. After three more interviews, he got a suitable job.

They were able to solve this problem because Bella was supportive instead of critical, she helped him feel more adequate and competent, and she got rid of his barriers of fear. Had she only tried to convince him to try harder to get a job, he wouldn't have.

Harvey often shirked his personal and family responsibilities but always helped his friends. When he had to choose, he put his friends ahead of his wife. This made Shirona furious, but his friends and acquaintances thought that he was wonderful. His freedom to socialize with friends who made few demands on him was more important than being with his critical wife.

Rather than attempt to change his need to be a social person, Shirona tried to work with it. It was useless trying to get him to give up being with his friends, so she stopped making him choose. She encouraged him to spend one night a week with them while she spent those evenings seeing her friends or playing the piano. When he wanted to go out more often, she asked him to help her get the kids to bed first and encouraged him to have a pleasant evening.

Knowing that he didn't have to choose between his wife and his friends made him feel less smothered. That improved his marriage, and he actually went out less often than he had previously. Once Shirona gave him "permission" to socialize and be free, he was more interested in being with her.

Elisheva was a computer programmer with three young children. She often stayed up very late making *Shabbat* food for poor families or baking pastries and cakes for parlor meetings. Her volunteer work exhausted her, but she thrived on the kudos that she got for it. Mitchell tried to convince her to stop doing this, but she wouldn't hear of it.

Rather than try to take away this source of social approval, Mitchell asked what it meant for her to do volunteer work. She replied that feeling admired and appreciated was important to her, and she rarely got this at home or at work. Baking also gave her a chance to be creative, and it relaxed her.

Now that he understood what motivated his wife to bake, Mitchell could think about how to propose a compromise that would keep her from being so tired and would also encourage her to spend more time with him. First he acknowledged how good it must feel to be appreciated by so many people. Next, he told her that he would prefer if she could find a way to do this that didn't take such a physical toll on her. Then he acknowledged that he was remiss in not telling her more often how much he enjoyed what she did as a mother and wife. Finally, he asked if she would consider altering her late-night baking so that they could spend more time together.

Elisheva was surprised by Mitchell's approach. She had previously resented him telling her to give up the one activity that gave her pleasure. She was pleased that he finally acknowledged her feelings in a supportive way. They decided to cook dinner together one night a week and go out one night a week. Mitchell also offered to put the kids to bed two nights a week so that she could bake then. Elisheva offered to close up shop by 11:00 those nights so she wouldn't be exhausted.

These vignettes illustrate how important it is to know what motivates a partner before you address issues. You must speak a spouse's language by using emotional arguments to persuade an emotional person, logical arguments to persuade a logical mate, and so forth, and then incorporate something that gratifies a spouse's needs into any solution you propose.

Lee wants his wife to visit his parents for a weekend, but Stephanie hates them. She will do whatever makes her comfortable and doesn't care what others think about her behavior. Although she loves Lee, she does not feel that she should endure visits to two people who disparage her. He will not convince her to go by telling her that it's really not so bad or that it's the right thing to do. She doesn't care about that. Instead, he should empathize with how unpleasant it is for her and suggest ways that he can make it nicer. He can suggest that they go on a picnic at a nearby lake, or to a romantic piano bar, or go shopping together at a mall if she will join him. She agrees because he made the trip more pleasant for her.

Maya and Dov want to buy a house. She likes one that costs $20,000 more than the one he wants, but they can afford either one. His considerations are financial while hers are esthetic and social. She won't convince him to buy the more expensive house by saying that she will be happier there. He thinks that she should be content with the cheaper house. But she can "sell" him on her house by speaking to his motivations and concerns. She tells him that its location makes it a better value, and, if they resell it, they will recoup their higher initial investment. She points out that its workmanship and insulation are better, making it cheaper to maintain and heat. She also reminds him that renovations on the cheaper house will increase its real cost and so on. She succeeds in convincing him.

Ken would like Felice to be more religious, but she won't if it interferes with her social life. If she doesn't relate to spirituality (yet), telling her that observant Judaism will make her life more meaningful will fall on deaf ears. She might, however, be open to his lifestyle if he first introduces her to interesting and enjoyable religious people. When she is comfortable with religious people, he can suggest inviting them to their home and make this pleasant for her by taking care of the kosher food himself. When she is comfortable with kosher food and new friends, she may not mind if they take the next step and make the kitchen kosher. By "speaking her language," Ken encourages Felice to try his new way of life without taking away an important part of hers. People are loathe to give up what they have before they have something comparable to replace it.

STEPS FOR PROBLEM SOLVING

The process of making decisions is at least as important as the decisions themselves. The Torah teaches us this lesson by saying that God consulted His "Heavenly entourage" before creating people.[1] Surely He did not need to ask anyone whether or not to create man! He did this to teach us the importance of consulting others whenever our actions will affect them.

Margie had invited twenty guests for the Passover *seder.* Although he didn't want extra work to do, Harvey asked how he could help her prepare. She felt good that he recognized how hard she worked and wanted to ease her burden. Had he waited for Margie to tell him what to do, Harvey's lack of sensitivity would have hurt her feelings and made her angry. What he ended up doing was less important than the fact that he offered to help.

Stanley asked Yonit to plan their vacation, but she didn't want to because she already had many other tasks to do. She resentfully did it, then bickered with him throughout their vacation.

He should have told her, "I know that it's not fair to ask you to plan our vacation, and you already have so much to do, but can you do it as a favor to me? (This shows empathy and understanding.) I'll try to make it worth your while by doing whatever you want while we're away, as long as it fits into our budget."

She planned a trip to Hawaii, replete with snorkeling and a helicopter ride. While he wouldn't normally have been so adventurous, he had a wonderful time. He treated her to a massage at the hotel as a thank-you. The way they resolved their problem left them with good feelings about each other, and they enjoyed their trip together.

Ideally, both partners should do the following when they negotiate issues:

1. Show sensitivity to each other's feelings.
2. Respect a partner's differences and ideas.
3. Make a partner feel loved and taken care of.

4. Share power and responsibilities.

5. Develop solutions that are realistic and specific.

When couples have a problem that they aren't resolving easily, they can do the following:

1. *Set a mutually convenient time to discuss the issue.*

This should be when neither partner will be a poor listener because she or he is too hungry, too tired, too angry, or preoccupied with other matters. It must also be when the couple will not be interrupted by telephone calls, children, and so on. (Put on the answering machine, or go for a walk.)

2. *Define the problem, trying to be as neutral as possible.*

For example, "We can't seem to agree about how to get Becky to do her homework," or "We disagree about the time frame in which we should get our tax returns completed." Don't blame, attack, or insult each other when you define the problem. Don't say things like, "You never take responsibility for helping Becky with her homework," or "I'm at my wit's end because you still haven't gotten your tax records in order."

Defining a problem shows couples that they have a common goal, although they may differ in the ways they want to get there.

3. *Take responsibility for what you each contribute to the problem.*

Don't tell your partner what she or he doesn't do right. Even if one person is only 5 percent responsible and the other partner is 95 percent, each needs to take responsibility for his or her contribution. Couples' problems are usually interactive problems, and it is useless to see them only as caused by one person.

For example, Leo and Beth defined their problem as, "We disagree about how much time Beth should spend with the baby and with Leo." Leo believed that the problem was Beth's over-involvement with the baby and neglect of him. Beth believed that the problem was Leo's jealousy and possessiveness. His admitting that he didn't do enough household chores or shopping to free Beth's time and her admitting that she spent most of her time with the baby when Leo was home put them on their way to finding a solution.

4. *List all of the things that you have done to try to solve the problem. Note which, if any, have been successful.*

When Leo and Beth did this, they determined that Leo often asked Beth to ignore the baby's fussing or crying. That angered her because it made her feel that Leo was insensitive. He also criticized her caretaking and yelled at her. The more critical and angry he became, the more Beth took comfort in the baby and withdrew from him. That made Leo feel even more neglected. They had never tried anything that made the problem better.

5. *Set specific goals, stating what you want in positive terms.*

Define your goals behaviorally, stating what each spouse wants more of. For example, Leo says that he wants to spend more time with Beth giving him her undivided attention. (A poorly stated goal is for Beth to spend less time with the baby.) Beth wants Leo to talk to her about subjects that are of interest to both of them. (A poorly stated goal would be that she wants Leo to stop criticizing her and being angry.)

The couple states what they want to accomplish, not what each is doing wrong, and they identify what each wants more of. Saying that they want more "affection" or "time together" is too vague. Leo specifies that he wants at least thirty minutes a day when Beth will talk to him without interruption, when she's not taking care of the baby.

Beth adds that she wants Leo to listen when she tells him about her day and empathize without giving advice. She also wants him to clean up the kitchen after dinner two nights a week so that she can have time to relax.

6. *Brainstorm, and write down all of the possible solutions that you can think of to help you achieve your goals, even if they seem unrealistic or silly.*

By putting their heads together without censoring themselves, couples can often find solutions to previously "unsolvable" problems. They might even laugh at some of these solutions.

Beth and Leo wrote down the following:

a. Beth can let the baby cry for ten minutes after putting her to sleep before picking her up.

b. Leo could do the dishes after dinner twice a week.

c. Leo could ask Beth about her day while she nurses the baby.

d. Leo could do more housework and shopping so that Beth will have more free time to spend with him.

e. They could go for evening walks with the baby in the stroller.

f. They could get a babysitter and go out once or twice a week.

g. Leo could tell Beth that she is a terrific mother when he feels like criticizing her, then add that he feels lonely.

h. They could make a date to spend time together every day.

7. *Discuss each solution.*

After brainstorming, discuss the pros and cons of each solution you came up with and whether it is likely to get you closer to your goal. For example, Leo and Beth decided that going for evening walks was not a great idea because Beth was too tired then, and Leo's cleaning the kitchen on a regular basis was not realistic because his work schedule was too erratic. Most of the other solutions seemed pretty good.

8. *Decide which one of the possible solutions you will try first.*

Although more than one solution may improve the problem, don't try to do too much too quickly. Start with one solution that seems reasonable and doable. Beth and Leo decided to try getting a babysitter so they could go out.

9. *Concretize how each of you will implement that solution by identifying the steps you must take to get to your goal.*

It is important not to be too general or vague. They decided that Beth would find a sitter for Tuesday nights from 7 to 10:30. Leo would pick her up and take her home. They would spend the evening going to a restaurant that Leo chose, and he would make the reservations. Beth would limit her time talking about the baby and problems at home to ten minutes on these dates, but Leo would show that he appreciated how she felt when she did this.

The couple whose problem was getting Becky to do her homework agreed that the husband, Tom, would get more involved. They concretized this by deciding that he would go over her homework with her from 7 to 7:30 every Monday, Wednesday, and Thursday night. Martha agreed not criticize the way that he explained things to Becky and to back him if Becky complained that he made her work too hard.

The couple with the tax problem agreed to work on the problem together. They concretized this by deciding that Sheldon would buy a small filing cabinet and a pack of twenty-five files on Sunday. Merle would help him set up a filing system with categories of deductions on the tax returns. They would then spend the rest of the day sorting through their records together and putting them in the appropriate files. Sheldon would take the files to the accountant the following Sunday.

10. *Set a time to assess your progress.*

In Leo and Beth's case, they set a "review date" for the fourth Tuesday night after they arrived at their solution. They thought that this would give them enough time to see if Leo was still feeling neglected. Martha and Tom decided that Sunday night, two weeks later, would be a good time to assess their progress. Sheldon and Merle decided that the following Sunday was their benchmark.

When couples set a date, they should decide what will be the signs that the problem is getting better. What will be happening more?

11. *When you review your progress, note the plans that worked and reinforce each other for your good work. Then note whatever still needs improvement and concretize how to do that.*

Leo and Beth decided that their plan worked very well, and their brainstorming had planted seeds in their minds about other things they could do. Leo had already stopped criticizing Beth when he felt neglected and occasionally complimented her on her good mothering instead. She made more of an effort to be attentive to him. They reinforced each other for their good work and concretized another plan for improving their relationship further.

This kind of problem solving tends to be very effective because it identifies a goal, makes spouses partners in finding a way to get there, and defines concrete and doable steps to make it happen.

UNDERSTANDING RESISTANCES

Couples can reach impasses solving problems when one spouse is not willing to do what the other one wants. While there are many possible reasons for this, it is often because the resistant spouse does not feel understood, or because what is asked of him or her is emotionally threatening or painful. For example, something that is no big deal to one spouse may feel like a major concession to the other. What makes one partner feel secure makes the other feel humiliated or powerless. One spouse may have strong feelings about a request that is emotionally neutral to the other. When a spouse isn't receptive to something we want, we need to check out what our request means to him or her.

Elliot, Peggy, and their five-year-old son Andy ate dinner with some friends. When Andy finished his meal, he made a beeline for the refrigerator and emerged with a prized dish of chocolate pudding. Halfway through, he offered the soggy remains to a guest. The guest assumed that his parents had taught him to be polite and that he was going through the motions of sharing his dessert with others.

Elliot told the guest otherwise. "Andy must really like you. Pudding is his favorite food, and he never shares it with anyone."

Until Elliot explained, the guest didn't realize how much Andy's gesture meant.

This same idea frequently plays out in marriage. A wife may think that she is asking for a small favor, while her husband sees it as a supreme sacrifice, and vice versa.

Marvin wanted marriage to be a partnership in which he and Betty shared everything. She wanted to share many things, but also wanted Marvin to respect her boundaries. One day, she ordered ice cream at a café while Marvin had coffee. When her dessert arrived, he wanted to share it. He was shocked and angry when she refused.

This scenario repeated itself every time they ate dessert. Marvin asked Betty to share what she had, she turned him down, and he got angry. Finally, he asked her why she never shared food with him, and she explained, "When I was growing up, I had to watch my diet very carefully, and rarely got treats. To this day, it makes me feel violated to have to share food that I really like with anyone." From then on, Marvin ordered his own dessert and offered some to his wife.

Betty asked Marvin to go skiing with her, but he felt that it was a waste of time. Not only didn't he enjoy it, they skied separately most of the time because she went down the expert slopes and he did not. Using time productively was extremely important to him, so he preferred to do things together that they both enjoyed. She decided to go skiing with a friend and went elsewhere with Marvin.

Betty viewed her long hair as part of her femininity, and it pained her to cut it. Marvin begged her to try a short haircut, but she wouldn't hear of it. He couldn't understand why she wouldn't do such a small thing for him, and she couldn't understand how he could ask so much of her. She would never ask him to amputate his leg, so why would he ask her to amputate her hair?!

Marvin can't understand how she can feel so strongly about hair. But instead of trying to argue her out of her feelings, he accepts it and stops asking her to change.

Betty asked Marvin to buy furniture with her, but he gave a million excuses to avoid going. He hated shlepping around while she decided what to buy. This upset Betty because buying furniture symbolized building a home, and she wanted to do it with her husband. Marvin thought that shopping was a necessary evil and preferred to avoid it. They compromised by shopping together two more times. He read a book while she looked at the furniture, and he gave his opinion when she had narrowed down her choices.

ENCOURAGING COMPROMISE

We encourage a partner to compromise if we offer something they want in return. It also helps if we acknowledge their concessions, even if they don't seem like a big deal to us. We need to put ourselves in a spouse's shoes to appreciate what they are giving up, not discount it because we would readily do the same. Telling a spouse that what we want is only reasonable or fair will backfire if our spouse thinks that we are actually asking for a lot.

Arnold wanted Fern to go to a weekly lecture series with him. That meant giving up her reading on those nights, which was a big concession for her. He didn't say, "It's no big deal to give up your reading." Nor did he say, "I don't ask much of you. How about indulging me just this once?" Fern believed that she already did a lot for him, so he encouraged her to join him by offering to make dinner the night they went out, allowing her time to read.

Tonya made dinner while the stereo blared in the living room. Saul wanted peace and quiet when he came home. His impulse was to shut off the stereo and scream, "I work hard all day in an office with phones ringing and printers making loud noise. I need quiet here." Luckily, he realized that would be counterproductive, and he spent a few minutes generating positive thoughts about his wife. It calmed him down to think that she had hard days and was probably bored cooking for the thousandth time. He also wasn't very sociable when he came home, so she used the stereo to keep her company.

He went into the kitchen, put his arms around her, and said, "You're a doll, making me dinner every night, but could you do me a favor? Can you lower the stereo volume? My nerves are so rattled by the time I get home that the noise really bothers me."

Since she couldn't hear the stereo if they lowered the volume, they resolved the problem by buying her a small radio to use in the kitchen when she cooked. From time to time, Saul kept her company instead or suggested that they listen to tapes together while she cooked and he looked through the mail.

NOT UNDERSTANDING

A major stumbling block to resolving conflicts occurs when one or both partners feel misunderstood. This commonly happens when one spouse believes that validating the other's needs or feelings will only reward the person's inappropriateness. For example, Brian had told Joy a million times to stop leaving her cosmetics and hair care products all over their bedroom and bathroom, but she found it inconvenient to put her things away. She tried to explain that to him, but he insisted that her messiness was intolerable and she should keep their room neat. As long as each tried to convince the other of his point of view and neither acknowledged the other's feelings, nothing got resolved.

Brian did not want to validate Joy's feelings because he thought that would reinforce her lack of discipline and disorganization. Joy didn't want to validate his feelings because she thought she would then have to agree to do what he wanted.

Validating a spouse's feelings only means that we can appreciate how they feel. It doesn't mean that we agree with their behavior or with their perceptions. Those are separate issues.

Not validating a spouse's feelings will make it impossible to resolve an issue. Brian could say to Joy, "I know that your life is very hectic and that it's hard for you to put your things away every day. Can you also appreciate that I'm used to living in a place where things are always neat? Just as it's hard for you to change what you do, it's hard for me to change my feelings about living in a place that isn't tidy."

Now that Joy doesn't have to mobilize all of her energy defending herself, she can finally hear Brian's point of view. "I'm sorry I make things uncomfortable for you. I guess it's not so easy for a man to live in the middle of curlers, blow dryers, hair gook, and women's stuff." In this atmosphere of understanding, they could finally discuss this issue and come to a resolution. Although she wasn't willing to clean up in the mornings, she was willing to do it when she came home. By the time Brian came home an hour later, the house was tidy.

When we are focused on solving a problem, it seems inefficient or even a waste of time to tune into a partner's feelings. *But being a good listener is probably the most important factor in solving any relationship problem.*

Rhonda told Simon that she had a suspicious lump and her doctor wanted her to get it biopsied and removed as soon as possible. She wanted to get a second opinion and more information before she got possibly catastrophic news. Her doctor had indicated that the lump might very well be malignant.

Simon exploded, "How can you even think about waiting? You must get biopsied as soon as possible. If you don't make an appointment now, I'll do it for you!"

She got angry at Simon for exploding and infantilizing her. She responded by withdrawing and being silent. He tried to revive their dialogue, but she clammed up.

Simon was perplexed. He had only shown concern for her. Why was she being so unreasonable?

The more upset someone is, the more she or he needs to feel understood. Rhonda first needed support and reassurance, not practical advice. Simon's intentions were good, but his method was terrible. He needed to ask Rhonda how she felt, empathize with and comfort her, and only afterwards make suggestions. He was so anxious that she might have cancer that all he could think about was "fixing" the problem.

Since Rhonda felt injured, he should apologize before doing anything else. He can get back on track by saying, "Rhonda, I'm terribly sorry that I hurt your feelings. The last thing that I wanted was to upset you. How about if we try this again?"

Rhonda feels better but is still sulking. "What's there to talk about?" she asks.

"Please tell me how you feel about going to the doctor." Simon takes her hand and caresses it.

Rhonda starts to cry. "I'm very scared, and a little angry that this is happening to me."

Simon holds her closer. "Tell me about it."

Tears stream down her face. "My grandmother died of cancer when I was a little girl. It was horrible. I don't want to go through what she did."

Simon kisses her on the forehead. "I promise you that I'll be here for you no matter what happens. You won't have to go through this alone." He holds her for a few minutes while she cries. When she stops crying he asks, "Is there anything that I can do to make you feel better?"

Rhonda now feels close to Simon because he has tuned into her feelings. He has apologized, empathized with, and supported her. Now she is ready to hear suggestions or advice. "I'd like to call a second doctor today but, until now, I was too scared to do it. Just be there with me when I make the call."

As things turned out, the second doctor told Rhonda that she only had an infected milk duct.

Notice that Simon did not try to get Rhonda to change her mind by assaulting her with cancer statistics or by using logic. When someone is very afraid or anxious, if we don't first make them feel secure and safe, they won't be ready to hear suggestions about what to do.

Using scare tactics with someone who is already panicked will usually cause them to shut out the information. People go into denial when they feel overwhelmed. Scare tactics only work when someone can handle anxiety productively. They are useless with people who are already emotionally flooded.

We can summarize how couples solve some problems and negotiate in the following way:

1. Spouse A states a problem.
2. Spouse B asks A for his or her feelings about the issue.
3. Spouse B acknowledges A's feelings and shares his or her feelings.
4. Spouse A validates B's feelings.
5. Both spouses dialogue about how to resolve the issue.
6. They negotiate and compromise without attacking or disrespecting each other.
7. If they reach an impasse, they try to identify what the solution or request means to each of them and renegotiate.
8. If the issue is nonnegotiable, they identify it as such and try to work around it, or table it for another discussion.

BARRIERS TO COMPROMISE

One of the most important qualities in marriage is the ability to adapt to changes. Couples need to compromise a lot during the first year of marriage because differences are greatest then, but compromising continues throughout life. Below are some things that make compromise difficult:

1. *Not wanting to give up what we want.*

We can be rigid and unyielding and not relinquish what's important to us. We have to believe that compromise will be worth it in the long run, or we won't give up what is meaningful to us in the short run.

Alita told Marcus that his eating behavior really bothered her. "I love being with you, but I have a problem with your table manners. I would really appreciate it if you would use a fork and knife instead of eating with your fingers, and wipe your face and hands on a napkin instead of on the tablecloth or your pants."

Marcus doesn't see why he shouldn't eat the way he wants. He says, "I don't tell you how to eat, you don't tell me how to eat. Etiquette is a ridiculous social convention, and my way of eating is just as valid as yours. Lots of people eat the way I do."

Unless he thinks that the long-term benefits of accommodating his wife are worth giving up some momentary comforts, he won't change. He is being penny-wise and pound-foolish, losing her goodwill over something so trivial, but that's not the way he sees it.

Were he willing to compromise, he could say, "I love you and don't want you to be miserable. How about if I eat the way you like on *Shabbat* and when we eat out? At other times, I'd like not to have to watch my table manners."

That would give Alita more of what she wants while allowing Marcus not to feel controlled. Alita would accept that and not expect perfection.

Couples need to be concerned with what's best for their marriage, not with what's best for them individually.

Eliezer insisted on driving when he and Susan went out. He was a reckless driver who drove frighteningly fast. If Susan offered to drive, he overruled her. If she asked him to slow down to sixty-five, he insisted that he could handle the roads at eighty-five. If she said that speed made her uncomfortable, he suggested that she try to get over her problem. He refused to let her drive. When Susan saw that he wouldn't allow her to be comfortable in the car, she stopped going places with him.

Victor wanted to spend Rosh Hashanah (Jewish New Year) with his parents, while Barbara wanted to spend it with hers. She had not spent the holidays with her family for the past three years because Victor thought that his in-laws' religious standards were too lax, and he had little in common with them. His in-laws were not comfortable staying in his house, and he didn't want to bring kosher food to theirs and stay in a nearby hotel. He ended up spending the holidays with his parents while Barbara stayed with hers.

2. *We believe that giving an inch now will cost us much more later.*

Some people believe that compromising now gives a spouse the message that she or he can manipulate us in the future. Some married men advise their engaged male friends to burn dinner or do a poor job cleaning up the kitchen when they first get married so that their wives will not ask them for future help. They also dig in their heels at the start of marriage to make sure that their spouse won't have the upper hand.

Showing an initial willingness to compromise makes a partner likely to give in on other issues, and vice versa. On the other hand, showing an initial unwillingness to compromise creates ill will from the start, usually with disastrous results later.

Bernard told Karen that he was inviting his parents for *Shabbat* dinner. She normally made an elaborate meal for the two of them anyway, so she surprised him by saying, "It's not my job to cook. If you want to buy take-out food for all of us, that's fine. But don't count on me to put together a fancy meal."

Instead of arguing, Bernard was smart enough to acknowledge that indeed cooking wasn't her job, and that he appreciated the wonderful food that she made. "Would you help me plan a menu of take-out food for *Shabbat?*" he asked his wife.

"No, I'll cook," Karen offered. "I just needed to know that you didn't take me for granted." When Karen saw that he didn't, she was happy to invite his parents for dinner.

Dave had an excuse whenever Esther asked him to wash the dishes. He assumed that once he helped her, she would expect him to help on a regular basis. He nipped the problem in the bud by refusing to help with anything. She got the message and stopped asking, but also resented him because of it.

Couples need to do uncomfortable things to preserve domestic harmony and maintain a loving atmosphere – not play war games. Marriage runs on goodwill, not on keeping the enemy at bay.

3. *We insist on being "right."*

Many of us believe that our ideas and feelings are "right" and that different opinions are "wrong." There are many facets to a situation, so there can be many valid opinions, feelings, and perspectives about it. Our Sages proved this by finding hundreds of theoretical ways to find ritually unclean lizards "clean." Even though lizards are, in fact, "unclean," the Sages had to be adept at viewing any situation from many different angles.

"Truth" is important in determining what is morally right and wrong, in formulating scientific theories, and in assessing facts. It is irrelevant to most personal relationships. What is important is how interactions affect the closeness between two people. Two people can have very different interpretations and feelings about the same experience and both be "right."

Malka and Nat took a vacation together. He enjoyed it so much that he can't wait to do it again. She thought that it was awful. He loved the cool weather and found the trip relaxing and enjoyable. She froze at night, was devoured by mosquitoes, and hated hiking on muddy trails where the high pollen counts played havoc with her allergies. When it was time to plan the next vacation, she wanted to go to Washington, D. C., and he wanted to go to a national park.

Whose perspective was "right?" Had their previous trip been great or terrible? Nat shouldn't insist that nature outings are fantastic and that Malka should learn to like them. Nor should she tell him that camping is stupid and that he should like cultural vacations. By admitting the legitimacy of their differences, they can find workable compromises.

We can't solve problems as long as we think that only our standards are right and reasonable and our partner is wrong. Even if a partner *is* objectively wrong, he or she won't change unless we admit the validity of his or her point of view.

How we discuss problems is more important than the issues themselves. We can quickly end most conflicts by agreeing with, or validating, our spouse's point of view and apologizing if he or she feels wronged. Refusing to acknowledge each other's feelings is a great way to escalate trivial issues into major blowups.

Gil went on a two-day business trip, and left three messages for Cindy the day he left. She had a lot of work to do and deliberately avoided returning his calls until she had finished what she had to do late that night.

When she called him, Gil was very angry. "I left you three messages. Why didn't you call me back until now?"

She retorted defensively, "I told you that I was going to be very busy today and couldn't call until late."

"Well, you could at least have called for two minutes and said that you didn't have time to talk. I would have understood. You got me very upset."

Instead of acknowledging his hurt, Cindy felt attacked and kept defending what she had done. "What are you complaining about? I'm calling you now." Then, she counterattacked, "Besides, when you call me and I'm busy, you keep me on the phone longer than I can spare. By the time I get back to what I was doing, I've lost at least half an hour and my concentration is shot!"

Since she still hasn't validated his feelings, Gil keeps asserting himself. "That's no excuse. You should be more sensitive to me. It wouldn't kill you to call me for five minutes." *Ad infinitum.*

Gil and Cindy each thought they were "right." Each felt attacked and misunderstood and wanted the other to admit that she or he was wrong. To get back on track, each needed to apologize and acknowledge the other's feelings.

When we feel hurt or misunderstood, we may expect our partner to apologize, yet be loathe to apologize ourselves. We should train ourselves to say, "I'm sorry for hurting your feelings," even if we don't believe that we did anything wrong. Our partner's feelings and harmony should be more important than being "right."

Cindy decided to eat humble pie and break their downward spiral. "I'm sorry that I didn't take a few minutes to let you know that I was thinking about you. I was insensitive. How about if we go on from here?"

"That's fine with me." Gil softened his tone. "I know that you feel pressured when I call you so often, but I like hearing your voice. If you would call me when I'm away, I won't keep you on the phone for more than sixty seconds. I'll also try to leave messages that make you feel loved instead of pressured." They then discussed how to do this.

They had a productive dialogue, even though neither really believed that he or she had acted badly in the first place. But they had the maturity to know that it was more important to say what was needed than to be "right."

Sometimes marriage requires acting. If we know how we want a scene to end, we can script a dialogue that will work, although it won't necessarily feel comfortable.

4. *We feel humiliated, criticized, or attacked.*

Sometimes a spouse's ideas or recommendations hurt or upset us, even if they had loving intentions. We have to find out what our spouse meant when we feel humiliated, criticized, or attacked, then clear the air by taking responsibility for our part of the problem.

Barry was fired from his job as a clothing store manager. After not finding work for six months due to a recession, Linda suggested that he take a pay cut and work in a friend's office for awhile.

Her idea humiliated and infuriated him. He had lost his job after eight years and wanted to believe that he would get a managerial offer any day. He misinterpreted her comment to mean that she didn't think much of his talents, and this led to a fight. He refused to consider any job that wasn't as good as his previous one.

After taking a break so that their tensions could subside, Linda clarified that she thought that Barry was very talented, and she was sure that he would get a managerial job when the economy improved. In the meantime, it would be helpful if he had a job to put on his resumé, and could help pay the rent. Once she bandaged his bruised ego, Barry admitted that he had overreacted because he felt so crushed by his unemployment. He agreed to look for a job that was a step down.

Jackie bought herself a computer and offered to show Herman how to use it. He prided himself on his technical expertise and said that he would figure out how to use it. Three weeks later, he was logging some business records when he erased everything on the hard drive. He was so humiliated that he didn't dare tell Jackie.

When she turned on the computer the next day, she realized what Herman had done. At first she was furious. She confronted him about it and told him that she expected him to reenter the software and her data that he had lost. He refused to take any responsibility for the fiasco. Being told what to do by a critical wife was intolerable for him. Jackie ended up doing the data reentry herself.

Had Jackie responded differently, Herman may have been more amenable to helping her. For example, when she realized what he did, she could have decided that it was easier to replace a few weeks of work than to find a new husband, and should have reminded herself of his many good qualities and what she loved about him. Creating these warm feelings would keep her from humiliating him further by interrogating him about what happened and ordering him about what to do. She could focus on ways to fix the problem instead of devising ways to punish him.

5. *We are afraid of losing power if we compromise and negotiate.*

We can view our spouses as allies or as adversaries. We feel allied when we sense our commonality and mutual commitment and adversarial when we think of our partner as critical, rejecting, or controlling. We lose nothing by compromising with a reasonable spouse, but we must believe that he or she won't take advantage of us. We feel this way if we remind ourselves of how much our spouse does for us, and why we have every reason to trust him or her.

Alex left his clothes on the floor every night, which made Melissa unhappy. She asked him to put them in the hamper, but he felt that she was trying to run his life. He reacted as if she was his adversary and told her that he was not going to be henpecked.

How we *interpret* what a spouse says or does is more important than what she or he *actually* says or does. Once we assume that our spouse is trying to control us, even if that is not the case, giving in to their requests makes us feel as if we are losing power.

Suzy told Rod that she'd like him to buy some items from the store for their son's birthday party. He adamantly refused. This was the sixth thing that she had told him to do that morning, and it wasn't even 10:00 yet. First she told him to mow the lawn. Then he had to clean up the living room. Next, she told him to call several of his relatives and confirm that they were coming to the party. . . . Now he was supposed to be her delivery boy! Enough was enough! As far as he was concerned, it was time to stand up for himself and stop letting her control him.

Harry asked Lynn to sew some buttons on his shirts and to mend two pairs of his pants. She refused, thinking that he could do it himself but apparently didn't want to be bothered. If he wanted to treat her like a maid, she was not going to indulge him.

Some spouses stay in control by refusing to do what a partner asks or by making unilateral decisions. This makes sure that a spouse has no real say or power.

Ronald kept Lucille in the dark about how much money he made and what he did with it. This gave him total control over their finances. She was a housewife with no income, and he gave her only as much money as he decided she needed. That prevented her from spending anything without his approval.

Passive–aggressive people seem flexible and easy-going, then do infuriating things to show that they are in control. They seem overtly agreeable, but their blood boils when a spouse tells them what to do. Then they subtly sabotage a spouse's plans or expectations by procrastinating, doing a half-baked job, or doing what they want instead of what their spouse wants.

Aryeh worked flexible hours, while Varda worked from 7 A.M. to 3 P.M., with Wednesdays off. When she said that she wanted to spend more time together, he agreed to arrange a new work schedule. He asserted himself by complying outwardly, then doing what he wanted. His new hours: 10 A.M.–6 P.M., with Fridays off.

Ezra drove to work every day, and Sally used the car on evenings and weekends. It desperately needed repairs, but Ezra was cheap. He didn't want to spend money fixing it. Sally insisted that he rent a car while she got the car repaired, but she wasn't going to force him to do things her way. So he agreed with her, then drove to work the next day. When she confronted him about it, he said that he "forgot." Each day he had a different excuse for not leaving her the car. Two months later, the car died and had to be scrapped.

Since passive–aggressive people like to appear agreeable and don't like to admit that they feel angry about being controlled, it's rarely useful to point out what they are doing. Ezra, for example, would not admit that he was angry at his wife or that he had done anything inappropriate. Instead of trying to get him to take responsibility for his actions, it is more productive to ask how he would like to resolve this issue. Once Sally tells him what to do, he won't do it. If he makes the suggestion on his own, he feels in control and doesn't need to assert his power by making her feel helpless and doing the opposite of what she wants.

Mark and Lenore agreed to take turns shopping for groceries every week. Mark kept "forgetting" when it was his turn and told Lenore that she needed to remind him. When she did, he told her that he was too tired, but he would do it the following day. When he didn't do it for the rest of the week, she asked him again. He told her that if she would stop nagging, he would do it. After this continued, she decided to buy the food herself.

Mark needs to feel that he has a real choice about how he contributes to the marriage. Otherwise, he is unlikely to follow through on chores that he agrees to do. By approaching him from a powerless position, Lenore is more likely to enlist his help. She can do this by saying, "I have a problem. I just can't manage to do all of the shopping, cooking, and cleaning for the house. Do you have any ideas about what to do about this?"

Mark is more likely to offer help, and give it, if she comes from a "subservient" position.

6. *We have poor timing.*

Communication is only effective if we do it when a spouse is receptive. It is best not to discuss important issues when he or she is hungry, angry, sick, tired, upset, or distracted. Instead of battering a spouse with a host of problems or critiques at once, or when he or she first walks in the door after work, we should only say as much as a spouse can hear. When in doubt, say too little rather than too much.

Janet thought that the house needed decorating. She mentioned it to Ricky when he was extremely busy at work, and he asked her to discuss it with him when he was less pressured. When his father had a heart attack two days later, they waited to talk to his doctor outside the Emergency Room. Janet saw this as the perfect opportunity to ask him about hiring a house painter and decorator. Needless to say, her timing could not have been worse.

Alice was the bookkeeper for her husband's business. She was in bed with pneumonia when Bert told her that the Internal Revenue Service was going to audit the business and that she needed to get their financial records in order. Could she have them ready in three days?

Alice was in no condition to hear this, and could do nothing about it then. She exploded, "I can't believe how insensitive you are. I'm sick as a dog, and all you care about is your business. You can do it all yourself." Bert should have asked the IRS for an extension, and asked Alice for help when she felt better.

Most people would like to feel safe and secure at home, and dislike being barraged with problems when they walk in the door. After getting a hug and a warm hello, having half an hour to unwind, and eating a good meal, they feel replenished and can discuss problems more reasonably.

Leslie's car was stolen while she was at work. It took two hours to give the police a report and go home. Meanwhile, the children had thrown a ball into the living room window and shattered the glass. When Doug came home half an hour later, she barraged him with a blow-by-blow description of the day's disasters, then asked him to help her look for a used car the next day. He said, "No. I don't have time." The more she insisted, the angrier he became. "Leave me alone already. You're old enough to buy a car by yourself," he snapped.

Doug reacted out of exhaustion and frustration. He really wouldn't have minded helping her buy a car, but he didn't want to think about it then. She should have let him settle down and eat dinner before telling him how her day was and asking him for help.

7. *We are too rigid, expect perfection, and denigrate our spouse whenever he or she falls short.*

If our spouse gets the sense that we have unrealistic expectations, often ask for too much, or are critical of his or her efforts, he or she is not likely to do much of what we want.

Natalie is a meticulous housekeeper and Sam is a slob. (Funny how these two types often marry each other, isn't it?) She can relax only when everything is clean and neat, while he needs to be casual to feel comfortable. He chafes every time she reminds him to put the cap on the toothpaste, wash his dirty dishes immediately after eating, and stack his newspapers and magazines in a neat pile. He is willing to be neater than when he was a bachelor, but not willing to live by her standards. Instead of appreciating that Sam will meet her halfway, Natalie feels that he is not compromising enough. Either he does everything she asks, or she reacts as if he has done nothing at all. Since she doesn't appreciate it when Sam makes an effort, he stops trying.

She needs to be more realistic about what Sam will do and not expect him to be perfect. Unless she starts appreciating his efforts, he won't compromise at all.

Shira was not very conscientious about turning off lights, heating, or air conditioning when she left the apartment. This upset Nosson, who asked her to be more careful so they didn't waste money. Still, she forgot at least once a week. When she suggested moving to a nicer place, he refused. "You're not responsible about electricity here, so why should I waste even more money on a bigger place?"

Shira's "negligence" cost them $10–15 a month. Nosson should accept that she is not going to totally change her lifetime habits. Nobody's perfect. Her wasting some electricity is a small flaw to overlook in an otherwise fine person. He should put her minor shortcoming into perspective.

8. *Certain issues aren't negotiable.*

Every couple has nonnegotiable issues. These can be cultural, physical, emotional, or religious, and are matters about which one spouse won't compromise. Couples should know what their nonnegotiable issues are so they don't waste time and energy trying to get a spouse to change in these areas.

Alfred believed that men should never do domestic work, and expected to come home and relax after a hard day's work. He assumed that Adelle would raise their three small children and run their home without his help. After all, his mother had raised seven children by herself.

He was raised in a traditional Eastern European community where women did housework and raised the children, while men earned money. It is fruitless for Adelle to tell him that his attitude went out of vogue fifty years ago or that she needs him to help her. His role is not negotiable. She can hire help if she can't manage on her own, but he won't help her.

Michelle insisted on living in a vibrant, religious Jewish community. When Howard got a wonderful job offer in a city with only five thousand Jews, he tried to convince her to move there. But nothing could entice her to budge. Her religious standards were not negotiable.

Nina loved the excitement and cultural life in New York City, where she had wonderful friends and enjoyed being in a stimulating community. After he was held up at gunpoint, Dennis insisted on moving but Nina resisted. She kept trying to convince him to stay, but her pleas fell on deaf ears.

Willy refused to waste money. His wife considered him cheap, yet he saw himself as frugal, responsible, and conscientious. He would not buy new clothes because he considered it wasteful, so it was pointless for Cheryl to try to convince him that he needed to buy himself a new wardrobe. On the other hand, he didn't mind wearing attractive clothes to make his wife happy. Instead of wasting her time trying to convince him to change his principles, Cheryl bought him new clothes herself when she felt he needed them.

THREATS AND INTIMIDATION

Some people say and do desperate things when they are frustrated, hurt, or angry. Domestic violence and spouse and child abuse are at all-time highs, even in Jewish families. Although Jewish law forbids couples to yell at, curse, or attack each other verbally or physically, people don't always act as they should. The casualness with which people threaten each other today is shocking.

Threats and "acting out" come in many forms. Some spouses try to punish a partner by staying away from home, threatening to leave, or talking about divorce. These tactics are so devastating that they should never be used by people who want to stay married. There are much better ways to convince a spouse that marital problems need to be addressed.

Melanie told Dean that she planned to go on a week-long business trip. Dean didn't want her to go and was angry that she had decided to go without consulting him. He was tempted to say, "If you go, I will divorce you." Instead, he thought for a few minutes and asked, "Can we discuss how I feel about your going?" He learned that the trip was necessary, and he was actually grateful for his wife's sacrifice. What he originally thought would be a vacation away from him, he discovered would be long days of hard work for his wife.

Randy bought a motorcycle, even though Sima thought that riding it was extremely dangerous. She decided not to threaten, "If you don't get rid of it, I will walk out on you." She conveyed the same concerns by saying, "I know that you have wanted to get a motorcycle for years, and that you are really excited about finally getting one. On the other hand, I think that riding a motorcycle is extremely dangerous, and it upsets me terribly that you might become a quadriplegic. What should we do, considering that you have a strong need to do this, and I consider it terribly dangerous?"

Randy argued that riding with a helmet was not unsafe, and she told him that she was concerned about other reckless drivers and poor road conditions. They finally compromised: He would ride it in a deserted state park, wearing his helmet, when the roads weren't slick or icy, and she wouldn't nag him to get rid of it.

There's always time to give an ultimatum or threats when all other tactics fail. On the other hand, broaching divorce even once can cause irreparable damage to a marriage by introducing mistrust, less commitment, and panic into the relationship. Threats of leaving, or moving out, sometimes do motivate an apparently uncaring spouse to be more loving, but they should only be used as a last resort. Divorce should only be mentioned when a couple has exhausted all other avenues for repairing a marriage and they can no longer tolerate the *status quo*.

Nadine was angry at Scott, who recently stopped being loving and helpful. When she cooked, he told her that the soup was too salty, the meat was overcooked, and the rice was too spicy. After dinner, he pointed out that she had left some dirty pots on the stove. Before going to sleep, he commented that there were dust balls under the furniture and the bathroom was dirty.

After three weeks of this, Nadine told Scott that she had had enough. "I'm sick and tired of your criticism. If you do it one more time, I'm going to divorce you."

Instead of being convinced that he should be more sensitive, Scott was shocked. It had never occurred to him that Nadine would leave him for any reason. Now she was threatening to walk out because he'd been grouchy for a few weeks?!

How could he ever trust her to go through bad times with him or stick by him if he ever got terribly sick, lost his job, or had a crisis?

Nadine used "big guns" when a fly-swatter would have worked. She should have said, "You're usually so loving, Scott, but lately you've hurt me a lot with your frequent criticism. Are you aware that you have been unusually critical of me lately? I need you to go back to your usual, loving self." That would have made Scott aware of how hurtful he had been, and he would have apologized and tried to do better. Instead, Nadine's divorce threat stopped his criticism but also made him withdraw for months because he could no longer trust that she wouldn't walk out on him.

"Big guns" can be appropriate when a spouse is abusive or won't get help for serious emotional problems or addictions. Under most circumstances, though, calm confrontations should be the first line of defense. If that fails, it may help to ask a friend, relative, or rabbi to intervene. If that doesn't work, it might be necessary to say, "Your problem is wreaking havoc on us, and I can't keep living like this. If you don't change or get help by next week, I will leave."

Threats and manipulations usually have no place in marriage. People who use them routinely need to learn how to communicate better and deal with their anger in more constructive ways.

LIGHTEN UP

Couples need to work out their differences, but they also need to enjoy being together. Marriage should be more than a series of problems that are worked out. This means putting some problems on hold so that couples have a chance to enjoy each other.

Roberta's parents told her that she was making the mistake of her life when she announced her engagement to Murry. The parents tried to destroy her marriage, and she became a nervous wreck keeping them at bay. As if that weren't enough, Roberta and Murry's business floundered, and she started having anxiety attacks when they went into major debt. All they talked about were problems. They stopped having fun and got little relief from their tensions.

As they stopped recharging their emotional batteries, their relationship started to deteriorate. When she contemplated separating, Roberta saw a psychologist. The therapist taught her to relax and manage her stress better. She stopped burdening Murry with a blow-by-blow description of her family problems and anxiety attacks and discussed them with her therapist instead.

She and Murry started scheduling dates together twice a week, when it was off-limits to talk about problems. They went to free concerts, parks, museums, and the like. If one of them slipped and brought up problems, the other suggested scheduling a time to discuss them. They became happier as they took care of each other and replenished their emotional reserves. This gave them the energy to solve the issues that needed their attention and allowed them to get their marriage back on track.

A good sense of humor is a great asset in marriage. Even though we should take a spouse's feelings seriously, laughter helps put some problems in perspective.

Norman and Louise couldn't agree about how to arrange their bedroom furniture. He wanted the beds near the window, and she wanted them against the opposite wall. She finally gave in and they moved the beds where he wanted.

Her family visited a week later and noticed that the room looked lopsided. When Norman went to buy a Sunday paper, Louise and her father rearranged the beds, hoping that Norman wouldn't notice.

When Norman came back, he went into the bedroom, while Louise and her parents waited to see if he would notice what they had done. He emerged five minutes later with a huge grin and exclaimed, "I can't believe it. While I was gone, someone moved the window."

Since husbands' and wives' internal thermostats rarely mesh, many couples stage a Home Thermostat Ballet. Wives turn up the heat when their husbands leave the house, and husbands create Arctic surroundings when their wives go out to run errands.

One steamy summer day, Aileen pushed the air conditioner thermostat to 72° from 65°. "I'm sorry I have to do this," she quipped to Moshe, who perspired when the mercury hit 68°. "But if you really love me, you'll stop sweating."

After enduring two hours of oppressive heat, Moshe couldn't take it any more. He reset the temperature to 68°. When she complained of frostbite, he playfully suggested, "You'll save us money by turning off the freezer and keeping everything cold with your hands!"

Viewing differences as comical instead of serious makes them easier to deal with.

Husbands who feel "henpecked" can chuckle instead of feeling angry by thinking about the following story:

Moe died and went to heaven. He saw a long line of men that extended as far as the eye could see. Next to them was a shriveled old man standing by himself. Not one to wait patiently, Moe asked the lone man, "What are these two lines for?"

The man replied with a heavy Yiddish accent, "Det long line is for all de men who vere hen-pecked vhile dey vere alive."

"And what is this line for?" Moe queried.

"De line det I'm in is for men who veren't hen-pecked," the man answered.

"Why are you standing here?" Moe asked.

The man shrugged, "My vife told me to."

When friends or family want to make plans, some men joke, "I have to check with the boss, then I'll get back to you." Everyone knows who "the boss" is.

Couples can find their different levels of religious observance painful, but a sense of humor can even help here. For example, a husband was invited to bring his wife to a party whose *kashrut* the wife might find objectionable. Instead of putting her in a compromising position, he told his friend, "Let me ask my rabbi, then I'll get back to you." The rabbi, of course, was his more observant partner.

HELPFUL EXERCISES

1. Think about what motivates each of you (truth, comfort, social approval, etc.) in different circumstances. For example, Rochel seeks comfort and approval from relationships, orderliness and organization at work or at home. Yossi seeks truth when he makes decisions; intellectual stimulation from friends; respect, acceptance, and love when he's with Rochel. Discuss sensitive issues, taking your spouse's point of view, before trying to resolve them.

2. Tell your spouse what you are trying to accomplish when you talk. For example, before relating a story, tell your spouse that you are sharing it because it makes you feel closer. You would like him or her to show interest in what you say by keeping eye contact and validating your feeling. If you get the response you wanted, compliment your spouse for being a good listener.

Alternatively, you might tell your spouse that you feel devastated by the events that you're about to relate, and would like to feel supported and loved.

3. If your spouse does not react the way you'd like when you speak, suggest what you would like him or her to say. For example, if your spouse gives you suggestions when you talk about your day, tell him that you want only a listening ear and understanding.

4. Try to solve a problem using the problem-solving outline in this chapter. When you reach impasses, ask your spouse if she or he feels understood and not judged, and don't go further until the answer is "yes."

5. Ask your spouse to validate a feeling of yours that she or he disagrees with. For example, Ted felt humiliated when Ronna contradicted him. Instead of insisting that he's too sensitive, she says that she can appreciate how embarrassed he feels when she says that he's wrong.

6. Identify two nonnegotiable issues for each of you.

7. Ask your spouse if she or he would like you to apologize for something that you said or did. If she or he identifies an issue, apologize for hurting their feelings without defending what you did. Your spouse should accept the apology and say that he or she appreciates your sensitivity. Then switch roles.

8. Review the section on "Barriers to Compromise" together. Identify which barriers apply to you and how you can overcome them. For example, if one of you has bad timing, the spouse can say when it is a good time to broach issues. If one of you feels that you compromise much more than your spouse does, discuss which compromises each one makes. One couple was surprised to discover that the husband compromised by *doing* things for his wife, while she compromised by *foregoing* activities that she liked.

9. Make one date a week where you interact for at least half an hour without discussing problems. Watching television, movies, shows, or concerts where you don't interact does not count. If you can't leave the house, make sure that children and telephone calls don't interrupt your time together.

10. Get a book that makes you laugh and read sections together. Try to remember funny incidents or jokes that you hear and share them.

SUMMARY

Our Sages said, "When the tongue is good, there is nothing better; and when bad, there is nothing worse."[2] By resolving marital issues in a way that leads to closeness, friendship, and compromise, we don't bear grudges (which is biblically forbidden[3]), or harbor anger about unresolved issues or hurt feelings. We are obliged to do "what's good and what's right"[4] with our spouses.

Our Sages said that Jerusalem was destroyed because judges based themselves only on the letter of the law.[5] Compromise is the preferred Jewish way to solve problems, and this certainly holds true for marriage.

NOTES

1. Rashi on Genesis 1:26.
2. *Vayikra Rabbah* 33:1.
3. Leviticus 19:81.
4. Deuteronomy 6:18.
5. *Bava Metziah* 30.

16

Money and Marriage

It is said that money makes the world go 'round, but married couples have more conflicts about it than anything else.[1] How we spend, save, and budget money reflects our feelings about trust, security, power, and being taken care of. Although some people use money to nurture and protect a spouse, others just as readily use it to express anger and control.

Poverty by itself rarely ruins marriages, but how couples deal with money and communicate about it can. Money conflicts often express emotional issues, such as poor self-esteem, getting nurtured or feeling deprived, anger, poor communication, irresponsibility, and power struggles.

Money tends to mean different things to different people. For example, men often use it to show power, adequacy, and to get respect, while women see it as a sign that they are loved and nurtured. Women once praised their husbands by saying, "He's a good provider," equating money with being taken care of.

Women with poor self-esteem or an inner emptiness often spend money on themselves to feel better. Men often save or lavish money on others to feel important and respected, and are less apt to buy items to bolster their self-esteem than women are. Some men resent their wives buying unnecessary items or wasting money, while some wives resent their husbands spending money on their friends or associates in order to get respect and admiration.

Conflicts about money often begin with the engagement ring. Many women gauge a man's love for them by the cost (and size) of the diamond (and other gifts) that he buys. They expect to show off at least a carat-sized rock, even if the man can't afford it.

In secular circles, a rule of thumb suggests that a man spend approximately one month's salary on an engagement ring. Borrowing a lot of money to buy a ring is a bad idea. New marriages have enough stresses without adding debt to the list.

Planning a wedding also raises money issues. While brides' families once paid for weddings, this is not always the case today. Many dual-career couples, and some parents of the groom, now pay for some or all of the wedding expenses. As many as six different people may contribute, and each expects to have a say in the wedding arrangements. The bride wants simple flower arrangements, but her mother thinks they look chintzy. The mother-in-law wants an afternoon wedding so that her relatives can get home that evening and not have to stay over in a hotel. The groom would rather put money into a nest egg than go on a $2,000 honeymoon. The father-in-law insists on an expensive photographer, but the bride wants her best friend to take pictures.

Even when these are not issues, deciding how many guests to invite and how opulent a wedding to have may pit couples against each other and against their families. The groom's parents want to invite more people than the bride's parents will allow. The bride's parents insist on bridesmaids' gowns, despite the fact that two bridesmaids can't afford them. The bride wants a caterer that costs $1,000 more than her parents will spend. She is willing to pay the difference out of her wedding gifts, but the groom objects. A groom buys a $400 *ketuvah,* and his in-laws criticize him for throwing away money. . . .

Couples may have to resolve many financial issues before the wedding that show how well equipped they are to resolve similar conflicts in the future. They can also get a sense of each other's financial personality type. Are they hoarders, savers, spenders, worriers, risk-takers, and so forth? Since opposite types tend to marry each other, this is a good time to take stock of your differences and consider how you will handle them.

For example, does the bride or groom want a "perfect" wedding that costs $50,000, while the other thinks that $15,000 should be the upper limit? How does the couple feel about their parents going into debt for their wedding, or making a gorgeous wedding with money that could be their nest egg? There is no shame in making a wedding for $10,000 or less, but does the couple believe that?

Neither Heddi nor her fiancé Dale had much money, nor did their families. But most of Heddi's friends were wealthy and had had extravagant weddings. Heddi pressured Dale to use all of his savings, plus all of their wedding cash, to make a wedding like her friends had. He wanted a simple reception, but Heddi was adamant that they go all out. So they squandered their savings. Instead of enjoying their first year of marriage, Dale had to work two jobs to make ends meet. In retrospect, Heddi wished that she had had a simpler wedding and had more time to spend with a less-pressured husband.

Ashley and Walter came from wealthy families, and her parents gave her a choice: She could have a $100,000 wedding, or a less expensive one plus a nest egg that would total $100,000. Ashley opted for a $25,000 wedding and a $75,000 wedding present, but Walter vetoed the idea. He figured that they had a combined income of six figures a year, so why not have a bash on their wedding day? She reluctantly agreed, and they had an opulent wedding for 250 guests that was the "Wedding of the Year."

Walter lost his lucrative job a year later, and had to settle for another that paid considerably less. When Ashley was driving that winter, she hit a patch of black ice, totalled the car, and had to stop working for two months as she recuperated. They doled out $40,000 for unreimbursed medical expenses and another car. By the time she had a baby a year later, they had no savings and a lot of debts. They had never imagined this might happen to them. Not a week went by that they didn't rue squandering their nest egg on their wedding.

PRENUPTIAL FINANCIAL AGREEMENTS

Although most engaged couples are sure that their marriages will last forever, it is prudent for people to protect themselves in case they don't. Fifty percent of first marriages, and 60 percent of second marriages, end in divorce. These often include vicious child custody and money battles.

When one or both spouses own a house, have children from a previous marriage, or expect to inherit or earn a lot of money, a prenuptial financial agreement can be worth its weight in gold. Without it, many couples will fight wrenching court battles, where some men will get stripped of their homes and life savings and make onerous alimony payments. Contrary to popular belief, only 15 percent of women end up getting child support and alimony after a divorce.[2] Moreover, many women become impoverished after divorce. On average, their standard of living decreases by 73 percent after divorce, while men's goes up by 42 percent.[3] While prenuptial agreements can't always make things equitable, at least they can keep couples from squandering their money on lawyers' fees, hurting their children, and wasting time in court.

Few people who should have financial prenuptial agreements do. Most people find it uncomfortable asking a fiancé(e) to sign a document that implies mistrust and anticipates divorce. Some people get angry and indignant when they are asked to waive their legal right to half a spouse's earnings or assets and settle for a smaller amount. But this temporary emotional discomfort should not deter people from protecting themselves. If a fiancé(e) refuses to sign a reasonable agreement and expects you to be totally vulnerable, she or he may have serious personality problems or ulterior motives for marriage.

It is beyond the scope of this book to discuss who needs a prenuptial financial agreement and what it should cover. Since laws vary according to state, and personal circumstances differ, consult a qualified attorney who has no vested interest in your decision.

Bernard was a workaholic surgeon who earned a great deal of money. He was forty years old with $2 million in assets by the time he met Doris. She was beautiful, twelve years his junior, and made him feel virile and desirable. When they got engaged, his friends advised him to get a prenuptial agreement. When he broached this with her, she was furious and accused him of not trusting her. She refused to marry him if he insisted on an agreement. He backed down and married her without one.

His friends took bets on how long he would wine and dine her, buy her beautiful things, and furnish a luxurious home for her before she got restless and divorced him. A year after their marriage, she confided that she was not cut out to be a mother and did not want to have children. His folly cost him a bundle by the time he finished paying her alimony and legal fees, even though they had only lived together for a year. Next time, he won't let his emotions dissuade him from protecting himself.

Howard was a hardworking man of modest means. When he and Gail married, he bought a house with his life savings and put it in both their names. After five years, she left him, but not before taking him to the cleaners. She had never put a penny into the house, but it was awarded to her in the divorce settlement, along with a lot of Howard's hard-earned money. He had to start over from scratch financially at the age of thirty-six. When he married his second wife, he made sure to get a prenuptial agreement, which he thankfully has not needed.

Maimon's mother was in her seventies and terminally ill. She had a house that was worth half a million dollars, which he was due to inherit. When he got engaged, he thought that his new wife might be able to force him to sell the house if they got divorced and he couldn't pay alimony. Since Maimon never expected to earn much money, he consulted an attorney to see if he needed a prenuptial agreement to protect his inheritance.

SPENDING AND SAVING

Rabbi Nachman of Bratzlav, *zt"l,* said, "A couple who saves wisely will have a fine home."[4] With this in mind, before they get married some couples should set up a financial game plan that includes how they will spend, save, and budget money. They should discuss their expectations about establishing a certain standard of living; providing for their children's education; having retirement plans; getting health, disability, and life insurance; and giving money to charity.

Income permitting, their budget should allow each to spend some money as each prefers. They should set up individual and/or joint checking account(s), decide which credit cards to use, and which large purchases and investments to make. Most couples have different ways of handling money and need to adapt to each other.

Sheldon and Baila figured out that their net (after-tax) combined income was $3,000 a month. They gave 10 percent of that, or $300 a month, to charity. Their other living, clothing, medical, and entertainment expenses totaled $2,200 a month. They decided to save $400 a month, and take $50 apiece every month to do with as each wished. Baila saved her money to purchase jewelry, kitchen gadgets, and gifts for Sheldon. While he ordinarily thought spending money on jewelry was wasteful, he didn't mind since she bought hers with discretionary money. He used his money to buy Jewish books and religious articles for the holidays.

Shira loved ice cream and bought a double dip on her way home from work every day during the spring and summer. She treated herself to a daily cup of coffee and a brownie from a vendor the rest of the year. Zvi realized that her small indulgence was costing them $40–$60 a month, and they needed that money for necessities. Shira pointed out that Zvi's snacks cost as much as hers did. They realized that they could save almost $1,000 a year by cutting out these "treats." Instead of giving them up entirely, they brought homemade coffee and snacks from home at a fraction of their former cost.

Mimi was a frugal, unmaterialistic woman. Her one indulgence was getting a manicure every week. Menachem thought that nail polish was silly and didn't know why she didn't do her nails herself. But they had enough money for her to spend $10 a week on manicures, so he didn't upset himself that she wasted $500 a year on her nails. He focused on being grateful that this was the only time she "wasted" money. They otherwise agreed about how to spend and save.

HOW TO DESIGN A BUDGET

It is a good idea for most couples to design a budget that estimates their disposable income and expenses. Then they can assess how to best spend their money while living within their means and accomplishing their financial goals.

If you want to design a budget, first figure out your annual income by listing for each spouse:

1. Annual salary after taxes, payroll deductions, union dues, and social security have been taken out = _____

2. Annual interest income on checking and savings accounts = _____

3. Annual interest on investments = _____

4. Stock dividends = _____

5. Other income = _____

Add totals for both spouses and divide by twelve. This is your real monthly income.

Now figure out how much money you spend by listing your typical monthly and yearly expenditures:

Expenses		Per Mo.	Per Yr.
Home	Rent or maintenance fees*		
	Mortgage*		
	Gas and electric		
	Heating oil		
	Water		
	Telephone		
	Homeowner taxes		
	Cable TV		
	Maid, housekeeper		
	Babysitters		
	Yard care, snow removal		
	Painting, maintenance, home repairs		
Domestic Items	Furnishings and furniture		
	Linens		
	Kitchenware and appliances		
	Cleaning supplies		
	Appliance repairs		
	Telephones, computers, electronic equipment (TV, VCR, stereo, etc.)		
	Miscellaneous (stationery, postage, etc.)		
Food	Groceries		
	Eating out, meals and snacks at work		
	Wine, beer, liquor		
	Home entertaining		
	Candy, gum, snacks		
Personal	Health and beauty aids		
	Haircuts, manicures, beauty salon, etc.		
	Cigarettes		
	Toiletries, perfume, makeup		
Clothing	Clothes, shoes, hose, hats, accessories		
	Wigs and wig styling		
	Special outfits for skiing, swimming, exercise, etc.		
	Jewelry		
	Cleaning and laundry bills		

*Use after-tax approximations, if part of this is tax-deductible.

Medical	Doctors' visits
	Dentist and orthodontist
	Chiropractor, physical therapy
	Lab and diagnostic tests
	Psychotherapy
	Allergy shots
	Medications
	Vitamins
Fees	Lawyer, accountant
	Organizational memberships*
Insurance	Medical
	Car
	Homeowner's
	Life
	Disability
Car	Gas and oil
or	Inspections
Transportation	Maintenance
	Repairs and parts
	Commuting expenses (tolls, mass transit, trains, taxis, parking)
Education	Tuition, fees for lectures
	Books, subscriptions, newspapers, magazines
	Writing supplies
Charity	All contributions
Entertainment	Movies, plays, concerts, etc.
and	Vacations
Recreation	Hobbies and sports supplies
	Club memberships
	Activity fees, lessons, classes
Gifts	Cards and presents (birthdays, special occasions, anniversaries, mother's and father's day, holidays like Chanukah)
	Bridal showers, weddings, baby gifts, *bar/bat mitzvahs*
	Flowers
Debts and Loans	Credit card interest and back payments
	Bank loans
	Student loans
	Other loans
Miscellaneous	Computer and printer supplies
	Alimony and child support payments
	Other _____

Add your monthly joint expenses with each spouse's monthly individual expenses. (Divide annual amounts by twelve to get the monthly amount.) This equals your total monthly expenses. Subtract it from your average joint monthly income. The difference will be your disposable monthly income. (Monthly income minus monthly expenses equals monthly disposable income.)

This number will be greater than zero if you make more money than you spend. Discuss with your spouse how to spend and/or save it.

If your monthly disposable income is less than zero, you spend more than you earn and might already be in debt.

Discuss with your spouse how to decrease your expenses or increase your income.

If you don't know what your expenses are, itemize them for a month. That will show you and your spouse how you spend money.

To determine their financial compatibility, couples should consider:

1. Are you spenders or savers?
2. How do each of you spend money?
3. Are either of you worried about money?
4. Do either of you spend money that you don't have, such as by using credit cards?
5. Do either of you resent having to limit your spending?
6. Do you basically agree about how to earn, spend, and save money? If not, can you live with your differences?
7. Are you willing to change your spending and saving habits, if necessary, when you have children?
8. Do you agree about whether to buy or rent a place to live? Do you agree on a ballpark amount to spend on rent or on mortgage payments?

Answering "yes" to numbers 3, 4, or 5, and "no" to numbers 6, 7, or 8 may be signs of future trouble. Couples with strong financial differences or who live beyond their means may benefit from personal or financial counseling.

Some dual-income couples prefer having separate bank accounts. (Those who do should follow the guidelines in the chapter on marital obligations.) When there is only one breadwinner, the nonworking spouse should always have spending money available without having to ask or beg for it.

When Hal gets angry at Rosemary, he stops depositing his paycheck in their joint account and puts it in his individual account. He controls his homemaker-wife by forcing her to ask for money, then deciding how much to dole out to her.

People who are controlling are uncomfortable trusting others, and sometimes expect a spouse to account for how they spend every dollar. Husbands are advised not to be overly exacting in supervising household expenses.[5]

Married couples may handle money in different ways, each of which is equally valid. For example, Davida likes to pay her bills as they come in, while Uri prefers to pay them on the first of every month. She doesn't like his system because they have to pay interest on their credit card and telephone bills. Uri likes his way because it saves him time. Instead of criticizing him, Davida pays bills that would otherwise accrue late charges, while Uri pays the others. Saving money is more important than convenience to her, but she respects the fact that the opposite is true for her husband.

Lolly bought a cake at the local bakery every week, but Morris thought that this was a terrible waste of $40 to $60 a month. When he pointed out that her habit cost them $500 a year, she agreed to limit her cake buying to rare occasions.

Jeannette had simple needs and was not a big spender, but she rarely denied herself something she wanted. It bothered Michel that she bought items on impulse instead of buying only what she needed. When she spent $50 on a handbag that he didn't think she needed, he lost his temper.

"What do you need another handbag for?" he shouted. "You already have six!"

Instead of answering his question, she addressed the real issue. "Michel, we make enough money that I can afford to spend $50 every other month buying treats for myself. Other women spend a lot of money on clothes, jewelry, perfume, eating out, and so on. I spend a total of $400 a year buying accessories for myself, and I've been wearing the same clothes for the last five years. Let's put things in perspective."

Even though Michel still wished that she wouldn't waste any money, her comment made sense and he decided it wasn't worth making an issue of it.

FINANCIAL IRRESPONSIBILITY

Many affluent Jews now lead lives of conspicuous consumption. Some young women expect prospective husbands to be affluent and rate their desirability by how much the men earn. Unfortunately, many men gauge their self-esteem by the same yardstick. When they get married, couples get on a merry-go-round of buying expensive homes, cars, clothes, furs, jewelry, vacations, and the like. The husbands become workaholics to support their lifestyles, and the wives spend their free time shopping and keeping up with the neighbors. The satisfaction of each novelty wears off quickly and they waste their lives chasing one materialistic goal after another.

When lottery winners have been polled, most say they were happier before they won their jackpots. Having a lot of money and possessions doesn't gratify people for long, and often brings many problems in its wake. Money doesn't buy happiness, although it can make people more comfortable if they know how to use it wisely.

Many couples today work long hours so that they can live comfortably and give their children a "good life." Their materialistic dreams often put enormous stress on their marriages and emotionally deprive their children. The children, and sometimes the spouse, would prefer to have less materially and spend more time with their family.

Bill was an executive who made $200,000 a year, and Catherine was an executive secretary. Despite his hefty salary, she managed to spend almost every dollar he made before he even deposited the paychecks. They rented an apartment for $3,500 a month, and she decorated it for $40,000. Two months later, they rented a suburban house for $4,000 a month. She hired a gardener for $600 a month, bought new appliances, a new car, new drapes, new linens, new carpets, new furniture, and so on. Her frenetic shopping and decorating left her too exhausted to cook, so they ate most meals out. She planned short vacations every two months that cost $3,000–4,000 each because she needed to get away from the stresses of her life.

She expected her husband to recharge her emotional batteries after running herself ragged every day, and she shopped to take away her underlying depression and emptiness. Her husband tried to take away her credit cards and limit her spending, but she threatened to divorce him if he did. He wanted to avoid divorce at all costs, and so he let his wife keep them on the brink of financial ruin.

Women like Catherine never feel good for long. They spend money to feel nurtured and distract themselves from their inner void and lack of meaning. But the good feelings from shopping never last very long, so they must shop continually to feel good. Women like this don't usually have a strong and meaningful identity. Professional and/or religious counseling can help them come to terms with that.

Any form of financial irresponsibility can ruin a marriage. People who can't balance a checkbook before marriage rarely do so afterwards, and people who spend money to feel good usually don't change just because it upsets a spouse.

Connie was from a well-to-do family and didn't like feeling deprived. Martin barely eked out a living as an electronics salesman, but this didn't deter Connie from living as she always had. She spent all of their wedding money furnishing their new apartment. She had no savings, so she charged new clothes and other unnecessary purchases on Martin's credit card. He could barely pay the rent, yet she saw nothing wrong with racking up $3,000 of charges in one month. She needed to modify her spending according to what they could afford.

Millions of Americans now have large credit card debts. Most of these people have emotional problems such as depression, poor self-esteem, anger, and a sense of entitlement that fuel their spending. Self-help groups like Debtors Anonymous give them emotional support while they learn to live with realistic budgets and pay off their existing debts.

Karen and James always struggled financially. She supported them both because he was frequently out of work during their six years of marriage. After she gave birth to their first child, she got fed up with him spending their rent and food money frivolously, and taking credit card cash advances at 21 percent interest when he ran out of money.

James refused to admit that he had a problem, and would not see a debt counselor or go to Debtor's Anonymous. Karen finally stopped enabling him by closing their joint credit card and bank accounts.

In marriage, one spouse's financial problems affect the other. A wife can be liable for debts that her husband incurs, and vice versa. Each can be denied a mortgage because of the other's bad credit rating. One spouse may squander the other's savings or incur debts for them both. Some spouses have no choice but to cancel joint credit cards, close all joint accounts, put their money in an individual account, and refuse to bail out a partner who gambles or spends recklessly.

Some compulsive spenders and gamblers jeopardize the family's house and assets. If they refuse to get help and keep creating financial havoc, divorce may be the only prudent option.

Jeffrey was a "nice Jewish boy" whose minor gambling problem became major after marriage. He cashed his paychecks at the racetrack and borrowed money from loan sharks who threatened his family. He asked friends to bail him out, which they did. He continued doing this for thirty years because so many people enabled him. Meanwhile, he ruined his family's lives because they lived with constant threats of bodily harm by loan sharks and with threatened eviction by landlords.

No one is equal to the task of treating a partner's addictions or compulsions. The best she or he can do is convince a partner to seek professional help or join a self-help group. People with pathological spending patterns will only change if they believe they have a problem and get help with it.

UNDEREMPLOYED SPOUSES

Some people aren't serious about earning a living and are often unemployed or underemployed. This can wreak havoc on their families.

Even though Jeremy wasn't religious, he insisted, "God provides financial sustenance," distorting a religious concept to justify his laziness. He never worked at the same job for more than a year, and took long breaks between one job and the next. Cindy tried to support them on her meager receptionist's salary, but couldn't. They lived in debt, paid their bills late, and were threatened with eviction several times a year. No matter how nicely Cindy discussed this, Jeremy refused to work harder. He rationalized his irresponsibility, then blamed her for being a worry-wart.

Cindy finally asked Jeremy to support them for six months to a year so that she could train for a better job. He refused. She even tried enlisting his father to convince him. That also failed. She finally threatened to move in with her parents if Jeremy didn't work consistently. When he got laid off a month later because he came late to work, she moved into a sympathetic friend's home with her three small children.

A chasidic woman with five children was married to a man who barely made ends meet. Even so, they were happily married for ten years until he decided to become "holier." He suddenly decided to change his entire way of life. He prayed so long every morning that he came late to work and lost customers. The wife had to run a nursery school in their home so that she could pay the rent. When they went into debt, she pleaded with her husband to work normal hours, but he refused.

He needed to address his emotional problems with a psychologically aware rabbi and/or therapist. He had an obligation to support his family and should have found a way to pray that was not at his family's expense.

People who are used to an opulent lifestyle often lose their jobs or savings, and must drastically change their way of life at some time. Countless millionaires have lost their fortunes due to poor health, economic recessions or depressions, dishonest partners, lawsuits, bad investments, and so on. But even people of modest means fall on hard times. When fortunes change drastically, people need to be equipped to deal with it.

Bryna and Anton had everything money could buy. He got a $250,000 bonus every December, in addition to his ample salary. They owned two gorgeous homes, three cars, a boat, expensive home furnishings, and the like. They had a full-time housekeeper. They spent $10,000 on private week-long cruises in the Caribbean, $500 on theater and dinner outings with friends, $10,000 on European trips every summer, and $15,000 a year on dinner parties for friends at their house.

Anton lost his job and most of his savings when the stock market crashed. He had mortgages on both homes, in addition to sizeable debts. One house was repossessed, and he sold the other at a $200,000 loss. He sold his boat for a fraction of what he paid for it, and had to give up dining out, vacations, and the housekeeper. He and Bryna rented a modest apartment and went through the humiliation of losing many of their wealthy friends. They could not believe that their dreams and way of life were shattered in the blink of an eye.

Instead of being supportive, Bryna was furious with Anton for investing in the stock market, and he was angry at her for not being understanding. Their strained marriage got more tenuous the longer he was unemployed. When he finally got a job that paid a fraction of his former salary, she left him.

Money and material things are merely loans that God gives us for spiritual ends. People who stake their marital happiness on money often find that their marriages crumble when their circumstances change. Couples need to support each other and feel like a team when they confront difficult financial circumstances.

Before they got married, Cynthia told George that she expected to have a house in an upscale, Jewish suburb, with a husband who earned at least $80,000 a year. At the time, he was earning $90,000 a year from his jewelry business, but there were no guarantees that things would stay that way. Four years later, he had a very bad year and took out $20,000 in loans. Cynthia was not very sympathetic. She only cared that her dreams had been shattered, and that her friends were living the life that she felt entitled to have.

MONEY AND CHILDREN

Children from materialistic families often learn to value appearances, super-ficiality, and immediate gratification. They tend to have poor self-esteem and quickly become bored with life because they never developed a meaningful identity or goals. Two twelve-year-old girls showed their values in the following conversation:

Girl #1: "And how much did your *bat mitzvah* dress cost?"

Girl #2: "It cost four hundred dollars, and my *bat mitzvah* cost fifty thousand dollars. How much did yours cost?"

Girl #1: "My dress cost more than four hundred dollars, and I'm sure my *bat mitzvah* cost as much as yours."

Will these girls develop any meaningful aspirations or identities when they become older?

Rhoda and Jerome were excited about moving to a wealthy community where he would be the rabbi. His $40,000 salary was considered good for an Orthodox congregational leader. The synagogue paid his rent, and his children got free tuition from the local Jewish day school.

The couple's happiness dissolved as they realized that their children were misfits in their new surroundings, and people looked down on them. Their neighbors had backyard swimming pools, expensive cars, and the latest electronic and entertainment systems. They wore expensive clothes, and their children had birthday parties that cost hundreds of dollars. They spent school and summer vacations in places the rabbi's children could only dream about.

Rhoda and Jerome soon moved to a less affluent community where good character traits, integrity, and spiritual growth were more important than fashion-able appearances and having money.

SUMMARY

Couples begin to deal with differences over money once they get engaged, if not before. Couples should have compatible ways of earning, spending, and saving money. When this isn't the case, counseling may help them reconcile their differences in ways they can both feel comfortable.

NOTES

1. Clifford Notarius and Howard Markman, *We Can Work It Out* (New York: G. P. Putnam's Sons, 1993), p. 56.

2. Michael McManus, *Marriage Savers* (Grand Rapids: Zondervan Publishing House, 1993), p. 29.

3. Michele Weiner-Davis, *Divorce Busting* (New York: Summit Books, 1992), p. 31.

    4. *Sefer Hamiddot* (Warsaw, 1912), p. 96.
    5. Eliezer Papo, *Pele Yoetz, Ahavat Ish V'Ishto.*

SUGGESTED READING

Forward, Susan. *Money Demons.* New York: Bantam Books, 1994.
Discusses financial issues in marriage and what to do about them.

17

Sexuality in Marriage

Many Americans view sex as the ultimate physical pleasure, and often relate to each other as objects who fulfill one another's fantasies.

Judaism enjoins us to become holy by separating ourselves from what can't be sanctified and by elevating what can. God created a physical world so that we would sanctify its permitted pleasures, abstain from pleasures that we can't make holy, and relate to the divine image in others. To this end, sex is supposed to be much more than a way to get physical and emotional pleasure.

Sex itself is morally and emotionally neutral. When we enjoy it in ways that God forbade, we degrade ourselves and our partner, no matter how good it feels. When we enjoy it with His blessing, He becomes a partner to our intimacy. This happens when we become givers who connect to the divine image in our partner and have relations in a state of holiness. Sexual intimacy is viewed as an act that integrates a Jewish couple's emotions, souls, and bodies, while the Divine Presence hovers above them.[1]

In medieval times, Nachmanides wrote, "God did not create anything that is inherently shameful. . . . He is pure of spirit, and nothing that comes from Him is intrinsically bad. . . . Whatever ugliness there is comes from people misusing what God gave them."[2]

How that contrasts with Christian views of sex! As Paul put it, "It is better to marry than to burn." Celibacy is the preferred state for Christians who want to be holy, and marriage is a concession to those who can't live up to that ideal.

By contrast, Judaism teaches that when a married couple experiences true intimacy, it gives them a taste of how profoundly God wants (so to speak) to have an intimate relationship with us, and how deeply we should want the same with Him.

This is why sexual maturity for a Jew is integrated with an intensified relationship with God. A Jewish boy's or girl's obligation to observe the Torah's commandments starts when he or she becomes sexually mature. In other words, the responsibilities of Jewish adulthood only begin when we can have a physical relationship with the opposite sex. This is because we cannot have a meaningful relationship with God until we feel the need to attach ourselves to, and unite with, another person. Once we yearn for such an intense connection with a person, we can channel those feelings into holy relationships with people and God.

Jewish men have permanent reminders on their sex organ (circumcisions) to uphold God's covenant with the Jewish people to bring holiness into the world. By sanctifying sexual relations, Jews insure the continuity of the Jewish nation as a holy people, devoted to God. By following the Jewish laws that govern sexual expression, couples bring children into this world in an atmosphere of holiness.

We feel a strong yearning to unite with a mate because of how God created humanity. The first human being was actually a male and female Siamese twin whom God later separated into Adam and Eve. When he separated them physically, he also separated them spiritually. By reuniting sexually, their souls reunited.

Since our soul was one with our life partner's before coming here, we feel incomplete until we reunite with our soul mate. Our sex drive is fueled by our soul's yearning to find completion with a spouse. Our bodies are vehicles that allow us to reunite two halves of one soul.

Thus, sex was intended to be an act of spiritual elevation, not one of self-service or hedonism. We are supposed to sanctify our desires and relate to a mate's divine soul, not have animalistic couplings.

Sanctified sex unifies our physical desires with our spiritual yearnings. One reason why the sex drive is so powerful is because of its inherent potential for sanctity. The more potential for holiness something has, the more it can potentially debase us. How we channel our sexuality has a far stronger spiritual effect than most people realize. The amount of holiness we create during marital intimacy even affects the quality of the soul that God puts into the resulting child.

A couple who wants to conceive should concentrate on bringing a child into this world who will make it a better place and fulfill his or her Godly mission here. The holier the intimacy that a couple creates during marital relations that lead to conception, the less limited their child will feel about what he or she can accomplish.

Sex is called *yediah* in biblical Hebrew, which means "knowledge." This is because marital relations were meant to be an outgrowth of a total understanding between a husband and wife. *Yediah* means intellectual knowledge, integrated with emotional understanding, that culminates in actions. When the Torah says that a man "knew" his wife,[3] it means that he expressed his love and understanding of her by nurturing her emotionally and physically. This expresses the idea that a couple should know and understand each other emotionally, intellectually, and spiritually before physically celebrating their intimacy. Such total unity helps promote the kind of spiritual and emotional development that God wanted us to have.

Using sex primarily for fun or pleasure divorces our souls and minds from our bodies and emotions. Judaism prohibits couples from having relations when they are not getting along, or when either is contemplating divorce, is drunk, is asleep, or does not want it.[4] This is because sex cannot be intimate or holy if a couple's mindset precludes being loving towards each other. Jewish marital relations are based on taking care of a partner whom we love and appreciate, not using a partner to gratify our lusts. Sex was intended to occur between two people who love each other, are fully aware of who they are with, and are totally focused on each other. Having sex while fantasizing about someone other than a spouse, being drunk, and so forth, are ways of relating to ourselves, not uniting two divine souls.

God wants us to invite Him into the most private part of our lives. Sanctifying sex is just as important as observing the Sabbath and eating kosher food. We make God our partner in every aspect of our lives, including in the bedroom.

This point is illustrated by a story that involved the Jewish Sage Rav. He taught his students that it was important to create intimacy with a wife by talking to her, making her laugh, and engaging in protracted foreplay before having marital relations. When he went home that night, he put his words into actions. After pleasuring his wife for a long time, a voice called out, "Hurry up already. How much of this do you need?"

The alarmed Sage peered under his bed, only to find Rav Kahana, one of his students, there. "What are you doing here?!" Rav asked.

The student replied, "In class, you taught us the theory of how to treat a wife in bed. I came here tonight to learn how to do it in practice."[5]

This story expresses that just as there are prescribed ways to pray, to celebrate Jewish holidays, and to keep kosher, there is also a uniquely Jewish way to sanctify sex.

Until recently in most Gentile societies, sex was a man's right and a woman's duty to provide. This is the opposite of what Judaism mandates. The Torah gives a wife sexual rights,[6] while her husband is obligated to satisfy her sexually.[7] Jewish men are required to temper their sex drives so as to give their wives physical and emotional pleasure.[8] Thus, husbands are supposed to have relations with a wife whenever she shows that she is interested, provided they are allowed to be intimate. Depriving a wife of relations for a prolonged period of time is grounds for divorce.

A man may not even take a job without his wife's consent if it will reduce the amount of time they spend together.[9] The first year of marriage he may not stay out-of-town overnight without her permission, and he is required to be especially attentive to her during those twelve months.[10]

Wives do not have parallel sexual obligations to their husbands, but they may not withhold sex as a weapon nor refuse to have relations for a long period of time.

Nachmanides described how a Jewish man is supposed to treat his wife when they have relations: He is supposed to initiate sexual intimacy with his wife by first talking to her lovingly, making her feel tranquil and happy to be with him, then arousing her with words that make her feel desire, emotional attachment, love, and passion.[11]

When he is ready for intimacy, he must make sure that she feels the same. He should not try to arouse her too quickly. He should be patient, try to please her, and make sure that she is sexually satisfied before he achieves his satisfaction.[12]

Jews must thank God before enjoying pleasures such as eating, drinking, or smelling fragrances. We must also say blessings before performing many religious duties, yet we don't say a blessing before having marital relations. If a husband is obligated to make love to his wife, one would think that he should say a blessing before he does it, yet he doesn't. This is because we never say a blessing when someone else's participation is needed, in case the recipient doesn't let us consummate the act.

However, we don't say a blessing over the pleasure of sex, either. Perhaps this is because our pleasure during marital relations comes from giving, not from taking. A Jewish man makes love by giving to his wife.[13] Jews don't make a blessing when they give pleasure, only when they take it.

Part of what makes sexual intimacy holy is the husband's sensitivity to his wife's emotional and physical needs. His desire to provide for her needs, rather than his own, sets the stage for a relationship where he is primarily a giver, like God, instead of a taker.

MARITAL ABSTINENCE

Jewish law forbids a husband and wife from touching each other when a woman has or expects her period, or has hormonally caused uterine bleeding. She is a *niddah* ("separated") at these times. Couples may not have a physical relationship until she properly immerses in a ritual bath, called a *mikvah,* a week after the bleeding stops. This is based on the biblical verses, "When a woman has a flow of blood, where blood flows from her body, she shall be separated for seven days . . ."[14] "And to a woman who is separated, [a man] should not approach to uncover her nakedness [i.e., to have sex]."[15] Once a young woman gets her first period, she remains a *niddah* until she properly immerses in a ritual bath just prior to her wedding.

Besides not touching each other when a woman is *niddah,* couples may not do things that could lead to physical contact, such as sleeping in the same bed, or handing or throwing objects to each other. These restrictions help couples realize that even seemingly insignificant actions and feelings towards each other are important to God. Also, it reinforces an awareness of how small actions are important in a relationship and can be used to foster intimacy.

When God oversees and is a partner to every aspect of a marriage, couples don't relate to each other in terms of, "What's best for me?" Instead they ask, "What's best for us, in God's eyes?" Learning to restrain ourselves and be sensitive to a partner with regard to sex sets the stage for being respectful and resolving differences in the rest of the relationship.

When a woman is *niddah,* she may not do "wifely" tasks for her husband. These include pouring him beverages, serving him food, or making his bed in the usual manner. If she wishes to serve him food, she places it slightly to the side of his place at the table instead of directly in front of him. She may make the bed if she wishes, but may not turn down the sheets. This reminds him every month of how many loving acts she customarily does for him, and it encourages him not to take her ongoing kindnesses for granted.

Women are always supposed to look attractive for their husbands—but not attracting to other men, even when the couple can't touch. In fact, the Talmud praised the wife of a Torah scholar who dressed in her nicest clothes before greeting him every night. Women who look unattractive for their husbands may encourage them to wonder if someone better is "out there."

The Talmud says that a woman becomes physically forbidden to her husband every month so that he will not grow tired of her.[16] This abstinence makes her as beloved to him every month as she was on their wedding day. Limiting a couple's physical relationship to approximately two weeks a month encourages them to celebrate a monthly emotional and spiritual honeymoon when she comes back from the *mikvah.* The related restrictions remind men not to view their wives as sex objects nor take them for granted. It also reminds couples to frequently perform little loving gestures for each other to preserve the romance in their marriage.

It does not take long for many couples to feel bored and stop appreciating each other. The "Seven Year Itch" reportedly takes only four years now, and as many as 60 percent of American men have cheated on their wives. Jewish marital laws can help keep the intimacy, excitement, and romance in marriage. Since "absence makes the heart grow fonder," and "forbidden fruit is sweetest," the patterns of separation and reunion help couples keep loving and desiring each other even after many years.

Our lives have cycles of intensity and withdrawal because emotions and physical sensations wax and wane. They don't stay constantly intense. Judaism regulates these cycles by giving us a built-in system for being intense, then separating, so that we can build an intensity again. By using these periods of separation to develop self-restraint and good verbal communication, we feed our marriages. Couples who can't tolerate physical separation will always lack a certain depth to their marriages.

Since the wife is the one who menstruates, she is the one who controls the sanctity of the marriage by telling her husband when they must separate or when they can resume physical intimacy. It is especially important for him to nurture her emotionally when she's *niddah,* and not think that the marriage is over for those two weeks. Physical separation should not trigger emotional distance, because staying emotionally connected during times of separation is critical to a marriage. It also makes reunion easy and pleasurable when it happens.

Since men and women often experience their physical relationship differently, their monthly separations may present different challenges to each of them. Since women may not feel like having sex during the first few days they are *niddah* anyway, relinquishing sex then may not be especially hard for them. But their husbands' sexual feelings do not run according to the wife's monthly cycle. Just as the men are getting comfortable after two weeks of sex, the wife "takes it away." This abrupt change in closeness is out of the husband's control, and is hard for some men to adjust to. It is not unusual for some men to take a year or longer to get used to this. Since men often associate acceptance with sexual intimacy, they may feel rejected or distanced when the wife abruptly makes sex off-limits every month.

Women, on the other hand, may find these prohibitions difficult because they can't touch or be held. Nonsexual closeness makes many women feel loved and calms them when they feel upset or stressed.

The quality of a marriage depends upon how many emotional "goodies" couples have in their relationship account. Using times of abstinence to say what they love and appreciate about each other, sharing warm memories, meaningful experiences and projects, giving gifts and treats, reading and writing each other poetry and love notes are all ways of using this time well. (See the chapter on "Keeping Love Alive.")

KEEPING THE INTIMACY

The more sex has become public and casual, the less intimacy it has retained. Strangers readily go to bed with one another, twelve-year-old children know all there is to know about sex, and nothing is left to the imagination in magazines, television, and movies.

For most Americans in the 1950s, sex was still a mystery before marriage. Sipping an ice cream soda from the same glass was an intimate experience. Holding hands was thrilling and exciting. The first kiss was a rapturous moment that could be recalled years later with fondness. Women, if not men, looked forward to the consummation of their marriage as an almost mystical union with their beloved. The sexual part of a physical relationship was reserved for a private, loving, lifetime partner.

The sexual revolution changed all that. Sex was cheapened and stripped of its privacy, exclusivity, and intimacy. The brush of two hands against each other was reduced to "nothing," instead of causing a flush of arousal and desire. Kisses between a husband and wife became dispassionate social greetings, except in the bedroom. The little rituals of intimacy, such as sharing food, were reduced to their functionality.

By making all forms of physical contact off-limits for two weeks every month, Judaism helps couples retain their excitement and passion. When couples become physically reacquainted every month, "casual" sharing, touching, and kissing have a renewed sense of allure that makes them anything but old hat.

Couples can be intimate on many levels. Having a physical encounter with no emotional preparation is like cashing a check on a bankrupt account. It feels empty. On the other hand, when couples use times of separation to make emotional contributions to their "relationship account," the caresses and kisses that follow feel like cashing a check for a million dollars. The more a physical relationship is backed by verbal expressions of love and warm feelings, the richer it becomes.

Couples can only be physically *intimate* if they feel emotionally intimate first. That can only happen if they communicate effectively in and out of the bedroom. Couples who can't let go of hurts and anger will bring these feelings into bed, making real intimacy impossible. We should use our monthly abstinence to communicate lovingly, "air out" differences, resolve problems, and create meaningful goals together. This strengthens a marriage enormously and sets the stage for feeling like newlyweds by the time the wife returns from the *mikvah*.

The laws of family holiness remind couples to evaluate their marriages every month. What do we need to work on? Are we making the most of our opportunities as a couple? If not, how can we do better? Instead of being embarrassed about starting over or admitting shortcomings, couples get monthly opportunities to put the past behind them and start their marriages anew.

When couples stop loving each other, they can always redevelop good feelings by acting as they did when they dated and grew in love.

This is expressed by a Torah law that requires us to help a Jew who needs our assistance.[17] If we don't like him but help him anyway, our altruistic act will make us overcome our dislike and stop perceiving him negatively.

The same happens in marriage. Couples often have times when they see their spouse as an enemy because discord is an inevitable part of marriage.[18] By acting lovingly, even when they don't feel like it, couples can overcome their distance and go back to being friends. The monthly cycles give couples ongoing chances to start over.

ENDING THE SEPARATION

When a married woman starts bleeding in a way that makes her *niddah,* this is day one of her cycle. On day five, or when the bleeding ends, whichever is longer, she determines that she is no longer bleeding by making an internal exam shortly before sunset. She does this by inserting a small ($2 \times 2''$ or $3 \times 3''$), white square of cloth into her vagina. If it has no bloodstains on it when she withdraws it, her period is over. She may use as many cloths as necessary to get a white specimen before sunset.

Once she gets an unstained cloth, she normally inserts another small, white cloth and leaves it inside her until nightfall. If it is unstained when she withdraws it, it shows definitively that she has stopped bleeding. The next day, she begins counting the first of seven "preparatory days." That entire week, she wears white underpants or white night garments so that bloodstains will be readily recognizable if her period has not really stopped.

She does an internal examination with a white cloth every morning and afternoon during these seven preparatory days. She does this to make sure that bleeding has not recurred. Some women spend a few minutes each of these days thinking about a different quality that they love in their husbands.

If a woman does not stain that week, she prepares for her immersion before sunset on the seventh preparatory day, finishing her preparations after dark. (Immersions on the Sabbath or Jewish holidays follow a slightly different protocol.)

This rough outline of how to observe the laws of family holiness may be altered for some women. They must speak to a qualified rabbi if they have breakthrough bleeding or spotting during the seven preparatory days; if they bleed for extended periods of time; if they have difficulty getting pregnant because they are *niddah* when they ovulate; if these observances create marital conflicts; and so on. The rabbi can recommend appropriate leniencies and/or practical suggestions.

To prepare for her immersion, a woman removes all of her jewelry, bandages, nail polish, and makeup, then takes a leisurely bath. She removes all dirt and loose pieces of skin from her body, as well as secretions in her eyes, ears, and nose. She cuts her fingernails and toenails and removes any dirt underneath. She brushes her teeth, shampoos her hair twice with a nonconditioning shampoo, and combs it free of tangles.

A woman may make these preparations in a private room at the *mikvah* building, or she may prepare at home. If she prepares at home, she needs to shower again in a private room at the *mikvah* before immersing to make sure that she is totally clean. She may immerse as early as forty-five or fifty minutes after sunset, or as late as 10 or 11 P.M., depending upon when the *mikvah* closes. Since *mikvahs* in every community have different hours, call your local *mikvah* to find out when they are open. Some are open by appointment only.

When a woman is ready to immerse, she slips into a bathrobe and slippers that are provided. She may say the following prayer, or other personal prayers, before immersing:

"May it be Your will, Lord our God, that Your Divine Presence rest between my husband and myself. May Your holy Name be unified through us, and cause a spirit of purity and holiness to enter our hearts. Distance me from all bad thoughts and fantasies, and give my husband and me pure and clean souls. Let neither of us desire anyone else, but let me desire my husband, and let him desire me. And let me feel that no man in the world is better, more handsome, and more gracious than my husband. . . . And so should I seem to him, that no woman in the world is more beautiful, gracious, and appropriate for him than me. Let him think only about me and no one else. . . . As it is said, 'Therefore shall a man leave his father and his mother and cleave unto his wife.'

"And may it be Your will, Lord our God, that our union be beautiful and proper, with love, unity, peace, and friendship, according to the law of Moses and Judaism, with proper fear of Heaven and fear of sin. Let our union result in healthy, deserving children who are righteous, perfect, and upright, whose bodies will not be damaged or lacking, and who will have no affliction, plague, sickness, disease, pain, trouble, weakness, or failing, but only goodness all the days of their lives. Let our union be blessed, as it says, 'Your wife shall be like a fruitful vine in your house, your children like planted olive trees around your table.'

"Our marriage should be one where my husband is happier with me than with all of the good things he has in the world. There should never be anger, quarreling, contention, or jealousy between us, only love, unity, peace, friendship, humility, modesty, patience, righteousness, charitable deeds, and doing good to [God's] creatures.

"Our souls, spirits, and bodies should form a union that will allow holiness and purity to flow in thought, speech, and action as befits proper Jews. Our union should accord with the Jewish laws of holiness, with success and blessing of Heaven above and of the deep below, blessings of the breasts and the womb. A union of holy and pure seed, good and beautiful, sweet and acceptable. . . ."[19]

When she finishes praying, she summons the *mikvah* attendant by pressing a buzzer, and steps into the adjoining *mikvah* room. Most preparation rooms open into the *mikvah* so that no one sees her except the attendant.

After the attendant makes sure that the woman has prepared properly, the woman steps out of her robe and slippers and walks down a few steps into the ritual bath. The bath looks like a tiny, private swimming pool, approximately five feet by eight feet by four feet deep. It is filled with clean, warm water.

She stands with her feet apart, her arms away from her body, and her fingers spread apart so that her fingers are separated. She quickly bends her knees so that her entire body is submerged for a few seconds. When she stands up, the attendant tells her "kosher" if she immersed properly. The attendant then hands her a clean washcloth, which the woman puts on her head before reciting, "Blessed are You, God, Ruler of the Universe, who has sanctified us with Your commandments and commanded us about the immersion." She hands the attendant the cloth and immerses at least two more times. She then walks up the steps and out of the water, where the attendant helps her into a robe. The woman returns to her preparation room and gets dressed.

The laws of family holiness are more detailed than can be summarized here. Readers who are interested in observing these beautiful laws can learn more about them from the "Suggested Readings," or by consulting a local *mikvah* association. Women customarily take individual or group instruction from a woman who is specially trained to teach this. Books do not give enough information to practice these laws properly.

MYTHS ABOUT FAMILY HOLINESS

God commanded us to observe the laws of family holiness so that we would be holy, not for hygienic reasons. It happens that couples who observe these laws get medical benefits from them but that is not why God gave them to us.

Some people think that the laws of family holiness originated with ancient taboos about menstruation. This is nonsense. Couples separate from each other when the woman is *niddah* so that they can ultimately draw closer to God, not because a *niddah* is "taboo" or contaminated by evil spirits. A husband is not forbidden to touch his *niddah* wife because she will make him "unclean" or "defiled," as is proven by the fact that she may touch male family members. Nor does she immerse to get rid of bad blood or evil spirits. She does it to change her status from being physically off-limits to her husband to being permitted and to remove spiritual blockages between her body and soul.

Some people confuse the concept of "ritual impurity" with poor hygiene. They erroneously think that modern hygiene makes the laws of *mikvah* obsolete. Some misinformed women even think that a bath or dip in a jacuzzi is as good as immersing in a *mikvah!*

The biblical words "ritual purity" and "impurity" are mistranslations of the Hebrew words *taharah* and *tumah,* respectively. *Taharah* actually means "spiritual blockage," and *tumah* means "spiritual free flow." Both men and women can become ritually impure, and, in fact, all Jews are so today. The implication for us today is that we are forbidden to enter the Temple Mount in Jerusalem.

A "ritually impure" person is spiritually blocked, not taboo, evil, or unacceptable. When the Temple stood, a ritually impure person was forbidden to enter it until he or she reinstated a fuller connection with their soul.

Ritual "impurity" occurs when our souls cannot fully influence our bodies. This happens most intensely when we encounter some form of death. The laws of ritual impurity remind us that we will all die some day, and should use this world to develop our spiritual sensitivities and not pursue physical pleasure as an end in itself.

Nothing that happens to us is accidental. God deliberately created menstrual cycles to teach us that the physical world is finite and limited. Its true purpose is to give us an opportunity to elevate it spiritually.

A Jewish couple is supposed to separate when the woman's period tells her that potential life (her egg) has died, and that physical life is finite. Everything physical eventually dies. Only our souls, our spiritual contributions to the world, and our connection to God are everlasting. A woman's period signals the couple to limit their physical relationship and develop the spiritual aspect of their marriage.

When a woman who wants to conceive menstruates, she feels a loss of potential life that makes her sad. She then experiences a spiritual blockage. Immersing in a *mikvah* allows her to reinstate a spiritual free flow so that she and her husband can reconnect fully with their spiritual Source.

What distinguishes a *mikvah* from a bathtub is that a *mikvah* has water that God put here without human intervention. Most *mikvahs* use rainwater that collects and flows inside the *mikvah,* where it mixes with regular water, and is heated. Natural bodies of water, such as lakes or oceans, may also be used as *mikvahs.*

The *mikvah*'s water symbolically dissolves our mortal barriers and connects us to God, who is infinite and eternal. Women may not have even a speck of dirt on them when they immerse because nothing can stand between them and the Source of spiritual blessing when they reconnect to Him. Once a woman is spiritually revitalized, she can renew her physical connection with her husband and bring spiritual blessing into her marriage and home.

The laws of family purity have been a foundation of Jewish life for 3,300 years and are a magnificent heirloom that has enhanced our families. The *mikvah* is so important that if a community has only enough money to build a synagogue or a *mikvah,* the *mikvah* takes precedence. While the synagogue is important, the sanctity of family life is paramount.

GOOD SEX

A good sex life requires a lot more than chemistry and special techniques. This is borne out by the fact that sexual problems are the second most distressing marital problem,[20] despite the fact that most Americans live together before marriage.

How we feel about our bodies and sex are strongly influenced by our upbringing, religious beliefs, and experiences. Guilt, mistrust, fear of losing control, fear of losing one's identity, difficulty integrating sexual and loving feelings, and anxiety about intimacy can all cause sexual problems. So can poor communication of feelings and needs and unresolved anger in and out of the bedroom. Sexual compatibility also requires tremendous sensitivity, as each partner tells or shows the other how to become more skilled at providing what each needs.

Because sex involves so much emotional and physical accommodation, satisfying sex for most couples may take one to three years. Differences over sexual needs and occasional sexual problems are common.

Good sex starts with a basic knowledge of a man's and woman's physiology, the mechanics of sex, and how sexual feelings are developed, heightened, and satisfied. Couples with no sexual experience should read a sex manual shortly before getting married so that they will know what to expect and do on their wedding night. The woman should ask her gynecologist how to make sex comfortable and what to expect initially.[21] Women's bodies change during pregnancy and when nursing, and the ways they affect sex should also be discussed with one's doctor.[22]

One in five or six couples who want to conceive will still not be pregnant after a year of trying. They should read a lay person's guide to infertility and consult a gynecologist. Couples who observe the laws of family holiness should explain their practices to the doctor. If a fertility workup is recommended for either spouse, a qualified rabbi should be consulted before proceeding. He may recommend specialists who are familiar with implementing tests and treatments in halachically acceptable and minimally disruptive ways.

SEXUAL DYSFUNCTIONS

Men have two primary kinds of sexual dysfunction. Those who are impotent cannot get or maintain an erection. Those who ejaculate prematurely climax before several minutes of intercourse, or before their wives are satisfied, whichever occurs first.

Most men occasionally have these problems. For example, they may ejaculate prematurely on their wife's *mikvah* night, or at other times when the couple has relations for the first time after a prolonged separation. The major cause of premature ejaculation is men's anxiety about performing. Removing their pressure to perform and building their self-confidence often remedies this.[23]

Some men become impotent when they are worried, distracted, emotionally overwhelmed, or exhausted. This is normal, unless it happens frequently. When impotence is due to ongoing emotional problems, such as unresolved anger toward a wife or fear of intimacy, professional help is in order.

Yonason felt like a total failure when he didn't get a raise at work. He became so preoccupied with feeling inadequate that he couldn't have relations with his wife. The more he worried about it and the more he thought about how inadequate he was, the less he was able to perform. Adina's response helped build his confidence instead of sending him on a downward spiral. Had she done nothing to take away his sense of inadequacy, his problem would have gotten worse. Had she been "honest" and shared her feelings that she felt cheated, disappointed, and dissatisfied, he would have felt even more inadequate and would have taken much longer to recover.

She took pressure off him by telling him that the sex act was not that important to her and that he could satisfy her in many other ways. She suggested that they abstain from sex for a few days and, instead, massage and touch each other in loving, nonsexual ways. Focusing on the pleasure of touching, rather than on having sex, took away his pressure to perform, and felt great to her. A week later, their sex life was back to normal.

As much as 50 percent of male impotence today is caused by medical factors. Prostate, heart and circulatory problems, aging, diabetes, and antihypertensive medications are frequent culprits in older men. Antidepressant medication, alcohol, and recreational drugs often cause problems for men of any age. Couples with sexual problems should rule out medical or drug factors before assuming that emotional problems are the cause. Both psychological and medical factors can occur simultaneously.

Morey battled depression off and on for years, and finally consulted a psychiatrist, who prescribed a daily antidepressant. A year later, he married Darlene. Much to their dismay, Morey became impotent within minutes of any amorous encounter. Before assuming that he had unresolved conflicts with her, he discussed the problem with his psychiatrist. Changing his medication solved the problem.

The most common sexual problem for women is the inability to have an orgasm. As with men, taking antidepressants can kill a woman's sex drive and functioning. When that is not the reason for the problem, women usually need to learn about their bodies and how sexual arousal and orgasm occurs. (See the "Suggested Readings.") Once women feel comfortable with their bodies and learn what feels good, they can teach or show their husbands what to do.

Some women are afraid of intimacy with men, or they fear letting go. Some feel that sex is shameful or disgusting, and/or are uncomfortable with their bodies and sexuality. They are unlikely to be sexually fulfilled if they don't change their feelings and may need professional help to do this.

Couples who aren't able to remedy their sexual problems after a month or two of trying should consult a marriage counselor. Discussing such intimate matters with friends or relatives usually causes more problems than it solves. They are prone to giving misinformation, feeling uncomfortable hearing these private details of your life, and may also share your confidences with others.

SEXUAL EXPECTATIONS

People often have a host of unrealistic expectations about sex, such as thinking that it should be great from the start.[24] Just figuring out how to coordinate schedules, adapt to a partner's needs, make the setting comfortable, touch and kiss a partner the way she or he likes, and feel comfortable with each other's bodies can easily take a year or more.

Men may need little physical or emotional stimulation to become aroused, while women are likely to need affection, loving talk, and lots of caressing to become aroused. Since women need emotional and physical preparation for sex, men should spend a *minimum* of ten to fifteen minutes setting an emotional or romantic mood, drawing a wife close with loving words, hugs, and kisses. When she is ready, foreplay should last at least another five to ten minutes.

Since men's and women's needs tend to be so different, couples need to show or tell each other what they want in bed, just as they do in other areas of marriage. Couples should never assume that a partner knows what pleases them. Spouses who find it hard to tell a partner how they want to be touched or kissed can guide the partner's hand or mouth. Those who feel uncomfortable even with this can write a note and give it to the spouse or leave it on his or her night table.

Carol pushed Sam away when he grabbed and kissed her, then tried to have sex soon after. She assumed that he knew that she needed conversation and cuddling to get her in the mood. She didn't know that men can feel close to a woman without conversation, and Sam did not know that she needed romance and caresses to feel loved.

She was convinced that he was selfish and didn't care about her feelings. Had she only told him what pleased her, he would have tried to make her happy.

One night they had a big fight. Carol was shocked and revolted that Sam wanted to have sex afterwards. She was still angry at him and could not believe that he wanted to have sex under the circumstances. She told this to a therapist-friend who explained, "Men often have a need to reconcile physically when they are criticized or hurt by their wives. After their wives have been distant, this makes men feel accepted and loved. Women can't imagine wanting to have sex when they are still angry at a man. Women reinstate closeness by reconciling first with words and nonsexual touching. Men may try to do it through sex first."

Women usually seek spiritual and emotional fulfillment in sex more than men do, and feel exploited, hurt, and/or angry when that is missing. If sex feels physically good to many men, it is automatically satisfying to them. Men are generally less in tune with feelings than women are, and may not even know what they feel, let alone know how to express warmth, love, and intimacy in words, or via sex. As the old adage goes, "Women have sex to get love; men give love to have sex."

Men often compartmentalize sex and emotions, so that they may not know how to use sex to express love. Without learning otherwise, foreplay may not seem gratifying to them, except as a means to the "real" goal, which is sex. For women, the real goal is intimacy with a partner, and sex is an outgrowth of that process.

Shlomo was emotionally unsophisticated and didn't understand how sex expressed love. Love and sex seemed like two different things to him. Tobi felt disconnected and hurt by his lack of romance and decided it was time to see a therapist because she often felt angry at him in bed.

The counselor taught Tobi that Shlomo was neither uncaring nor selfish, but he needed Tobi's help to know how to express his feelings lovingly. While she knew how to express love through sex, he did not. Their physical relationship improved dramatically once she told and showed him how to treat her in bed.

Besides having sexual intimacy, couples also need to enjoy physical closeness and intimacy without sex. Touching, caressing, holding hands, and massage are ways of being affectionate that can be enjoyed with or without sex.

SUMMARY

The quality of one's sex life is unrelated to how many orgasms a couple has, how often they have sex, or how many positions they try. What is important is how sensitively they communicate and respond to each other's emotional and physical needs and how much they bring God into their relationship.

NOTES

1. *Sotah* 17a.
2. Nachmanides, *Iggeret Hakodesh,* chapter 3.
3. As in Genesis 4:1; 4:17 and 4:25.
4. *Gittin* 90a.
5. *Berakhot* 62b.
6. Deuteronomy 24:5.
7. *Niddah* 71a.
8. Tosefot Rid to *Yevamot* 12b.
9. This is derived from the verse in Exodus (21:10) "He may not diminish her food allowance, clothing provisions and time spent having intimate relations."
10. Based on Deuteronomy (24:15), "He must remain free for his home for one year and gladden the wife that he took."
11. *Iggeret Hakodesh,* quoted by Maimonides, ed. Chavel, 2:336.
12. Ibid.
13. The word *ahavah* comes from the root *hav,* which means "to give." From a kabbalistic point of view, when a couple has marital relations, the man gives his seed and the woman receives and nurtures it.
14. Leviticus 15:19.
15. Leviticus 18:19.
16. *Niddah* 31b.
17. Based on Exodus 23:5 and Deuteronomy 22:4.
18. *Shabbat* 130a.
19. From *Chupat Chasanim.*
20. Clifford Notarius and Howard Markman, *We Can Work It Out* (New York: G. P. Putnam's Sons, 1993), p. 56.
21. Some women need to use lubricants. All of them, except egg whites or saliva, may prevent conception because they immobilize or kill sperm, although lubricants are not reliable contraceptives. Women who are over thirty-five, or who are nursing, often need lubricants to make sex comfortable.
22. For example, even weeks or months after giving birth, many mothers find that sex is either uncomfortable or painful. This is common and should be discussed with one's obstetrician before it causes marital problems.
23. Judaism recommends marital relations with the man on top of the woman, especially when conception is possible. But this position exacerbates men's sexual dysfunctions. Sex therapists usually recommend positions with the couple side by side, or with the woman on top. Consult your rabbi if this presents halachic problems for you.

Premature ejaculation and impotence are usually remedied, at least in part, by taking pressure off the man to have sex. The couple touches each other only in nonsexual ways for a few days, then adds sexual caresses to their repertoire. After a week or so, the couple has relations with the wife on top, stopping the stimulation before the man climaxes. They repeat the stimulation, then stop several more times before he climaxes. As his self-control improves, they resume less structured intimacy.

24. One common misconception, promoted by novels and movies, is that women usually climax during intercourse. Men usually do, but most women do not, unless the man somehow stimulates his wife at the same time.

SUGGESTED READING

Abramov, Tehilla. *The Secret of Jewish Femininity.* Brooklyn: Targum Press, 1988.

Kaplan, Aryeh. *Waters of Eden.* New York: Union of Orthodox Jewish Congregations of America, 1982.

Lamm, Norman. *A Hedge of Roses.* New York: Feldheim, 1977.

Masters, William, Johnson, Virginia, and Kolodny, Robert. *Heterosexuality.* New York: Harper Perennial, 1994. A sexuality textbook covering topics such as love and intimacy, sex and sensuality, sexual problems, and infertility. Some infertility information is outdated, and some ideas contradict Jewish law. The factual information and self-help exercises for sexual problems are otherwise very helpful.

Renshaw, Domeena. *Seven Weeks to Better Sex.* New York: Random House, 1995. A self-help book for couples with sexual problems. Recommended exercises need to be adapted to accord with Jewish law.

18

In-Laws

D espite the fact that in-laws were once reputedly the third major reason for divorce, few singles consider their impact before marriage. While many in-laws are wonderful and fully accept new members of their family, others are nasty and critical, intrusive, or offensive. Some parents have such a hard time separating from their children (and vice versa) that they pit the child against his or her spouse, and interfere with raising the grandchildren. Some newlyweds realize only too late how intertwined a spouse is with his or her parents.

Ilene and Yaakov were very much in love – until a month before their wedding. Her parents rightfully insisted that she have him sign a prenuptial agreement, but it was terribly biased in her favor. When Yaakov refused, the parents insisted that their daughter call off the wedding, and she dutifully complied. For years, Yaakov has rued the fact that he didn't sign the agreement, thinking that they would have had an ideal life together. He doesn't realize that Ilene is so enmeshed with her parents that their controlling her prenuptially was a portent of things to come. They will continue ruling her when she gets married because she is unable and unwilling to go against their wishes, and they have very definite ideas about how she should live and be treated by a husband.

When a couple gets married, their primary emotional bond and loyalty should be to their spouse, not to their parents. The Torah expresses this by saying, "Therefore shall a man leave his father and his mother, and cling unto his wife, and they shall be one flesh."[1] Singles must separate from parents and make their own decisions once they get married. Unfortunately, some people refuse to do this. Others may make their own decisions, but keep seeking emotional "goodies" from parents that they should have given up.

Itzi made a good living as an engineer, but still lived at home at the age of thirty-one. He didn't have to do laundry, shop, or cook, and his mother was pleased to take care of him. When he got married, he expected Charlene to do the same for him. She was quite nurturing but having a career made it difficult to find the time or energy to do everything he wanted. Instead of helping at home, Itzi stopped by his mother's house on his way home from work and ate dinner there most weeknights. He also gave her his dirty laundry, and she washed and ironed it for him.

Charlene initially felt insulted and angry about her husband and mother-in-law's inability to separate from each other. By accepting that neither Itzi nor his mother were ready to cut the apron strings, Charlene stopped trying to change them. Instead of cooking for him when she came home early, she went out to eat by herself or made herself a nice meal at home. When he came home later than she did, she went out to lectures, read, chatted with girlfriends on the telephone, or took a nice, long bath. Three months after they got married, Itzi finally stopped going to his mother's so often, although he did talk to her every few days by phone. Charlene decided that if she couldn't beat them, she would join them. She gave Itzi her laundry to take to his mother's along with his. Two years later, Mama decided that she'd been doing laundry for two families long enough. Itzi had no choice but to do laundry himself.

Some parents wreak havoc on a marriage by manipulating their child or trying to divide and conquer the couple. These parents are desperate to keep their child's loyalty and dependence, and feel threatened by their child replacing them with a spouse.

Faith's mother called every day, and never lost an opportunity to criticize Faith and her husband. By the time she hung up, Faith felt awful. Jim couldn't tolerate this intrusiveness and hung up on Mother when she called. Mother then called repeatedly until Faith picked up the phone, only to hear Mother cry about Jim's viciousness. Mother's manipulation wreaked havoc on Faith, and she asked Jim to be more tolerant. He insisted that Mother was acting inappropriately and that he wouldn't tolerate her abuse. This happened at least once a week and made Faith a nervous wreck as she tried to mediate between her husband and mother.

Faith needed to distance herself emotionally from her mother and set firm limits on Mother's manipulation and criticism. When Mother became manipulative or critical on the phone, Faith respectfully changed the subject. If Mother continued being inappropriate, Faith ended the conversation and let the answering machine pick up Mother's plaintive cries for the rest of the evening. When Mother refused to stop destroying Faith and her marriage, Faith had no choice but to screen all of her phone calls and set painful limits on her Mother.

Couples are often surprised and devastated by in-laws' intrusiveness, especially when there are grandchildren. These problems are often compounded when the couple is religious, but their parents are not.

When Deena became a *baalat teshuva* (observant Jewess), her parents were terrified that she would marry a religious fanatic with a long beard, sidecurls, and black hat who eschewed secular education and work. They were relieved when she got engaged to Baruch, an attractive, clean-shaven, well-educated school administrator.

But their relief was short-lived. Deena grew to love Baruch's parents, and liked them better than her own. The newlyweds spent every *Shabbat* and all Jewish holidays with his observant and warm family. Deena consulted her mother-in-law about how to set up a Jewish home, where to buy home furnishings, kosher food, and religious items. Deena also went clothes shopping with her mother-in-law, which only compounded her mother's sense of rejection.

Deena didn't like spending time with her parents because they were so critical of her, and they had little in common. They believed that traditional Jews lived in the Dark Ages, that Baruch was a male chauvinist, and that he didn't treat her well. Their negative comments made Deena even less inclined to visit.

Had Deena been more sensitive to her parents' feelings, her parents could have felt less threatened. She could have included her mother more as she planned the wedding, and realized that her mother wanted to share her homemaking knowledge and ideas with her married daughter. Most mothers find it very painful to be shut out—or worse, to be supplanted in their daughters' affection by strangers. Some of this hurt can be minimized if a married child invites parents to join them occasionally for visits. Some in-laws are even happy to invite the other in-laws (*machatenesters*) for family gatherings, holidays, or *Shabbat* meals.

Unless your mother is so opinionated that spending time together is a nightmare, invite her to join you when you shop. Most mothers appreciate being asked for suggestions about what to buy for your new home, even if you don't follow the advice.

Since most secular parents are intimidated by the "bizarre" behaviors and beliefs of their *baalei teshuva* children, a sensitive rabbi or rebbetzin can do wonders to help smooth things over. Very often, a stranger can accomplish what the child cannot. Children who show sensitivity to secular parents and try to accommodate them within the parameters of Jewish law go a long way towards making parents feel less threatened. Time, and having grandchildren, also helps.

Leah was so excited when she got engaged to Moti, but her mother wasn't enthused. Not only wasn't Moti the kind of man she had hoped her daughter would marry, but Selma had many fears. Would her beloved daughter become estranged from her? Would the family stop spending Passover and Rosh Hashana together? Selma ran a traditional home, yet her daughter was now saying that Selma's standards weren't good enough. Would Leah abandon her mother in favor of her new husband, community, rebbetzin, and in-laws?

Leah was sensitive to her mother's anxieties, and told her that she would like her mother to help her plan the wedding. She also reassured her mother that as long as Leah could clean Selma's house the way Leah wanted, and use new pots, pans, and utensils, Leah and Moti would continue to spend Passover with her parents. Leah then suggested that they read a book about Jewish weddings together and meet the rabbi. The rabbi explained what the ceremony would entail, and stressed the role that Selma would play at the *tenaim* and *chupah*. This made Selma feel wanted and important. The rebbetzin also met with her and explained what *sheva brachot* were, and suggested ways that Selma could help Leah set up a Jewish home. Demystifying the rituals and treating the mother as a person who deserved respect went a long way toward allaying her fears. By the time Leah's wedding came, Selma actually enjoyed it!

Unfortunately, some parents inflict their emotional problems on their child and new spouse, causing untold misery. But it is hard for them to break up a marriage unless the couple already has problems of their own. By forming a united front and not letting parents divide or manipulate them, spouses won't end up siding with their parents against each other.

Neither Chaya nor Chaim were emotionally ready for marriage when they tied the knot in their mid-twenties. Each had many dreams and expectations, and were very distraught when they weren't fulfilled. To vent her feelings, Chaya reported Chaim's shortcomings to her mother every day. Mom readily reinforced Chaya's dissatisfaction by telling Chaya how much better Chaya's sisters' and friends' husbands were and how hopeless Chaya's marriage sounded. Meanwhile, Chaim's mother called every few days to criticize Chaya to him.

Chaim loved his mother, but Chaya hated everything about her. If Chaya refused to spend *Shabbat* at her in-laws, Chaim got angry and felt deprived. If Chaim accepted his mother's invitations, Chaya got angry. Before long, Chaya and Chaim hated each other. The fragile love that they once felt for each other never had a chance to be nurtured.

Parents can easily kill a marriage before the couple is able to build a strong connection to each other. Parents and children should never disparage the spouse, and should quickly end any conversations that do. Couples must also not allow parents to interfere with their marital harmony nor reinforce their doubts about each other, except when abuse is likely or occurring.

Arlene and Marty ran a business together. When they ran into financial difficulties, she asked her wealthy parents for a $10,000 loan to tide them over for a year. Her parents took this opportunity to tell Arlene for the hundredth time what a mistake she had made by ignoring their warnings and marrying her inadequate husband. They offered her a loan at 12 percent interest (which is forbidden by Jewish law, apart from being nasty), with the stipulation that she repay them within the year. Marty was enraged at his in-laws for treating his wife so shabbily and insisted that she desist from any future contact with them.

The Torah says that we must honor[2] and fear our parents. It doesn't say that we must love them.[3] We must act and speak respectfully to them, but not let them abuse us or ruin our marriages.

Arlene knew that her parents were abusive but wasn't prepared to sever ties with them. She and Marty argued for two months about how to deal with this. When Arlene sought professional help, the therapist suggested a way to get a loan that neither Arlene nor Marty had known about. The counselor also suggested that Arlene distance herself from her parents for a year. At that time, Arlene could reassess the situation. This advice saved their marriage.

Shelly and Bob moved a mile away from her parents when they got married. Shelly and her mother talked on the telephone every day and saw each other twice a week. Bob was dismayed at how enmeshed Shelly and her mother were, especially since his mother-in-law criticized and bossed them both around. He boiled inside every time he came home and found Momma there. She was sure to tell him or Shelly what to do several times an hour.

After a year of this, Bob told Shelly that they needed to move. Shelly wouldn't hear of it. Bob then asked Shelly to limit her phone calls to Momma because Momma encouraged her daughter to spend too much money and made Bob look bad.

Jewish law was on Bob's side. A wife's first loyalty is to her husband, not to her parents. She is not allowed to let her parents interfere with her marriage. If the wife thinks that her husband is being unduly possessive or unreasonable, they should discuss this with a rabbi or therapist.

When Shelly was pregnant with their first child, she was confined to bed for a few months. Momma took care of her and cleaned the house every day. Bob was grateful for the help, which he otherwise could not have afforded, but he also felt like he was in boot camp. Momma told him to hang up his coat, not to leave his dishes in the sink, not to put his feet up on the coffee table, and so forth. She kept "straightening" his papers and threw out what she considered junk. A month before Shelly was due, Bob had had it with Matilda, the Mum.

Bob realized that things would only get worse after the baby arrived. He told Shelly that she must tactfully set limits on her mother's intrusiveness, and learn to deal with her mother's consequent anger and disapproval. Shelly said that she couldn't change her mother and refused to get professional help for her inability to disengage. Bob decided to stand up to his mother-in-law and respectfully told her to leave the house when he got home at night. He also locked the door to his den so that she couldn't clean it. After the baby came, he got volunteer help from neighbors and friends in the community. He told Momma that she could no longer come on *Shabbat* because he and Shelly needed time alone together. Both Momma and Shelly were very angry at him for putting his foot down, and his wife resented him doing this for years.

The above scenarios illustrate how important it is for couples to form a united front and set firm limits on parents when the latter are intrusive. Couples should see a sensitive rabbi or therapist as soon as possible, and as often as is necessary, to nip explosive marital problems in the bud. They must also not discuss their problems or criticize their spouse to their parents, unless the parents are exceptionally objective and adept at suggesting solutions.

THE SANDWICH GENERATION

Many couples today are, or will be part of, the "Sandwich Generation." They will be stuck in the middle between parents who need their help and support and the needs of their spouses and children. If parents become debilitated, severely depressed, have ongoing health problems, or need home care, one child often becomes their financial support and coordinates the needed services. Needless to say, this can be a full-time job and can severely strain a marriage emotionally and financially.

Adults in the "Sandwich Generation" have to divide their time, money, and energy between their aging parents, their spouse, and children. While husbands typically help their parents financially, wives are more apt to give personal care, even when they work full-time, run a home, and raise children. If the parents' intensive needs continue for years, their married children have many difficult choices to make.

Lou's mother had Alzheimer's disease, and he wasn't willing to put her in a nursing home. He moved her into his house against Marla's wishes (which is forbidden by Jewish law). His mother's forgetfulness and lack of self-control soon became a serious problem. She was sometimes hostile to her grandchildren, frequently left the stove burners on, and got locked in the bathroom twice. Bubbie required almost constant supervision, which Marla couldn't provide. After Bubbie wandered out of the house unnoticed one day, Marla fought bitterly with Lou about putting Bubbie in a nursing home. They could not afford home nursing care, yet Lou wanted to believe that his mother could live at home if Marla only tried harder to supervise her. After six months of fighting with his wife, he finally put his mother in a nursing home, then felt guilty when she died two weeks later. Part of him blamed Marla for his mother's death.

Evelyn's mother fell and broke her hip, then had a series of medical complications resulting in a four-month hospitalization. Since Mother didn't get adequate medical or nursing care in the hospital, Evelyn stopped by there every day on her way home from work. After making sure that her mother had clean linens, homemade food, necessary medication, and was comfortable, Evelyn went home to her husband and six children. Needless to say, she was exhausted, the children were bouncing off the walls, and her husband, Barry, was at his wits' end. To make matters worse, Mother's house developed a leaky roof during the winter and desperately needed repairs. Evelyn thought she would have a nervous breakdown, and she and her husband became ships passing in the night. He was angry at her for neglecting him and the children, and for not making her sister share responsibilities with her. Evelyn was angry at him for not being more understanding.

SUMMARY

While parents shouldn't interfere with their children's marriages, they often do. When it happens, children need to set limits on their parents, create a united front, and put their marriage first. When they are unable to do this, professional help is in order.

NOTES

1. Genesis 2:24.
2. Exodus 20:12; Deuteronomy 5:16.
3. Rambam, Responsa #369.

19

Children and Marriage

Some people think that having children makes a good marriage better and a bad marriage worse. There is nothing as wonderful as feeling a child's love, excitement about life, and innocence, as parents help him or her develop. Raising a little person together makes some couples feel even more bonded, yet it can also highlight their differences and bring out their worst character deficiencies.

Jewish men are required to have children so that they will bring Jewish souls into the world who will serve God. In the process of raising children, both parents develop their inner Godliness and spiritual potentials by giving, and hopefully improve their own character traits.

Jewish parents have an awesome responsibility, being partners with the Almighty each time they create a child.[1] They are responsible for teaching and modeling to children how to do *mitzvot* (commandments), sanctify daily life, relate to people, and feel the Almighty's presence in everything they do. They should inspire children to love God and Judaism, taking the child's age and personality into account. Parents need to help develop each child's character, including the practice of kindness and charity. In short, parents show their children how to be *menschen* and live holy lives.

When God responded to Eve after she ate the forbidden fruit in the Garden of Eden, He told her that raising children would be painful.[2] Parents feel pained when they see their children imitating the parents' bad behavior. This hopefully motivates parents to improve themselves for their children's sake.

Annette heard her three-year-old son Larry cursing like a sailor. She ran over to him and demanded, "Who taught you those words?"

"Daddy did, Mommy," he replied.

"Daddy did?" she asked, taken aback.

"Yeah, he tripped over my shoes this morning, and this is what he said when it happened!"

Children learn from parents' "casual" remarks, negative comments about others, inconsistencies between what they say and do, and parental fights. Parents become more aware of who they are, and who they should be, when children hear, see, and imitate them.

Whether we like it or not, we are stand-ins for God in this world. We constantly model to children what He is like and how He relates to us. If we are patient, compassionate, loving, respectful, fair, and give children what they need, children believe that a Heavenly Parent is also this way. If parents have serious shortcomings, children assume that God has the same problems.

Thus, raising Jewish children is an awesome responsibility that gives us a chance to be almost godlike. By being who we are supposed to be, parents can help children realize their potential, and both can grow in the process.

A couple's world is never the same once they have children. Parents must get used to being emotionally and physically exhausted and being out-of-control. A good night's sleep and predictable schedules are a thing of the past. (As the author wrote this, a friend called. Her son had pushed his sister down a flight of stairs and broke her leg. They had spent the morning in the Emergency Room.) Parents need to be flexible, creative, patient, and giving, in ways that constantly stretch them to improve.

Even when couples love each other, having children is almost invariably stressful. Studies have shown that almost all new parents feel that their marriages suffer once they have a child. For example, one study showed that 92 percent of new parents had less marital satisfaction and more conflicts than before they had children.[3] Another study showed that only 19 percent of couples thought their marriages had improved after having children.[4] While almost all of these couples expected a new baby to bring them closer, nearly all new parents grew further apart and became more self-centered, as strain and chronic fatigue took their toll.

After having a baby, it is a challenge to make time to be together in pleasant ways, and managing time well becomes essential. Husbands often feel that they are competing with their children for a wife's attention. When the wife always has time for the children, but not much for him, he may feel jealous or angry that he is no longer a priority.

Since children need a lot of attention, and will take as much as parents give, couples must be careful not to make a spouse feel short-changed. They can do this by getting a babysitter and going on weekly dates, or getting away periodically for a weekend. If a wife spends most of her time nursing a baby and/or taking care of small children, she should not make her husband feel like an afterthought. Letting him know that she thinks about him and that he is important to her, asking him to spend time with her (not only to do things for her or the children), and greeting him with enthusiasm when he comes home are some ways of doing this.

After Nicole had their second baby, Steve came home night after night to a messy house. Nicole didn't even keep food in the refrigerator or pantry, so he got used to shopping on his way home from work. Then he made his own meals while she took care of the children. He felt completely neglected. He even lost his attraction to her because she wore dirty sweatsuits or stained, shapeless house-coats around the house. To make matters worse, they couldn't even have a physical relationship for three months because of her post-partum bleeding. That only added to their tension.

Even though she claimed to be too tired to take care of Steve, Nicole doted on the baby. Steve began to resent both his wife and their son because the baby had usurped all of her attention.

Nicole needed to tend to her husband's emotional needs and stop treating him like a dormitory resident. She could put on attractive clothes before he came home. Even if she was busy, she could greet Steve warmly when he came home and make him feel loved and special. She could call him briefly at work and say that she missed him. She could leave one-sentence love notes on the door for him when he came home. She could ask him to spend time with her while she nursed the baby, and use that time to chat, share ideas, express affection, or learn Torah. Instead, she usually told him things that he needed to do and problems she had during the day.

Nicole needed to organize her time better and/or discuss with Steve how they could keep house better and enjoy quality time together.

TIME MANAGEMENT

Time management is important when a couple gets married, but becomes critical once they have children, especially if both spouses are employed. Many couples have almost no time together once they have children, and, if they do, they talk about schedules, problems, and "important" matters, not romance, affection, and intimate feelings.

Managing time well makes balancing work, children, and marriage a little easier. Here are a few tips:

1. Make a chart of what you need to do each week and how long each activity takes. Be realistic. Remember that almost nothing *really* takes only five minutes. For example, how often do you *not* wait at the bank, post office, or store? When is the last time that everything went exactly as you planned, without any hitches? How often do your five-minute phone calls last much longer?

Paying bills, cleaning up after meals, running errands, taking a shower, and doing your nails all take time. You can't miraculously fit them into your day without taking away time from other things. Doing errands also requires travel time. Add that into your time budget, remembering that just because you are in a hurry, others aren't going to move faster to accommodate you.

Make sure that your list includes quality time with your spouse and children every day.

2. Think about your long-term goals and decide what you *don't* need to do. Save your time and energy for tasks that are really important. Forego nonessential tasks, if necessary. For example, it would be nice to make a frosted chocolate cake from scratch for *Shabbat* lunch, but that means taking time away from something else. Would it be better to spend that forty-five minutes with your husband than give your family a piece of cake? How about serving fresh fruit instead?

3. Do your hardest tasks when your energy level is high, and do trivial or mindless tasks when you're tired.

4. Make a list of things that you can do when you only have five or ten minutes of free time. Refer to the list when appropriate.

5. Be flexible and creative. If you can't get everything you want done, either do less or get help. Rework your schedule and reprioritize your commitments as necessary.

6. Make time to relax or take naps when you need them. Taking care of yourself is important. It is hard to be nice to others if you are overwhelmed or chronically exhausted. You should be able to enjoy your family, not only take care of them.

7. Delegate some tasks to others, even if you do them better and faster. Little tasks add up, so learn to accept less than perfection when others do it their way. It may take you longer in the short-run to train others to help you, but it will be better for all concerned in the long-run. Other family members need to feel that they are helping out and that they make meaningful contributions to the family.

8. Use your time efficiently by planning ahead. Be practical and realistic. Run errands that are in the same location at one time, and consider when traffic jams are least likely and lines are shortest. For example, go to the bank in the late morning instead of at 8:30, so that you can go to the nearby pharmacy to pick up your prescription, which won't be ready until ten o'clock.

Instead of doing your shopping when stores are most crowded, or when traffic is worst, try to organize your week so that you can go during off-hours. If the bakery is mobbed on Friday mornings, go on Thursday. If the phone lines are busiest when you try to straighten out your credit card bill at 9:30 A.M., try calling in the early evening.

9. Do several tasks simultaneously. For instance, clean up the house or cook while you make phone calls or help the children with homework. Listen to Torah tapes while you drive, run errands, stand in lines, and so forth. Ask your husband to keep you company while you mend clothes or pack lunches for the kids.

Pesha and Yechezkel both worked full-time and were raising three young children. They had almost no time to be together so they reserved 10:30 every night for that. They put on background music, sometimes lit a candle, talked about the day's events, and/or used the time for intimacy.

When Yechezkel went on business trips, they got up at 5:30. She did not feel like getting dressed so early, but did put on a beautiful robe, a touch of makeup, and covered her hair attractively. Meanwhile, Yechezkel made coffee, and they spent the next hour enjoying each other's company. That gave them lovely memories to hold onto until he came back a few days later.

Raising children should never cause couples to stop loving each other, although it often does. This typically happens because couples stop working on their marriage, or because they let their children play one parent against the other.

Parents must be careful not to argue about their differences in front of children, especially when it comes to discipline and childrearing. Parents can respectfully disagree in ways that teach children that it is okay to have differences, but they should never fight with, or scream at, each other in front of children. That kind of behavior erodes children's security and respect for their parents. Parents should support each other in front of their children and privately discuss their differences concerning the children.

Parents have to set appropriate limits on children, and teach children to respect and honor them without using threats, abuse, or excessive force. Children should not hit their parents, call them by their first names, shame, or talk back to them. They are supposed to serve parents food and beverages if the parents want them, as a sign of honor. Children should do some household chores so that they will learn a sense of responsibility.

Parents are supposed to live in a way that earns respect. This can't happen if parents can't control their anger, or if they undermine or disrespect each other to their children. Parents also erode their credibility by acting unfairly, unpredictably, or disrespectfully with their children.

Some secular Jews want children to treat them as friends and call them by their first names. This is not healthy. Jewish parents are required to teach children to appreciate the status differences between parents and children so that children will honor them.

Parents must discipline their children with love so that they become decent adults. Children should be punished or rewarded appropriately so that they associate good behavior with reward and bad behavior with punishment.

Ideally, parents should not hold their children to a higher standard than they themselves live by. Instead, parents should improve themselves and set a proper example.

Detailed ideas about raising children are beyond the scope of this book. Interested readers should see the recommended readings.

SUMMARY

Raising children is a tremendous challenge, yet can be infinitely rewarding. Even though children need enormous amounts of time, energy, and self-sacrifice, couples should not allow their marriages to disintegrate in the process. One of the greatest gifts that parents can give their children is the knowledge that their parents love each other very much.

NOTES

1. *Niddah* 31a.
2. Genesis 3:16.
3. "A Lens On Matrimony," *U.S. News and World Report* (February 21, 1994), p. 68.
4. Ibid.

SUGGESTED READING

Adahan, Miriam. *Raising Children to Care: A Jewish Guide to Childrearing.* New York: Feldheim, 1988.
Aiken, Lisa. "Raising Jewish Children." In *To Be a Jewish Woman.* New Jersey: Jason Aronson, 1992.

20

Building a Jewish Home

A goal of Jewish marriage is to make God our partner. We draw down His presence as we express Jewish values in the way we relate to our spouses, children, community, and Creator, and we make our homes into mini-Temples.

Doing this as a couple can be exciting and challenging, given that partners typically have differences in religious attitudes and observances, even if both are "Orthodox," "observant," or even "Reform." They may also have different motivations for their styles of living. For instance, some people follow the Torah because it is the right way to live. They are motivated by truth. Others enjoy the family rituals and communal closeness. They are motivated by feeling good. Others observe the rituals because they were raised to do so and it makes them comfortable. Others are motivated by a spiritual yearning to feel closer to God and to be spiritually affected by Judaism's rituals.

Many Jews find a "flavor" of Judaism that combines one or more of the above factors. Once we understand what motivates a spouse's approach to Judaism, we can know if it is open to compromise or change. If it is, we can also know what kind of approach is most likely to be successful.

We don't encourage people who are motivated by comfort to become more observant by telling them that what they already do is insufficient. Someone will only take on more religious obligations if he is motivated by truth or spiritual yearning. Nor will someone who is motivated by comfort be encouraged to observe more rituals by being told that he or she will gain more spiritual rewards that way. On the other hand, they might observe more if the rituals were made more meaningful or enjoyable.

Irwin was raised in an observant home and attended yeshiva until college, but was lax in many of his observances. He ate "vegetarian" food and candy that weren't necessarily kosher. He went to the synagogue more to chat with his friends than to pray. Although he didn't drive on the Sabbath, he did other prohibited acts.

Jenny was upset by Irwin's behavior and tried to get him to adopt more stringent standards, but he was comfortable and felt no need to change. Instead of trying to get him to change his attitude, which is never easy, she can get better results by trying to make greater observance more comfortable. She can make the kind of kosher food and buy kosher snacks that he likes so that he will eat them instead of questionably kosher products. She can ask him to study Judaism with her, which might make consistent observance more meaningful to him. She can set up the house in such a way that properly observing the Sabbath will be easier, or offer to do things that he especially likes if he will refrain from doing prohibited activities.

She is unlikely to change his attitudes, but she can encourage him to adopt new behaviors that are more congruent with hers.

Many people relate to Judaism only insofar as it feels good. They enjoy the family rituals and togetherness, the warm, caring community, and the rich traditions. They relate to the "emotional goodies" of Judaism, but not to divine punishment, details of Jewish law, nor rabbinic authority. They pick and choose what feels good. Such people are likely to become more observant only if there is a strong emotional payoff.

Most people resent anyone criticizing their religious practices. While someone who is motivated by truth may change if someone nicely points out to him the error of his ways, that will not encourage someone who is motivated by emotions to change. It will only make him defensive or annoyed.

Regina so enjoyed eating pizza in nonkosher restaurants that she was not willing to give it up. When Hirsh objected and his rabbi backed him, she felt angry and betrayed that he had brought an outsider into their marriage. Eating food that she enjoyed was important to her, and she resented Hirsh's lack of respect for her way of life.

People like Regina equate being "religious" with doing things that are "emotionally satisfying" or they simply eschew rituals and limitations that are uncomfortable. If something feels good, they assume that that is what God wants, even if Jewish law says differently. Such people are loathe to give up doing things that make them comfortable, unless the new behavior is even more gratifying. If someone tries to change them by telling them that what they are doing is wrong, such people are likely to assert that they have as much authority to interpret the law as the rabbis do, that the law doesn't apply to them, or that they don't care what Jewish law says.

People like Regina value pleasure and comfort more than truth. Hirsh should not try to convince her that she is wrong. Instead, he can try to make her feel good about an alternative that is more to his liking. He can do this by telling her that he knows what a sacrifice it would be for her to stop eating in her favorite pizzeria, but that he will make her pizza at home if she would like. If that's not feasible, he can tell her that it would mean a lot to him if she would stop eating out, or eat in a kosher pizzeria instead. If she still won't compromise, he can ask if there's anything he can do to make it worth her while to give up her pleasure, or anything that will make her feel less deprived.

Some people use their own logic to decide what they should observe or not. Since their beliefs and practices often reflect their principles, these can be difficult to change. It is rarely productive to reason with people whose principles differ from yours, and people are loathe to change behaviors that reflect their principles. Behaviors that are not rooted in principles are the most amenable to change.

This also applies to people whose religious practices are rooted in the truth of Judaism. They believe that God gave Jews the Torah and gave the rabbis license to interpret its laws in specific ways. To the extent that their practices are rooted in Jewish law or principles, they will be resistant to changing them. But if they are shown that their principles or understanding of the law are incorrect, they will change.

Robert wore his father's *tefillin* (phylacteries) after his father died, and they became a daily connection to Dad. When he had the *tefillin* checked a few years later, they turned out to be improperly made and could not be used. Robert was devastated, but he stopped wearing them because his adherence to God's law overrode sentimentality.

Couples who want to resolve their religious differences must speak each other's language. We won't change someone's religious observances that are based on truth by using emotional arguments. Nor can we use reason to convince emotional people to change their religious practices.

Shari is Conservative and Al is Orthodox. Although she agrees not to cook nonkosher foods at home, she eats foods that are acceptable only by Conservative standards. Instead of asking her to change her beliefs and lifestyle because they are wrong, Al asks her if she would stop driving on *Shabbat* so that they can be together. She agrees and sleeps in on Saturday mornings while he goes to services. Then they spend the rest of the day with each other. Several months later, when she is used to not driving, Al asks her to join him at his synagogue once a month. She agrees but doesn't like the services. He then suggests that she try a beginner's service, which she enjoys. A few months later, he asks if she would stop bringing nonkosher foods into the house and suggests kosher alternatives.

This was much more productive than arguing with her about the merits of observant Judaism. Shari slowly changed some of her attitudes as she changed her practices, and she came to enjoy Al's way of life, although their philosophies still differed significantly.

Even though they rarely admit it, people's emotional makeup, rather than logic or truth, often determines which religious strictures or leniencies they accept.

Avraham consulted a respected authority on Jewish law when his kitchen sink backed up on Passover, and the water overflowed onto his dishes. When the rabbi told him that the dishes were not disqualified for Passover use, Avraham would not accept it. He wanted the rabbi to say that the dishes had become *chometz* (contaminated by leavened food) and had to be discarded.

Avraham's need to be stringent under the circumstances reflected a personality problem, not an objective search for truth. The Sages never intended Judaism to be as uncomfortable as possible, nor are we supposed to deny ourselves everything that raises questions about its permissibility. We are supposed to discuss such matters with an expert in Jewish law who is qualified to determine if the law allows or prohibits using the item, or doing the act, in question. Ruling for oneself that something permitted is prohibited is an act of ignorance, not piety. And acting stringently after a qualified rabbi tells you not to is prohibited.

Rabbi Chaim Vital wrote that a man is judged in the next world by how he treats his wife. A man is not supposed to adopt religious stringencies at his wife's expense.

Simcha surprised Shaindy by becoming even stricter in his religious observances after they got married. Not only did she think his strictures were unnecessary, she was angry that he showed extreme religious "piety" about keeping kosher, yet did not fulfill his basic marital obligations to her. He readily spent $400 on a new oven because a rabbi told him that a minority opinion held that theirs could not be made kosher. Yet he wouldn't buy her flowers for the Sabbath because he considered that wasteful. He was scrupulous about going to services every morning, no matter how tired he was, yet didn't spend minimal time with Shaindy. He never lifted a finger to help her do chores, yet criticized her for not properly checking vegetables for bugs. His stringencies were rooted in his character, not in Judaism, since he wasn't willing to apply them to his marital obligations.

Certain leniencies in Jewish law must be used when marital harmony is at stake. They may only be applicable in these circumstances and must be recommended by a qualified rabbi. Other couples with a similar problem cannot assume that the same *psak* (legal ruling) applies to them because each couple is unique, and extenuating circumstances or details that are relevant to one couple may be irrelevant to another. This is especially true when *taharat hamishpacha* (family holiness) matters are at issue. If these leniencies were not meant to be used, they would not exist.

Craig and Ruth were married for ten years when she became interested in observant Judaism. That year, she decided to *kasher* her home, observe the Sabbath, and be fully observant. Her new lifestyle was completely foreign to her husband and their three children, but she tried to make this new way of life enjoyable for them. After she went to study in a women's seminary for a month, she told Craig that she was going to cover her hair, and he hit the roof. He had been willing to stop driving and playing golf on Saturdays. He went to the synagogue with her and gave up the pleasure of eating out since their town had no kosher restaurants. He studied Torah a few hours a week, gave ten percent of his income to charity, and fasted on Yom Kippur and Tisha B'Av. He even sent their children to a Jewish school at a cost of $18,000 a year. He had said nothing when Ruth stopped wearing blue jeans, even though he thought it was crazy to wear skirts during the bitter mid-Western winters. But enough was enough. If she insisted on covering her hair, he would divorce her.

Ruth, who was now using her Hebrew name Batya Rut, discussed this with her rabbi. He told her that she should not even think about covering her hair and should be grateful that her husband had already accepted the many major changes that she had made.

Barry and Joan were *baalei teshuva*. He observed numerous stringencies for Passover, and drove her crazy by telling her that she did not prepare the house and the food properly. She got so fed up by his attitude and criticism that she was ready to walk out on him when she asked a rabbi to mediate. He told Barry that only one of his concerns about the kitchen was well-founded and suggested a simple solution. He also told Barry that the foods that Joan bought were completely acceptable and that Barry should not take any future stringencies upon himself without first consulting the rabbi.

Rose and Drew grew up in nonreligious Jewish homes, and started taking beginner classes in Judaism when they were in their thirties. As they studied, they started becoming more observant. After hearing a lecture about *taharat hamishpacha*, they decided that it would be nice if she went to the *mikvah*, but they were not willing to stop all physical contact and abide by the other separations when she was *niddah*. Her rabbi told her to go to the *mikvah* and refrain from sex when she was *niddah*, but not to observe any other restrictions. If and when she and Drew felt ready to observe more, they should consult the rabbi.

God showed how important preserving domestic peace is (*shalom bayit*) by foregoing His honor for its sake. We learn this (among other places) from the *Sotah* ceremony. It took place if a woman gave her husband good reason to suspect her of adultery, after he had warned her not to sequester herself with a suspected lover. She was told to confess if she had sinned, but if she maintained her innocence, the High Priest wrote God's Name on a piece of parchment, then dissolved the writing in water. When she drank this solution, she and her husband soon had a child together if she had not sinned. If she had committed adultery, both she and the adulterer died.

God allowed His Name to be obliterated, an act which is normally forbidden, in order to restore peace between a couple. That shows how much we should bend over backward to restore domestic tranquility. This is especially important for couples who resist using allowable leniencies in Jewish law that can restore or preserve marital harmony.

RELIGIOUS GROWTH

Spouses often grow Jewishly at different paces and in different ways. One may want to study the details of the laws while the other wants to understand its symbolism. One is drawn to spiritual concepts and philosophy, the other to practical requirements of how to live. He wants to study Talmud and intellectual commentaries, she wants to open her heart by plumbing the depths of the prayers and psalms and by practicing Jewish meditation.

Couples should expect to differ in their rates of growth, in their religious-intellectual development, in the topics they study, and in their particular leniencies and customs. This is because God gave each of us a unique soul, and we each have slightly different, legitimate avenues for developing it. When people see their differences in terms of "I'm right and you're wrong," or fear that a more religious spouse will reject them, they are unlikely to bridge differences with each other. It is common for the less-observant spouse to feel anxious if he or she sees a partner moving further and further away and to worry that they will eventually separate completely. The more religious spouse may need to allay the partner's fears and reassure him or her that religious growth will not ruin their marriage. Giving the partner the space to grow at a different pace can actually foster growth and keep him or her from being immobilized by anger and fear. When religious differences threaten the marriage, a sensitive, observant rabbi should be consulted.

We cannot respect and appreciate a partner's legitimate differences from us if we see them as being self-serving, unhealthy, overly restrictive, lax, ignorant, and so on. For example, one spouse washes his hands in a basin of water near the bed every morning, while the other gets angry that some water spills on the carpet. She eats before praying on *Shabbat* morning, while he gets upset that she won't wait until after services to have breakfast. The *baal teshuva* husband eats only *shmurah matzah* (made from wheat that has been guarded since it was reaped) on Passover, while his always-observant wife thinks that is ridiculous, and resents him spending $12 a pound for it. A wife refuses to eat at her in-laws' home because she considers their *kashrut* questionable, yet her husband expects her to eat there with him. Some couples end the Sabbath at different times. Others differ in how modestly they want the wife to dress. Couples can have endless religious differences in the course of a marriage. These should be addressed with a rabbi, who may legitimize each's point of view and/or suggest constructive ways to resolve the conflict.

Shoshana was upset that her husband did not accept some basic Jewish ideas and had unorthodox ideas and practices. She was so upset by this that she asked her rabbi to "straighten him out." Much to her surprise, the rabbi told her that, although Eric's ideas and practices were quite different than hers, they were perfectly legitimate. Once her rabbi sanctioned Eric's attitudes and behavior, Shoshana was able to feel close to him again.

How we feel about religious differences depends upon what they mean to us. If we think that a spouse's observances are stupid, obsessive, dogmatic, or irrational, we may feel threatened, distant, or even resentful.

Couples should expect to have different religious customs when they get married. One spouse might pray the Ashkenazic service, while the other says Sephardic prayers. One may be accustomed to saying Friday night *kiddush* (sanctification of the Sabbath) standing, while the other stands for the first half and sits for the rest. One eats *gebrokst* (foods cooked with *matzah* or *matzah* meal) on Passover while the other doesn't. One eats seven special foods on the first night of Rosh Hashana (New Year's), while the other never heard of this custom.

Religious compromises involve much more than good communication and problem-solving skills. We have to know when Jewish law requires us to compromise for the sake of marriage and when we shouldn't waver in our convictions and practices. We must know when not to impose our perspectives on a spouse and when to encourage a spouse to adopt our observances. Smoothing out religious differences is hardest when the issues are intertwined with strong emotions and nonnegotiable principles, as they usually are.

Most couples need to bring these issues to a sensitive, qualified rabbi who knows the couple and Jewish law well and who both partners respect. If this is the husband's rabbi, the wife should feel that he is understanding and sympathetic to her. If not, they should find a different rabbi.

Jill had a severe bout of Krohn's disease shortly before she got married, and wanted to use birth control for six months while she regained her strength. Lawrence did not think this was halachically justified and consulted a rabbi who Jill felt was insensitive to women. When the rabbi gave his opinion, Jill refused to accept it. After talking to a married mentor couple, they found a different rabbi who was more sensitive to women.

Ideally, couples should agree before marriage which rabbi they will consult and discuss their differences and potential religious problems with him before the wedding. An ounce of prevention is worth a pound of cure.

ADOPTING THE HUSBAND'S CUSTOMS

Judaism reduces marital frictions by requiring a wife (and their children) to follow her husband's religious customs if their practices differ. This does not mean that if he is not properly observant, she should be similarly lax or that she should follow customs that he adopted out of ignorance. But if they have mutually exclusive traditions, such as when one is Ashkenazic and the other Sephardic, she adopts his way of life. This smooths over some religious differences and gives the children one set of religious rules to follow.

But adopting a husband's customs can bring its own tensions. A wife can intellectually accept the need to form a united front when building a family and home but miss her lifelong way of life.

Hadassah missed the warmth, songs, closeness, and emotional rituals of the Sephardim when she married her Ashkenazic husband. The Ashkenazic prayers on the High Holidays and Tisha B'Av (the Jewish national day of mourning) were foreign to her and left her feeling cold. Her husband's friends prayed in a rote and emotionless way, and their rituals lacked the emotional richness that she loved so much. She also missed the Passover meals in her family's house and relinquishing Sephardic foods that her husband didn't like.

She worked through these issues during her first few years of marriage. She prayed at home most of the time but went to the synagogue for the latter part of the Sabbath and holiday services. She invited her family and Sephardic friends for meals, when they had a chance to share familiar melodies, and she got a collection of cassettes of her rabbi's classes. It wasn't long before she stopped missing her previous way of life.

COMPROMISING OVER RELIGIOUS DIFFERENCES

Our actions have spiritual effects on us and others, but they often have pragmatic consequences as well. For example, a husband's eating nonkosher food at work has no direct, pragmatic effects on his wife. If she has to choose religious battles with him, she might prefer to focus on behaviors that directly affect her or their children.

Suzanne felt strongly about properly observing the laws of family holiness. Ariel was willing not to have sex but refused to abstain from other forms of touching when she was *niddah*. When they consulted a rabbi, he told Ariel not to touch Suzanne when she was *niddah* but allowed them to hand things to each other and to do other things that were normally prohibited (such as pouring each other wine.) The rabbi also addressed their need to communicate better and show more affection to each other without having physical contact.

Suzanne agreed to greet Ariel at the door when he came home, be enthusiastic to see him, and join him for dinner every night without talking on the telephone. They also agreed to go on two dates every week when they were not allowed to touch.

Ariel agreed to bring Suzanne flowers when she went to the *mikvah,* help her get the children to bed so that they could have time alone together, and write her a love note once a week. Feeling more loved and being more loving made it easier for Ariel to refrain from physical contact when it was off-limits.

Some spouses object to a partner's religious laxity because they believe that it reflects negatively on them. They think that a loving or respectful spouse would gladly adopt their religious practices, but this is not the case, and they shouldn't take it personally when they don't.

Gail enjoyed reading novels on the Sabbath, but Ike disapproved, and wanted her to read Torah books instead. When she continued to read novels despite his objections, he felt angry and disrespected. She appreciated how he felt, but pleasure reading helped her unwind. Ike kept fueling his upset by discussing his situation with *yeshivish* friends, who agreed that his wife should not be reading novels.

It would have been more useful for Ike to ask Gail if there were any Torah topics that she would enjoy learning, then learn them with her on the Sabbath. He might also offer to do the dishes, then go for a walk with her so that she could unwind with him. If neither offer helped, he should accept it and focus on Gail's positive points.

Couples who have religious differences should know which issues are negotiable and which are not.

Bella had a very stressful office job, and also raised four children under the age of ten. After a debilitating miscarriage, she wanted to recuperate for a long weekend at a place where she could swim and get some sun. Zev would not go because there would be no *minyan* (quorum for prayer with ten men) there. Since she wanted to go away to a specific place where he was not willing to go, they decided that she would go alone, and he would watch the kids. After she came back, she made a list of warm get-away spots with deserted beaches and nearby *minyans* so they could travel together in the future.

Besides identifying issues that are not negotiable, we should know what compromises mean to a partner. That allows us to acknowledge his or her feelings and to offer compensation for what the other person gives up for us.

Pat is not yet Sabbath-observant, and enjoys relaxing, doing errands, and spending time with her parents fifty miles away on Saturdays. Jacob is Sabbath-observant and tries to make observance more attractive to her instead of telling her what not to do on the Sabbath. He invites her to join him at Friday night services, makes a tasty *Shabbat* dinner for her, and gets them invited for *Shabbat* lunch at the homes of religious families. He suggests that she invite her parents to join them for *Shabbat* meals so that Pat won't drive to see them on Saturday. He also suggested that they visit her parents together on Sundays instead of her going alone on Saturdays.

This legitimized Pat's feelings, instead of telling her that being spiritual is more important than driving or running errands. Validating her feelings set the stage for encouraging her to change. Jacob sweetened the pot by offering something she valued in return for what she would give up. Two years later, Pat loved observing the Sabbath and had no regrets about giving up her former lifestyle.

LIFE CYCLES

The Jewish holidays can be rejuvenating and exciting opportunities to regain a spiritual focus, relax, and spend time with family and friends. But they are also times of great stress, especially for women, and are times of enormous discord for many families. While men often prefer to stay home for Jewish holidays, their wives are exhausted by endless shopping, cooking, serving meals, and cleaning up. Women often prefer to go to the homes of friends or relatives, or to resorts for holidays.

Phyllis likes to spend Jewish holidays with her family because she enjoys their company, but she also gets to relax there because her mother does the cooking and a maid cleans up. Frank likes to stay home where he can sleep in his own bed, relax in his living room, and have things his way. He dislikes his mother-in-law's cooking and prefers his modern *shul* to their "old-folks" synagogue. They compromise by going to her parents every other holiday. Since no solution will please them both, they accept that one of them will be slightly uncomfortable every holiday.

The stress of cleaning, cooking, marathon eating, and washing dishes made Francine irritable every Passover, and it was a difficult time for her and Bill. He was a tax accountant who worked fifteen-hour days for two months before Passover, then collapsed when the holiday began. When they first got married, he told Francine that she overdid things, and shouldn't wash the drapes, shampoo the carpets, clean out the attic, or make elaborate meals for the holidays. This made her angry; she felt that he didn't understand her, and she did her usual cleaning undeterred. She spent the holiday resentful and exhausted. It took Bill a long time to accept that telling her to do less would not solve the problem. He finally hired help for her.

Some couples are stressed getting the house and children ready for the Sabbath and holidays. They yell a lot because they have short fuses and unrealistic expectations of their children. They snap at the children for taking too long to get ready, then get angry when the children misbehave at meals where they are bored and ignored. Parents should include the children in conversation, singing, sharing what they learned in school that week, serving food, and cleaning up. Parents also have to be realistic about how long children can sit for a meal.

Couples who lose their tempers around the holidays or Sabbath need to make more realistic schedules, manage time better, and have more realistic expectations of themselves and others. It is a lot easier and more appropriate for adults to change their expectations than to expect children always to do what parents want. Hiring help may also be in order.

Both Cindy and Ricky worked full-time. He had his own business, and came home moments before the Sabbath. During the winter, she rarely managed to get the house, kids, and meals ready before *Shabbat,* and she yelled at everybody for not being ready on time and being disorganized. The children started dreading *Shabbat* because they knew that Mom would punish and yell at them.

Cindy never allotted enough time to accomplish all that needed to be done. She had unrealistic expectations of her children. She needed a housekeeper to start getting them ready when they came home from school, to straighten the house, and to start making food before Cindy got home.

Gary and Michelle were recently married, and went away for the High Holidays. After missing three days of work, they focused on making it up, and lost track of time. The day before Succot (the holiday of Tabernacles, five days after Yom Kippur), Michelle asked Gary if he had bought a *lulav* (a date palm branch bound to myrtle and willow branches), *etrog* (a citron), and *succah* (an outdoor booth for the holiday of Tabernacles). He had been so busy working that he had completely forgotten. They managed to buy a *lulav* at the last minute, but had to carry food to the synagogue *succah* a mile away for the holiday meals. This experience taught them to consult a Jewish calendar every week to remind them about upcoming events.

Shmuel and Raizy were on a shoestring budget and fought about her purchases before every holiday. She bought more expensive food than usual because of the *mitzvah* to spend extra money in honor of the festivals. He felt that she overdid it. She bought bakery desserts instead of baking cakes herself, whole chickens instead of dark meat, wine instead of grape juice, and nice paper plates so that she didn't have to wash dishes. Shmuel wanted her to forego these "luxuries," but she wouldn't. He couldn't enjoy meals that made him wonder how he would make ends meet for the next month.

Some couples argue about where, and how, to spend each holiday. The wife expects the husband to spend extra time with her, or watch the kids so that she can nap. Meanwhile, he expects to study, read, or take a nap himself. She wants to go to friends' homes, where he feels uncomfortable. She wants to go to a resort, but he thinks it costs too much money. The possible conflicts are endless.

While there are no guaranteed ways to resolve these matters to everyone's satisfaction, it helps if couples discuss their expectations and plans a few weeks before every holiday. Once you know how your partner feels, and what you agree and disagree about, you can negotiate compromises. No one likes unpleasant *faits accomplis* at the last minute.

Discussing holiday and *Shabbat* plans well in advance also helps couples divide chores and delegate responsibilities. Newly married couples should not make assumptions about who will shop, cook, clean, and extend or accept invitations without discussing it first. Eventually, they can set up a system whereby they decide who does what, and how often they want to go away or eat meals with friends. Keep checklists and reminders on the refrigerator, or on a bulletin board in the kitchen.

SUMMARY

Virtually every couple has some religious differences. Some can be healthy and may enrich the marriage, while others may harm the marriage or children if they are not bridged. Discuss with a rabbi which ones are which, and what to do about them.

A less observant spouse is more likely to grow when observances are made more appealing than when criticized for his or her laxity. Criticism usually causes defensiveness, not change. No one likes to be told that what she or he is doing is wrong, or that she or he is inadequate.

Empathize with how your observance or laxity affects your partner. If you want your spouse to change, first consider how you would feel if you were in your spouse's shoes.

Don't ask a spouse to compromise religious principles. It won't work, and it's not appropriate. When necessary, ask a spouse to change a few behaviors, not an attitude or a belief. Changing behaviors often results in people ultimately generating new attitudes that are consistent with the new actions.

Remember that Rome wasn't built in a day. Don't try to overhaul a spouse's belief system, or make major lifestyle changes. It is hard enough to change one or two behaviors at a time.

Finally, spouses with different observances should agree about what to teach and model to their children, including respecting legitimate differences. For example, if the mother only drinks *cholov Yisrael* (milk that was supervised by a Jew during milking) and the father drinks regular milk, the children should be told that both practices are legitimate and that they can follow their father's custom. Disparaging the other spouse's beliefs or practices discredits both parents and Judaism to children.

21

Keeping Love Alive

Being in love is much easier than staying in love. Being in love just happens; staying in love takes a lot of work!

Unfortunately, the "highs" of being crazy about someone don't last forever. They are replaced by the boredom, disappointments, and tensions of daily life. Some husbands think that earning a living and buying a wife food, clothes, a house, supporting their children, and paying for vacations will make her feel eternally grateful and loving. Men are shocked by how quickly wives take their hard work and occasional presents for granted, or even resent their husbands for working such long hours!

Wives are also surprised when their husbands stop complimenting them and take for granted their cooking, running a home, and raising children. Both men and women tend to expect certain things, and unfortunately, their appreciation doesn't last very long after they get them.

Activities that take most couples' time, such as working, sleeping, running errands, and doing household chores, do not foster affection between them. Love depends upon doing specific acts that go way beyond fulfilling basic needs. Discussing which pediatrician to use, who will do the dishes, what to buy at the supermarket, and watching television don't build affection and intimacy. Couples must actively love each other by sharing funny and emotional stories, warm memories, deep feelings, hopes, dreams, and spiritual ideas for their love to stay vibrant.

This takes work, especially for couples with busy careers, young children, and/ or many extracurricular activities. Many couples don't eat meals together today. When they do, they often interrupt the meal by taking telephone calls or rushing out to evening activities. Some couples don't even spend ten or fifteen minutes a day of uninterrupted time together and spend their limited free time discussing problems or tasks to be done.

Couples who stop acting lovingly drift apart. This is why many couples need to reserve uninterrupted, relaxed time together when the children are occupied or asleep, and the answering machine is on. Instead of using this time to discuss problems, schedules, tasks, and so forth, they use it to share loving feelings, compliments, ideas, experiences, and memories. They look at and sit close to each other, make eye contact, and enjoy each other's company and warmth.

Some people think that it is ludicrous to schedule loving time together. They think that loving should be spontaneous, not contrived. That is true for couples who have loving conversations anyway, but most do not. After the wedding, work and domestic demands slowly but surely pull many couples apart.

Judaism prescribes three formal prayer services every day. This reminds us to talk to our Partner three times a day, whether the spirit moves us or not. This also makes us aware that our Partner yearns to hear from us periodically.

The same applies to marriage. If we wait to feel loving before expressing it, our loving interactions may be few and far between. Scheduling loving time every day ensures that we are often affectionate with a partner, even when we aren't in the mood or have other things that we would rather do.

Chuck and Helaine made time to work on their marriage after they put the kids to bed every night. Some nights they relaxed on the living room sofa or in the bedroom, and other times they went for a walk, or hired a babysitter so they could go out. He would make comments like, "Your eyes look especially beautiful tonight. You always look pretty, but you look really stunning today."

"You're so sweet," Helaine responded coyly. "You always know just what to say. I love you even more now than when we got married."

During these times together, they complimented each other, and discussed what they appreciated in each other. Sometimes they shared happy or funny memories. At other times, they enjoyed reading each other poetry or romantic stories. They occasionally reminisced over photographs or shared thoughts and feelings. No matter what happened during the day, they always looked forward to these times of sharing.

Becky was reading in bed when Herman sat down beside her. Instead of ignoring him and treating him like an interruption, she put down her book. He caressed her tenderly and told her that he was madly in love with her.

She smiled with pleasure. "You still look like a beautiful bride to me." He kissed her gently on the forehead, and murmured, "You fascinate me. You're so good at knowing just the right things to say and do for me. Today, you did a great job calming me down when I came home after a terrible day. I'm so glad I married you.

Becky blushed as she enjoyed basking in his love. "You always make me feel so good about myself. I'm so lucky to have you."

People who think that no one talks this way probably need to start doing it themselves!

It's not easy being affectionate when spouses are tired, upset, or preoccupied with children who need them, but it is well worth the effort. Sharing loving words recharges a couple's emotional batteries and renews their marriage. The need to earn a living, do errands, raise children, and so on, shouldn't be an excuse to stop giving affection and warmth to a spouse.

Scheduling time to be affectionate doesn't mean that couples shouldn't be loving at other times. But creating islands of tranquility is important in a marriage, and it's nice to associate being home with finding a refuge and haven from the abuses and stresses of life.

Every marital interaction can potentially bring a couple closer, and spouses need to use these opportunities. Even if couples get along, they need to keep stoking the fires of romance, warmth, and love or their relationship will suffer. As we train ourselves to act kind or loving, even when we don't feel like it, we become more loving. A good place to start is by starting and ending each day on a positive note.

Bracha was at her best late at night, while Benjy was the opposite. He was bright-eyed and bushy-tailed in the mornings, long before Bracha felt like talking to anyone. She gave him the message to leave her alone when he got up, which hurt his feelings.

They finally discussed this. "I'm sorry that I'm so curt with you in the morning, Benjy. I love you very much, but I hate talking when I'm half-asleep. How can I show you that I love you without having to talk to you when you get up?"

Benjy suggested cuddling for a few minutes before he got out of bed, or giving him a make-believe kiss when she couldn't do that. She started leaving short love notes on the refrigerator for him to find when he came home, and he reciprocated.

Couples have many mundane interactions that can reinforce their love. Why have a mediocre marriage when, with a little effort, you can make it great?

Colette and Harry were in their late twenties. She had a bad back and he had hay fever. They started most days sounding like two decrepit invalids.

"How are you feeling?" Harry asked as he blew his nose.

"Ugh, what a night!" Colette moaned. "I hardly slept. My neck is stiff and hurts, and my legs feel sore from exercising yesterday."

"I don't feel so great my ACHOO! self," Harry sneezed, as he reached for another tissue. "These allergy pills make me drowsy but don't seem to do much good. My eyes still feel itchy and my ACHOO! nose won't stop running . . ."

They started their days complaining about their aches and pains, until they realized that this wasn't very useful. They finally broke their unproductive cycle by discussing more pleasant matters.

After Harry asked Colette how she was, she told him, "I'm a little stiff and sore, thank you. Did you sleep well?"

"Could have been better," Harry responded, "but I'm used to it by now. When I was tossing and turning at 5 A.M., I looked at you sleeping and had such tender feelings for you."

When they were doing chores around the house, Colette asked, "Have you seen the screwdriver?"

"No, sweetie," he replied. Using that little term of endearment brightened her day and made her feel warmly toward her husband.

As she made dinner she told Harry, "I'm making your favorite dish for dinner."

"You're my favorite dish," he replied.

Even the most trivial conversations can be warm and loving if couples make them so.

TELEPHONE CALLS

Some rain must fall in everyone's life, but we don't have to constantly focus on it. No one wants to hear daily litanies of complaints or problems. We should try to spend more time discussing what's positive than discussing what's negative. That keeps our spouse from dreading to listen to us.

Loren liked to call Sally on his lunch break to tell her that he loved her, but she used these times to complain. He pointed this out and asked if she could share her complaints after dinner and be warmer to him on the telephone.

She called him the next day. He cautiously answered, "Hi, Sally. What's up?"

Instead of complaining, she tried being pleasant. "I just called to say that I missed you and felt a warm rush thinking about you."

"Oh, that's so nice to hear," Loren responded. "I love you very much and you make me very happy."

"I've got to run now, but I'm looking forward to seeing you later. Bye."

Loren started looking forward to coming home instead of anticipating a barrage of complaints as he walked in the door. Sally discovered that it wasn't so bad being more pleasant and bonding with her husband through pleasant interactions instead of by complaining. She still told Loren about the day's tribulations after dinner, but much less than before she realized how she sounded. And when she really had to discuss problems with him during the day, she did it on a separate call.

Even a few moments on the phone can be a chance to share warm feelings.

Lewis called Hanna every day in case she needed to discuss pressing problems at home. He had little time to talk, and she was likely to be nursing the baby while the two-year old howled in the background. Lewis felt so overwhelmed just imagining what his wife went through every day that he dreaded calling her. So he did it in a detached and abbreviated way.

"Hi, Hanna," he mumbled between mouthfuls of lunch. "How are you?"

"Terrible." He could hear the baby screaming as his wife tried to calm her down. "The baby is running a fever and the dishwasher overflowed a few minutes ago. I have a million dirty dishes from the weekend and there's soapy water all over the kitchen. I just put clean clothes on Bobby and he's already filthy from playing in the puddles. Oh, no, now he's tracking dirty water all through the house!"

Lewis put her on his speaker-phone, and looked for his bottle of aspirin. "Why don't you see if Allison will let you use her housekeeper today? Anything else?"

Bobby was putting soap suds in his hair. "No, I guess not," Hanna said, feeling Lewis' detachment. "I'll talk to you later. Bye."

"Bye," Lewis said, relieved to hang up.

Lewis could have been more loving, as in the following scenario:

"Hi, Hanna. I'm sorry that I'm calling you while I'm eating, but this is my only free time today. I wanted you to know that I was thinking about you and missed you."

"You're a doll. I miss you, too."

"How is your day going?" Lewis asked.

"Terrible," Hanna confessed, almost at the point of tears. "I'm so overwhelmed. The baby's sick, the dishwasher broke, there are suds all over the kitchen, and Bobby's playing in them."

"I'm so sorry. I wish I could be there to give you a hug and some help. Can I do anything to help you now, or would you like to tell me all about it when I come home?"

"I could really use a hug now, but I guess that will have to wait. It means a lot just to know that you care about me when I have days like this." Bobby started putting suds in his hair. "I'm sorry, Lew, but Bobby's getting into trouble. I love you. Thanks for calling."

"Here's a quick hug and kiss over the phone," Lewis offered. "I'll deliver them in person later."

It doesn't take much to make a spouse feel special during routine interactions.

Elizabeth was a saleswoman who was usually unreachable, and Todd was a teacher who was usually in the classroom. Since they couldn't easily connect during the day, they left loving messages for each other on their answering machine. It felt wonderful to hear, "I just called to say I love you. I can't wait to see you around 8 tonight."

"I feel so happy thinking about you today."

"You made me feel great by putting that love note and my favorite dessert in my lunch bag."

"I'm having a very hard day today, but just knowing that I'll see you when I get home makes it bearable."

With a little forethought and creativity, couples can spice most mundane encounters with loving words and gestures, although some times are better for this than others.

Dawn worked in a busy health clinic, and often did three things at once. Paul worked in a busy office but took a short break every afternoon to call her. Dawn wished that he wouldn't do this because his calls put her even further behind at work, and the hectic atmosphere made it hard for her to be pleasant.

She told Paul, "I'm glad that you want to be loving while I'm at work, but the timing doesn't work for me. How about if we put love notes in each other's lunches instead?"

Paul didn't see why she couldn't talk to him for a few minutes every day, but tried her suggestion. He was pleased that she appreciated his daily notes, weekly cards, and monthly flowers, and he enjoyed her notes and the funny cartoons that she drew with them. She even called him once in a while when things were slow to say that she loved him. He turned out not to mind giving up calling her at work.

ENDING THE DAY PLEASANTLY

It is especially difficult for some people to be pleasant at the end of the day when they are worn out. They want to decompress and be taken care of, not have to take care of someone else. When both spouses expect the other to take care of them at the same time, neither is likely to get nurtured.

Some people are so used to complaining or talking about unpleasant topics with their spouse that they need to prepare pleasant things to discuss. Marriages should not be prolonged therapy sessions or toxic waste dumps for personal problems. People who are chronically pessimistic, unhappy, depressed, or who have poor self-esteem should see a therapist. They may need to dilute their emotional baggage among friends, not expect their spouse to hear all of their problems.

We don't have to be Pollyannas, but research has shown that most people actually feel *worse* when they keep reliving situations that made them unhappy or angry. Doing this repeatedly is hard on a spouse, too. It is one thing to complain for fifteen minutes every day, get support, and move on to neutral or pleasant topics. It is another matter to wallow in pain, upset, or anger and not be content until we have dragged our spouse into our misery.

Bernie routinely complained about his day when he and Goldie ate dinner. His secretary sent out memos without proofreading them. His computer went down and he couldn't find the backup disks. A client blew up at him. . . . Goldie couldn't wait for him to finish sharing his day's traumas so that she could tell him hers. Their son poured syrup in his hair, gave his baby sister a black eye, and broke the bedroom lamp. She spent an hour and a half straightening out last month's credit card bill. The baby threw up all over her favorite blouse. . . . Each had a good half-hour of complaints to share.

One day, they realized how wasteful this was, and decided to change their pattern. Most upsets were not catastrophes, some were not worth dwelling on, and others were even funny in retrospect. Bernie put his daily upsets into perspective on his drive home, then thought about how to relate some of them to Goldie in a pleasant or funny way.

Goldie found mothering stressful, and appreciated having a good laugh more than hearing complaints. Bernie brightened her mood by bringing her interesting articles and cartoons from the office so that she would know what was going on in the world, or at least laugh about something.

She found it helpful to put most of her upsets on hold until she and Bernie had a chance to share some pleasantries. More often than not, once they felt close by laughing or relaxing together, she had less need to complain! When she did discuss problems, she stopped making them the major focus of their time together. They felt better sharing positive events and feelings than reliving every day's injuries and upsets for an entire evening.

The last part of the day is the only "quality" time that some couples have together, and it sets the emotional tone for how they remember the entire day. If bedtime is used for loving and pleasant interactions, couples will feel better than if they go to bed feeling distant, drained, or tense.

It is especially important to associate bedtime with warmth and togetherness, not with criticism, aggravation, and tantrums. Giving a spouse the silent treatment or criticism at the end of the day, before he or she falls asleep, is never productive. Defer discussing emotional issues that can't be resolved at bedtime for a more opportune moment. If there never seems to be an opportune time, ask your spouse to plan a time with you when you can have a productive discussion.

GET MORE BY GIVING

When a spouse is critical, cold, or unappreciative, some people get emotional gratification from work, hobbies, or friends, and avoid being home.

Yonah expected Neima to greet him at the door when he came home, yet she rarely did. She usually stayed in the kitchen making dinner and talked on the phone. He felt like a dormitory resident instead of like a cherished husband.

By discussing this, they resolved that Neima would make every effort to greet him with a smile and a warm hello when he came home. If she was on the phone, she would interrupt to say, "Hi, Yonah, I'm so happy to see you," blow him a kiss, and tell him that she would be with him in five minutes.

Instead of expecting Neima to always greet him, Yonah also extended himself. When she was busy making dinner or taking care of the baby, he kept her company or gave her a hand. These small changes made Yonah feel good about coming home, and made Neima look forward to his return.

Helen spent at least three nights a week going to meetings and charity events. Manny felt neglected and angry. She had time for every needy person in the world except him. He told her that charity begins at home and that she should be there when he came home. This only made Helen more determined to avoid him.

A few days later, Manny tried a different approach. Instead of demanding that she take care of him, he said, "Helen, I'm very proud of what you do for the community. You're a wonderful woman with a good heart, and I'm glad that you're my wife. On the other hand, I need you and miss spending time with you. Is there some way that I can make you feel as good as your friends do?"

Helen was taken aback by his question because he usually took her for granted. He only seemed to care that she had left him dinner and made sure that he had clean clothes.

She responded, "Since you asked, everyone makes a fuss about me when I go out. They tell me how beautiful I look. They notice that I've lost fifteen pounds and encourage me to keep it off. They think that I'm talented and show an interest in what I have to say. You don't do these things.

"I need you to compliment me on how I look and on what I do for you. Take the initiative by giving me a hug and kiss when you come home and tell me that you find me attractive. Show that you're interested in my life, not only in what I do for you. Ask me how I feel, and how my day was. Smile at me and tell me that you love me. If you do these things, I would be happy to stay home more often."

There are many ways to take care of a spouse. It can cost $15 to buy a wife some cleaning products and toilet paper. But if he buys a $15 pair of earrings instead, or in addition, she feels loved. Unlike the household items, jewelry is personal and not expected. When she runs errands, does laundry, or cleans the house, he doesn't attach much personal meaning to it, but he does take it personally when she *doesn't* do it! We feel loved when someone does things for us in a personal way, especially if they go above and beyond the call of duty.

Affectionate touching, using terms of endearment, giving chocolate, jewelry, and flowers make most women feel loved. Making men their favorite food, showing appreciation and acceptance, and letting them know that they are attractive and make you happy does the same for men.

Norman's mother came to the United States on the *S. S. Kinderlach* (Yiddish for "Eat, eat, my child"). His memories of the gefilte fish, flanken, and kugel she made him when he was young made these his favorite foods forever. When Norman asked Stephanie to make them for him, he wanted her to show that she loved him as much as his mother did. He didn't want a lecture from her about the high cholesterol in flanken, and the lack of food value in the kugel. She can acknowledge the symbolic meaning of these foods and make them for him on special occasions.

When Lonnie asked Tuvia to rub her back, she wanted more than relief from sore muscles. Her mother used to rub her back when she was a little girl, and backrubs still made Lonnie feel loved and special. She wanted Tuvia to bring back all those warm memories by showing her affection the way her mother once did.

As happens in other areas, if we don't tell a spouse what our requests mean, or ask what theirs mean, we can't know when hidden wishes underlie the obvious ones.

As Ronnie dressed for the Sabbath, he asked Sarita where his favorite suit was. She replied that she hadn't yet taken it to the cleaners, and it was in a bag of dirty clothes. He was very angry and thought, "What kind of wife lets her husband run out of clean clothes?!" What Sarita thought was a mere oversight Ronnie interpreted as a lack of caring for him.

Many men feel loved when their wives serve them dinner and have the house tidy and quiet when they come home and feel unloved when that doesn't happen. Many wives only feel loved when their husbands tell them loving words, regardless of how helpful the men are at home. The best gift of love is giving what a spouse wants from us.

RENEWING GOOD FEELINGS

Most couples need to share enjoyable activities throughout their marriage. Weekly dates and intimate getaways are two opportunities for doing this. Some couples, though, have actually forgotten what they once enjoyed doing together! Here are some suggestions (several involve other people):

- Walk, swim, or go boating; snorkel or scuba dive; stroll along a beach or lake.
- Visit a museum, art gallery, craft show, street or county fair, antique show, photography exhibit, or historical site.
- Have a picnic in a scenic spot; visit a botanical garden or nature park; go hiking.
- Eat out; have a cup of coffee in a cafe or coffee shop; go out for drinks in a beautiful hotel, piano bar, or place with a view.
- See a movie, concert, play, or show in a comedy club.
- Play racketball, squash, tennis, volleyball, or softball.
- Ride bicycles, jog, hike, ice skate, ski, exercise, or roller blade.
- Take a walking tour; go bird watching; take photographs and display them in your house.
- Go to a weekly class or lecture series.

The following are for couples who prefer to stay home:

- Garden and landscape your yard; make crafts or refinish furniture; write poetry, short stories, or books together.
- Play musical instruments; sing; listen to music.
- Paint, renovate, or decorate the house.
- Cook; host dinners for friends; have a candlelit dinner at home with stereo music in the background.
- Dance or exercise.
- Cuddle or massage each other.
- Play chess, checkers, cards, or board games.
- Collect coins, stamps, or scrapbook items.
- Read poetry, articles, or books.
- Learn Torah.

Exercise is important for couples to be physically and mentally healthy. It helps get rid of tension and causes chemicals to be released in our bodies that make us happy and give us energy. People who are in good shape and happy are more pleasant to be with than lethargic people who are in poor health and who feel blah or depressed. Exercise is also a great outlet for stress.

Today, hectic lifestyles and taking care of children can make it especially important for couples to relax and have fun together and to remember what they like and admire in each other.

Bert and Valerie learned Torah together once a week. She once felt neglected when he went out to study two nights a week, but now she feels good about his learning because she sees how much progress he's made. They both feel enriched by the spiritual dimension that Torah study adds to their marriage.

Diana and Marc decided to plant a vegetable garden. He gave her a running commentary at the plant nursery, and she was amazed at how much he knew. She discovered that he once had studied herbal medicine and organic gardening. This gave them new topics for conversation and made her respect him even more.

Jean was very modest and shy. Jeff suggested that they write each other a poem once a week. When he read hers, he couldn't believe how beautiful it was. "You should write a book of poetry," he told her.

"I once did," she admitted.

"Why didn't you ever tell me?" Jeff asked.

"I never thought enough of it to say anything about it."

"I would love to see it," he encouraged. "Do you still have it?"

"Sure. I keep it in a drawer with my other mementos."

They spent the rest of that evening, and many others, reading poetry together. He encouraged her to write some more, and she did, eventually publishing it. Had Jeff never suggested that they write each other poems, he would not have known that his wife was so talented, and she probably would never have written again.

Sharing enjoyable activities reinforces a couple's bonds. When couples are too exhausted to create good feelings with words, having a repertoire of ways to create warmth and affection is important. When one avenue isn't available, others are.

Couples can also revive warm feelings by going through a photo album or memento box. They should put in engagement and wedding pictures; photographs from trips together; funny or loving cards and letters from friends, family, and each other; petals from flowers that he gave her, and so forth. They can continually fill the box with new mementos, poems, love notes, and photos throughout their marriage.

Some people like to keep a love diary that records their happy feelings and experiences with a spouse. They may not make entries every day, but their collected writings remind them of how wonderful their spouse is, and how good their marriage has been.

They can review their "memory box" or love diary every anniversary, or any time they want to feel warm and happy. This is especially helpful when they have rough times and need to rekindle the warmth and love they once felt for each other. When one spouse feels neglected or upset, she or he can always go to the box and replace negative feelings with positive ones.

One of the best ways to destroy a relationship is to take a partner for granted, and not praise, admire, or show pleasure with him or her. Although we never tire of getting compliments or having a happy spouse, we do get tired being cheerful and complimentary ourselves. Unless we are careful, we can easily take a spouse for granted instead of regularly mentioning what we appreciate about him or her.

It only takes a few seconds to say, "That hat looks fabulous on you," "Thanks for helping me with the children tonight," "It was so sweet of you to buy my favorite dessert," "You did a great job cleaning up the house," "I loved your *dvar Torah* [words of Torah] at dinner," "I appreciate how supportive you've been during my work crisis," and so on. Complimenting a spouse even when she or he is not so nice to be with might motivate the person to improve.

Pinchas' behavior infuriated Mona. He rarely cleaned up after himself or helped with household chores. He ate and dressed like a slob, and could not be depended upon to take care of daily problems. No matter how much she asked him to act like a mensch, he did what he pleased.

When criticism, nagging, and "reminders" failed, she tried to compliment him when he did what she liked. He wore a rumpled shirt to work, but at least it was clean, so she told him how nice he looked. He came home on time, so she told him how much she appreciated that. She served him a meal that he couldn't eat with his fingers, or spill, then complimented him for eating so neatly. After a few weeks, Pinchas did more of what she wanted and even took more initiative to please her.

It wasn't worth it for Pinchas to sacrifice his independence to stop her nagging, but it was worth it for him to change when he got positive feedback for it.

Some people feel that it is wrong to praise someone who is "substandard." They think that only someone who is outstanding or special deserves compliments. While that is true in contests, that attitude doesn't work in marriage.

Jews are required to thank God for every pleasure we enjoy. We say a blessing before we eat food, smell fragrant flowers or spices, or see an exceptionally beautiful sight. We formally thank God at least three times a day for sustaining us, besides thanking Him for everything we eat. We even thank Him every time we use the bathroom! We train ourselves to take nothing for granted by acknowledging every divine gift, big and small.

We are supposed to do the same with people. Just as we frequently thank God for being good to us, we should do the same with a spouse. We don't ignore God's kindness because He is only doing His job. We are supposed to be thankful for every kindness we receive, even when it's a spouse's job to provide it.

It is easy for husbands to take their wives for granted instead of thanking them for doing laundry, making the beds, cooking meals, cleaning the house, running the home, taking care of the children, and giving husbands a listening ear, love, and comfort. Wives who fall short in some areas should still get compliments for what they do well.

Wives also take their husbands for granted by not appreciating how hard they work to earn a living. They should compliment their husbands for this, and thank them whenever they contribute to the family's wellbeing and happiness. This includes buying a wife clothes, food, gifts, flowers, candy, treats, taking her out, and paying for vacations.

Appreciation should be verbal and behavioral. For example, a husband should not assume that his wife knows that he enjoyed her cooking by the fact that he cleaned his plate. He needs to thank her for her efforts. Likewise, a wife shouldn't think her husband feels appreciated for supporting the family by the fact that she doesn't complain about his long hours away from home. By telling a spouse that we appreciate his or her efforts, we also remind ourselves how much he or she does for us, and we feel closer to our mate as a result.

It is hard to love someone who isn't interested in us. We want a spouse to support and encourage us and feel frustrated and pained when a spouse doesn't share our excitement or interests.

We should show interest in a spouse's conversation, even if we don't share his or her feelings. Being a good marriage partner often requires acting. There are times when we must act pleasant even when we feel grumpy and should compliment a spouse even if we feel disappointed or angry. We say loving words when our spouse needs to hear them, even if we don't feel affectionate. And we sometimes feign interest in a spouse's conversation to show that we care about him or her, even though the topic bores us.

Magda was so excited about her Jewish philosophy class that she couldn't wait to come home and share her new insights with her husband. Marshall had absolutely no interest in metaphysical concepts or discussions of spiritual energy. He liked rationalist philosophies, not the esoterica that Magda gushed about.

Instead of ignoring or belittling her, he shared her excitement. He was genuinely happy that she finally found a teacher who made Judaism come alive for her. He loved watching her face glow with pleasure. He was pleased that she was intellectually stimulated by her classes.

After summarizing her latest class, she asked what he thought about it.

"It sounds fascinating," he replied enthusiastically. "I'm so glad that you're getting a lot out of it. Your excitement is contagious." He responded to what Magda needed to hear, not to how he felt about the content of her question.

Carla was tired of hearing her husband talk about computers every night. Instead of saying this, she put herself in his shoes. He was isolated at work, and had few friends with whom he could share his excitement. He so much wanted Carla to feel proud of him and share his enthusiasm, and would be terribly hurt if she didn't.

Carla asked, "Can you help me understand more about computers so that I can know how they work and appreciate more about your latest project?"

He was happy to oblige, and Carla discovered that he was actually doing some interesting work.

Murry hated coming home to Shonnie because all she talked about were problems with the kids and the house. He was tired of hearing about their son throwing up, the white sales at department stores, and the latest cleaning products. She was so boring!

One night he said, "Shonnie, it must be hard for you to spend all day running our home and raising our children. Do you ever miss the stimulation that you used to get at work?"

"Truthfully," Shonnie admitted, "I do. I often feel exhausted, and sometimes I wish that someone else would take over my responsibilities. I long to read a book, or go to a class, or get some exercise, but my daydreams only last until the kids come home from school and I come back to my senses."

Murry felt so sad for her. "I heard that there's a terrific lecture series for women on Sunday mornings. How would you like me to take care of the kids so that you can go?"

"I would love that," she beamed.

Over the next few months, Murry convinced Shonnie to hire a part-time housekeeper so that she could go out three afternoons a week. He clipped newspaper articles that he thought she would enjoy and got her two Torah tapes to listen to every week when she ran errands or cooked. He encouraged her to discuss more interesting topics and fewer unpleasant details of daily life. His patience and support paid off for both of them as his wife expanded her horizons, and their marriage reaped the benefits.

SUMMARY

Affection and intimacy are like fires. They can burst into flame or peter out if they aren't stoked and fueled. We need to learn what makes a spouse feel loved, and must enlighten him or her about what we need. Then we can structure our lives so that we have the time and energy to nurture our marriages on a regular basis.

Keeping love alive is important in making the difference between having a functional, or a truly great, marriage. If you've gone so far as to get married, why not make it last a lifetime?

SUGGESTED READING

Kreidman, Ellen. *Light Her Fire*. New York: Dell Publishing, 1991.
Kreidman, Ellen. *Light His Fire: How to Keep Your Man Passionately and Hopelessly in Love with You*. New York: Villard Books, 1992.

22

If You Feel Hopeless about Your Marriage

Y ou may be reading this book because you have a troubled marriage. If you have tried using the techniques presented earlier and your marriage is still not improving, don't give up! This chapter is for you.

Couples with troubled marriages typically have a number of destructive communication and problem-solving patterns. They tend to focus on problems instead of on solutions; on what is wrong instead of what is right; they fight about issues without resolving them, invalidate each others' feelings, and blame each other for their marital problems. They continue to pursue a spouse who is already flooded, impute all kinds of negative intentions to a partner's behavior, and assume that a spouse will fail to respond in ways that can lead to a satisfying marriage.

This chapter was designed to help people identify their destructive interactive patterns, help them develop solutions, and give concrete ideas about how to stay on the right track. They can do this whether or not a spouse is willing to work on the marriage. By making small changes in what one person does, positive responses from a spouse are likely to result that can vastly improve a relationship.

First, diagnose a marital problem. Instead of assuming that it is a spouse's fault and blaming his or her personality disorder, upbringing, or undernourished "child," take the point of view that marital problems result from what you *both* do. Research has shown that if one spouse changes whatever is maintaining the negative interactions, the second spouse is likely to react better.

For example, Yaffa assumed that Adin was at fault for their unsatisfying marriage. She had tried for five years to get him to talk to her when he came home from work. She had explained to him that wives want to be asked how their day was, have their husbands make eye contact with them, and give them undivided attention when they talk. Instead, Adin made comments like, "Why should I care what you have to say?" He would bring magazines and mail to the dinner table and read them while she tried to talk to him. She would indicate that she was interested in going to bed early so that they could be intimate, and he would come to bed hours later, long after she had fallen asleep waiting for him. She would ask him to dress nicely for Friday night dinner, and he would deliberately wait until he was good and ready to change out of his work clothes.

She was at her wits' end after enduring this for so long. By that time, Adin was so fed up with their constant fighting that he might actually have changed if she had changed her style of relating. Unfortunately, he had already been so emotionally abusive that she no longer appreciated any of the nice things he did. When he washed the dishes, she didn't see why she should compliment him for it. After all, she did everything else around the house. When he bought her a dress or piece of jewelry, she assumed that he did it so that their friends would not know what a rotten husband he really was and would think that he was wonderful.

While there happened to be some truth in everything Yaffa thought, focusing only on these negatives guaranteed that Adin would never be an adequate husband. Once she was convinced that he would never act better, she waited for him to come home and ignore her. When he did, it just confirmed her view that he was incorrigible, and that their marriage was doomed. She responded by generating many negative thoughts about him and their relationship. First, she overgeneralized that he *never* acted like a normal, loving husband. He had *no* social skills. He *never* cared about her feelings. She had tried *everything* to get him to be a *mensch,* and *everything* failed. Every time she did this for a few minutes, she was flooded by anger and ready to find fault with anything he did.

He actually did try to make conversation sometimes when they sat down for dinner, but she attacked him almost immediately.

Adin: "What did you make for dinner?"

Yaffa: "Hamburgers, salad, and corn."

Adin: "Do we have any ketchup?"

Yaffa: "I don't know. I never use ketchup. If you used up the last of it, you should have gotten more when you went to the store yesterday."

Adin: "But you're the one who makes up the shopping list and you're the one who knows what we're missing."

Yaffa: "Since when is it my job to know when you've used up all the ketchup? I'm not your mother."

Adin: "At least my mother would know if there was ketchup in the house or not."

Yaffa: "What are you talking about? Your mother didn't even know if *you* were in the house."

Adin: "I guess that I got stuck with a woman just like my mother, then, didn't I?"

Yaffa: "You've made me into a woman like your mother. You're just as sick as your father. You wouldn't know how to be a decent husband if your life depended on it."

Adin: "You should talk. You and your family make the Addams family look normal."

Adin and Yaffa ended up getting divorced, but it didn't need to happen. If they had worked hard to follow the rules for communication and problem-solving that appear earlier in this book, they could have nipped these kinds of fights in the bud and spent their energy enjoying each other. Let's see how that could have happened, even if Adin had not decided that he should change:

Adin: "What did you make for dinner?"

Yaffa: "Hamburgers, salad, and corn. I went to the farm store to get fresh corn because I know how much you like it. How is it?"

Adin: (takes a bite) "It's actually pretty good. By the way, is there any ketchup for the hamburgers?"

Yaffa: "I don't know. Didn't you finish it last week?"

Adin: "Yeah, I guess I did. Can you get some the next time you go shopping?"

Yaffa: (gritting her teeth while smiling) "Yeah, I'll put it on my list, and you put it on your list if you go shopping first. Anything else I can do for you?"

Adin: (He is stunned by the question, and actually looks up from his magazine and makes eye contact with her.) "No, there's nothing I can think of." (Goes back to his magazine.)

Yaffa: "I'm glad you're home. I missed you today."

Adin: "You did?" (He turns the page.)

Yaffa: "Yeah. I thought about your dry sense of humor, and how you make me laugh at the end of my long days."

Adin: "I'm glad you appreciate that." (Still reading)

Yaffa: "Is there anything you'd like to talk about tonight?"

Adin: "Nah, I'm pretty tired from work. I'd just like to finish my meal and relax."

Yaffa: "Okay. Enjoy your dinner."

Note that even though Adin was still acting inappropriately, Yaffa continued to communicate nicely. Even if nothing else happens, this will keep hostility at a minimum. Not only is it more pleasant to live in a less hostile environment, it sets the stage for the couple to (1) see that they can interact without fighting, and (2) not erase the goodwill and positive feelings that will build as they do nice things for and with each other.

The next step is for Yaffa to do something different than she usually does, such as asking Adin to talk to her during dinner, since that has failed. She has tried being very attentive to him, but once he finishes talking about what interests him, he ignores her and goes back to his magazine. She decides to do what he does, and she reads a magazine at the dinner table.

As he tells her about his day, she picks up *Redbook* and leafs through the pages.

Adin: "I had a really rough day today."

Yaffa: "Umh-hm." (She tears out a coupon for skin lotion.)

Adin: (a little insulted) "Did you hear me?"

Yaffa: (turning the page) "Yeah. You said that you had a really rough day today."

Adin: (looks over at her magazine) "What are you reading?"

Yaffa: (not looking up) "A ladies' magazine. This has some really interesting articles, and I never have time to read them because I'm so busy working and taking care of the house."

Adin: "What kind of interesting articles do they have?"

Yaffa: (still buried in the magazine) "Oh, things like what to do in medical emergencies, how to manage time and stress better, different uses for your home computer, how to do basic home repairs . . . things like that."

Adin: (intrigued) "Really? I thought it was only a bunch of recipes, fashion, and beauty articles."

Yaffa: (engrossed in an article about anaphylactic reactions to bee and wasp stings) "That's really good to know."

Adin: "What is?"

They end up having a ten-minute conversation.

The next night, Adin sits down for dinner without his magazine.

If that hadn't worked after a week, Yaffa would have left dinner for Adin on the stove and gone out with her friends for the evening. Sooner or later, he is likely to want to talk and listen to her in a nicer way rather than be ignored.

Let's see how a therapist might work with a couple when both partners are willing to go for help, although each is expecting the other to change:

Renee was a "pursuer" and Rob was a "withdrawer." (Many couples have one spouse who wants to talk issues out while the other wants to avoid them. Eighty percent of "pursuers" are women and 20 percent are men.) Rob and Renee came from totally opposite families. Hers was Mediterranean, warm, and effusive; his was American, stoic, and unemotional. Her mother and three sisters talked everything out, while Rob was an only child whose parents largely neglected him emotionally. Throughout their marriage, Renee felt uncared for by Rob. Whenever he came home from work, he would eat dinner with her, rarely initiating conversation and volunteering little about his day. He then spent the rest of the evening watching television in the living room. The more ignored she felt, the more she "pursued" him in the living room by asking his opinion about problems and trying to get an interested and warm response from him. Instead, he felt annoyed that she kept interrupting his television viewing with small talk and problems that she could easily handle herself. Not infrequently, her persistent attempts to get loving attention ended with him blowing up at her or telling her to leave him alone. As their emotional life deteriorated, so did their sex life. They had not had relations in two years. They finally decided to get divorced after twenty years of marriage.

But before they did, they came to therapy at a friend's suggestion. They were convinced that their marriage was not salvageable. The first thing the therapist asked was what each wanted from, and didn't like about, their spouse. Rob wanted his freedom. He was tired of being nagged and criticized, and longed to spend his days fishing in blessed silence. Renee wanted some caring conversation and shows of affection from him. Despite the fact that their wants seemed unbridgeable, they developed a very happy marriage after only four months of weekly or biweekly therapy.

Once the therapist identified what each wanted and did not want, she asked each of them why they married the other. Rob had found Renee attractive, and thought that she would make a pleasant homemaker and good mother. He did not have any other expectations of marriage. When asked if she had been nice during their courtship and early months of marriage, Rob said that she had. Their marriage began to deteriorate four or five years later when she began criticizing and pursuing him for being aloof and unemotional. The therapist asked if he would stay married if Renee would go back to the way she had been during their courtship—less critical, more accepting of him, and satisfied with what he offered. He agreed to consider it but couldn't imagine how that would be possible.

The therapist then asked Renee why she had married Rob. She said that he was attractive, kind, a real gentleman, and they had had great talks into the wee hours of the morning when they courted. The therapist asked what Rob had done then that he no longer did, and Renee said that he used to bring her flowers, opened doors for her, talked about his feelings, and gave her little gifts. He pretty much stopped doing all of these things once they married. The therapist asked if there were things about Rob that Renee still appreciated or admired, and she said that he was a terrific father. In fact, she thought that he was a better father than she was a mother.

Rob was surprised that she appreciated him. She had never mentioned that she thought he was a good father during their entire marriage. But when she had a serious post-partum depression after the birth of their son, Rob raised Brian for the first six months of life. This opened the door for them to discuss how good he was at handling their teenage daughter Donna. Renee said that she (Renee) was such a pushover, she could not put limits on Donna, and Rob always did that well. Donna respected him and asked his opinions. Rob was warm and affectionate with his children, yet was also a good disciplinarian. He was especially adept at handling Donna's volatile emotions and tantrums. Renee tended to get overwhelmed by her daughter's anger and attempts at manipulation.

For the first time, Renee realized that Donna had been a major source of tension in the marriage. A lot of Renee's unpleasantness with Rob was triggered by Renee's fights with Donna on the telephone. The parents agreed that, when Donna called to discuss her problems, Rob would work the problems out with her. Then Renee would talk to Donna about issues such as her social life. This started the couple reinforcing to each other what they loved and appreciated in each other.

Next, the therapist taught them to use the techniques in the chapter on "Communication." Their first challenge was finding a time to talk, inasmuch as Rob liked to watch television all evening and much of the weekend. They finally agreed that they would set aside from 9 to 9:15 every evening to talk, usually with Renee initiating the conversation. She started these interactions by complimenting Rob and/or telling a pleasant story or joke. This changed his perception that all of their interactions would be unpleasant and made him more interested in conversing with her.

Both Renee and the therapist told Rob that he was also fulfilling Renee's needs by actively listening to her without trying to solve her problems. That allowed him to feel good about listening without offering advice. Had they not told him this, he would have felt useless and ineffectual listening to her upsets and complaints as long as he couldn't solve the "real" problem. Once he stopped offering advice when she wanted empathy, she stopped shooting it down. Her rejecting his advice always made him feel hurt and angry and convinced him that listening to her was an exercise in futility. Once they created a more pleasant atmosphere for talking, he was more responsive and she was more relaxed and less critical. They soon stopped watching the clock to see when the fifteen minutes would be up and often chatted for more than half an hour.

One of the challenges they had to overcome was breaking a fifteen-year pattern of him watching television all evening. They decided that the best reminder that it was time for their nightly chat was to set an alarm clock every evening when they came home from work. When it went off, they turned off the television. That way, Renee didn't have to be the bad guy who constantly deprived Rob of his relaxation. It was a joint decision, with a neutral object helping them implement it.

The therapist asked Rob what he wanted Renee to do to show that she cared about him and was willing to work on their marriage. He said that he wanted her to leave him alone for fifteen minutes when he got home so that he could unwind and would not have to listen to problems or make conversation. When Renee was posed the same question, she said that she wanted Rob to bring her flowers, just as he did when they dated. Rob was quite willing to do this. He hadn't brought her flowers after they got married because he had no idea that husbands did that. After all, his father never gave his mother flowers, or any gifts, for that matter. Renee asked him to buy her flowers every Friday but told him not to spend more than $10 on them, except for special occasions. He gave her chrysanthemums every week for the next two months. She then told him that she loved the flowers but asked if he would mind varying what he bought. He was happy to oblige. He had not known that variety mattered, so it was good that she told him.

Soon Rob and Renee were going for evening walks together, enjoying meals in inexpensive restaurants once a week, and having almost no fights with Donna, or with each other. The couple was communicating well and felt affectionate towards each other. They no longer had any thoughts of divorce and had rediscovered what they once loved about each other. Yet they still weren't having sex. Talking through their issues was not enough to get their intimate life back on track. The therapist surmised that Rob had not had sex in such a long time that he probably had a lot of performance anxiety. The therapist helped them set aside a time every week when they could relax in bed together without distractions, and talk and caress each other without having sex. Two weeks later, they dutifully ignored the therapist's instructions about not having relations and the rest of their marriage got back to normal.

Not every marriage can be saved, but many "hopeless" marriages can, especially with a good therapist and two motivated spouses. Yet even without therapy or with only one motivated spouse, a lot can be done to improve a marriage that seems doomed.

Before detailing some of the techniques that can turn a bad marriage around, a few words must be said about marriages that shouldn't be salvaged. If your spouse hits you, or throws objects at you, or there is reason to fear that you or your children will be harmed, consult a professional as soon as possible. The professional can advise you about how serious your problem is, and tell you if you should contact the police, leave the house, change the locks on the doors, find shelter, get financial assistance, counseling, or protection for your children and yourself. There are now a number of shelters for battered Jewish women, as well as confidential hotlines that provide a listening ear, counseling, and practical advice. (See "Resource Agencies" at the end of this chapter.)

Some violent men (and women) respond well to anger-control therapy, while others remain explosive, unpredictable, and dangerous. If you are unwilling to consider getting divorced from a violent spouse, a separation is in order until this person is willing and able to control himself. Do not convince yourself that, if only you were a better wife, your husband would not hurt you. No man should ever hit a wife (except for self-defense) or harm his children physically or sexually. Acknowledging that a spouse's violence and sexual abuse is abnormal, and *is not your fault,* is half of the solution. Separating does not preclude the possibility that you might reconcile if your spouse gets professional help. Meanwhile, any temporary social embarrassment that you might face is better than being battered until you lose your teeth, hearing, eyesight, dignity, and/or your life.

Unfortunately, child molesters rarely get better with therapy. If your spouse has sexually abused your children, you must protect them by getting them away from your spouse as soon as possible. Call a professional to find out what you can and should do.

FIXING YOUR TROUBLED MARRIAGE

If you want to start improving your troubled marriage, consider the following:

1. *What do each of you need to feel satisfied with your marriage?*
Specify the goals that you want to achieve in your relationship. Once you have written what you need to feel satisfied, ask what your spouse wants you to change in order for him or her to be satisfied.

Yaffa wrote that she wanted Adin to be more responsible and to listen to her more attentively in order for her to be satisfied with their marriage.

Adin wanted Yaffa to stop telling him what to do and to stop criticizing him when he didn't do things her way.

2. *What do each of you need to change in order to have a satisfying marriage?*

Yaffa needed to stop criticizing Adin and to post a list on the refrigerator of tasks that needed to be done. Adin needed to do the tasks in a timely way and to listen to Yaffa when she talked to him.

If you don't know what each of you needs to change, ask yourself what was happening when your relationship was good, such as when you were dating. Identify what each of you did or didn't do then. Did you spend more time together? Were you more solicitous of each other? Did you give each other little presents or compliment each other more? Did you go out more or share more activities that you both enjoyed? Did you complain or nag less? Did you avoid discussing every problem or address problems without invalidating each other's feelings? Did you argue less? Did you help each other more? Were you both more involved with the children?

3. *What does your partner do that makes you feel good? Bad?*

It is important to identify not only what you don't like about your partner, but also what is right with him or her and what is good about your marriage.

Yaffa wrote that when Adin used his sense of humor, looked attractive, and gave her creative presents, she felt good. When he didn't pay his bills, help out at home, keep his car in good working order, keep current insurance, and follow through with commitments that he had made to her, she felt bad. She also felt bad when he ignored her, or complained about the way his father and his boss treated him when he was irresponsible.

Adin felt good when Yaffa cooked, did his laundry, paid the bills, invited him to join her at business parties, gave him greeting cards, looked beautiful, and followed his religious strictures. He felt bad when she criticized and nagged him, or told him what to do.

4. *Describe what happens in a typical cycle when you interact negatively.*

Yaffa would ask Adin to fill out some necessary forms, call someone, make an appointment to straighten out a problem, or pay bills by a certain time. When Adin didn't, Yaffa criticized him, and he withdrew. She then pursued him angrily because he ignored her—at which point he defended himself, causing her to explode and verbally attack him. He would keep defending himself, instead of validating her feelings, and criticize her about extraneous issues. She then brought up his irresponsible behavior during their past fifteen years. He finally locked himself in the bathroom and ran the water so that he couldn't hear her.

Identify what each of you does, says, and thinks that contributes to your destructive or unproductive interactions. Write down productive thoughts and actions that you could use instead.

For instance, instead of assuming that Adin deliberately tuned her out because he didn't take her seriously, Yaffa started to think that he must be getting flooded.

Instead of continuing her unproductive "pursuing," she asked him when they could discuss an issue at a better time.

Rather than concluding that all Yaffa wanted was to take away his freedom and henpeck him, Adin told himself that she was hurt and anxious and needed him to show that he cared about her. He agreed to discuss issues that were important to her, if they followed the rules for problem-solving in this book, including the use of a frowning, happy, and neutral card, so that she would know how she came across before he got flooded.

5. *How have you tried to fix your marriage? What have you done that makes things better? What have you done that makes things worse?*

We tend to keep communicating the same way with a spouse, even if it is totally ineffective, because that is all we can think of doing at the time. For example, Yaffa recognized that pursuing her husband when they had an argument never got him to resolve the issue at hand. It *always* ended in a stalemate or fight. Yet she did it anyway. She was sure that the problem was Adin's refusal to accept responsibility, and that if she only convinced him to do that, things would get better. She did not realize that her criticism only pushed his passive–aggressive button, and pursuing him always caused him to get flooded. That made him incapable of responding to her in a validating or constructive way. Since her criticism got him so angry, he retaliated by not listening to her even when she was calm.

People who become frustrated when they fail to solve a problem often keep doing the same useless thing, only more intensively. If it doesn't work, doing more of it won't help. What it will do is cause the spouse to intensify his or her negative reaction, further fueling upset feelings.

In other words, couples who can't resolve problems often get in cycles like this: Spouse A tries to fix the problem → Spouse B responds in a way that upsets A → A repeats the same negative behavior, but more strongly → B intensifies the response that upset A in the first place.

If this happens when you try to resolve conflicts with your spouse, stop blaming your spouse and try changing yourself.

a. Define what you want to accomplish when you interact with your spouse. Make it realistic, reasonable, and doable.

Yaffa wanted Adin to admit that he was irresponsible. Since he will never do this, she should redefine her goal.

She decides to try to get him to do a certain behavior in a timely way, such as paying his student loans when the bills come every month. This is not realistic, either, so she changes her expectation again. She wants him to pay the bills the same month they come in. She would like not to have to remind him to do this and would like him to guarantee that he will take care of things without her checking up on him.

Adin would like to interact with Yaffa without her telling him what to do and would like her to compliment him every day.

b. Don't expect your spouse to be a mind-reader, or to change an attitude. Focus on a behavior that you want more or less of, and think about *how your spouse might be convinced to do it.*

Yaffa wants to raise issues only once with Adin. She realizes that she must first validate his feeling, so she writes down a possible scenario. She tells him, "It must be hard for you to have me coming after you almost every day, nagging and criticizing you. I'm sorry I've done that, and I know that it's really hurt our relationship. I really don't want to keep doing this. I do it because I feel anxious when our bills aren't paid on time, or I have to deal with the consequences of your doing things on your own timetable. I'd like to trust that you will take care of your responsibilities in a timely way so that I don't have to feel anxious. If you can reassure me by working out an arrangement that satisfies both of us, I will stop criticizing and nagging you. How does that sound?"

c. Don't argue about whose perspective, needs, or wants are more correct. Focus on getting a reasonable solution to the problem.

d. Think about when your interactions stop being amicable and become fights. What happens just before things turn sour? For example, do you accuse, blame, or back your spouse into a corner? Do you denigrate his or her opinions or actions? Do you overgeneralize, digress, mind-read, or talk about everything your spouse has done wrong since the day you met? Do you tell him or her what to do in a negative way?

People who fight destructively often try to bully each other into changing; refuse to change unless the spouse first does what they want; or refuse to accept changes or solutions that aren't exactly what they want. Think about whether you do any of these things. If you tend to bully, make a point of validating your spouse's feelings, and ask him or her to suggest a solution to various problems. Or, work it out together in a non-threatening way.

If you refuse to change until your spouse does first, you are asking for misery. If you take the first step, your spouse is likely to follow, and you'll be on your way to improving your marriage. Even if your spouse never changes, you can always make changes that will result in your being happier. Instead of staking your happiness on your spouse's doing what you want, think about what you can do to make yourself more satisfied.

Yaffa decided to pay the bills and to fill out necessary forms herself. If Adin refused to take care of tasks at home in a timely way, she stopped nagging him and did them herself. When she went on a three-week vacation without him, he miraculously took care of all of his responsibilities in her absence! When she returned, she continued to let him open the mail and take care of bills and correspondence by himself.

If you tend to belittle small changes that your spouse makes, your marriage will not improve. Show a lot of appreciation for small changes when they happen, and they are likely to grow rapidly. Compliments are not likely to make your spouse think that he doesn't have to do more than the minimum. If changing feels good, he or she will keep doing things that are rewarded.

Once you identify what causes your conversations to turn sour, stop doing it. What can you do differently that will improve things?

Yaffa realized that the turning point with Adin came as soon as she spoke in an angry tone of voice, or expressed anger to him. She resolved to tell him, with a smile on her face, that she had a problem and wondered if he could help her with it. She then complimented him before stating matter-of-factly that she got a letter from a collection agency, or a letter from the insurance company threatening to terminate their policy. Instead of telling Adin what to do, she asked if he had any ideas about what to do.

e. Identify what happens differently when you come to a truce, agree to disagree, or something constructive comes out of your conflicts or disagreements.

For example, does your spouse collaborate with you when you say, "I have a problem. Can you help me figure out a way to deal with it?" Do issues get resolved better when you ask your spouse to set a time to discuss them or when you change your usual place for discussions? Do issues get resolved better when you are sensitive to your spouse's flooding or when you call a time-out because you are too angry to respond constructively?

Yaffa realized that when she asked Adin, instead of telling him, what he thought would be a reasonable way to handle a problem, it was most likely to get resolved.

Adin realized that when he focused on solving a problem, instead of assuming that Yaffa was trying to control him and he had to hold his own, they resolved issues.

6. *When, where, and under what circumstances do most of your negative interactions occur?*

Yaffa noticed that most of her arguments with Adin occurred at home, when Adin tried to relax in the living room after coming home from work. She tended to tell him what she wanted him to do or criticized what he hadn't done. He then ignored her, and an argument almost invariably ensued.

When you have identified what makes things worse, *stop doing it.* Some people fight most when they are both tired, when they are pressured, hungry, or have many problems to deal with all at once. Some couples resolve issues best on the living room sofa when they can cuddle together and worst when they sit in opposite chairs in the den. Some couples argue most when a stepchild is over or when one of them has just spoken to his or her mother, and so on.

7. *Identify what you do as a couple when things go well, which you haven't been doing, and start doing them.*

Yaffa remembered that, when they were first married, she would snuggle up to Adin when he first came home. He would hold her for fifteen or twenty minutes while they read the newspaper together to unwind. They also used to go out to eat once a week. They used to sing together while Yaffa played the piano or he played his guitar. They went bicycling on Sundays or went on long walks on a nearby beach. She realized that they almost never did any of those things any more, and she started to change that.

Doing this exercise should help you identify what you each need to do more and less of, to make your marriage more satisfying and to communicate better.

If you want your spouse to do more of something:

a. *Write down as specifically as possible what distresses you about your spouse and your marriage.*

For example, don't say "He's narcissistic," or "He's got to stop getting angry." Try, "He doesn't make eye contact with me most of the time that I speak to him, and he doesn't ask me about my day or listen to me at night." "I'd like him not to yell at me when I don't clean up the kids' toys and to compliment me when I cook for him."

b. *Identify times and situations when the problem doesn't occur, happens less often, less intensely, for less time, or upsets you less than usual.*

Yaffa noted that Adin would ask her about her day when she didn't respond with a litany of problems; he would listen to her more before 8 P.M. and when he wasn't watching television; and she was least upset about his not listening when she had had an interesting day and had spent time with her friends.

c. *Identify what you do to make these exceptions occur.*

Yaffa noted that when she talked without complaining, or refrained from talking about upsetting situations, Adin tended to listen. She could time their conversations around dinner instead of waiting for him to unwind in front of the television. She could also spend time with her friends, instead of expecting Adin to provide her with all of her emotional support.

d. *Try doing the things that work and keep repeating them if they continue to help.*

e. *If what you try doesn't work, try something else.*

OVERCOMING HOPELESSNESS

When couples have focused on their failures for a long time, they develop the perception that nothing they do will make things improve. If you have not yet developed the tools to make your relationship better, you are going to start now.

1. Instead of thinking that you and your spouse can't improve your marriage, change your perception by focusing on how you can change your marriage if you do _____ more often and _____ less often.

Yaffa realized that she could improve her marriage by complaining less, doing more for herself, and having better timing.

2. Ponder the following: My spouse does more of what I want when I do _____ or when _____ occurs.

3. I will know that my spouse is doing more of what I want when she or he does _____, says _____, or says or does _____ less.

It is very important that spouses notice when their partner is doing more of the right things. They must not discount this. Do not expect your spouse to do perfectly and exactly everything you want, as soon as you want. Set realistic goals that will let you notice that she or he is moving in the right direction. Yaffa will know that Adin is doing more of what she wants when he makes eye contact with her three or four times during dinner; asks her about one thing that she said; or listens to one or two minutes of her conversation. She will try her new behavior for a week before evaluating if Adin's desired behaviors occur. As he does more of what she wants, she can slowly raise her expectations.

4. My spouse would like me to change _____. She or he will notice that I have started to change when I do or say _____, or stop doing _____.

Yaffa decided to tell Adin that she was turning over a new leaf, and would start talking more about topics that interested him. After discussing a topic for a few minutes, she asked if he wanted to continue with it, or wished to talk about something else. If Adin seemed engaged in the topics that she raised, she would ask him a week later if he thought their interactions had improved.

People in troubled marriages often wait to see if their spouse changes in the manner they want instead of accepting the reality that both spouses have to change. Have you changed appreciably in any ways that your spouse would like, or do you think that he or she is entirely to blame?

Once you identify what you can do to improve your marriage, and your spouse sees that he or she is getting more of what he or she wants from you, you are already on the way to finding a solution.

Remember, no marriage is perfect. Expect small changes and some backsliding, and anticipate how you will react constructively when one or both of you goes back to your old ways from time to time. Don't expect failure, but do be realistic about minor setbacks, and prepare to overcome them. Think about how to constructively meet the challenges in your marriage, and you are likely to succeed.

AS A LAST RESORT

If you have tried all of the techniques in this book, and your marriage is still floundering, read the "Suggested Readings" and see a marriage counselor.

SUGGESTED READING

Notarius, Clifford and Markman, Howard. *We Can Work It Out*. New York: G. P. Putnam's Sons, 1993.
Weiner-Davis, Michele. *Divorce Busting*. New York: Summit Books, 1992.

RESOURCE AGENCIES

Family Violence Resources (Jewish sponsored)
  Assists battered women by giving shelter, legal or medical aid, and individual or couple counseling. The following are contacts for more information:
    In Los Angeles: Family Violence Project (818) 908–5007
                    Shiloh (818) 783–6754
    In Chicago: Project Shalva (312) 583–HOPE (24–hour hotline)
    In Baltimore: Chana Weinberg (410) 486–0322
    In New York: The Transition Center (718) 520–8045
                 Center for Family Violence (718) 237–1337
    In Houston: Avda (713) 520–8620
    In Montreal: Auberge Shalom Pour Femmes (514) 733–3217
    In Toronto: ASTEH (416) 638–7800
    In Jerusalem: Tas Zahav (02) 223–237
                  Maon Horim (02) 827–805
Jewish Board of Family and Children's Services (718) 435–5700
  This branch of JBFCS offers psychotherapy by qualified Orthodox therapists.
Jewish Family Service of Los Angeles—6505 Wilshire Boulevard, Los Angeles, CA 90048, (213) 852–7723
  Has an Orthodox Counseling Program staffed by observant Jewish therapists and supervised by rabbis.
Jewish Information and Referral Service of the United Jewish Appeal–Federation, (212) 753–2288
Shalom Task Force, P. O. Box 900127, Far Rockaway, NY 11690–0127, (718) 337–3700
  Confidential hotline for abused women and their families.
Yittie Leibel Help Line, (718) HELP–NOW, 1276 50th Street, Brooklyn, NY 11219
  Telephone hotline that offers free, anonymous professional help to Jews who have emotional and family problems.

Appendix:

Premarital Questionnaire

Certain factors are highly predictive of divorce:[1] a husband's lack of fondness and affection for his wife; seeing himself as independent in marriage instead of being part of a team; remembering few details about how he met his wife and what happened during their courtship; being vague about what attracted him to her; expressing negative feelings about her and disagreeing with her frequently; being disappointed in her; and a tendency for him to withdraw from problem-solving arguments. A man's tendency to stonewall was related to his wife having health problems.

Divorce rates are also high for wives who have little sense of togetherness with their husbands, and/or who are very disappointed in them.[2]

"PREPARE" (Premarital Personal and Relationship Evaluation) is a set of 125 questions developed by David Olson at the University of Minnesota. It has been given to more than a half million couples worldwide and is reported to predict with 80–85 percent accuracy which couples will divorce.

Couples who do not want to take formal questionnaires that are computer scored can use the following questionnaire to get a sense of what their areas of conflict are and to assess their compatibility in certain areas. It can be taken by either married or unmarried couples.

QUESTIONNAIRE

Decide if each item is true (T) or false (F), and mark items accordingly. After both of you complete the questionnaire individually, compare and discuss your answers. The number of items you agree about is not as important as the severity of the differences or concerns in important areas. True answers generally show compatibility, and False answers can be areas for concern.

Work Issues

1. I am satisfied with my job, salary, schedule, and work environment.
2. I am satisfied with the same about my spouse's job.
3. We agree about how each of us will work (or not) after having children.
Other Work Issues: _____

Parenting

1. I think that I will be a good parent.
2. I think that my spouse will be a good parent.
3. We agree about what each of our roles will be raising children.
4. We generally agree about how to discipline our children.
5. We agree about what kind of schooling we want our children to have.
6. We agree about the values that we want our children to have.
7. We agree about the kind of home, peer group, and neighborhood in which we would like to raise our children.
8. I am not concerned that my spouse will pressure me to have children (or more children) before I am ready.
9. We have (or expect to have) conflicts over stepchildren.
10. We agree about what we will do if we cannot have children.
Other Parenting Issues: _____

Parents and In-laws

1. I am not concerned about problems that parents or in-laws will cause us.
2. My spouse and I agree about how we will spend time with our parents and in-laws, especially on holidays and weekends.
3. Our families approve of our choice of spouse and welcome our mate.
4. Neither my spouse nor I need to work out emotional issues with our parents.
Other Relevant Issues: _____

Personal Compatibilities

1. My spouse and I communicate well, and can disarm each other when disagreements get heated.

2. My spouse and I are rarely depressed or anxious.

3. My spouse and I are rarely moody or unpredictable.

4. I am not concerned that I will be bored with my spouse.

5. Neither my spouse nor I feel that we should make up to each other for past hurts.

6. We are comfortable compromising for each other.

7. Neither of us tends to put the other down or uses sarcasm frequently.

8. We find each other attractive.

9. My spouse's hygiene rarely concerns me.

10. Neither my spouse nor I are too concerned with others' opinions.

11. My spouse treats me with consideration and is not overly self-centered.

12. We have compatible tastes in clothes, food, home furnishings, and so forth.

13. I am not bothered by my spouse's personal habits, such as being late, not finishing tasks, being disorganized, being sloppy, or procrastinating.

14. I respect my spouse's ambition and initiative.

15. My spouse is outgoing enough.

16. My spouse is not rigid, inflexible, or unable to relax.

17. My spouse is decisive.

18. My spouse is not bossy, controlling, or a nag.

Other Relevant Issues: _____

Friends and Social Interactions

1. My spouse and I like each other's friends.

2. We like similar kinds of people.

3. I feel secure when my spouse is around members of the opposite sex.

4. My spouse's behavior or manners rarely embarrass me.

5. My spouse respects me.

6. My spouse does not spend too much time talking on the phone or socializing with friends.

7. We agree about how much time we should spend away from each other.

8. My spouse approves of my spending time with my friends and family.

9. My spouse has close friends.

Other Relevant Issues: _____

Decision Making and Communication

1. When we disagree or fight, we are comfortable talking things out.

2. We generally respect each other's opinions.

3. I am satisfied with the way we make decisions and resolve conflicts.

4. We are careful to soothe each other's feelings and apologize when we disagree or hurt each other's feelings.

5. We easily and diplomatically disclose our feelings to each other.

6. We communicate affection often and easily.

7. We are good listeners.

8. We express caring and intimacy much more than we fight.

9. Neither of us tries to avoid confrontations or disagreements at any cost.

10. We each get our way equally often.

11. Neither of us gets violent when upset.

12. We don't think that if we only express ourselves the right way, the other person will eventually do what we want.

Other Relevant Issues: _____

Problems with Anger, Getting Along, and Bad Habits

1a. I don't have strong reservations about getting married.

1b. (if married) I don't think that we should get divorced.

2. I have no concerns about how my spouse or I express anger, and/or lose our temper.

3. Neither my spouse nor I use drugs nor drink too much alcohol.

4. Neither of us expects our problems to automatically disappear when we marry.

5. I don't expect my spouse to change what I don't like about him or her once we are married.

6. I don't feel that my spouse is too possessive.

7. No one whose opinions I respect has objected to our marriage.

8. I am not getting married because of outside pressures (age, family, social, etc.).

9. I don't feel intimidated or find it hard to stand up for myself and my opinions when we are together.

10. Neither my spouse nor I are bringing a lot of past problems and emotional baggage into our marriage.

11. I don't feel that I am settling by marrying my spouse.

12. I am not concerned about my spouse's relationship with an ex-spouse or former girl/boyfriend.

13. When we are angry, we rarely say or do hurtful things to each other.

14. If we are hurt, we don't harbor angry feelings and explode later.

15. My spouse gets very angry over matters that I consider trivial.

16. I often get the sense that my spouse is trying to control or smother me.

Other Relevant Issues: _____

Interests, Activities, Lifestyles, Spending Time

1. We have many common interests and enjoy doing things together.

2. We enjoy each other's company and feel comfortable and secure with each other.

3. We are satisfied with the amount of time we spend together and alone.

4. We are satisfied with the way our partner spends his or her free time.

5. We are both energetic at the same time of day.

6. We have similar lifestyles and goals.

Other Relevant Issues: _____

Sex and Expressing Affection

1. We both have similar feelings about sex.

2. My spouse makes me feel loved.

3. We have compatible sex drives.

4. Neither of us has emotional or physical problems that will interfere with being a good sex partner.

5. When we don't feel loving towards each other, we keep working on our relationship until the feelings come back.

6. We can count on each other to give support when either of us needs it.

7. We feel comfortable discussing our sexual feelings and needs with each other.

Other Relevant Issues: _____

Money Issues

1. We largely agree about how we will each spend and save money.

2. I am not concerned about my spouse's debts or inability to handle money and pay bills responsibly.

3. I do not worry that we will have serious financial problems.

Other Money Issues: _____

Backgrounds, Future Goals, and Expectations

1. We agree about where to live.

2. We have discussed how we expect our lives to change with marriage and children, and the adaptations that we will need to make.

3. Each of us feels ready for marriage.

4. Our socioeconomic or cultural differences will not cause problems.

5. I am not concerned about our intellectual or educational differences.

6. I am not concerned about how we will deal with my, or my spouse's, medical or emotional problems.

7. We have compatible expectations of marriage.

8. We agree about how we will divide domestic responsibilities.

Other Relevant Issues: _____

Religion

1. We do not have worrisome religious differences.
2. We agree about which rabbi we will consult to resolve our religious conflicts.
3. We agree about the kinds of charities we will support, and what percent of our income we will donate.

Other Religious Issues: _____

NOTES

1. "A Hundred Twenty-Five Questions May Answer the Big One: Will the Couple Divorce?" *New York Times,* 11 August 1992, pp. C1, C9.
2. John Gottman, *Why Marriages Succeed or Fail* (New York: Simon and Schuster, 1994).

RECOMMENDED

Jewish *Marriage Encounter* weekends.
PAIRS Foundation—Offers Practical Application of Intimate Relationship Skills in semester-long classes. Given in fifty U.S. cities.

Index

About the Author

Lisa Aiken received her Ph.D. in clinical psychology from Loyola University of Chicago. She was the chief psychologist at Lenox Hill Hospital in New York City and clinical assistant professor at New York Medical College, Long Island University, and St. John's University. She currently does psychotherapy with individuals and couples in Manhattan and Great Neck, New York.

Dr. Aiken coauthored the *The Art of Jewish Prayer* with Rabbi Yitzchok Kirzner and is the author of *To Be a Jewish Woman* and *Why Me God?: A Jewish Guide for Coping with Suffering*. She gives lectures throughout the world on diverse Jewish and psychological topics and has appeared on radio and television.